PEARSON ALWAYS LEARNING

Supply Chain and Operations Management

REVISED Sixth Custom Edition for Conestoga College
Compiled by Tracey Lopers and Brian Watson

Taken from:
Operations Management, Canadian Edition
by Jay Heizer, Barry Render and Paul Griffin

Introduction to Operations and Supply Chain Management, Third Edition
by Cecil C. Bozarth and Robert B. Handfield

Cover Art: Courtesy of Conestoga College

Taken from:

Operations Management, Canadian Edition
by Jay Heizer, Barry Render and Paul Griffin
Copyright © 2014 by Pearson Canada, Inc.
Toronto, Canada

Introduction to Operation and Supply Chain Management, Third Edition
by Cecil C. Bozarth and Robert B. Handfield
Copyright © 2013, 2008, 2006 by Pearson Education, Inc.
Published by Prentice Hall
Upper Saddle River, New Jersey 07458

Pearson Learning Solutions, 501 Boylston Street, Suite 900, Boston, MA 02116
A Pearson Education Company
www.pearsoned.com

Printed in the United States of America

9 10 11 12 13 VOUD 19 18 17 16 15

000200010271861345

SJ

PEARSON

ISBN 10: 1-269-71915-7
ISBN 13: 978-1-269-71915-5

Table of Contents

[1] *Operations Management*, Canadian Edition by Jay Heizer, Barry Render and Paul Griffin.
[2] *Introduction to Operations and Supply Chain Management*, Third edition by Cecil C. Bozarth and Robert B. Handfield.

Students Profile

Fairen Moore Sourcing Analyst – Business Operations Procurement, TD Bank Group
Business Administration – Materials & Operations Management Program 2012.

Obtaining a diploma in the Materials & Operations Management field has proven to be invaluable as I pursued my career with TD Bank Group in their Strategic Sourcing Department. I have spent the last 10 months providing value-added research, analysis, and reporting for one of the largest and most respected financial institutions in North America. I utilize the skills and knowledge learned throughout my time at Conestoga College on a daily basis, and I believe the commitment and expertise of the program's faculty has prepared me to become an expert in many aspects of my job's roles and responsibilities. The course material is applicable not only to manufacturing careers, but also many service focused organizations. I strongly believe that this program's focus on continuous improvement is what will propel me forward throughout my career.

Nathan Woods CSCMP, BCom.
Commodity Manager, Christie Digital Systems
Business Administration – Materials Management (CO-OP) Diploma Program 1999–2002.

To this day, I clearly remember my final year at Elmira District Secondary School, going in and out of the guidance counselor's office with various reading material, hoping to narrow down and figure out what my future career path would be. This is a big decision for any 18-year old, and I especially felt the pressure because I wanted nothing more than to choose an education that upon graduation would offer a high probability of landing me a job! After talking to my parents, a few friends, and attending an information session at Conestoga College for the Materials Management program, there was no turning back! Materials Management was a specific business program I had interest in, and I was especially excited about the high success rate of students finding jobs after graduation.

While taking the Materials Management program at Conestoga, I worked hard, always kept my end goal in mind (to land a good job), and reaped the benefits as a result. Overall, the program did an excellent job teaching, developing and applying skills in purchasing, planning, operations, logistics, project planning and much more.

The Materials Management program was a launching pad to what so far has been a successful career for me in supply chain management. My first jobs (McNeil Consumer Healthcare & NCR) came out of the Co-op program. After that, I worked at BlackBerry (formerly known as "RIM") for over 8 years; starting out as a buyer and moving my way up to the Commodity Manager position. With BlackBerry's support, I obtained my CSCMP designation in 2007, as well as a Bachelor of Commerce degree in 2009 (by taking courses online so I did not have to leave or quit my job). Last summer, I decided to grow my professional experience by taking on a new Commodity Manager opportunity at Christie Digital. After 10 months at Christie, I've had the opportunity to take on new and exciting challenges; which as a result has expanded my overall skill set.

My career has allowed me to travel, meet people and companies all over the world. This has been an invaluable experience in today's world of global supply, and much of it has to do with the credibility of the Materials Management program at Conestoga College

1

Operations and Productivity

Chapter Outline

10 OM Strategy Decisions

- Design of Goods and Services
- **Managing Quality**
- **Process Strategy**
- **Location Strategies**
- **Layout Strategies**
- **Human Resources**
- **Supply-Chain Management**
- **Inventory Management**
- **Scheduling**
- **Maintenance**

Operations Management at Hard Rock Cafe

Operations managers throughout the world are producing products every day to provide for the well-being of society. These products take on a multitude of forms. They may be auto parts at Magna International, motion pictures at Dreamworks, rides at Disney World, or food at Hard Rock Cafe. These firms produce thousands of complex products every day—to be delivered as the customer ordered them, when the customer wants them, and where the customer wants them. Hard Rock does this for over 35 million guests worldwide every year. This is a challenging task, and the operations manager's job, whether at Magna International, Dreamworks, Disney, or Hard Rock, is demanding.

Orlando-based Hard Rock Cafe opened its first restaurant in London in 1971, making it over 4 decades old and the granddaddy of theme restaurants. Although other theme restaurants have come and gone, Hard Rock is still going strong, with 150 restaurants in more than 53 countries—and new restaurants opening each year. Hard Rock made its name with rock music memorabilia, having started when Eric Clapton, a regular customer, marked his favourite bar stool by hanging his guitar on the wall in the London cafe. Now Hard Rock has millions of dollars invested in memorabilia. To keep customers coming back time and again, Hard Rock creates value in the form of good food and entertainment.

The operations managers at Hard Rock Cafe at Universal Studios in Orlando provide more than 3500 custom products, in this case meals, every day. These products are designed, tested, and then analyzed for cost of ingredients, labour requirements, and customer satisfaction. On approval, menu items are put into production—and then only if the ingredients are available from qualified suppliers. The production process, from receiving, to cold storage, to grilling or baking or frying, and a dozen other steps, is designed and maintained to yield a quality meal. Operations managers, using the best

Hard Rock Cafe in Orlando, Florida, prepares over 3500 meals each day. Seating more than 1500 people, it is one of the largest restaurants in the world. But Hard Rock's operations managers serve the hot food hot and the cold food cold.

Operations managers are interested in the attractiveness of the layout, but they must be sure that the facility contributes to the efficient movement of people and material with the necessary controls to ensure that proper portions are served.

Efficient kitchen layouts, motivated personnel, tight schedules, and the right ingredients at the right place at the right time are required to delight the customer.

people they can recruit and train, also prepare effective employee schedules and design efficient layouts.

Managers who successfully design and deliver goods and services throughout the world understand operations. In this text, we look not only at how Hard Rock's managers create value but also at how operations managers in other services, as well as in manufacturing, do so. Operations management is demanding, challenging, and exciting. It affects our lives every day. Ultimately, operations managers determine how well we live.

Chapter 1 Learning Objectives

What is Operations Management?

AUTHOR COMMENT Let's begin by defining what this course is about.

Operations management (OM) is a discipline that applies to restaurants like Hard Rock Cafe as well as to factories like Ford and Whirlpool. The techniques of OM apply throughout the world to virtually all productive enterprises. It doesn't matter if the application is in an office, a hospital, a restaurant, a department store, or a factory—the production of goods and services requires operations management. And the *efficient* production of goods and services requires effective application of the concepts, tools, and techniques of OM that we introduce in this book.

LO1: Define operations management

VIDEO 1.1 Operations Management at Hard Rock

VIDEO 1.2 Operations Management at Frito-Lay

As we progress through this text, we will discover how to manage operations in a changing global economy. An array of informative examples, charts, text discussions, and pictures illustrates concepts and provides information. We will see how operations managers create the goods and services that enrich our lives.

In this chapter, we first define *operations management*, explaining its heritage and exploring the exciting role operations managers play in a huge variety of organizations. Then we discuss production and productivity in both goods- and service-producing firms. This is followed by a discussion of operations in the service sector and the challenge of managing an effective and efficient production system.

Production is the creation of goods and services. **Operations management (OM)** is the set of activities that creates value in the form of goods and services by transforming inputs into outputs. Activities creating goods and services take place in all organizations. In manufacturing firms, the production activities that create goods are usually quite obvious. In them, we can see the creation of a tangible product such as a Sony TV or a Harley-Davidson motorcycle.

Production
The creation of goods and services.

Operations management (OM)
Activities that relate to the creation of goods and services through the transformation of inputs to outputs.

In an organization that does not create a tangible good or product, the production function may be less obvious. We often call these activities *services*. The services may be "hidden" from the public and even from the customer. The product may take such forms as the transfer of funds from a savings account to a chequing account, the transplant of a liver, the filling of an empty seat on an airplane, or the education of a student. Regardless of whether the end product is a good or service, the production activities that go on in the organization are often referred to as operations, or *operations management*.

Organizing to Produce Goods and Services

AUTHOR COMMENT Operations is one of the three functions that every organization performs.

To create goods and services, all organizations perform three functions (see Figure 1.1). These functions are the necessary ingredients not only for production but also for an organization's survival. They are:

1. *Marketing*, which generates the demand, or at least takes the order for a product or service (nothing happens until there is a sale).
2. *Production/operations*, which creates the product.

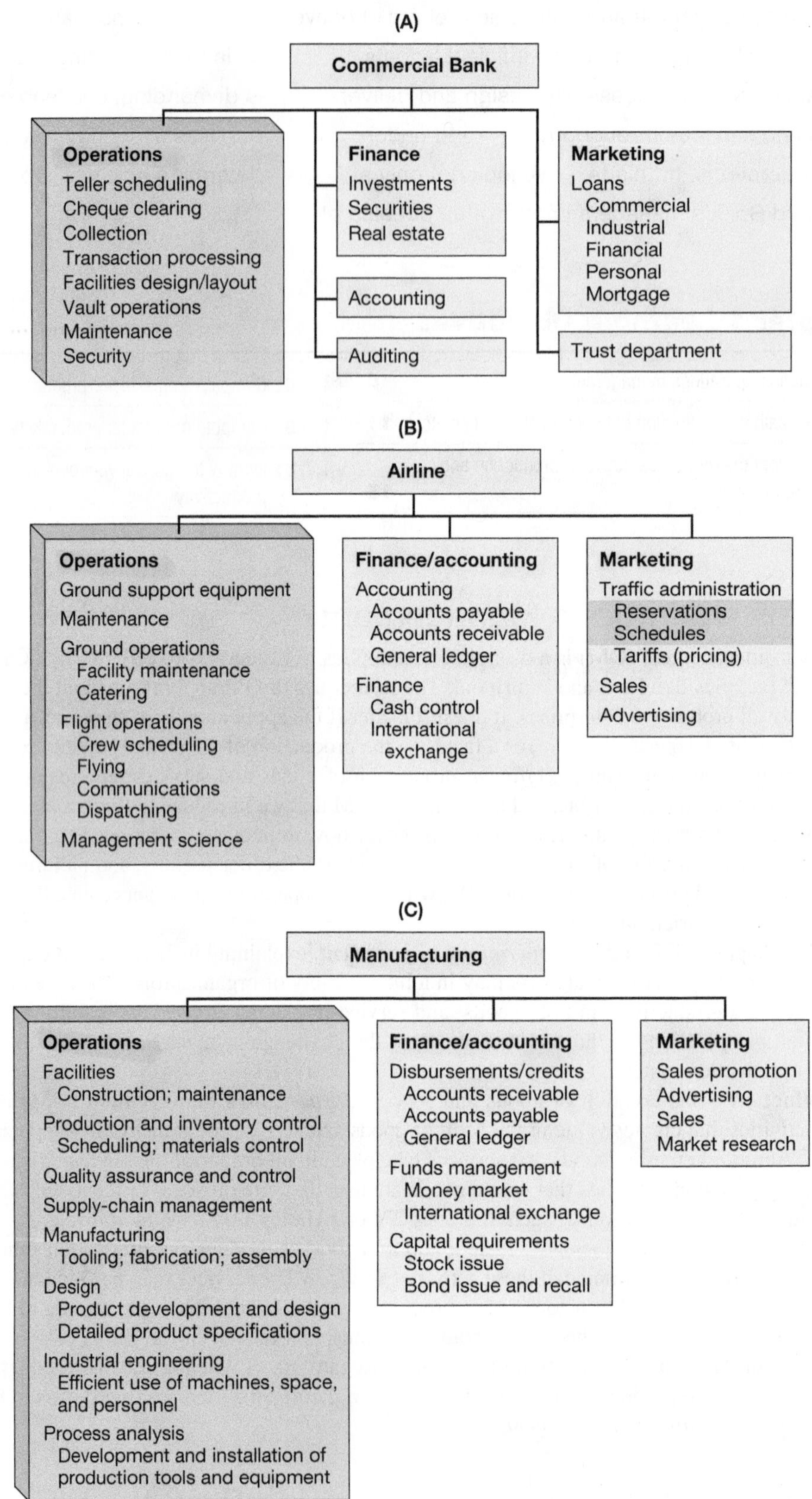

FIGURE 1.1
Organization Charts for Two Service Organizations and One Manufacturing Organization
(A) A bank, (B) an airline, and (C) a manufacturing organization. The blue areas are OM activities.

3. *Finance/accounting*, which tracks how well the organization is doing, pays the bills, and collects the money.

Universities, places of worship, and businesses all perform these functions. Even a volunteer group such as Scouts Canada is organized to perform these three basic functions. Figure 1.1 shows how a bank, an airline, and a manufacturing firm organize themselves to perform these functions. The blue-shaded areas of Figure 1.1 show the operations functions in these firms.

Why Study OM?

We study OM for four reasons:

1. OM is one of the three major functions of any organization, and it is integrally related to all the other business functions. All organizations market (sell), finance (account), and produce (operate), and it is important to know how the OM activity functions. Therefore, we study *how people organize themselves for productive enterprise.*
2. We study OM because we want to know *how goods and services are produced.* The production function is the segment of our society that creates the products and services we use.
3. We study OM to *understand what operations managers do.* Regardless of your job in an organization, you can perform better if you understand what operation managers do. In addition, understanding OM will help you explore the numerous and lucrative career opportunities in the field.
4. We study OM *because it is such a costly part of an organization.* A large percentage of the revenue of most firms is spent in the OM function. Indeed, OM provides a major opportunity for an organization to improve its profitability and enhance its service to society. Example 1 considers how a firm might increase its profitability via the production function.

AUTHOR COMMENT
Good OM managers are scarce and, as a result, career opportunities and pay are excellent.

EXAMPLE 1

Examining the options for increasing contribution

Fisher Technologies is a small firm that must double its dollar contribution to fixed cost and profit in order to be profitable enough to purchase the next generation of production equipment. Management has determined that if the firm fails to increase contribution, its bank will not make the loan and the equipment cannot be purchased. If the firm cannot purchase the equipment, the limitations of the old equipment will force Fisher to go out of business and, in doing so, put its employees out of work and discontinue producing goods and services for its customers.

APPROACH ▶ Table 1.1 shows a simple profit-and-loss statement and three strategic options (marketing, finance/accounting, and operations) for the firm. The first option is a *marketing option,* where good marketing management may increase sales by 50%. By increasing sales by 50%, contribution will in turn increase 71%. But increasing sales 50% may be difficult; it may even be impossible.

TABLE 1.1
Options for Increasing Contribution

		Marketing Option[a]	*Finance/ Accounting Option*[b]	*OM Option*[c]
	Current	**Increase Sales Revenue 50%**	**Reduce Finance Costs 50%**	**Reduce Production Costs 20%**
Sales	$100 000	$150 000	$100 000	$100 000
Costs of goods	–80 000	–120 000	–80 000	–64 000
Gross margin	20 000	30 000	20 000	36 000
Finance costs	–6 000	–6 000	–3 000	–6 000
Subtotal	14 000	24 000	17 000	30 000
Taxes at 25%	–3 500	–6 000	–4 250	–7 500
Contribution[d]	$10 500	$18 000	$12 750	$22 500

[a]Increasing sales 50% increases contribution by $7500, or 71% (7500/10 500).
[b]Reducing finance costs 50% increases contribution by $2250, or 21% (2250/10 500).
[c]Reducing production costs 20% increases contribution by $12 000, or 114% (12 000/10 500).
[d]Contribution to fixed cost (excluding finance costs) and profit.

The second option is a *finance/accounting option,* where finance costs are cut in half through good financial management. But even a reduction of 50% is still inadequate for generating the necessary increase in contribution. Contribution is increased by only 21%.

The third option is an *OM option,* where management reduces production costs by 20% and increases contribution by 114%.

SOLUTION ▶ Given the conditions of our brief example, Fisher Technologies has increased contribution from $10 500 to $22 500. It may now have a bank willing to lend it additional funds.

(Continued)

INSIGHT ▶ The OM option not only yields the greatest improvement in contribution but also may be the only feasible option. Increasing sales by 50% and decreasing finance costs by 50% may both be virtually impossible. Reducing operations costs by 20% may be difficult but feasible.

LEARNING EXERCISE ▶ What is the impact of only a 15% decrease in costs in the OM option? [Answer: A $19 500 contribution; an 86% increase.]

Example 1 underscores the importance of an effective operations activity of a firm. Development of increasingly effective operations is the approach taken by many companies as they face growing global competition.

AUTHOR COMMENT
An operations manager must successfully address the 10 decisions around which this text is organized.

What Operations Managers Do

All good managers perform the basic functions of the management process. The **management process** consists of *planning*, *organizing*, *staffing*, *leading*, and *controlling*. Operations managers apply this management process to the decisions they make in the OM function. The 10 major decisions of OM are shown in Table 1.2. Successfully addressing each of these decisions requires planning, organizing, staffing, leading, and controlling. Typical issues relevant to these decisions and the chapter in which each is discussed are also shown.

Management process
The application of planning, organizing, staffing, leading, and controlling to the achievement of objectives.

WHERE ARE THE OM JOBS? How does one get started on a career in operations? The 10 OM decisions identified in Table 1.2 are made by individuals who work in the disciplines shown in the blue areas of Figure 1.1. Competent business students who know their accounting, statistics, finance, and OM have an opportunity to assume entry-level positions in all of these areas. As you

TABLE 1.2
Ten Critical Decisions of Operations Management

Ten Decision Areas	Issues	Chapter(s)
1. Design of goods and services	What good or service should we offer? How should we design these products?	
2. Managing quality	How do we define the quality? Who is responsible for quality?	
3. Process and capacity design	What process and what capacity will these products require? What equipment and technology are necessary for these processes?	
4. Location strategy	Where should we put the facility? On what criteria should we base the location decision?	
5. Layout strategy	How should we arrange the facility? How large must the facility be to meet our plan?	
6. Human resources and job design	How do we provide a reasonable work environment? How much can we expect our employees to produce?	
7. Supply-chain management	Should we make or buy this component? Who should be our suppliers and how can we integrate them into our strategy?	6, Supplement 7
8. Inventory, material requirements planning, and JIT (just-in-time)	How much inventory of each item should we have? When do we reorder?	
9. Intermediate and short-term scheduling	Are we better off keeping people on the payroll during slowdowns? Which job do we perform next?	
10. Maintenance	Who is responsible for maintenance?	

AUTHOR COMMENT
Current OM emphasis on quality and supply chain has increased job opportunities in these 10 areas.

read this text, identify disciplines that can assist you in making these decisions. Then take courses in those areas. The more background an OM student has in accounting, statistics, information systems, and mathematics, the more job opportunities will be available. About 40% of all jobs are in OM.

The following professional organizations provide various certifications that may enhance your education and be of help in your career:

- APICS, the Association for Operations Management (**www.apics.org**)
- Standards Council of Canada (**www.scc.ca**)
- Institute for Supply Management (ISM) (**www.ism.ws**)
- Project Management Institute (PMI) (**www.pmi.org**)
- Council of Supply Chain Management Professionals (**www.cscmp.org**)

Figure 1.2 shows some possible job opportunities.

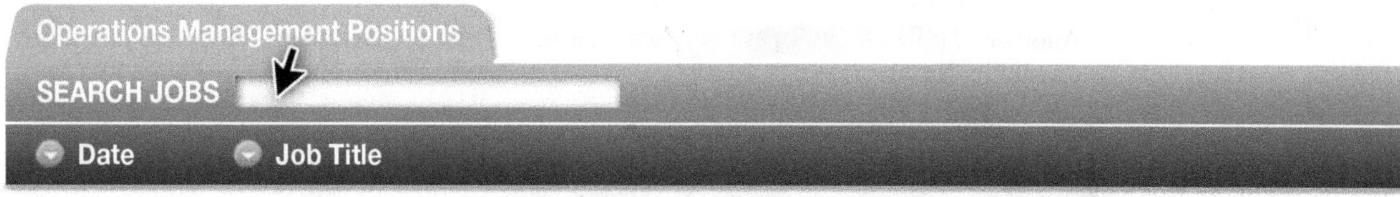

1/15 **Plant Manager**
Division of Fortune 1000 company seeks plant manager for plant located in the Vancouver area. This plant manufactures loading dock equipment for commercial markets. The candidate must be experienced in plant management including expertise in production planning, purchasing, and inventory management. Good written and oral communication skills are a must, along with excellent application of skills in managing people.

2/23 **Operations Analyst**
Expanding national coffee shop: top 10 "Best Places to Work" wants junior-level systems analyst to join our excellent store improvement team. Business or I.E. degree, work methods, labour standards, ergonomics, cost accounting knowledge a plus. This is a hands-on job and excellent opportunity for a team player with good people skills. West coast location. Some travel required.

3/18 **Quality Manager**
Several openings exist in our small package processing facilities in Montreal and Winnipeg for quality managers. These highly visible positions require extensive use of statistical tools to monitor all aspects of service, timeliness, and workload measurement. The work involves (1) a combination of hands-on applications and detailed analysis using databases and spreadsheets, (2) process audits to identify areas for improvement, and (3) management of implementation of changes. Positions involve night hours and weekends. Send resume.

4/6 **Supply Chain Manager and Planner**
Responsibilities entail negotiating contracts and establishing long-term relationships with suppliers. We will rely on the selected candidate to maintain accuracy in the purchasing system, invoices, and product returns. A bachelor's degree and up to 2 years related experience are required. Working knowledge of MRP, ability to use feedback to master scheduling and suppliers and consolidate orders for best price and delivery are necessary. Proficiency in all PC Windows applications, particularly Excel and Word, is essential. Knowledge of Oracle business systems is a plus. Effective verbal and written communication skills are essential.

5/14 **Process Improvement Consultants**
An expanding consulting firm is seeking consultants to design and implement lean production and cycle time reduction plans in both service and manufacturing processes. Our firm is currently working with an international bank to improve its back office operations, as well as with several manufacturing firms. A business degree required; APICS certification a plus.

FIGURE 1.2 Many Opportunities Exist for Operations Managers

The Heritage of Operations Management

The field of OM is relatively young, but its history is rich and interesting. Our lives and the OM discipline have been enhanced by the innovations and contributions of numerous individuals. We now introduce a few of these people, and we provide a summary of significant events in operations management in Figure 1.3.

Eli Whitney (1800) is credited for the early popularization of interchangeable parts, which was achieved through standardization and quality control. Through a contract he signed with the U.S. government for 10 000 muskets, he was able to command a premium price because of their interchangeable parts.

Frederick W. Taylor (1881), known as the father of scientific management, contributed to personnel selection, planning and scheduling, motion study, and the now popular field of ergonomics. One of his major contributions was his belief that management should be much more resourceful and aggressive in the improvement of work methods. Taylor and his colleagues, Henry L. Gantt and Frank and Lillian Gilbreth, were among the first to systematically seek the best way to produce.

Another of Taylor's contributions was the belief that management should assume more responsibility for:

1. Matching employees to the right job.
2. Providing the proper training.
3. Providing proper work methods and tools.
4. Establishing legitimate incentives for work to be accomplished.

Cost Focus

Early Concepts 1776–1880
Labour Specialization (Smith, Babbage)
Standardized Parts (Whitney)

Scientific Management Era 1880–1910
Gantt Charts (Gantt)
Motion & Time Studies (Gilbreth)
Process Analysis (Taylor)
Queuing Theory (Erlang)

Mass Production Era 1910–1980
Moving Assembly Line (Ford/Sorensen)
Statistical Sampling (Shewhart)
Economic Order Quantity (Harris)
Linear Programming
PERT/CPM (DuPont)
Material Requirements Planning (MRP)

Quality Focus

Lean Production Era 1980–1995
Just-in-Time (JIT)
Computer-Aided Design (CAD)
Electronic Data Interchange (EDI)
Total Quality Management (TQM)
Baldrige Award
Empowerment
Kanbans

Customization Focus

Mass Customization Era 1995–2015
Globalization
Internet/E-Commerce
Enterprise Resource Planning
International Quality Standards (ISO)
Finite Scheduling
Supply-Chain Management
Mass Customization
Build-to-Order
Sustainability

FIGURE 1.3 Significant Events in Operations Management

By 1913, Henry Ford and Charles Sorensen combined what they knew about standardized parts with the quasi-assembly lines of the meatpacking and mail-order industries and added the revolutionary concept of the assembly line, where men stood still and material moved.

Quality control is another historically significant contribution to the field of OM. Walter Shewhart (1924) combined his knowledge of statistics with the need for quality control and provided the foundations for statistical sampling in quality control. W. Edwards Deming (1950) believed, as did Frederick Taylor, that management must do more to improve the work environment and processes so that quality can be improved.

Operations management will continue to progress with contributions from other disciplines, including *industrial engineering* and *management science*. These disciplines, along with statistics, management, and economics, contribute to improved models and decision making.

Innovations from the *physical sciences* (biology, anatomy, chemistry, and physics) have also contributed to advances in OM. These innovations include new adhesives, faster integrated circuits, gamma rays to sanitize food products, and higher-quality glass for LCD and plasma TVs. Innovation in products and processes often depends on advances in the physical sciences.

Especially important contributions to OM have come from *information technology*, which we define as the systematic processing of data to yield information. Information technology—with wireless links, internet, and e-commerce—is reducing costs and accelerating communication.

Decisions in operations management require individuals who are well versed in management science, in information technology, and often in one of the biological or physical sciences. In this textbook, we look at the diverse ways a student can prepare for a career in operations management.

Operations in the Service Sector

AUTHOR COMMENT
Services are especially important because almost 80% of all jobs are in service firms.

Manufacturers produce a tangible product, while service products are often intangible. But many products are a combination of a good and a service, which complicates the definition of a service. Even the Canadian government has trouble generating a consistent definition. Because definitions vary, much of the data and statistics generated about the service sector are inconsistent. However, we define **services** as including repair and maintenance, government, food and lodging, transportation, insurance, trade, financial, real estate, education, law, medicine, entertainment, and other professional occupations.

Services
Economic activities that typically produce an intangible product (such as education, entertainment, lodging, government, financial, and health services).

DIFFERENCES BETWEEN GOODS AND SERVICES

Let's examine some of the differences between goods and services:

- Services are usually *intangible* (for example, your purchase of a ride in an empty airline seat between two cities) as opposed to a tangible good.
- Services are often *produced and consumed simultaneously*; there is no stored inventory. For instance, the beauty salon produces a haircut that is "consumed" simultaneously, or the doctor produces an operation that is "consumed" as it is produced. We have not yet figured out how to inventory haircuts or appendectomies.
- Services are often *unique*. Your mix of financial coverage, such as investments and insurance policies, may not be the same as anyone else's, just as the medical procedure or a haircut produced for you is not exactly like anyone else's.
- Services have *high customer interaction*. Services are often difficult to standardize, automate, and make as efficient as we would like because customer interaction demands uniqueness. In fact, in many cases this uniqueness is what the customer is paying for; therefore, the operations manager must ensure that the product is designed (i.e., customized) so that it can be delivered in the required unique manner.
- Services have *inconsistent product definition*. Product definition may be rigorous, as in the case of an auto insurance policy, but inconsistent because policyholders change cars and policies mature.
- Services are often *knowledge based*, as in the case of educational, medical, and legal services, and therefore hard to automate.
- Services are frequently *dispersed*. Dispersion occurs because services are frequently brought to the client/customer via a local office, a retail outlet, or even a house call.

LO2: Explain the distinction between goods and services

The activities of the operations function are often very similar for both goods and services. For instance, both goods and services must have quality standards established, and both must be designed and processed on a schedule in a facility where human resources are employed.

Having made the distinction between goods and services, we should point out that, in many cases, the distinction is not clear-cut. In reality, almost all services and almost all goods are a mixture of a service and a tangible product. Even services such as consulting may require a tangible report. Similarly, the sale of most goods includes a service. For instance, many products have the service components of financing and delivery (e.g., automobile sales). Many also require after-sale training and maintenance (e.g., office copiers and machinery). "Service" activities may also be an integral part of production. Human resource activities, logistics, accounting, training, field service, and repair are all service activities, but they take place within a manufacturing organization. Very few services are "pure," meaning they have no tangible component. Counselling may be one of the exceptions.

GROWTH OF SERVICES

Services constitute the largest economic sector in postindustrial societies. Until about 1900, many Canadians were employed in agriculture. Increased agricultural productivity allowed people to leave the farm and seek employment in the city. Similarly, manufacturing employment has decreased in North America in the past 30 years. The Canadian market tends to follow U.S. trends, as can be seen in the following comparison. The changes in U.S. manufacturing and service employment, in millions, are shown in Figure 1.4(a). Interestingly, as Figure 1.4(b) indicates, the number of people employed in manufacturing has decreased since 1950, but each person is now producing almost 20 times more than in 1950. Services became the dominant employer in the early 1920s, with manufacturing employment peaking at about 32% in 1950. The huge productivity increases in agriculture and manufacturing have allowed more of our economic resources to be devoted to services, as shown in Figure 1.4(c). Consequently, much of the world can now enjoy the pleasures of education, health services, entertainment, and myriad other things that we call services. Examples of firms and percentage of employment in the Canadian **service sector** are shown in Table 1.3. The table also provides employment percentages for the nonservice sectors of manufacturing, construction, utilities, agriculture, and mining on the bottom five lines.

Service sector
The segment of the economy that includes trade, financial, lodging, education, legal, medical, and other professional occupations.

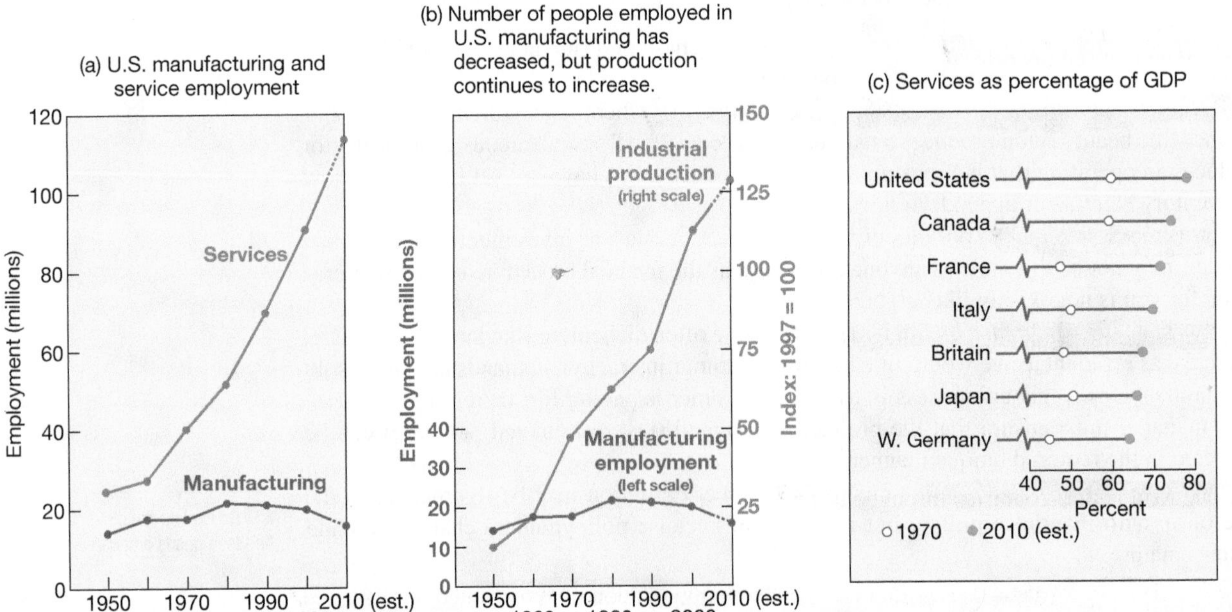

FIGURE 1.4 Development of the Service Economy and Manufacturing Productivity

Sources: U.S. Bureau of Labor Statistics; Federal Reserve Board, Industrial Production and Capacity Utilization (2009); and Statistical Abstract of the United States (2008).

TABLE 1.3
Examples of Organizations in Each Sector

Sector	Example	Percent of All Jobs
Service-Producing Sector		
Trade	Hudson Bay Company; Real Canadian Superstore	15%
Transportation and warehousing	WestJet; Maritime–Ontario Freight Lines Limited	5%
Finance, insurance, real estate, and leasing	Royal Bank; Manulife	6%
Professional, scientific, and technical services	Borden Ladner Gervais Law Firm	8%
Business, building and other support services[1]	Edmonton Waste Management Centre; Carlson Wagonlit Travel	4%
Educational services	McGill University	7%
Health care and social assistance	Sick Kids Hospital	12%
Information, culture, and recreation	Calgary Flames; Princess of Wales Theatre	5%
Accommodation and food services	Tim Hortons; Royal York Hotel	6%
Other Services	Joe's Barber Shop; ABC Landscaping	4%
Public administration	Province of Manitoba; City of Hamilton	6%
Goods-Producing Sector		22%
Agriculture	Farming Operations	2%
Forestry, fishing, mining, quarrying, oil, and gas[2]	Canadian Mining Company Inc.; Dome Pacific Logging Ltd.	2%
Utilities	Ontario Power Generation	1%
Construction	PCL Construction Management Inc.	7%
Manufacturing	Magna International Inc.	10%

[1]Formerly "Management of companies, administrative, and other support services."

[2]Also referred to as "Natural resources."

Source: Statistics Canada, CANSIM, table 282-0008 and Catalogue no. 71F0004XCB.

SERVICE PAY

AUTHOR COMMENT
Service jobs with their operations component are growing as a percentage of all jobs.

Although there is a common perception that service industries are low paying, in fact, many service jobs pay very well. Operations managers in the maintenance facility of an airline are very well paid, as are the operations managers who supervise computer services to the financial community. However, the accommodation and food services sectors followed by the arts, recreation, and entertainment sectors offer the lowest average weekly pay levels in Canada.

Exciting New Trends in Operations Management

AUTHOR COMMENT
One of the reasons OM is such an exciting discipline is that an operations manager is confronted with ever-changing issues, from technology to sustainability.

OM managers operate in an exciting and dynamic environment. This environment is the result of a variety of challenging forces, from globalization of world trade to the transfer of ideas, products, and money at electronic speeds. The direction now being taken by OM—where it has been and where it is going—is shown in Figure 1.5. Let's look at some of these challenges:

- *Ethics:* Operations managers' roles of buying from suppliers, transforming resources into finished goods, and delivering to customers places them at critical junctures where they must frequently make ethical decisions.
- *Global focus:* The rapid decline in communication and transportation costs has made markets global. Similarly, resources in the form of capital, materials, talent, and labour are now also global. As a result, countries throughout the world are contributing to globalization as they vie for economic growth. Operations managers are rapidly responding with creative designs, efficient production, and quality goods.
- *Rapid product development:* Rapid international communication of news, entertainment, and lifestyles is dramatically chopping away at the lifespan of products. Operations managers are responding with management structures, technology, and alliances (partnerships) that are more responsive and effective.

Traditional Approach		Reasons for Change		Current Challenges
Ethics and regulation not at the forefront	➡	*Public concern over pollution, corruption, child labour, etc.*	➡	High ethical and social responsibility; increased legal and professional standards (chapters, 1, 2, 5, 6 and 7)
Local, regional, national focus	➡	*Growth of reliable, low-cost communication and transportation*	➡	Global focus; international collaboration (Chapters 2, 6)
Lengthy product development	➡	*Shorter life cycles; growth of global communication; CAD; internet*	➡	Rapid product development; design collaboration
Low-cost production, with little concern for environment; free resources (air, water) ignored	➡	*Public sensitivity to environment; ISO 14000 standard; increasing disposal costs*	➡	Environmentally sensitive production; green manufacturing; sustainability
Low-cost standard products	➡	*Rise of consumerism; increased affluence; individualism*	➡	Mass customization
Emphasis on specialized, often manual tasks	➡	*Recognizing the importance of the employee's total contribution; knowledge society*	➡	Empowered employees; enriched jobs
"In-house" production; low-bid purchasing	➡	*Rapid technology change; increasing competitive forces*	➡	Supply-chain partnering; joint ventures; alliances (Chapter 6, Supplement 7)
Large-lot production	➡	*Shorter product life; increasing need to reduce inventory*	➡	Just-in-time performance; lean production; continuous improvement

FIGURE 1.5 Changing Challenges for the Operations Manager

- *Environmentally sensitive production:* Operation managers' continuing battle to improve productivity is increasingly concerned with designing products and processes that are ecologically sustainable. That means designing products and packaging that minimize resource use, are biodegradable, can be recycled, and are generally environmentally friendly.
- *Mass customization:* Once managers recognize the world as the marketplace, the cultural and individual differences become quite obvious. In a world where consumers are increasingly aware of innovation and options, substantial pressure is placed on firms to respond. And operations managers are responding with creative product designs and flexible production processes that cater to the individual whims of consumers. The goal is to produce customized products, whenever and wherever needed.
- *Empowered employees:* The knowledge explosion and more technical workplace have combined to require more competence in the workplace. Operations managers are responding by moving more decision making to individual workers.
- *Supply-chain partnering:* Shorter product life cycles, demanding customers, and fast changes in technology, material, and processes require supply-chain partners to be more in tune with the needs of end users. And because suppliers can contribute unique expertise, operations managers are outsourcing and building long-term partnerships with critical players in the supply chain.
- *Just-in-time performance:* Inventory requires financial resources and impedes response to rapid changes in the marketplace. These forces push operations managers to viciously cut inventories at every level, from raw materials to finished goods.

These trends are part of the exciting OM challenges that are discussed in this text.

AUTHOR COMMENT
Why is productivity important? Because it determines our standard of living.

The Productivity Challenge

Productivity
The ratio of outputs (goods and services) divided by one or more inputs (such as labour, capital, or management).

The creation of goods and services requires changing resources into goods and services. The more efficiently we make this change, the more productive we are and the more value is added to the good or service provided. **Productivity** is the ratio of outputs (goods and services) divided

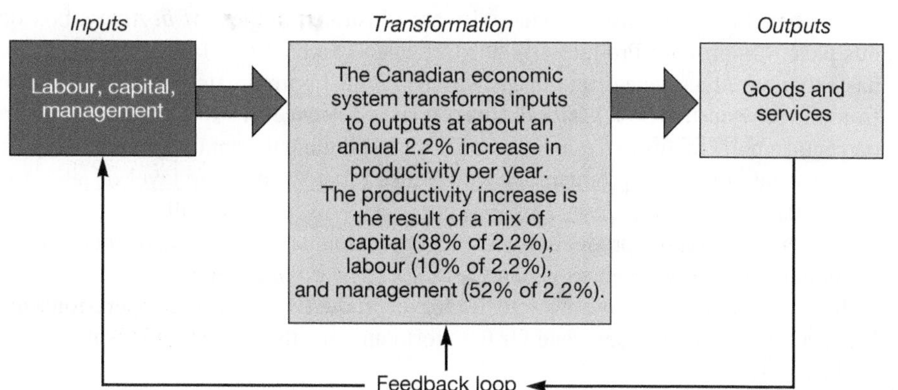

FIGURE 1.6
The Economic System Adds Value by Transforming Inputs to Outputs
An effective feedback loop evaluates performance against a strategy or standard. It also evaluates customer satisfaction and sends signals to managers controlling the inputs and transformation process.

by the inputs (resources, such as labour and capital) (see Figure 1.6). The operations manager's job is to enhance (improve) this ratio of outputs to inputs. Improving productivity means improving efficiency.[1]

This improvement can be achieved in two ways: reducing inputs while keeping output constant or increasing output while keeping inputs constant. Both represent an improvement in productivity. In an economic sense, inputs are labour, capital, and management, which are integrated into a production system. Management creates this production system, which provides the conversion of inputs to outputs. Outputs are goods and services, including such diverse items as guns, butter, education, improved judicial systems, and ski resorts. *Production* is the making of goods and services. High production may imply only that more people are working and that employment levels are high (low unemployment), but it does not imply high *productivity*.

LO3: Explain the difference between production and productivity

Measurement of productivity is an excellent way to evaluate a country's ability to provide an improving standard of living for its people. *Only through increases in productivity can the standard of living improve.* Moreover, only through increases in productivity can labour, capital, and management receive additional payments. If returns to labour, capital, or management are increased without increased productivity, prices rise. On the other hand, downward pressure is placed on prices when productivity increases, because more is being produced with the same resources.

OM *in Action* Improving Productivity at Starbucks

"This is a game of seconds . . ." says Silva Peterson, whom Starbucks has put in charge of saving seconds. Her team of 10 analysts is constantly asking themselves: "How can we shave time off this?"

Peterson's analysis suggested that there were some obvious opportunities. First, stop requiring signatures on credit-card purchases under $25. This sliced 8 seconds off the transaction time at the cash register.

Then analysts noticed that Starbucks's largest cold beverage, the Venti size, required two bending and digging motions to scoop up enough ice. The scoop was too small. Redesign of the scoop provided the proper amount in one motion and cut 14 seconds off the average time of one minute.

Third were new espresso machines; with the push of a button, the machines grind coffee beans and brew. This allowed the server, called a "barista" in Starbucks's vocabulary, to do other things. The savings: about 12 seconds per espresso shot.

As a result, operations improvements at Starbucks outlets have increased the average yearly volume by nearly $200 000, to about $940 000 in the past 6 years. This is a 27% improvement in productivity—about 4.5% per year. In the service industry, a 4.5% per year increase is very tasty.

Sources: The Wall Street Journal (August 4, 2009): A1, A10 and (April 12, 2005): B2:B7; *Industrial Engineer* (January 2006): 66; and www.finfacts.com, October 6, 2005.

[1]*Efficiency* means doing the job well—with a minimum of resources and waste. Note the distinction between being *efficient*, which implies doing the job well, and *effective*, which means doing the right thing. A job well done—say, by applying the 10 decisions of operations management—helps us be *efficient;* developing and using the correct strategy helps us be *effective*.

The benefits of increased productivity are illustrated in the *OM in Action* box on the previous page, "Improving Productivity at Starbucks." Since 1973, labour productivity in Canada has experienced an annual rate of growth averaging approximately 1.25%, down considerably from the previous level of 3.00% during the period between 1961 and 1973. An increase of one percentage point in this performance would almost double the annual growth rate to 2.25%. Such a growth rate in labour productivity would mean that the average level of labour productivity in Canada would double every 32 years, not every 58 years as it will with a 1.25% growth rate. Moreover, if our labour productivity level were to double every 32 years, then (in the absence of major demographic effects) so would Canada's standard of living.[2]

In this text, we examine how to improve productivity through operations management. Productivity is a significant issue for the world and one that the operations manager is uniquely qualified to address.

LO4: Compute single-factor productivity

PRODUCTIVITY MEASUREMENT

The measurement of productivity can be quite direct. Such is the case when productivity is measured by labour-hours per ton of a specific type of steel. Although labour-hours is a common measure of input, other measures such as capital (dollars invested), materials (tons of ore), or energy (kilowatts of electricity) can be used.[3] An example of this can be summarized in the following equation:

$$\text{Productivity} = \frac{\text{Units produced}}{\text{Input used}} \tag{1-1}$$

For example, if units produced = 1000 and labour-hours used is 250, then:

$$\text{Productivity} = \frac{\text{Units produced}}{\text{Labour-hours used}} = \frac{1000}{250} = \text{units per labour-hour}$$

Single-factor productivity Indicates the ratio of one resource (input) to the goods and services produced (outputs).

Multifactor productivity Indicates the ratio of many or all resources (inputs) to the goods and services produced (outputs).

The use of just one resource input to measure productivity, as shown in Equation (1-1), is known as **single-factor productivity**. However, a broader view of productivity is **multifactor productivity**, which includes all inputs (e.g., capital, labour, material, energy). Multifactor productivity is also known as *total factor productivity*. Multifactor productivity is calculated by combining the input units as shown here:

$$\text{Productivity} = \frac{\text{Output}}{\text{Labour} + \text{Material} + \text{Energy} + \text{Capital} + \text{Miscellaneous}} \tag{1-2}$$

To aid in the computation of multifactor productivity, the individual inputs (the denominator) can be expressed in dollars and summed as shown in Example 2.

EXAMPLE 2

Computing single-factor and multifactor gains in productivity

Collins Title wants to evaluate its labour and multifactor productivity with a new computerized title-search system. The company has a staff of four, each working 8 hours per day (for a payroll cost of $640/day) and overhead expenses of $400 per day. Collins processes and closes on 8 titles each day. The new computerized title-search system will allow the processing of 14 titles per day. Although the staff, their work hours, and pay are the same, the overhead expenses are now $800 per day.

APPROACH ▶ Collins uses Equation (1-1) to compute labour productivity and Equation (1-2) to compute multifactor productivity.

SOLUTION: ▶

$$\text{Labour productivity with the old system: } \frac{8 \text{ titles per day}}{32 \text{ labour-hours}} = .25 \text{ titles per labour-hours}$$

$$\text{Labour productivity with the new system: } \frac{14 \text{ titles per day}}{32 \text{ labour-hours}} = .4375 \text{ titles per labour-hour}$$

[2]See www.parl.gc.ca.

[3]The quality and time period are assumed to remain constant.

$$\text{Multifactor productivity with the old system: } \frac{8 \text{ titles per day}}{\$640 + 400} = .0077 \text{ titles per dollar}$$

$$\text{Multifactor productivity with the new system: } \frac{14 \text{ titles per day}}{\$640 + 800} = .0097 \text{ titles per dollar}$$

Labour productivity has increased from .25 to .4375. The change is (.4375 – .25) / .25 = 0.75, or a 75% increase in labour productivity. Multifactor productivity has increased from .0077 to .0097. This change is (.0097 – .0077) / .0077 = 0.26, or a 26% increase in multifactor productivity.

INSIGHT ▶ Both the labour (single-factor) and multifactor productivity measures show an increase in productivity. However, the multifactor measure provides a better picture of the increase because it includes all the costs connected with the increase in output.

LEARNING EXERCISE ▶ If the overhead goes to $960 (rather than $800), what is the multifactor productivity? [Answer: .00875.]

RELATED PROBLEMS ▶ 1.1, 1.2, 1.5, 1.6, 1.7, 1.8, 1.9, 1.11, 1.12, 1.14, 1.15

LO5: Compute multifactor productivity

Use of productivity measures aids managers in determining how well they are doing. But results from the two measures can be expected to vary. If labour productivity growth is entirely the result of capital spending, measuring just labour distorts the results. Multifactor productivity is usually better, but more complicated. Labour productivity is the more popular measure. The multifactor-productivity measures provide better information about the trade-offs among factors, but substantial measurement problems remain. Some of these measurement problems are:

1. *Quality* may change while the quantity of inputs and outputs remains constant. Compare an HDTV of this decade with a black-and-white TV of the 1950s. Both are TVs, but few people would deny that the quality has improved. The unit of measure—a TV—is the same, but the quality has changed.
2. *External elements* may cause an increase or a decrease in productivity for which the system under study may not be directly responsible. A more reliable electric power service may greatly improve production, thereby improving the firm's productivity because of this support system rather than because of managerial decisions made within the firm.
3. *Precise units of measure* may be lacking. Not all automobiles require the same inputs: Some cars are subcompacts, others are 911 Turbo Porsches.

Productivity measurement is particularly difficult in the service sector, where the end product can be hard to define. For example, economic statistics ignore the quality of your haircut, the outcome of a court case, or service at a retail store. In some cases, adjustments are made for the quality of the product sold but *not* the quality of the sales presentation or the advantage of a broader product selection. Productivity measurements require specific inputs and outputs, but a free economy is producing worth—what people want—which includes convenience, speed, and safety. Traditional measures of outputs may be a very poor measure of these other measures of worth. Note the quality-measurement problems in a law office, where each case is different, altering the accuracy of the measure "cases per labour-hour" or "cases per employee."

PRODUCTIVITY VARIABLES

As we saw in Figure 1.6, productivity increases are dependent on three **productivity variables**:

Productivity variables
The three factors critical to productivity improvement—capital, and the art and science of management.

1. *Labour*, which contributes about 10% of the annual increase.
2. *Capital*, which contributes about 38% of the annual increase.
3. *Management*, which contributes about 52% of the annual increase.

These three factors are critical to improved productivity. They represent the broad areas in which managers can take action to improve productivity.

LABOUR Improvement in the contribution of labour to productivity is the result of a healthier, better-educated, and better-nourished labour force. Some increase may also be attributed to a shorter workweek. Historically, about 10% of the annual improvement in productivity is

LO6: Identify the critical variables in enhancing productivity

attributed to improvement in the quality of labour. Three key variables for improved labour productivity are:

1. Basic education appropriate for an effective labour force.
2. Diet of the labour force.
3. Social overhead that makes labour available, such as transportation and sanitation.

Illiteracy and poor diets are major impediments to productivity, costing countries up to 20% of their productivity. Infrastructure that yields clean drinking water and sanitation is also an opportunity for improved productivity, as well as an opportunity for better health, in much of the world.

In developed nations, the challenge becomes *maintaining and enhancing the skills of labour* in the midst of rapidly expanding technology and knowledge. Recent data suggest that the average American 17-year-old knows significantly less mathematics than the average Japanese person of the same age, and about half cannot answer the questions in Figure 1.7. Moreover, more than 38% of U.S. job applicants tested for basic skills were deficient in reading, writing, or math.[4]

Overcoming shortcomings in the quality of labour while other countries have a better labour force is a major challenge. Perhaps improvements can be found not only through increasing competence of labour but also via *better utilized labour with a stronger commitment*. Training, motivation, team building, and the human resource strategies, as well as improved education, may be among the many techniques that will contribute to increased labour productivity. Improvements in labour productivity are possible; however, they can be expected to be increasingly difficult and expensive.

CAPITAL Human beings are tool-using animals. Capital investment provides those tools. Capital investment has increased in Canada most years except during a few very severe recession periods. Accumulated capital investment has increased in Canada at a compound annual growth rate of 4.5%.

Inflation and taxes increase the cost of capital, making capital investment increasingly expensive. When the capital invested per employee drops, we can expect a drop in productivity. Using labour rather than capital may reduce unemployment in the short run, but it also makes economies less productive and therefore lowers wages in the long run. Capital investment is often a necessary, but seldom a sufficient ingredient in the battle for increased productivity.

The trade-off between capital and labour is continually in flux. The higher the cost of capital, the more projects requiring capital are "squeezed out": they are not pursued because the potential return on investment for a given risk has been reduced. Managers adjust their investment plans to changes in capital cost.

MANAGEMENT Management is a factor of production and an economic resource. Management is responsible for ensuring that labour and capital are effectively used to increase productivity.

FIGURE 1.7
About Half of the 17-Year-Olds in the U.S. Cannot Correctly Answer Questions of This Type

AUTHOR COMMENT
Perhaps as many as 25% of North American workers lack the basic skills needed for their current job.

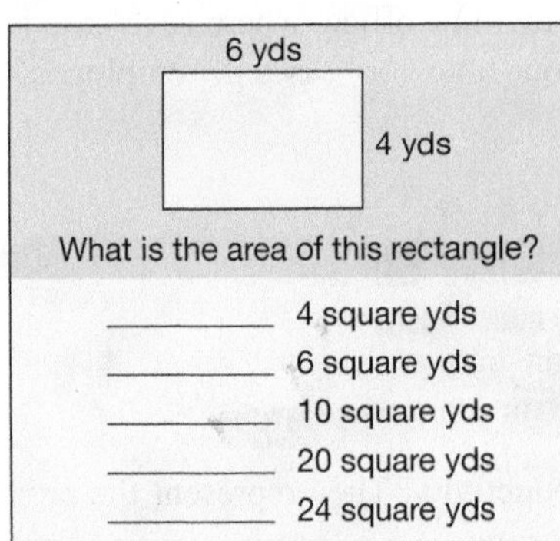

If $9y + 3 = 6y + 15$ then $y =$

_____ 1   _____ 4
_____ 2   _____ 6

Which of the following is true about 84% of 100?

_____ It is greater than 100
_____ It is less than 100
_____ It is equal to 100

[4]"Can't Read, Can't Count," *Scientific American* (October 2001): 24; and "Economic Time Bomb: U.S. Teens Are among Worst at Math," *The Wall Street Journal* (December 7, 2004): B1.

The effective use of capital often means finding the proper trade-off between investment in capital assets (automation, left) and human assets (a manual process, right). While there are risks connected with any investment, the cost of capital and physical investments is fairly clear-cut, but the cost of employees has many hidden costs, including fringe benefits, social insurance, and legal constraints on hiring, employment, and termination.

Siemens, the multi-billion-dollar German conglomerate, has long been known for its apprentice programs in its home country. Because education is often the key to efficient operations in a technological society, Siemens has spread its apprentice-training programs to its international plants. These programs are laying the foundation for the highly skilled workforce that is essential for global competitiveness.

Management accounts for over half of the annual increase in productivity. This increase includes improvements made through the use of knowledge and the application of technology.

Using knowledge and technology is critical in postindustrial societies. Consequently, post-industrial societies are also known as knowledge societies. **Knowledge societies** are those in which much of the labour force has migrated from manual work to technical and information-processing tasks requiring ongoing education. The required education and training are important high-cost items that are the responsibility of operations managers as they build organizations and workforces. The expanding knowledge base of contemporary society requires that managers use *technology and knowledge effectively.*

Knowledge society
A society in which much of the labour force has migrated from manual work to work based on knowledge.

More effective use of capital also contributes to productivity. It falls to the operations manager, as a productivity catalyst, to select the best new capital investments as well as to improve the productivity of existing investments.

The productivity challenge is difficult. A country cannot be a world-class competitor with second-class inputs. Poorly educated labour, inadequate capital, and dated technology are second-class inputs. High productivity and high-quality outputs require high-quality inputs, including good operations managers.

PRODUCTIVITY AND THE SERVICE SECTOR

The service sector provides a special challenge to the accurate measurement of productivity and productivity improvement. The traditional analytical framework of economic theory is based primarily on goods-producing activities. Consequently, most published economic data relate to goods production. But the data do indicate that, as our contemporary service economy has increased in size, we have had slower growth in productivity.

Productivity of the service sector has proven difficult to improve because service-sector work is:

1. Typically labour intensive (for example, counselling, teaching).
2. Frequently focused on unique individual attributes or desires (for example, investment advice).
3. Often an intellectual task performed by professionals (for example, medical diagnosis).
4. Often difficult to mechanize and automate (for example, a haircut).
5. Often difficult to evaluate for quality (for example, performance of a law firm).

The more intellectual and personal the task, the more difficult it is to achieve increases in productivity. Low-productivity improvement in the service sector is also attributable to the growth of low-productivity activities in the service sector. These include activities not previously a part of the measured economy, such as child care, food preparation, house cleaning, and laundry service. These activities have moved out of the home and into the measured economy as more and more women have joined the workforce. Inclusion of these activities has probably resulted in lower measured productivity for the service sector, although, in fact, actual productivity has probably increased because these activities are now more efficiently produced than previously.

However, in spite of the difficulty of improving productivity in the service sector, improvements are being made. And this text presents a multitude of ways to make these improvements. Indeed, what can be done when management pays attention to how work actually gets done is astonishing!

Although the evidence indicates that all industrialized countries have the same problem with service productivity, the U.S. remains the world leader in overall productivity *and* service productivity. Retailing is twice as productive in the U.S. as in Japan, where laws protect shopkeepers from discount chains. The U.S. telephone industry is at least twice as productive as Germany's. However, because productivity is central to the operations manager's job and because the service sector is so large, we take special note in this text of how to improve productivity in the service sector. (See, for instance, the *OM in Action* box, "Taco Bell Improves Productivity and Goes Green to Lower Costs.")

OM *in Action* Taco Bell Improves Productivity and Goes Green to Lower Costs

Founded in 1962 by Glenn Bell, Taco Bell seeks competitive advantage via low cost. Like many other services, Taco Bell relies on its operations management to improve productivity and reduce cost.

Its menu and meals are designed to be easy to prepare. Taco Bell has shifted a substantial portion of food preparation to suppliers who could perform food processing more efficiently than a stand-alone restaurant. Ground beef is precooked prior to arrival and then reheated, as are many dishes that arrive in plastic boil bags for easy sanitary reheating. Similarly, tortillas arrive already fried and onions arrive prediced. Efficient layout and automation has cut to 8 seconds the time needed to prepare tacos and burritos and has cut time in the drive-thru lines by one minute. These advances have been combined with training and empowerment to increase the span of management from one supervisor for 5 restaurants to one supervisor for 30 or more.

Operations managers at Taco Bell believe they have cut in-store labour by 15 hours per day and reduced floor space by more than 50%. The result is a store that can handle twice the volume with half the labour.

In 2010, Taco Bell will have completed the rollout of its new Grill-to-Order kitchens by installing water- and energy-savings grills that conserve over a billion litres of water and 200 million KwH of electricity each year. This "green"-inspired cooking method also saves the company's 5600 restaurants $17 million per year.

Effective operations management has resulted in productivity increases that support Taco Bell's low-cost strategy. Taco Bell is now the fast-food low-cost leader with a 73% share of the Mexican fast-food market.

Sources: Energy Business Journal (May 12, 2008): 111; *Harvard Business Review* (July/August 2008): 118; and J. Hueter and W. Swart, *Interfaces* (January–February 1998): 75–91.

Ethics and Social Responsibility

AUTHOR COMMENT
Ethics must drive all of a manager's decisions.

Operations managers are subjected to constant changes and challenges. The systems they build to convert resources into goods and services are complex. The physical and social environments change, as do laws and values. These changes present a variety of challenges that come from the conflicting perspectives of stakeholders such as customers, distributors, suppliers, owners, lenders, and employees. These stakeholders, as well as government agencies at various levels, require constant monitoring and thoughtful responses.

Identifying ethical and socially responsible responses while building productive systems is not always clear-cut. Among the many ethical challenges facing operations managers are:

- Efficiently developing and producing safe, quality products.
- Maintaining a sustainable environment.
- Providing a safe workplace.
- Honouring stakeholder commitments.

Managers must do all of this in an ethical and socially responsible way while meeting the demands of the marketplace. If operations managers have a *moral awareness and focus on increasing productivity* in a system where all stakeholders have a voice, then many of the ethical challenges will be successfully addressed (for example, see the *OM in Action* box, "Magna International"). The organization will use fewer resources, the employees will be committed, the market will be satisfied, and the ethical climate will be enhanced. Throughout this text, we note ways in which operations managers can take ethical and socially responsible actions while successfully addressing these challenges of the market. We also conclude each chapter with an *Ethical Dilemma* exercise.

OM *in Action* Magna International

In operations management, balancing the interests of the various stakeholders associated with a company can be challenging at the best of times. To add to the challenge, progressive organizations are now placing the needs of society high on the priority list and have declared their corporate social responsibility. Automotive parts manufacturer Magna International is an example of one of these companies.

Magna has publicly stated that they are committed to supporting the basic fabric of society through a number of programs, volunteer work, and charitable activities. Their "Corporate Constitution" allocates a maximum of two percent of their pre-tax profits to support charitable and non-profit organizations and they have pledged support to many programs dealing with health, culture, education, sports, and politics. They expressed their desire to continuously improve the quality of life in each of the communities in which their employees work and live.

Magna International's "Corporate Constitution" publicly declares and defines the rights of their employees and investors to participate in their profits and growth, while also imposing specified disciplines on management. This constitution strikes a balance between employees, investors, society, and management. This business philosophy was introduced by the company founder, Frank Stronach, in 1971—it is known as "Fair Enterprise" and is at the heart of Magna's operating structure.

Source: www.magna.com/about-magna/our-culture/corporate-constitution

Magna International actively supports the concept of corporate social responsibility.

CHAPTER SUMMARY

Operations, marketing, and finance/accounting are the three functions basic to all organizations. The operations function creates goods and services. Much of the progress of operations management has been made in the twentieth century, but since the beginning of time, humankind has been attempting to improve its material well-being. Operations managers are key players in the battle to improve productivity.

As societies become increasingly affluent, more of their resources are devoted to services. In Canada, more than three-quarters of the workforce is employed in the service sector. Productivity improvements are difficult to achieve, but operations managers are the primary vehicle for making improvements.

Key Terms

Production (p. 5)
Operations management (OM) (p. 5)
Management process (p. 8)
Services (p. 11)
Service sector (p. 12)
Productivity (p. 14)
Single-factor productivity (p. 16)
Multifactor productivity (p. 16)
Productivity variables (p. 17)
Knowledge society (p. 19)

Ethical Dilemma

Major corporations with overseas subcontractors (such as IKEA in Bangladesh, Unilever in India, and Nike in China) have been criticized, often with substantial negative publicity, when children as young as 10 have been found working in the subcontractor's facilities. The standard response is to perform an audit and then enhance controls so it does not happen again. In one such case, a 10-year-old was terminated. Shortly thereafter, the family, without the 10-year-old's contribution to the family income, lost its modest home, and the 10-year-old was left to scrounge in the local dump for scraps of metal. Was the decision to hire the 10-year-old ethical? Was the decision to terminate the 10-year-old ethical?

Discussion Questions

1. Why should one study operations management?
2. Identify four people who have contributed to the theory and techniques of operations management.
3. Briefly describe the contributions of the four individuals identified in the preceding question.
4. Figure 1.1 outlines the operations, finance/accounting, and marketing functions of three organizations. Prepare a chart similar to Figure 1.1 outlining the same functions for one of the following:
   a. a newspaper
   b. a drugstore
   c. a college library
   d. a summer camp
   e. a small costume-jewellery factory
5. Answer Question 4 for some other organization, perhaps an organization where you have worked.
6. What are the three basic functions of a firm?
7. Name the 10 decision areas of operations management.
8. Name four areas that are significant to improving labour productivity.
9. Canada, and indeed much of the world, has been described as a *knowledge society*. How does this affect productivity measurement and the comparison of productivity between Canada and other countries?
10. What are the measurement problems that occur when one attempts to measure productivity?
11. Mass customization and rapid product development were identified as current trends in modern manufacturing operations. What is the relationship, if any, between these trends? Can you cite any examples?
12. What are the five reasons productivity is difficult to improve in the service sector?
13. Describe some of the actions taken by Taco Bell to increase productivity that have resulted in Taco Bell's ability to serve "twice the volume with half the labour."

Solved Problems Virtual Office Hours help is available at MyOMLab.

▼ SOLVED PROBLEM 1.1

Productivity can be measured in a variety of ways, such as by labour, capital, energy, material usage, and so on. At Modern Lumber, Inc., Art Binley, president and producer of apple crates sold to growers, has been able, with his current equipment, to produce 240 crates per 100 logs. He currently purchases 100 logs per day, and each log requires 3 labour-hours to process. He believes that he can hire a professional buyer who can buy a better-quality log at the same cost. If this is the case, he can increase his production to 260 crates per 100 logs. His labour-hours will increase by 8 hours per day. What will be the impact on productivity (measured in crates per labour-hour) if the buyer is hired?

▼ **SOLUTION**

(a) Current labour productivity $= \dfrac{240 \text{ crates}}{100 \text{ logs} \times 3 \text{ hours/log}}$

$= \dfrac{240}{300}$

$= .8$ crates per labour-hour

(b) Labour productivity with buyer

$= \dfrac{260 \text{ creates}}{(100 \text{ logs} \times 3 \text{ hours/log}) + 8 \text{ hours}}$

$= \dfrac{260}{308}$

$= .844$ crates per labour-hour

Using current productivity (.80 from [a]) as a base, the increase will be 5.5% (.844/.8 = 1.055, or a 5.5% increase).

▼ **SOLVED PROBLEM 1.2**

Art Binley has decided to look at his productivity from a multifactor (total factor productivity) perspective (refer to Solved Problem 1.1). To do so, he has determined his labour, capital, energy, and material usage and decided to use dollars as the common denominator. His total labour-hours are now 300 per day and will increase to 308 per day. His capital and energy costs will remain constant at $350 and $150 per day, respectively. Material costs for the 100 logs per day are $1000 and will remain the same. Because he pays an average of $10 per hour (with fringes), Binley determines his productivity increase as follows:

▼ **SOLUTION**

	Current System		System with Professional Buyer	
Labour:	300 hrs. @10 = 3000		308 hrs. @10 =	$3080
Material:	100 logs/day 1000			1000
Capital:	350			350
Energy:	150			150
Total Cost:	$4500			$4580

Multifactor productivity of current system:
= 240 crates/4500 = .0533 crates/dollar

Multifactor productivity of proposed system:
= 260 crates/4580 = .0568 crates/dollar crates/dollar

Using current productivity (.0533) as a base, the increase will be .066. That is, .0568/.0533 = 1.066, or a 6.6% increase.

Problems*

•• **1.1** John Lucy makes wooden boxes in which to ship motorcycles. John and his three employees invest a total of 40 hours per day making the 120 boxes.

a) What is their productivity?
b) John and his employees have discussed redesigning the process to improve efficiency. If they can increase the rate to 125 per day, what will be their new productivity?
c) What will be their unit *increase* in productivity per hour?
d) What will be their percentage change in productivity? PX

•• **1.2** Riverside Metal Works produces cast bronze valves on a 10-person assembly line. On a recent day, 160 valves were produced during an 8-hour shift.

a) Calculate the labour productivity of the line.
b) The manager at Riverside changed the layout and was able to increase production to 180 units per 8-hour shift. What is the new labour productivity per labour-hour?
c) What is the percentage of productivity increase? PX

•• **1.3** This year, Benson, Inc., will produce 57 600 hot water heaters at its plant in Yulee, Florida, in order to meet expected global demand. To accomplish this, each labourer at the Yulee plant will work 160 hours per month. If the labour productivity at the plant is 0.15 hot water heaters per labour-hour, how many labourers are employed at the plant?

*Note: PX means the problem may be solved with POM for Windows and/or Excel OM.

•• **1.4** As a library or internet assignment, find the U.S. productivity rate (increase) last year for the (a) national economy, (b) manufacturing sector, and (c) service sector.

•• **1.5** Lori produces "Final Exam Care Packages" for resale by her sorority. She is currently working a total of 5 hours per day to produce 100 care packages.

a) What is Lori's productivity?
b) Lori thinks that by redesigning the package, she can increase her total productivity to 133 care packages per day. What will be her new productivity?
c) What will be the percentage increase in productivity if Lori makes the change? PX

•• **1.6** Eric Johnson makes billiard balls in his New England plant. With recent increases in his costs, he has a newfound interest in efficiency. Eric is interested in determining the productivity of his organization. He would like to know if his organization is maintaining the manufacturing average of 3% increase in productivity. He has the following data representing a month from last year and an equivalent month this year:

	Last Year	Now
Units produced	1 000	1 000
Labour (hours)	300	275
Resin (pounds)	50	45
Capital invested ($)	10 000	11 000
Energy (BTU)	3 000	2 850

Show the productivity percentage change for each category and then determine the improvement for labour-hours, the typical standard for comparison. PX

•• **1.7** Eric Johnson (using data from Problem 1.6) determines his costs to be as follows:

- *Labour:* $10 per hour
- *Resin:* $5 per pound
- *Capital expense:* 1% per month of investment
- *Energy:* $.50 per BTU

Show the percent change in productivity for one month last year versus one month this year, on a multifactor basis with dollars as the common denominator. PX

•• **1.8** Kleen Karpet cleaned 65 rugs in October, consuming the following resources:

Labour:	520 hours at $13 per hour
Solvent:	100 gallons at $5 per gallon
Machine rental:	20 days at $50 per day

a. What is the labour productivity per dollar?
b. What is the multifactor productivity? PX

•• **1.9** David Upton is president of Upton Manufacturing, a producer of Go-Kart tires. Upton makes 1000 tires per day with the following resources:

Labour:	400 hours per day @ $12.50 per hour
Raw material:	20 000 pounds per day @ $1 per pound
Energy:	$5000 per day
Capital costs:	$10 000 per day

a) What is the labour productivity per labour-hour for these tires at Upton Manufacturing?
b) What is the multifactor productivity for these tires at Upton Manufacturing?
c) What is the percent change in multifactor productivity if Upton can reduce the energy bill by $1000 per day without cutting production or changing any other inputs? PX

•• **1.10** Sawyer's, a local bakery, is worried about increased costs—particularly energy. Last year's records can provide a fairly good estimate of the parameters for this year. Judy Sawyer, the owner, does not believe things have changed much, but she did invest an additional $3000 for modifications to the bakery's ovens to make them more energy efficient. The modifications were supposed to make the ovens at least 15% more efficient. Sawyer has asked you to check the energy savings of the new ovens and also to look over other measures of the bakery's productivity to see if the modifications were beneficial. You have the following data to work with:

	Last Year	Now
Production (dozen)	1 500	1 500
Labour (hours)	350	325
Capital investment ($)	15 000	18 000
Energy (BTU)	3 000	2 750

PX

•• **1.11** Cunningham Performance Auto, Inc., modifies 375 autos per year. The manager, Peter Cunningham, is interested in obtaining a measure of overall performance. He has asked you to provide him with a multifactor measure of last year's performance as a benchmark for future comparison. You have assembled the following data. Resource inputs were: labour, 10 000 hours; 500 suspension and engine modification kits; and energy, 100 000 kilowatt-hours. Average labour cost last year was $20 per hour, kits cost $1000 each, and energy costs were $3 per kilowatt-hour. What do you tell Mr. Cunningham? PX

•• **1.12** Lake Charles Seafood makes 500 wooden packing boxes for fresh seafood per day, working in two 10-hour shifts. Due to increased demand, plant managers have decided to operate three 8-hour shifts instead. The plant is now able to produce 650 boxes per day.

a) Calculate the company's productivity before the change in work rules and after the change.
b) What is the percentage increase in productivity?
c) If production is increased to 700 boxes per day, what is the new productivity? PX

•• **1.13** Charles Lackey operates a bakery in Idaho Falls, Idaho. Because of its excellent product and excellent location, demand has increased by 25% in the last year. On far too many occasions, customers have not been able to purchase the bread of their choice. Because of the size of the store, no new ovens can be added. At a staff meeting, one employee suggested ways to load the ovens differently so that more loaves of bread can be baked at one time. This new process will require that the ovens be loaded by hand, requiring additional manpower. This is the only thing to be changed. If the bakery makes 1500 loaves per month with a labour productivity of 2.344 loaves per labour-hour, how many workers will Lackey need to add? (*Hint:* Each employee works 160 hours per month.)

•• **1.14** Refer to Problem 1.13. The pay will be $8 per hour for employees. Charles Lackey can also improve the yield by purchasing a new blender. The new blender will mean an increase in his investment. This added investment has a cost of $100 per month, but he will achieve the same output (an increase to 1875) as the change in labour-hours. Which is the better decision?

a) Show the productivity change, in loaves per dollar, with an increase in labour cost (from 640 to 800 hours).
b) Show the new productivity, in loaves per dollar, with only an increase in investment ($100 per month more).
c) Show the percent productivity change for labour and investment.

•• **1.15** Refer to Problems 1.13 and 1.14. If Charles Lackey's utility costs remain constant at $500 per month, labour at $8 per hour, and cost of ingredients at $0.35 per loaf, but Charles does not purchase the blender suggested in Problem 1.14, what will the productivity of the bakery be? What will be the percent increase or decrease?

•• **1.16** In December, General Motors produced 6600 customized vans at its plant in Detroit. The labour productivity at this plant is known to have been 0.10 vans per labour-hour during that month. Three hundred labourers were employed at the plant that month.

a) How many hours did the average labourer work that month?
b) If productivity can be increased to 0.11 vans per hour, how many hours would the average labourer work that month?

•• **1.17** Natalie Attired runs a small job shop where garments are made. The job shop employs eight workers. Each worker is paid $10 per hour. During the first week of March, each worker worked 45 hours. Together, they produced a batch of 132 garments. Of these garments, 52 were "seconds" (meaning that they were flawed). The seconds were sold for $90 each at a factory outlet store. The remaining 80 garments were sold to retail outlets at a price of $198 per garment. What was the labour productivity, in dollars per labour-hour, at this job shop during the first week of March?

▶ **Refer to MyOMLab for these additional homework problems: 1.18–1.19**

Case Studies

National Air Express

National Air is a competitive air-express firm with offices around the country. Mohammed Chaudry, the Ottawa station manager, is preparing his quarterly budget report, which will be presented at the Eastern regional meeting next week. He is very concerned about adding capital expense to the operation when business has not increased appreciably. This has been the worst first quarter he can remember: snowstorms, freezing rain, and bitter cold. He has asked Martha Lewis, field services supervisor, to help him review the available data and offer possible solutions.

Service Methods

National Air offers door-to-door overnight air-express delivery within Canada. Chaudry and Lewis manage a fleet of 24 trucks to handle freight in the Ottawa area. Routes are assigned by area, usually delineated by postal codes, major streets, or key geographical features, such as the Ottawa River. Pickups are generally handled between 3:00 P.M. and 6:00 P.M., Monday through Friday. Driver routes are a combination of regularly scheduled daily stops and pickups that the customer calls in as needed. These call-in pickups are dispatched by radio to the driver. Most call-in customers want as late a pickup as possible, just before closing (usually at 5:00 P.M.).

When the driver arrives at each pickup location, he or she provides supplies as necessary (an envelope or box if requested) and must receive a completed air waybill for each package. Because the industry is extremely competitive, a professional, courteous driver is essential to retaining customers. Therefore, Chaudry has always been concerned that drivers not rush a customer to complete his or her package and paperwork.

Budget Considerations

Chaudry and Lewis have found that they have been unable to meet their customers' requests for a scheduled pickup on many occasions in the past quarter. Although, on average, drivers are not handling any more business, they are unable on some days to arrive at each location on time. Chaudry does not think he can justify increasing costs by $1200 per week for additional trucks and drivers while productivity (measured in shipments per truck/day) has remained flat. The company has established itself as the low-cost operator in the industry but has at the same time committed itself to offering quality service and value for its customers.

Discussion Questions

1. Is the productivity measure of shipments per day per truck still useful? Are there alternatives that might be effective?
2. What, if anything, can be done to reduce the daily variability in pickup call-ins? Can the driver be expected to be at several locations at once at 5:00 P.M.?
3. How should package pickup performance be measured? Are standards useful in an environment that is affected by the weather, traffic, and other random variables? Are other companies having similar problems?

Source: Adapted from a case by Phil Pugliese under the supervision of Professor Marilyn M. Helms, University of Tennessee at Chattanooga. Reprinted by permission.

Frito-Lay: Operations Management in Manufacturing

Frito-Lay, the massive Dallas-based subsidiary of PepsiCo, has 38 plants and 48 000 employees in North America. Seven of Frito-Lay's 41 brands exceed $1 billion in sales: Fritos, Lay's Cheetos, Ruffles, Tostitos, Doritos, and Walker's Potato Chips. Operations is the focus of the firm—from designing products for new markets, to meeting changing consumer preferences, to adjusting to rising commodity costs, to subtle issues involving flavours and preservatives—OM is under constant cost, time, quality, and market pressure. Here is a look at how the 10 decisions of OM are applied at this food processor.

In the food industry, product development kitchens experiment with new products, submit them to focus groups, and perform test marketing. Once the product specifications have been set, processes capable of meeting those specifications and the necessary quality standards are created. At Frito-Lay, quality begins at the farm, with onsite inspection of the potatoes used in Ruffles and the corn used in Fritos. Quality continues throughout the manufacturing process, with visual inspections and with statistical process control of product variables such as oil, moisture, seasoning, salt, thickness, and weight. Additional quality evaluations are conducted throughout shipment, receipt, production, packaging, and delivery.

The production process at Frito-Lay is designed for large volumes and small variety, using expensive special-purpose equipment, and with swift movement of material through the facility. Product-focused facilities, such as Frito-Lay's, typically have high capital costs, tight schedules, and rapid processing. Frito-Lay's facilities are located regionally to aid in the rapid delivery of products because freshness is a critical issue. Sanitary issues and necessarily fast processing of products put a premium on an efficient layout. Production lines are designed for balanced throughput and high utilization. Cross-trained workers, who handle a variety of production lines, have promotion paths identified for their particular skill set. The company rewards employees with medical, retirement, and education plans. Its turnover is very low.

The supply chain is integral to success in the food industry; vendors must be chosen with great care. Moreover, the finished food product is highly dependent o[illegible]rishable raw materials. Consequently, the supply chain b[illegible]w material (potatoes, corn, etc.) to the plant securely and rapidly to meet tight production schedules. For instance, from the time that potatoes are picked in St. Augustine, Florida, until they are unloaded at the Orlando plant, processed, packaged, and shipped from the plant is under 12 hours. The requirement for fresh product requires on-time, just-in-time deliveries combined with both low raw material and finished goods inventories. The continuous-flow nature of the specialized equipment in the production process permits little work-in-process inventory. The plants usually run 24/7. This means that there are four shifts of employees each week.

Tight scheduling to ensure the proper mix of fresh finished goods on automated equipment requires reliable systems and effective maintenance. Frito-Lay's workforce is trained to recognize problems early, and professional maintenance personnel are available on every shift. Downtime is very costly and can lead to late deliveries, making maintenance a high priority.

Discussion Questions*

1. From your knowledge of production processes and from the case and the video, identify how each of the 10 decisions of OM is applied at Frito-Lay.
2. How would you determine the productivity of the production process at Frito-Lay?
3. How are the 10 decisions of OM different when applied by the operations manager of a production process such as Frito-Lay versus a service organization such as Hard Rock Cafe? (See the Hard Rock Cafe video case below.)

*You may wish to view the video that accompanies this case before addressing these questions.

Sources: Professors Beverly Amer (Northern Arizona University), Barry Render (Rollins College), and Jay Heizer (Texas Lutheran University).

Hard Rock Cafe: Operations Management in Services

In its 39 years of existence, Hard Rock has grown from a modest London pub to a global power managing 150 cafes, 15 hotels/casinos, live music venues, and a huge annual Rockfest concert. This puts Hard Rock firmly in the service industry—a sector that employs over 75% of the people in the United States Hard Rock moved its world headquarters to Orlando, Florida, in 1988 and has expanded to more than 40 locations throughout the U.S., serving over 100 000 meals each day. Hard Rock chefs are modifying the menu from classic American—burgers and chicken wings—to include higher-end items such as stuffed veal chops and lobster tails. Just as taste in music changes over time, so does Hard Rock Cafe, with new menus, layouts, memorabilia, services, and strategies.

At Orlando's Universal Studios, a traditional tourist destination, Hard Rock Cafe serves over 3500 meals each day. The cafe employs about 400 people. Most are employed in the restaurant, but some work in the retail shop. Retail is now a standard and increasingly prominent feature in Hard Rock Cafes (since close to 48% of revenue comes from this source). Cafe employees include kitchen and wait staff, hostesses, and bartenders. Hard Rock employees are not only competent in their job skills but are also passionate about music and have engaging personalities. Cafe staff is scheduled down to 15-minute intervals to meet seasonal and daily demand changes in the tourist environment of Orlando. Surveys are done on a regular basis to evaluate quality of food and service at the cafe. Scores are rated on a 1 to 7 scale, and if the score is not a 7, the food or service is a failure.

Hard Rock is adding a new emphasis on live music and is redesigning its restaurants to accommodate the changing tastes. Since Eric Clapton hung his guitar on the wall to mark his favourite bar stool, Hard Rock has become the world's leading collector and exhibitor of rock 'n' roll memorabilia, with changing exhibits at its cafes throughout the world. The collection includes thousands of pieces, valued at $40 million. In keeping with the times, Hard Rock also maintains a website, **www.hardrock.com**, which receives over 100 000 hits per week, and a weekly cable television program on VH-1. Hard Rock's brand recognition, at 92%, is one of the highest in the world.

Discussion Questions*

1. From your knowledge of restaurants, from the video, from the *Global Company Profile* that opens this chapter, and from the case itself, identify how each of the 10 decisions of operations management is applied at Hard Rock Cafe.
2. How would you determine the productivity of the kitchen staff and wait staff at Hard Rock?
3. How are the 10 decisions of OM different when applied to the operations manager of a service operation such as Hard Rock versus an automobile company such as Ford Motor Company?

*You may wish to view the video that accompanies this case before addressing these questions.

Additional Case Study: Visit **MyOMLab** for this free case study:
Zychol Chemicals Corp.: The production manager must prepare a productivity report, which includes multifactor analysis.

Bibliography

Broedner, P., S. Kinkel, and G. Lay. "Productivity Effects of Outsourcing." *International Journal of Operations and Production Management* 29, no. 2 (2009): 127.

Hounshell, D. A. *From the American System to Mass Production 1800–1932: The Development of Manufacturing.* Baltimore: Johns Hopkins University Press, 1985.

Lewis, William W. *The Power of Productivity.* Chicago: University of Chicago Press, 2004.

Maroto, A., and L. Rubalcaba. "Services Productivity Revisited." *The Service Industries Journal* 28, no. 3 (April 2008): 337.

Sahay, B. S. "Multi-factor Productivity Measurement Model for Service Organization." *International Journal of Productivity and Performance Management* 54, no. 1–2 (2005): 7–23.

San, G., T. Huang, and L. Huang. "Does Labor Quality Matter on Productivity Growth?" *Total Quality Management and Business Excellence* 19, no. 10 (October 2008): 1043.

Sprague, Linda G. "Evolution of the Field of Operations Management," *Journal of Operations Management* 25, no. 2 (March 2007): 219–238.

Tangen, S. "Demystifying Productivity and Performance." *International Journal of Productivity and Performance Measurement* 54, no. 1–2 (2005): 34–47.

Taylor, F. W. *The Principles of Scientific Management.* New York: Harper & Brothers, 1911.

van Biema, Michael, and Bruce Greenwald. "Managing Our Way to Higher Service-Sector Productivity." *Harvard Business Review* 75, no. 4 (July–August 1997): 87–95.

Wren, Daniel A. *The Evolution of Management Thought*, New York: Wiley, 1994.

CHAPTER 1 Rapid Review

Main Heading	Review Material	MyOMLab
WHAT IS OPERATIONS MANAGEMENT? (p. 5)	• **Production**—The creation of goods and services. • **Operations management (OM)**—Activities that relate to the creation of goods and services through the transformation of inputs to outputs. Videos 1.1 **AND** 1.2	OM at Hard Rock OM at Frito-Lay
ORGANIZING TO PRODUCE GOODS AND SERVICES (pp. 5–6)	All organizations perform three functions to create goods and services: 1. *Marketing*, which generates demand 2. *Production/operations,* which creates the product 3. *Finance/accounting,* which tracks how well the organization is doing, pays the bills, and collects the money	
WHY STUDY OM? (pp. 7–8)	We study OM for four reasons: 1. To learn how people organize themselves for productive enterprise 2. To learn how goods and services are produced 3. To understand what operations managers do 4. Because OM is a costly part of an organization	
WHAT OPERATIONS MANAGERS DO (pp. 8–9)	• **Management process**—The application of planning, organizing, staffing, leading, and controlling to achieve objectives. Ten major OM decisions are required of operations managers: 1. Design of goods and services 2. Managing quality 3. Process and capacity design 4. Location strategy 5. Layout strategy 6. Human resources, job design, and work measurement 7. Supply-chain management 8. Inventory, material requirements planning, and JIT (just-in-time) 9. Intermediate and short-term scheduling 10. Maintenance About 40% of *all* jobs are in OM. Operations managers possess job titles such as plant manager, quality manager, process-improvement consultant, and operations analyst.	
THE HERITAGE OF OPERATIONS MANAGEMENT (pp. 10–11)	Significant events in modern OM can be classified into five eras: 1. Early concepts (1776–1880)—Labour specialization (Smith, Babbage), standardized parts (Whitney) 2. Scientific management (1880–1910)—Gantt charts (Gantt), motion and time studies (Gilbreth), process analysis (Taylor), queuing theory (Erlang) 3. Mass production (1910–1980)—Assembly line (Ford/Sorensen), statistical sampling (Shewhart), economic order quantity (Harris), linear programming (Dantzig), PERT/CPM (DuPont), material requirements planning 4. Lean production (1980–1995)—Just-in-time, computer-aided design, electronic data interchange, total quality management, Baldrige Award, empowerment, kanbans 5. Mass customization (1995–present)—Globalization, internet/e-commerce, enterprise resource planning, international quality standards, finite scheduling, supply-chain management, mass customization, build-to-order, sustainability	
OPERATIONS IN THE SERVICE SECTOR (pp. 11–13)	• **Services**—Economic activities that typically produce an intangible product (such as education, entertainment, lodging, government, financial, and health services). Almost all services and almost all goods are a mixture of a service and a tangible product. • **Service sector**—The segment of the economy that includes trade, financial, lodging, education, law, medicine, and other professional occupations. Services now constitute the largest economic sector in postindustrial societies. The huge productivity increases in agriculture and manufacturing have allowed more of our economic resources to be devoted to services. Many service jobs pay very well.	
EXCITING NEW TRENDS IN OPERATIONS MANAGEMENT (pp. 13–14)	Some of the current challenges for operations managers include: • High ethical and social responsibility; increased legal and professional standards • Global focus; international collaboration • Rapid product development; design collaboration	

Main Heading	Review Material	MyOMLab
	• Environmentally sensitive production; green manufacturing; sustainability • Mass customization • Empowered employees; enriched jobs • Supply-chain partnering; joint ventures; alliances • Just-in-time performance; lean production; continuous improvement	
THE PRODUCTIVITY CHALLENGE (pp. 15–20)	Virtual Office Hours for • **Productivity**—The ratio of outputs (goods and services) divided by one or more inputs (such as labour, capital, or management). High production means producing many units, while high productivity means producing units efficiently. Only through increases in productivity can the standard of living of a country improve. U.S. productivity has averaged 2.5% per year for over a century. $$\text{Productivity} = \frac{\text{Units produced}}{\text{Input used}} \quad (1.1)$$ • **Single-factor productivity**—Indicates the ratio of one resource (input) to the goods and services produced (outputs). • **Multifactor productivity (total factor productivity)**—Indicates the ratio of many or all resources (inputs) to the goods and services produced (outputs). Multifactor Productivity $$= \frac{\text{Output}}{\text{Labour} + \text{Material} + \text{Energy} + \text{Capital} + \text{Miscellaneous}} \quad (1.2)$$ Measurement problems with productivity include: (1) the quality may change, (2) external elements may interfere, and (3) precise units of measure may be lacking. • **Productivity variables**—The three factors critical to productivity improvement are labour (10%), capital (38%), and management (52%). • **Knowledge society**—A society in which much of the labour force has migrated from manual work to work based on knowledge.	Problems: 1.1–1.17 Solved Problems: 1.1, 1.2
ETHICS AND SOCIAL RESPONSIBILITY (p. 21)	Among the many ethical challenges facing operations managers are (1) efficiently developing and producing safe, quality products; (2) maintaining a clean environment; (3) providing a safe workplace; and (4) honouring stakeholder commitments.	

Self Test

• **Before taking the self-test,** refer to the learning objectives listed at the beginning of the chapter and the key terms listed at the end of the chapter.

LO1. Productivity increases when:
- **a)** inputs increase while outputs remain the same.
- **b)** inputs decrease while outputs remain the same.
- **c)** outputs decrease while inputs remain the same.
- **d)** inputs and outputs increase proportionately.
- **e)** inputs increase at the same rate as outputs.

LO2. Services often:
- **a)** are tangible.
- **b)** are standardized.
- **c)** are knowledge based.
- **d)** are low in customer interaction.
- **e)** have consistent product definition.

LO3. Productivity:
- **a)** can use many factors as the numerator.
- **b)** is the same thing as production.
- **c)** increases at about 0.5% per year.
- **d)** is dependent upon labour, management, and capital.
- **e)** is the same thing as effectiveness.

LO4. Single-factor productivity:
- **a)** remains constant.
- **b)** is never constant.
- **c)** usually uses labour as a factor.
- **d)** seldom uses labour as a factor.
- **e)** uses management as a factor.

LO5. Multifactor productivity:
- **a)** remains constant.
- **b)** is never constant.
- **c)** usually uses substitutes as common variables for the factors of production.
- **d)** seldom uses labour as a factor.
- **e)** always uses management as a factor.

LO6. Productivity increases each year in the United States are a result of three factors:
- **a)** labour, capital, management
- **b)** engineering, labour, capital
- **c)** engineering, capital, quality control
- **d)** engineering, labour, data processing
- **e)** engineering, capital, data processing

Answers: LO1. b; LO2. c; LO3. d; LO4. c; LO5. c; LO6. a

The problems marked in red can be found on MyOMLab. Visit MyOMLab to access cases, videos, downloadable software, and much more. MyOMLab also features a personalized Study Plan that helps you identify which chapter concepts you've mastered and guides you towards study tools for additional practice.

Student Profile

Owen Moir Senior Consultant – Project Procure
Procurement Analyst, Queensland Rail
Bachelor of Business – Logistics and Supply Chain Management, 2010 (Griffith University)
Business Administration – Materials and Operations Management, 2007 (Conestoga College)

Following the completion of the Materials and Operations Management program at Conestoga College it wasn't long before I found myself working as an Expeditor for Hitachi Truck Construction. Having been equipped with the right tools I was able to quickly surpass the responsibilities involved in my role and begin expanding within the organization.

Following an 18 month term with Hitachi, I made the decision to pursue further education and took advantage of one of Conestoga's articulation agreements with Griffith University in Brisbane, Australia. The agreement allowed me to obtain a Bachelor of Business degree with a major in Logistics and Supply Chain Management in just one year thanks to my previous studies.

The quality of education provided to me during my time at Conestoga not only prepared me for the working world but put me in a position to achieve honours grades while enrolled at University. Upon graduation I was fortunate to survey multiple opportunities before deciding on a direction to pursue. That direction was Queensland Rail where I remained for two years beginning as a procurement analyst and later shifting into a buyer role.

Three years following my arrival to Australia I am now working as a Senior Consultant for a boutique supply chain firm called Project Procure. My role as a consultant involves consistently taking on different challenges and delivering value added solutions to clients across various industries. To this day I thank Conestoga College for providing me with the building blocks and the confidence necessary to take on the professional world in the pursuit of an exciting career path.

2

)perations Strategy
ı a Global Environment

Chapter Outline

GLOBAL COMPANY PROFILE: **BOEING**

10 OM Strategy Decisions

- Design of Goods and Services
- **Managing Quality**
- **Process Strategy**
- **Location Strategies**
- **Layout Strategies**
- **Human Resources**
- **Supply-Chain Management**
- **Inventory Management**
- **Scheduling**
- **Maintenance**

Boeing's Global Strategy Yields Competitive Advantage

Boeing's strategy for its 787 Dreamliner is unique from both an engineering and global perspective.

The Dreamliner incorporates the latest in a wide range of aerospace technologies, from airframe and engine design to superlightweight titanium graphite laminate, carbon fibre and epoxy, and composites. Another innovation is the electronic monitoring system that allows the airplane to report maintenance requirements to ground-based computer systems. Boeing has also worked with General Electric and Rolls-Royce to develop more efficient engines. The advances in engine technology contribute as much as 8% of the increased fuel/payload efficiency of the new airplane, representing a nearly two-generation jump in technology.

Some of the International Suppliers of Boeing 787 Components

Latecoere	France	Passenger doors
Labinel	France	Wiring
Dassault	France	Design and PLM software
Messier-Bugatti	France	Electric brakes
Thales	France	Electrical power conversion system and integrated standby flight display
Messier-Dowty	France	Landing gear structure
Diehl	Germany	Interior lighting
Cobham	UK	Fuel pumps and valves
Rolls-Royce	UK	Engines
Smiths Aerospace	UK	Central computer system
BAE Systems	UK	Electronics
Alenia Aeronautica	Italy	Upper centre fuselage and horizontal stabilizer
Toray Industries	Japan	Carbon fibre for wing and tail units
Fuji Heavy Industries	Japan	Centre wing box
Kawasaki Heavy Industries	Japan	Forward fuselage, fixed sections of wing, landing gear wheel well
Teijin Seiki	Japan	Hydraulic actuators
Mitsubishi Heavy Industries	Japan	Wing box
Chengdu Aircraft Group	China	Rudder
Hafei Aviation	China	Parts
Korean Airlines	South Korea	Wingtips
Saab	Sweden	Cargo and access doors

Boeing's collaborative technology enables a "virtual workspace" that allows engineers on the 787, including partners in Australia, Japan, Italy, Canada, and across the United States, to make concurrent design changes to the airplane in real time. Designing, building, and testing the 787 digitally before production reduced design errors and improved production efficiencies.

State-of-the-art composite sections of the 787 are built around the world and shipped to Boeing for final assembly.

Components from Boeing's worldwide supply chain come together on an assembly line in Everett, Washington. Although components come from throughout the world, about 35% of the 787 structure comes from Japanese companies.

This state-of-the-art Boeing 787 is also *global*. Led by Boeing at its Everett, Washington facility, an international team of aerospace companies developed the airplane. New technologies, new design, new manufacturing processes, and committed international suppliers are helping Boeing and its partners achieve unprecedented levels of performance in design, manufacture, and operation.

The 787 is global not only because it has a range of 13 800 km but also because it is built all over the world—with a huge financial risk of over $5 billion (USD), Boeing needed partners. The global nature of both technology and the aircraft market meant finding exceptional developers and suppliers, wherever they might be. It also meant finding firms willing to step up to the risk associated with a very expensive new product. These partners not only spread the risk but also bring commitment to the table. Countries that have a stake in the 787 are more likely to buy from Boeing than from the European competitor Airbus Industries.

Boeing teamed with more than 20 international systems suppliers to develop technologies and design concepts for the 787. Boeing found its 787 partners in over a dozen countries; a few of them are shown in the accompanying table on the previous page.

The Japanese companies Toray, Teijin Seiki, Fuji, Kawasaki, and Mitsubishi are producing over 35% of the project, providing whole composite fuselage sections. Italy's Alenia Aeronautica is building an additional 10% of the plane.

Many U.S. companies, including Crane Aerospace, Fairchild Controls, Goodrich, General Dynamics, Hamilton Sundstrand, Honeywell, Moog, Parker Hannifin, Rockwell Collins, and Triumph Group are also suppliers. Boeing has 70% to 80% of the Dreamliner built by other companies. And even some of the portion built by Boeing is produced at Boeing facilities outside the United States, in Australia and Canada.

The Dreamliner is efficient, has a global range, and is made from components produced around the world. The result: a state-of-the-art airplane reflecting the global nature of business in the 21st century and one of the fastest-selling commercial jets in history.

Chapter 2 Learning Objectives

A Global View of Operations

AUTHOR COMMENT
As Prof. Thomas Sewell observed, "No great civilization has developed in isolation."

Today's operations manager must have a global view of operations strategy. Since the early 1990s, nearly 3 billion people in developing countries have overcome the cultural, religious, ethnic, and political barriers that constrain productivity and are now players on the global economic stage. As these barriers disappear, simultaneous advances are being made in technology, reliable shipping, and cheap communication. The unsurprising result is the growth of world trade (see Figure 2.1), global capital markets, and the international movement of people. This means increasing economic integration and interdependence of countries—in a word, globalization. In response, organizations are hastily extending their operations globally with innovative strategies. For instance:

- Boeing is competitive because both its sales and production are worldwide.
- Italy's Benetton moves inventory to stores around the world faster than its competition by building flexibility into design, production, and distribution.

FIGURE 2.1
Growth of World Trade (world trade as a percentage of world GDP)

*Author estimate for 2010.

Source: Based on a speech by Mark A. Wynne, Federal Reserve Bank of Dallas, June 2009.

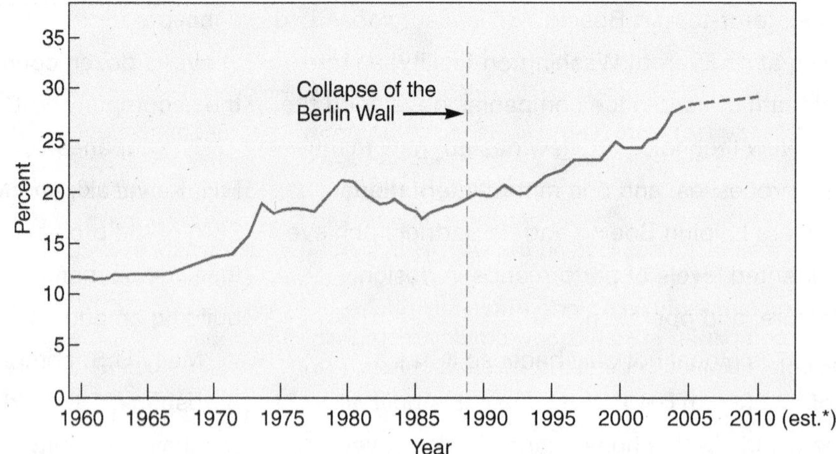

- Sony purchases components from suppliers in Thailand, Malaysia, and elsewhere around the world for assembly in its electronic products.
- Volvo, considered a Swedish company, was recently controlled by a U.S. company (Ford) and has been subsequently acquired by Geely of China. But the current Volvo S40 is built in Belgium on a platform shared with the Mazda 3 (built in Japan) and the Ford Focus (built and sold in Europe.)

Globalization means that domestic production and exporting may no longer be a viable business model; local production and exporting no longer guarantee success or even survival. There are new standards of global competitiveness that impact quality, variety, customization, convenience, timeliness, and cost. The globalization of strategy contributes efficiency and adds value to products and services, but it also complicates the operations manager's job. Complexity, risk, and competition are intensified; companies must carefully account for them.

We have identified six reasons why domestic business operations decide to change to some form of international operation. They are:

1. Reduce costs (labour, taxes, tariffs, etc.).
2. Improve the supply chain.
3. Provide better goods and services.
4. Understand markets.
5. Learn to improve operations.
6. Attract and retain global talent.

Let us examine, in turn, each of the six reasons.

REDUCE COSTS Many international operations seek to take advantage of the tangible opportunities to reduce their costs. Foreign locations with lower wages can help lower both direct and indirect costs. (See the *OM in Action* box, "Cartoon Production at Home in Manila.") Less stringent government regulations on a wide variety of operations practices (e.g., environmental control, health and safety, etc.) reduce costs. Opportunities to cut the cost of taxes and tariffs also encourage foreign operations. In Mexico, the creation of **maquiladoras** (free trade zones) allows manufacturers to cut their costs of taxation by paying only on the value added by Mexican workers. If a Canadian manufacturer brings a $500 machine to a maquiladora operation for assembly work costing $25, tariff duties will be charged only on the $25 of work performed in Mexico.

Maquiladoras
Mexican factories located along the U.S.–Mexico border that receive preferential tariff treatment.

Shifting low-skilled jobs to another country has several potential advantages. First, and most obviously, the firm may reduce costs. Second, moving the lower-skilled jobs to a lower-cost location frees higher-cost workers for more valuable tasks. Third, reducing wage costs allows the savings to be invested in improved products and facilities (and the retraining of existing workers, if necessary) at the home location. The impact of this approach is shown in the *OM in Action* box, "Going Global to Compete" on the next page.

OM *in Action* Cartoon Production at Home in Manila

Fred Flintstone is not from Bedrock. He is actually from Manila, capital of the Philippines. So are Tom and Jerry, Aladdin, and Donald Duck. More than 90% of North American television cartoons are produced in Asia and India, with the Philippines leading the way. With their competitive advantage of English as an official language and a strong familiarity with North American culture, animation companies in Manila now employ more than 1700 people. Filipinos understand Western culture, and "you need to have a group of artists that can understand the humour that goes with it," says Bill Dennis, a Hanna-Barbera executive.

Major studios like Disney, Marvel, Warner Brothers, and Hanna-Barbera send *storyboards*—cartoon action outlines—and voice tracks to the Philippines. Artists there draw, paint, and film about 20 000 sketches for a 30-minute episode. The cost of $130 000 to produce an episode in the Philippines compares with $160 000 in Korea and $500 000 in the United States.

Sources: Journal of Global Information Technology Management (2007): 1–6; *The New York Times* (February 26, 2004): A29; and *The Wall Street Journal* (August 9, 2005): D8.

Trade agreements have also helped reduce tariffs and thereby reduce the cost of operating facilities in foreign countries. The **World Trade Organization (WTO)** has helped reduce tariffs from 40% in 1940 to less than 3% today. Another important trade agreement is the **North American Free Trade Agreement (NAFTA)**. NAFTA seeks to phase out all trade and tariff barriers among Canada, Mexico, and the United States. Other trade agreements that are accelerating global trade include APEC (the Pacific Rim countries), SEATO (Australia, New Zealand, Japan, Hong Kong, South Korea, New Guinea, and Chile), MERCOSUR (Argentina, Brazil, Paraguay, and Uruguay), and CAFTA (Central America, Dominican Republic, and United States).

World Trade Organization (WTO)
An international organization that promotes world trade by lowering barriers to the free flow of goods across borders.

NAFTA
A free trade agreement between Canada, Mexico, and the United States.

Another trading group is the **European Union (EU)**.[1] The European Union has reduced trade barriers among the participating European nations through standardization and a common currency, the euro. However, this major Canadian trading partner, with almost 500 million

European Union (EU)
A European trade group that has 27 member states.

OM *in Action* Going Global to Compete

Headquartered in Montreal and founded in 1880, Bell Canada is one of Canada's prominent players in wireless telecommunications, controlling about 30% of the domestic market. Approximately 50% of Bell Canada's revenue stems from its wireless initiatives. It is active in contracting suitable vendors as part of outsourcing key voice-based projects for its satellite TV, Bell Mobility, Solo Mobility, and internet divisions. Bell Canada intends to outsource these particular projects via fixed payouts as part of a deal worth roughly between $25 and $30 million (CAD) per year. India is the beneficiary of these outsourced contracts, and the projects include inbound customer contact. Bell remains watchful for outsourcing partners with strong competencies in managing this type of front-end work.

In a similar fashion, the Canadian Bar Association reported through its in-house magazine about the "commoditization" of legal services, and noted a trend toward outsourcing certain aspects of legal work. Although the concept is fairly new to Canadian lawyers, firms that do engage in it suggest they provide hourly savings of up to 75%.

Resourceful organizations, such as Bell Canada and these law firms, use a global perspective to become more efficient, which allows them to develop new products, retrain employees, and invest in new plant and equipment.

Sources: Ottawa Citizen (2006); and *www.bell.ca*.

[1]The 27 members of the European Union (EU) as of 2013 were Austria, Belgium, Bulgaria, Cyprus, Czech Republic, Denmark, Estonia, Finland, France, Germany, Greece, Hungary, Ireland, Italy, Latvia, Lithuania, Luxembourg, Malta, the Netherlands, Poland, Portugal, Romania, Slovakia, Slovenia, Spain, Sweden, and the United Kingdom. Not all have adopted the euro. In addition, Croatia, Macedonia, and Turkey are candidates for entry into the EU.

people, is also placing some of the world's most restrictive conditions on products sold in the EU. Everything from recycling standards to automobile bumpers to hormone-free farm products must meet EU standards, complicating international trade.

IMPROVE THE SUPPLY CHAIN The supply chain can often be improved by locating facilities in countries where unique resources are available. These resources may be expertise, labour, or raw material. For example, a trend is evident in which precious metals companies are relocating to the mining regions of northern Ontario. Auto-styling studios from throughout the world are migrating to the auto mecca of southern California to ensure the necessary expertise in contemporary auto design. Similarly, world athletic shoe production has migrated from South Korea to Guangzhou, China: this location takes advantage of the low-cost labour and production competence in a city where 40 000 people work making athletic shoes for the world. And a perfume essence manufacturer wants a presence in Grasse, France, where much of the world's perfume essences are prepared from the flowers of the Mediterranean.

PROVIDE BETTER GOODS AND SERVICES Although the characteristics of goods and services can be objective and measurable (e.g., number of on-time deliveries), they can also be subjective and less measurable (e.g., sensitivity to culture). We need an ever better understanding of differences in culture and of the way business is handled in different countries. Improved understanding as the result of a local presence permits firms to customize products and services to meet unique cultural needs in foreign markets.

Another reason to have international operations is to reduce response time to meet customers' changing product and service requirements. Customers who purchase goods and services from Canadian firms are increasingly located in foreign countries. Providing them with quick and adequate service is often improved by locating facilities in their home countries.

UNDERSTAND MARKETS Because international operations require interaction with foreign customers, suppliers, and other competitive businesses, international firms inevitably learn about opportunities for new products and services. Europe led the way with cell phone innovations, and now the Japanese lead with the latest cell phone fads. Knowledge of these markets not only helps firms understand where the market is going but also helps them diversify their customer base, add production flexibility, and smooth the business cycle.

Another reason to go into foreign markets is the opportunity to expand the *life cycle* of an existing product. While some products in Canada are in a "mature" stage of their product life cycle, they may represent state-of-the-art

A worldwide strategy places added burdens on operations management. Because of regional differences, designers and manufacturers must adapt their products to suit their various markets. A common example of the market differences involves automobiles and the need to place the driver on either the right or the left due to the local roadways and infrastructure.

products in less developed countries. For example, the Canadian market for personal computers could be characterized as "mature" but as in the "introductory" stage in many developing countries, such as Albania, Vietnam, and Myanmar (Burma).

LEARN TO IMPROVE OPERATIONS Learning does not take place in isolation. Firms serve themselves and their customers well when they remain open to the free flow of ideas. For example, General Motors found that it could improve operations by jointly building and running, with the Japanese, an auto assembly plant in San Jose, California. This strategy allowed GM to contribute its capital and knowledge of North American labour and environmental laws while the Japanese contributed production and inventory ideas. Similarly, operations managers have improved equipment and layout by learning from the ergonomic competence of the Scandinavians.

ATTRACT AND RETAIN GLOBAL TALENT Global organizations can attract and retain better employees by offering more employment opportunities. They need people in all functional areas and areas of expertise worldwide. Global firms can recruit and retain good employees because they provide both greater growth opportunities and insulation against unemployment during times of economic downturn. During economic downturns in one country or continent, a global firm has the means to relocate unneeded personnel to more prosperous locations.

So, to recap, successfully achieving a competitive advantage in our shrinking world means maximizing all of the possible opportunities, from tangible to intangible, that international operations can offer.

CULTURAL AND ETHICAL ISSUES

AUTHOR COMMENT
As the owner of a Guatemala plant said, "The ethics of the world markets is very clear: Manufacturers will move wherever it is cheapest or most convenient to their interests."

While there are great forces driving firms toward globalization, many challenges remain. One of these challenges is reconciling differences in social and cultural behaviour. With issues ranging from bribery, to child labour, to the environment, managers sometimes do not know how to respond when operating in a different culture. What one country's culture deems acceptable may be considered unacceptable or illegal in another. It is not by chance that there are fewer female managers in the Middle East than in India.

In the last decade, changes in international laws, agreements, and codes of conduct have been applied to define ethical behaviour among managers around the world. The WTO, for example, helps to make uniform the protection of both governments and industries from foreign firms that engage in unethical conduct. Even on issues where significant differences between cultures exist, as in the area of bribery or the protection of intellectual property, global uniformity is slowly being accepted by most nations.

In spite of cultural and ethical differences, we live in a period of extraordinary mobility of capital, information, goods, and even people. We can expect this to continue. The financial sector, the telecommunications sector, and the logistics infrastructure of the world are healthy institutions that foster efficient and effective use of capital, information, and goods. Globalization, with all its opportunities and risks, is here and will continue. It must be embraced as managers develop their missions and strategies.

Developing Missions and Strategies

AUTHOR COMMENT
Getting an education and managing an organization both require a mission and strategy.

An effective operations management effort must have a *mission* so it knows where it is going and a *strategy* so it knows how to get there. This is the case for a small domestic organization, as well as a large international organization.

MISSION

Economic success, indeed survival, is the result of identifying missions to satisfy a customer's needs and wants. We define the organization's **mission** as its purpose—what it will contribute to society. Mission statements provide boundaries and focus for organizations and the concept around which the firm can rally. The mission states the rationale for the organization's existence.

Mission
The purpose or rationale for an organization's existence.

FIGURE 2.2
Mission Statements for Three Organizations

Sources: Human Resources materials for new employees; courtesy of Arnold Palmer Children's Care Team.

Royal Canadian Mounted Police
The RCMP is Canada's national police service. Proud of our traditions and confident in meeting future challenges, we commit to preserve the peace, uphold the law and provide quality service in partnership with our communities.
Hard Rock Cafe
Our Mission: To spread the spirit of rock 'n roll by creating authentic experiences that rock.
Arnold Palmer Hospital
Arnold Palmer Hospital for Children provides state of the art, family-centered healthcare focused on restoring the joy of childhood in an environment of compassion, healing and hope.

LO 1: Define mission and strategy

Developing a good strategy is difficult, but it is much easier if the mission has been well defined. Figure 2.2 provides examples of mission statements.

Once an organization's mission has been decided, each functional area within the firm determines its supporting mission. By *functional area* we mean the major disciplines required by the firm, such as marketing, finance/accounting, and production/operations. Missions for each function are developed to support the firm's overall mission. Then within that function, lower-level supporting missions are established for the OM functions. Figure 2.3 provides such a hierarchy of sample missions.

STRATEGY

Strategy
How an organization expects to achieve its missions and goals.

With the mission established, strategy and its implementation can begin. **Strategy** is an organization's action plan to achieve the mission. Each functional area has a strategy for achieving its mission and for helping the organization reach the overall mission. These strategies exploit opportunities and strengths, neutralize threats, and avoid weaknesses. In the following sections, we will describe how strategies are developed and implemented.

LO 2: Identify and explain three strategic approaches to competitive advantage

VIDEO 2.1
Operations Strategy at Regal Marine

Firms achieve missions in three conceptual ways: (1) differentiation, (2) cost leadership, and (3) response. This means operations managers are called on to deliver goods and services that are (1) *better*, or at least different, (2) *cheaper*, and (3) more *responsive*. Operations managers translate these *strategic concepts* into tangible tasks to be accomplished. Any one or combination of these three strategic concepts can generate a system that has a unique advantage over competitors. For example, Hunter Fan has differentiated itself as a premier maker of quality ceiling fans that lower heating and cooling costs for its customers. Nucor Steel, on the other hand, satisfies customers by being the lowest-cost steel producer in the world. And Dell achieves rapid response by building personal computers with each customer's requested software in a matter of hours.

Clearly, strategies differ. And each strategy puts different demands on operations management. Hunter Fan's strategy is one of *differentiating* itself via quality from others in the industry. Nucor focuses on value at *low cost*, and Dell's dominant strategy is quick, reliable *response*.

AUTHOR COMMENT
For many organizations, the operations function provides *the* competitive advantage.

Achieving Competitive Advantage through Operations

Competitive advantage
The creation of a unique advantage over competitors.

Each of the three strategies provides an opportunity for operations managers to achieve competitive advantage. **Competitive advantage** implies the creation of a system that has a unique advantage over competitors. The idea is to create customer value in an efficient and sustainable way. Pure forms of these strategies may exist, but operations managers will more likely be called

Sample Company Mission	
To manufacture and service an innovative, growing, and profitable worldwide microwave communications business that exceeds our customers' expectations.	
Sample Operations Management Mission	
To produce products consistent with the company's mission as the worldwide low-cost manufacturer.	
Sample OM Department Missions	
Product design	To design and produce products and services with outstanding quality and inherent customer value.
Quality management	To attain the exceptional value that is consistent with our company mission and marketing objectives by close attention to design, procurement, production, and field service opportunities.
Process design	To determine, design, and produce the production process and equipment that will be compatible with low-cost product, high quality, and a good quality of work life at economical cost.
Location	To locate, design, and build efficient and economical facilities that will yield high value to the company, its employees, and the community.
Layout design	To achieve, through skill, imagination, and resourcefulness in layout and work methods, production effectiveness and efficiency while supporting a high quality of work life.
Human resources	To provide a good quality of work life, with well-designed, safe, rewarding jobs, stable employment, and equitable pay, in exchange for outstanding individual contribution from employees at all levels.
Supply-chain management	To collaborate with suppliers to develop innovative products from stable, effective, and efficient sources of supply.
Inventory	To achieve low investment in inventory consistent with high customer service levels and high facility utilization.
Scheduling	To achieve high levels of throughput and timely customer delivery through effective scheduling.
Maintenance	To achieve high utilization of facilities and equipment by effective preventive maintenance and prompt repair of facilities and equipment.

FIGURE 2.3
Sample Missions for a Company, the Operations Function, and Major OM Departments

on to implement some combination of them. Let us briefly look at how managers achieve competitive advantage via *differentiation*, *low cost*, and *response*.

COMPETING ON DIFFERENTIATION

Safeskin Corporation is number one in latex exam gloves because it has differentiated itself and its products. It did so by producing gloves that were designed to prevent allergic reactions about which doctors were complaining. When other glove makers caught up, Safeskin developed hypoallergenic gloves. Then it added texture to its gloves. Then it developed a synthetic disposable glove for those allergic to latex—always staying ahead of the competition. Safeskin's strategy is to develop a reputation for designing and producing reliable state-of-the-art gloves, thereby differentiating itself.

Differentiation is concerned with providing *uniqueness*. A firm's opportunities for creating uniqueness are not located within a particular function or activity but can arise in virtually everything the firm does. Moreover, because most products include some service, and most services include some product, the opportunities for creating this uniqueness are limited only

Differentiation
Distinguishing the offerings of an organization in a way that the customer perceives as adding value.

by imagination. Indeed, **differentiation** should be thought of as going beyond both physical characteristics and service attributes to encompass everything about the product or service that influences the value that the customers derive from it. Therefore, effective operations managers assist in defining everything about a product or service that will influence the potential value to the customer. This may be the convenience of a broad product line, product features, or a service related to the product. Such services can manifest themselves through convenience (location of distribution centres, stores, or branches), training, product delivery and installation, or repair and maintenance services.

Experience differentiation
Engaging a customer with a product through imaginative use of the five senses, so the customer "experiences" the product.

In the service sector, one option for extending product differentiation is through an *experience*. Differentiation by experience in services is a manifestation of the growing "experience economy." The idea of **experience differentiation** is to engage the customer—to use people's five senses so they become immersed, or even an active participant, in the product. Disney does this with the Magic Kingdom. People no longer just go on a ride; they are immersed in the Magic Kingdom—surrounded by a dynamic visual and sound experience that complements the physical ride. Some rides further engage the customer by having them steer the ride or shoot targets or villains.

VIDEO 2.2
Hard Rock's Global Strategy

Theme restaurants, such as Hard Rock Cafe, likewise differentiate themselves by providing an "experience." Hard Rock engages the customer with classic rock music, big-screen rock videos, memorabilia, and staff who can tell stories. In many instances, a full-time guide is available to explain the displays, and there is always a convenient retail store so the guest can take home a tangible part of the experience. The result is a "dining experience" rather than just a meal. In a less dramatic way, both Tim Hortons and your local supermarket deliver an experience when they provide music and the aroma of brewing coffee or freshly baked bread.

COMPETING ON COST

Porter Airlines has been a consistent success while other North American airlines have lost billions. Porter has done this by fulfilling a need for low-cost and short-hop flights. Its operations strategy has included use of secondary airports and terminals, few fare options, smaller crews, and no expensive ticket offices.

Additionally, and less obviously, Porter has very effectively matched capacity to demand and effectively utilized this capacity. It has done this by designing a route structure that matches the capacity of its Bombardier Dash-8 Q400, the only plane in its fleet. Second, it achieves more air miles than other airlines through faster turnarounds—its planes are on the ground less.

One driver of a low-cost strategy is a facility that is effectively utilized. Porter and others with low-cost strategies understand this and utilize resources effectively. Identifying the optimum size (and investment) allows firms to spread overhead costs, providing a cost advantage. For instance, Walmart continues to pursue its low-cost strategy with superstores that are open 24 hours a day. For 20 years, it has successfully grabbed market share. Walmart has driven down store overhead costs, shrinkage, and distribution costs. Its rapid transportation of goods, reduced warehousing costs, and direct shipment from manufacturers have resulted in high inventory turnover and made it a low-cost leader. Franz Colruyt, as discussed in the *OM in Action* box, is also winning with a low-cost strategy.

Low-cost leadership
Achieving maximum value, as perceived by the customer.

Low-cost leadership entails achieving maximum *value*, as defined by your customer. It requires examining each of the 10 OM decisions in a relentless effort to drive down costs while meeting customer expectations of value. A low-cost strategy does *not* imply low value or low quality.

COMPETING ON RESPONSE

Response
A set of values related to rapid, flexible, and reliable performance.

The third strategy option is response. Response is often thought of as *flexible* response, but it also refers to *reliable* and *quick* response. Indeed, we define **response** as including the entire range of values related to timely product development and delivery, as well as reliable scheduling and flexible performance.

Flexible response may be thought of as the ability to match changes in a marketplace where design innovations and volumes fluctuate substantially.

OM *in Action* Low-Cost Strategy Wins at Franz Colruyt

Belgian discount food retailer Franz Colruyt NV is so obsessed with cutting costs that there are no shopping bags at its checkout counters, the lighting at its stores is dimmed to save money on electricity, and employees clock out when they go on 5-minute coffee breaks. And to keep costs down at the company's spartan headquarters on the outskirts of Brussels, employees don't have voice mail on their phones. Instead, two receptionists take messages for nearly 1000 staffers. The messages are bellowed out every few minutes from loudspeakers peppered throughout the building.

This same approach is evident at all 160 of Colruyt's shopping outlets, which are converted factory warehouses, movie theaters, or garages, with black concrete floors, exposed electrical wires, metal shelves, and discarded boxes strewn about. There is no background music (estimated annual cost saving: € 2 million, or $2.5 million), nor are there bags for packing groceries (estimated annual cost saving: € 5 million). And all the store's freezers have doors, so the company can save about € 3 million a year on electricity for refrigeration.

The company also employs a team of 30 "work simplifiers"—in Colruyt jargon—whose job is to come up with new ways to improve productivity. One recently discovered that 5 seconds could be shaved from every minute it takes customers to check out if they paid at a separate station from where groceries are scanned, so that when one customer steps away from the scanner, another can step up right away.

Chief Executive Rene De Wit says Colruyt's strategy is simple: cut costs at every turn and undersell your competitors. In an industry where margins of 1% to 2% are typical, Colruyt's cost cutting is so effective that a profit margin of 6.5% dwarfs those of rivals.

A low-cost strategy places significant demands on operations management, but Franz Colruyt, like Walmart, makes it work.

Sources: The Wall Street Journal (January 5, 2005): 1 and (September 22, 2003): R3, R7.

Hewlett-Packard is an exceptional example of a firm that has demonstrated flexibility in both design and volume changes in the volatile world of personal computers. HP's products often have a life cycle of months, and volume and cost changes during that brief life cycle are dramatic. However, HP has been successful at institutionalizing the ability to change products and volume to respond to dramatic changes in product design and costs—thus building a *sustainable competitive advantage*.

The second aspect of response is the *reliability* of scheduling. One way the German machine industry has maintained its competitiveness despite having the world's highest labour costs is through reliable response. This response manifests itself in reliable scheduling. German machine firms have meaningful schedules—and they perform to these schedules. Moreover, the results of these schedules are communicated to the customer and the

Whether it is because of a busy lifestyle or other reasons, customers can shop at home for groceries by placing an order with grocerygateway.com and arranging for a delivery time within a 90 minute window. Reliability is vital for this type of service.

OM *in Action* Response Strategy at Hong Kong's Johnson Electric

Patrick Wang, managing director of Johnson Electric Holdings, Ltd., walks through his Hong Kong headquarters with a micromotor in his hand. This tiny motor, about twice the size of his thumb, powers a Dodge Viper power door lock. Although most people have never heard of Johnson Electric, we all have several of its micromotors nearby. This is because Johnson is the world's leading producer of micromotors for cordless tools, household appliances (such as coffee grinders and food processors), personal care items (such as hair dryers and electric shavers), and cars. A luxury Mercedes, with its headlight wipers, power windows, power seat adjustments, and power side mirrors, may use 50 Johnson micromotors.

Like all truly global businesses, Johnson spends liberally on communications to tie together its global network of factories, R&D facilities, and design centres. For example, Johnson Electric installed a $20 million videoconferencing system that allows engineers in Cleveland, Ohio and Stuttgart, Germany to monitor trial production of their micromotors in China.

Johnson's first strength is speed in product development, speed in production, and speed in delivering—13 million motors a month, mostly assembled in China but delivered throughout the world. Its second strength is the ability to stay close to its customers. Johnson has design and technical centres scattered across the United States, Europe, and Japan. "The physical limitations of the past are gone" when it comes to deciding where to locate a new centre, says Patrick Wang. "Customers talk to us where they feel most comfortable, but products are made where they are most competitive."

Sources: Hoover's Company Records (January 1, 2006): 58682; *Far Eastern Economic Review* (May 16, 2002): 44–45; and *Just Auto* (November 2008): 18–19.

customer can, in turn, rely on them. Consequently, the competitive advantage generated through reliable response has value to the end customer. This is also true for organizations such as grocerygateway.com, where reliability in scheduling and adhering to these schedules is an expectation of customers.

The third aspect of response is *quickness*. Johnson Electric, discussed in the *OM in Action* box, competes on speed—in design, production, and delivery. Whether it is a production system at Johnson Electric, a pizza delivered in 5 minutes by Pizza Hut, or customized phone products delivered in three days from Motorola, the operations manager who develops systems that respond quickly can have a competitive advantage.

AUTHOR COMMENT These 10 decisions are used to implement a specific strategy and yield a competitive advantage.

In practice, differentiation, low cost, and response can increase productivity and generate a sustainable competitive advantage (see Figure 2.4). Proper implementation of the following decisions by operations managers will allow these advantages to be achieved.

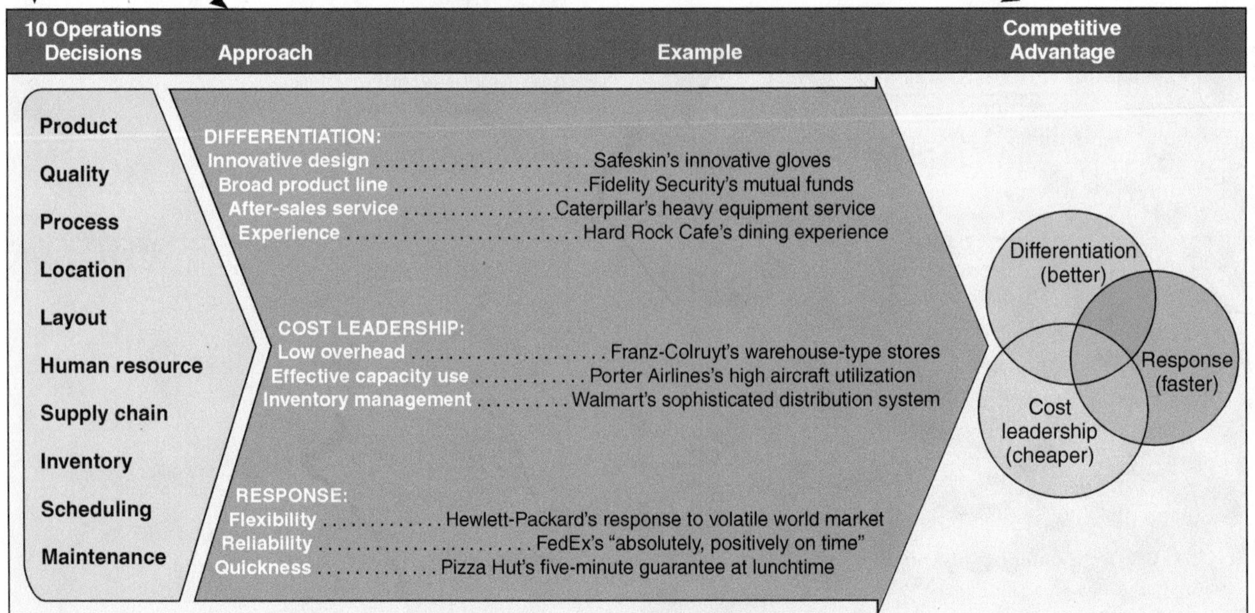

FIGURE 2.4 Achieving Competitive Advantage through Operations

Ten Strategic OM Decisions

AUTHOR COMMENT
This text is structured around these 10 decisions.

Differentiation, low cost, and response can be achieved when managers make effective decisions in 10 areas of OM. These are collectively known as **operations decisions**. The 10 decisions of OM that support missions and implement strategies are:

Operations decisions
The strategic decisions of OM are goods and service design, quality, process and capacity design, location selection, layout design, human resources and job design, supply-chain management, inventory, scheduling, and maintenance.

LO3: Identify and define the 10 decisions of operations management

1. *Goods and service design:* Designing goods and services defines much of the transformation process. Costs, quality, and human resource decisions are often determined by design decisions. Designs usually determine the lower limits of cost and the upper limits of quality.
2. *Quality:* The customer's quality expectations must be determined and policies and procedures established to identify and achieve that quality.
3. *Process and capacity design:* Process options are available for products and services. Process decisions commit management to specific technology, quality, human resource use, and maintenance. These expenses and capital commitments determine much of the firm's basic cost structure.
4. *Location selection:* Facility location decisions for both manufacturing and service organizations may determine the firm's ultimate success. Errors made at this juncture may overwhelm other efficiencies.
5. *Layout design:* Material flows, capacity needs, personnel levels, technology decisions, and inventory requirements influence layout.
6. *Human resources and job design:* People are an integral and expensive part of the total system design. Therefore, the quality of work life provided, the talent and skills required, and their costs must be determined.
7. *Supply-chain management:* These decisions determine what is to be made and what is to be purchased. Consideration is also given to quality, delivery, and innovation, all at a satisfactory price. Mutual trust between buyer and supplier is necessary for effective purchasing.
8. *Inventory:* Inventory decisions can be optimized only when customer satisfaction, suppliers, production schedules, and human resource planning are considered.
9. *Scheduling:* Feasible and efficient schedules of production must be developed; the demands on human resources and facilities must be determined and controlled.
10. *Maintenance:* Decisions must be made regarding desired levels of reliability and stability, and systems must be established to maintain that reliability and stability.

Operations managers implement these 10 decisions by identifying key tasks and the staffing needed to achieve them. However, the implementation of decisions is influenced by a variety of issues, including a product's proportion of goods and services (see Table 2.1 on page 47). Few products are either all goods or all services. Although the 10 decisions remain the same for both goods and services, their relative importance and method of implementation depend on this ratio of goods and services. Throughout this text, we discuss how strategy is selected and implemented for both goods and services through these 10 operations management decisions.

Let's look at an example of strategy development through one of the 10 decisions.

EXAMPLE 1

Strategy development

Pierre Alexander has just completed culinary school and is ready to open his own restaurant. After examining both the external environment and his prospective strengths and weaknesses, he makes a decision on the mission for his restaurant, which he defines as, "To provide outstanding French fine dining for the people of Calgary."

APPROACH ▶ Alexander's supporting operations strategy is to ignore the options of ***cost leadership*** and ***quick response*** and focus on ***differentiation***. Consequently, his operations strategy requires him to evaluate product designs (menus and meals) and selection of process, layout, and location. He must also evaluate the human resources, suppliers, inventory, scheduling, and maintenance that will support his mission as well as a differentiation strategy.

SOLUTION ▶ Examining just one of these 10 decisions, ***process design***, requires that Alexander consider the issues presented in the following figure.

(Continued)

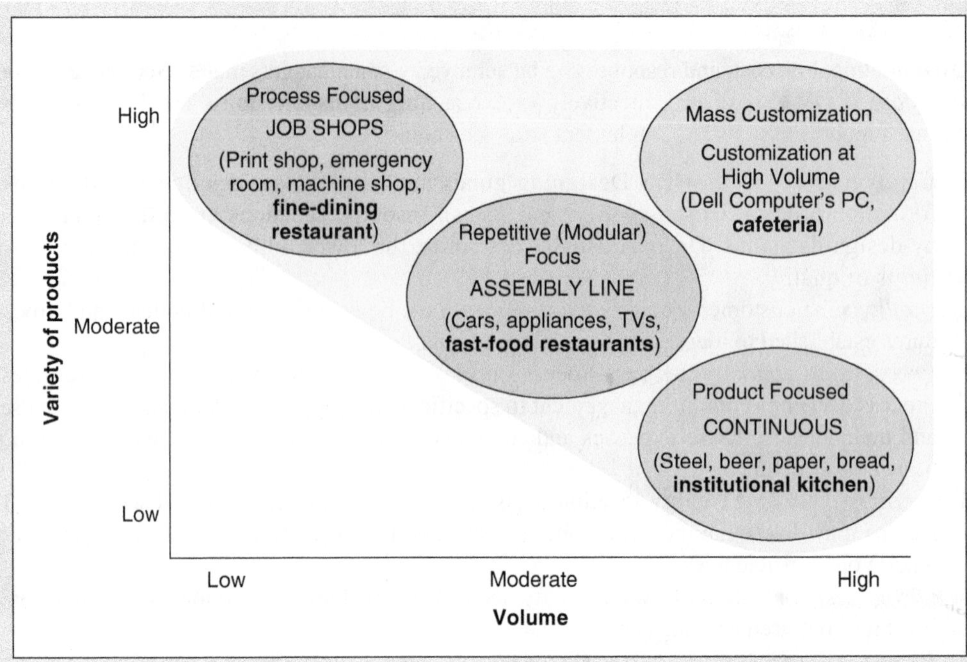

The first option is to operate in the lower right corner of the figure above, where he could produce high volumes of food with a limited variety, much as in an institutional kitchen. Such a process could produce large volumes of standard items such as baked goods and mashed potatoes prepared with state-of-the-art automated equipment. Alexander concludes that this is not an acceptable process option.

Alternatively, he can move to the middle of the figure, where he could produce more variety and lower volumes. Here, he would have less automation and use prepared modular components for meals, much as a fast-food restaurant does. Again, he deems such process designs inappropriate for his mission.

Another option is to move to the upper right corner and produce a high volume of customized meals, but neither Alexander nor anyone else knows how to do this with gourmet meals.

Finally, Alexander can design a process that operates in the upper left corner of the figure, which requires little automation but lends itself to high variety. This process option suggests that he build an extremely flexible kitchen suitable for a wide variety of custom meals catering to the whims of each customer. With little automation, such a process would be suitable for a huge variety. This process strategy will support his mission and desired product differentiation. Only with a process such as this can he provide the fine French-style gourmet dining that he has in mind.

INSIGHT ▶ By considering the options inherent in each of the 10 OM decisions, managers—Alexander, in this case—can make decisions that support the mission.

LEARNING EXERCISE ▶ If Alexander's mission were to offer less expensive meals and reduce the variety offered but still do so with a French flair, what might his process strategy be? [Answer: Alexander might try a repetitive (modular) strategy and mimic the La Madeleine cafeteria-style restaurants. The La Madeleine chain has more than 60 locations and would be a good model for Alexander to mirror. It has the approach, atmosphere, style, and menu he is seeking.]

The 10 decisions of operations management are implemented in ways that provide competitive advantage, not just for fine-dining restaurants, but for all the goods and services that enrich our lives. How this might be done for two drug companies, one seeking a competitive advantage via differentiation, and the other via low cost, is shown in Table 2.2.

AUTHOR COMMENT
An effective strategy finds the optimum fit for the firm's resources in the dynamic environment.

Issues in Operations Strategy

Resources view
A method managers use to evaluate the resources at their disposal and manage or alter them to achieve competitive advantage.

Whether the OM strategy is differentiation, cost, or response (as shown earlier in Figure 2.4), OM is a critical player. Therefore, prior to establishing and attempting to implement a strategy, some alternate perspectives may be helpful. One perspective is to take a **resources view**. This means thinking in terms of the financial, physical, human, and technological resources available

TABLE 2.1
The Differences between Goods and Services Influence How the 10 Operations Management Decisions Are Applied

Operations Decisions	Goods	Services
Goods and service design	Product is usually tangible (a computer).	Product is not tangible. A new range of product attributes (a smile).
Quality	Many objective quality standards (battery life).	Many subjective quality standards (nice colour).
Process and capacity design	Customer is not involved in most of the process (auto assembly).	Customer may be directly involved in the process (a haircut). Capacity must match demand to avoid lost sales (customers often avoid waiting).
Location selection	May need to be near raw materials or labour force (steel plant near ore).	May need to be near customer (car rental).
Layout design	Layout can enhance production efficiency (assembly line).	Can enhance product as well as production (layout of a classroom or a fine-dining restaurant).
Human resources and job design	Workforce focused on technical skills (stone mason). Labour standards can be consistent (assembly line employee). Output-based wage system possible (garment sewing).	Direct workforce usually needs to be able to interact well with customer (bank teller); labour standards vary depending on customer requirements (legal cases).
Supply-chain management	Supply chain relationships critical to final product.	Supply chain relationships important but may not be critical.
Inventory	Raw materials, work-in-process, and finished goods may be inventoried (beer).	Most services cannot be stored; so other ways must be found to accommodate fluctuations in demand (can't store haircuts, but even the barber shop has an inventory of supplies).
Scheduling	Ability to inventory may allow levelling of production rates (lawn mowers).	Often concerned with meeting the customer's immediate schedule with human resources.
Maintenance	Maintenance is often preventive and takes place at the production site.	Maintenance is often "repair" and takes place at the customer's site.

AUTHOR COMMENT
The production of both goods and services requires execution of the 10 OM decisions.

AUTHOR COMMENT
Notice how the 10 decisions are altered to build two distinct strategies in the same industry.

TABLE 2.2
Operations Strategies of Two Drug Companies

	Brand Name Drugs, Inc.	Generic Drug Corp.
Competitive Advantage	**Product Differentiation**	**Low Cost**
Product Selection and Design	Heavy R&D investment; extensive labs; focus on development in a broad range of drug categories	Low R&D investment; focus on development of generic drugs
Quality	Quality is major priority; standards exceed regulatory requirements	Meets regulatory requirements on a country-by-country basis, as necessary
Process	Product and modular production process; tries to have long product runs in specialized facilities; builds capacity ahead of demand	Process focused; general production processes; "job shop" approach, short-run production; focus on high utilization
Location	Still located in city where it was founded	Recently moved to low-tax, low-labour-cost environment
Layout	Layout supports automated product-focused production	Layout supports process-focused "job shop" practices
Human Resources	Hire the best; nationwide searches	Very experienced top executives provide direction; other personnel paid below industry average
Supply Chain	Long-term supplier relationships	Tends to purchase competitively to find bargains
Inventory	Maintains high finished goods inventory primarily to ensure all demands are met	Process focus drives up work-in-process inventory; finished goods inventory tends to be low
Scheduling	Centralized production planning	Many short-run products complicate scheduling
Maintenance	Highly trained staff; extensive parts inventory	Highly trained staff to meet changing demands

Value-chain analysis
A way to identify those elements in the product/service chain that uniquely add value.

Five forces model
A method of analyzing the five forces in the competitive environment.

and ensuring that the potential strategy is compatible with those resources. Another perspective is Porter's value-chain analysis.[2] **Value-chain analysis** is used to identify activities that represent strengths, or potential strengths, and may be opportunities for developing competitive advantage. These are areas where the firm adds its unique *value* through product research, design, human resources, supply-chain management, process innovation, or quality management. Porter also suggests analysis of competitors via what he calls his **five forces model.**[3] These potential competing forces are immediate rivals, potential entrants, customers, suppliers, and substitute products.

In addition to the competitive environment, the operations manager needs to understand that the firm is operating in a system with many other external factors. These factors range from political, to legal, to cultural. They influence strategy development and execution and require constant scanning of the environment.

The firm itself is also undergoing constant change. Everything from resources, to technology, to product life cycles is in flux. Consider the significant changes required within the firm as its products move from introduction, to growth, to maturity, and to decline (see Figure 2.5). These internal changes, combined with external changes, require strategies that are dynamic.

In this chapter's *Global Company Profile*, Boeing provides an example of how strategy must change as technology and the environment change. Boeing can now build planes from carbon fibre, using a global supply chain. Like many other OM strategies, Boeing's strategy has changed with technology and globalization. Microsoft has also had to adapt quickly to a changing

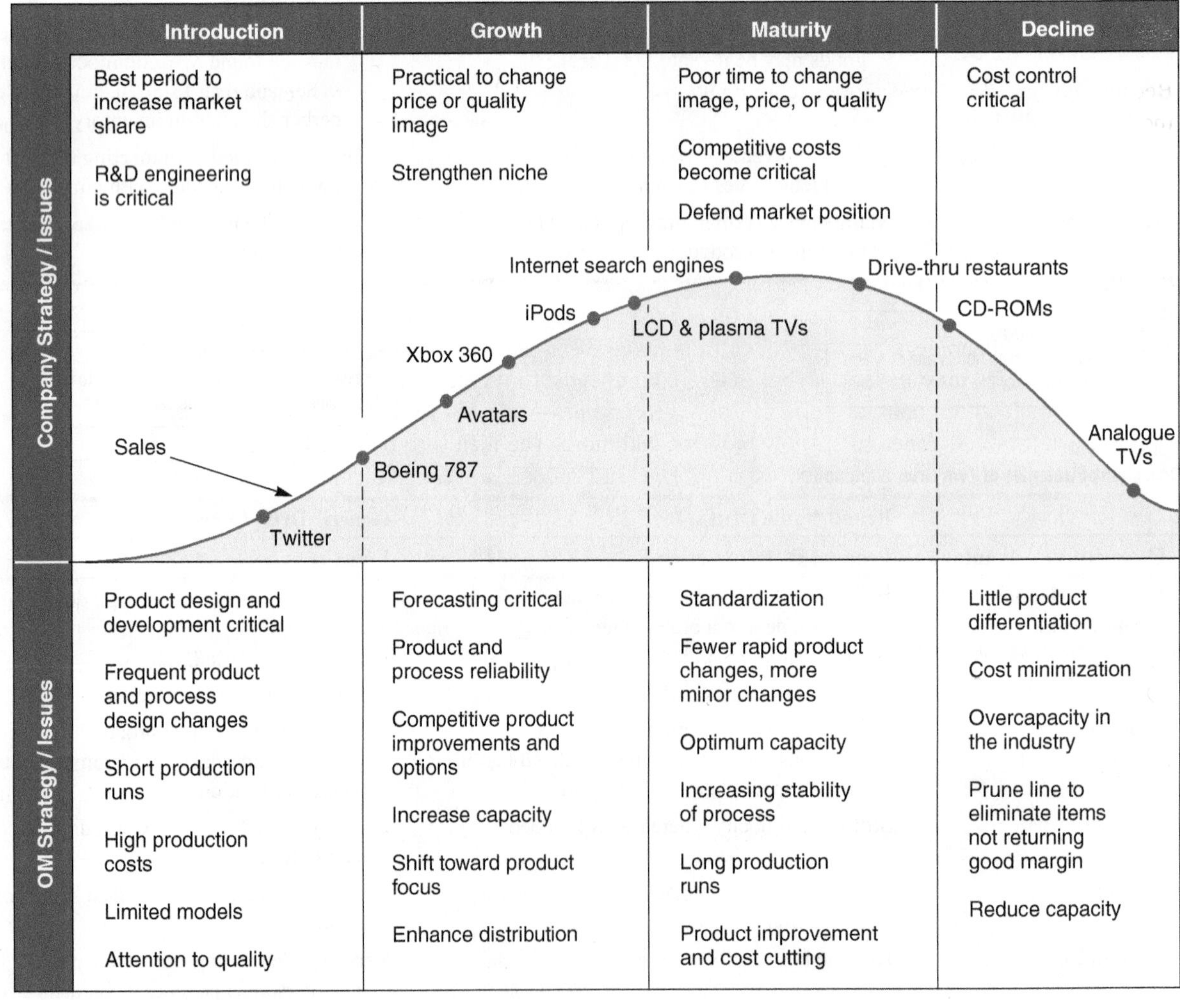

FIGURE 2.5 Strategy and Issues During a Product's Life

[2]M. E. Porter, *Competitive Advantage: Creating and Sustaining Superior Performance.* New York: The Free Press, 1985.
[3]Michael E. Porter, *Competitive Strategy: Techniques for Analyzing Industries and Competitors.* New York: The Free Press, 1980, 1998.

environment. Faster processors, new computer languages, changing customer preferences, increased security issues, the internet, and Google have all driven changes at Microsoft. These forces have moved Microsoft's product strategy from operating systems to office products, to internet service provider, and now to integrator of computers, cell phones, games, and television.

The more thorough the analysis and understanding of both the external and internal factors, the more likely that a firm can find the optimum use of its resources. Once a firm understands itself and the environment, a SWOT analysis, which we discuss next, is in order.

Strategy Development and Implementation

AUTHOR COMMENT
A SWOT analysis provides an excellent model for evaluating a strategy.

A **SWOT analysis** is a formal review of the internal Strengths and Weakness and the external Opportunity and Threats. Beginning with SWOT analyses, organizations position themselves, through their strategy, to have a competitive advantage. A firm may have excellent design skills or great talent at identifying outstanding locations. However, it may recognize limitations of its manufacturing process or in finding good suppliers. The idea is to maximize opportunities and minimize threats in the environment while maximizing the advantages of the organization's strengths and minimizing the weaknesses. Any preconceived ideas about mission are then reevaluated to ensure they are consistent with the SWOT analysis. Subsequently, a strategy for achieving the mission is developed. This strategy is continually evaluated against the value provided customers and competitive realities. The process is shown in Figure 2.6. From this process, key success factors are identified.

SWOT analysis
A method of determining internal strengths and weaknesses and external opportunities and threats.

KEY SUCCESS FACTORS AND CORE COMPETENCIES

Because no firm does everything exceptionally well, a successful strategy requires determining the firm's critical success factors and core competencies. **Key success factors (KSFs)** are those activities that are necessary for a firm to achieve its goals. Key success factors can be so significant that a firm must get them right to survive in the industry. A KSF for McDonald's, for example, is layout. Without a play area, an effective drive-thru, and an efficient kitchen, McDonald's cannot be successful. KSFs are often necessary, but not sufficient for competitive advantage. On the other hand, **core competencies** are the set of unique skills, talents, and capabilities that a firm does at a world-class standard. They allow a firm to set itself apart and develop a competitive advantage. Organizations that prosper identify their core competencies and nurture them. While McDonald's KSFs may include layout, its core competency may be consistency and quality. Honda Motors's core competence is gas-powered engines—engines for automobiles, motorcycles, lawn mowers, generators, snow blowers, and more. The idea is to build KSFs and core competencies that provide a competitive advantage and support a successful strategy and mission. A core competence may be a subset of KSFs or a combination of KSFs. The operations manager begins this inquiry by asking:

Key success factors (KSFs)
Activities or factors that are *key* to achieving competitive advantage.

Core competencies
A set of skills, talents, and activities in which a firm is particularly strong.

- "What tasks must be done particularly well for a given strategy to succeed?"
- "Which activities will help the OM function provide a competitive advantage?"
- "Which elements contain the highest likelihood of failure, and which require additional commitment of managerial, monetary, technological, and human resources?"

LO4: Understand the significance of key success factors and core competencies

Analyze the Environment
Identify the strengths, weaknesses, opportunities, and threats.
Understand the environment, customers, industry, and competitors.

Determine the Corporate Mission
State the reason for the firm's existence and identify the value it wishes to create.

Form a Strategy
Build a competitive advantage, such as low price, design or volume flexibility, quality, quick delivery, dependability, after-sale services, or broad product lines.

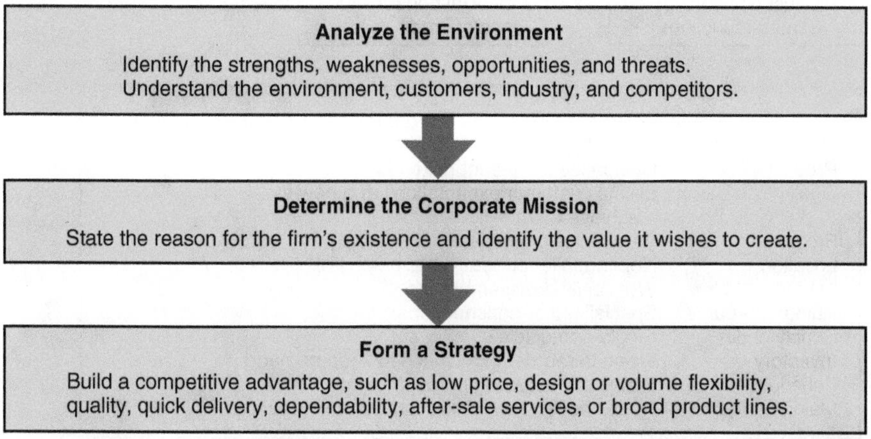

FIGURE 2.6
Strategy Development Process

Honda's core competence is the design and manufacture of gas-powered engines. This competence has allowed Honda to become a leader in the design and manufacture of a wide range of gas-powered products. Tens of millions of these products are produced and shipped around the world.

Only by identifying and strengthening key success factors and core competencies can an organization achieve sustainable competitive advantage.

In this text, we focus on the 10 OM decisions that typically include the KSFs. Potential KSFs for marketing, finance, and operations are shown in Figure 2.7. The 10 OM decisions we develop in this text provide an excellent initial checklist for determining KSFs and identifying core competencies within the operations function. For instance, the 10 decisions, related KSFs, and core competencies can allow a firm to differentiate its product or service. That differentiation may be via a core competence of innovation and new products, where the KSFs are product design and speed to market, as is the case for 3M and Rubbermaid. Similarly, differentiation may be via quality, where the core competence is institutionalizing quality, as at Toyota. Differentiation may also be via maintenance, where the KSFs are product reliability and after-sale service, as is the case at IBM and Canon.

Activity map
A graphical link of competitive advantage, KSFs, and supporting activities.

Whatever the KSFs and core competences, they must be supported by the related activities. One approach to identifying the activities is an **activity map**, which links competitive advantage, KSFs, and supporting activities. For example, Figure 2.8 shows how Porter Airlines, whose core competence is operations, built a set of integrated activities to support its low-cost competitive advantage. Notice how the KSFs support operations and in turn are supported by other activities. The activities fit together and reinforce each other. And the better they

FIGURE 2.7
Implement Strategy by Identifying and Executing Key Success Factors That Support Core Competences

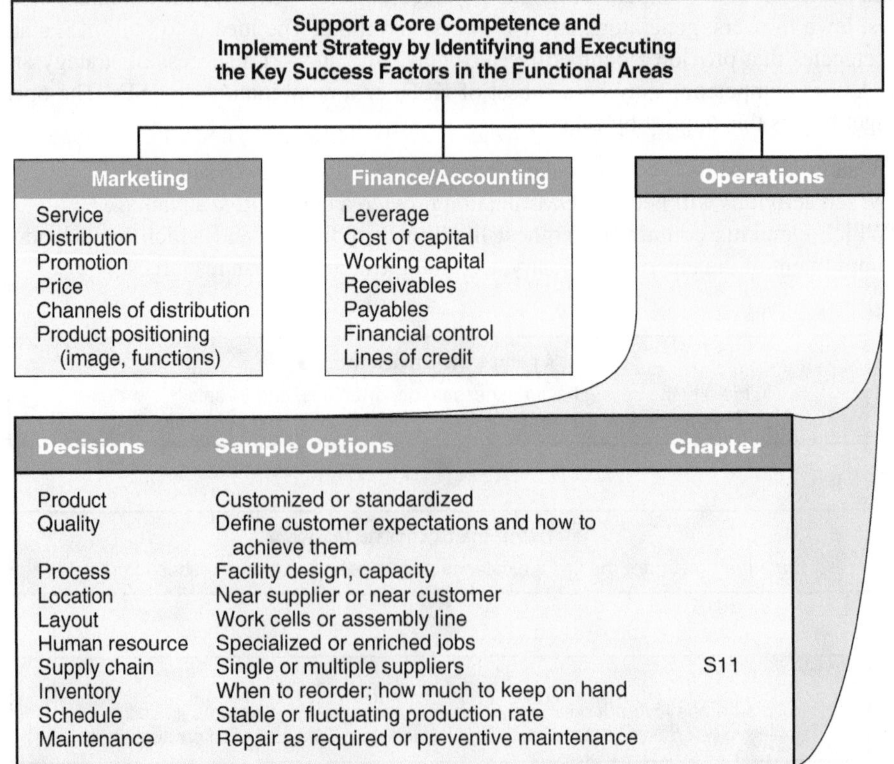

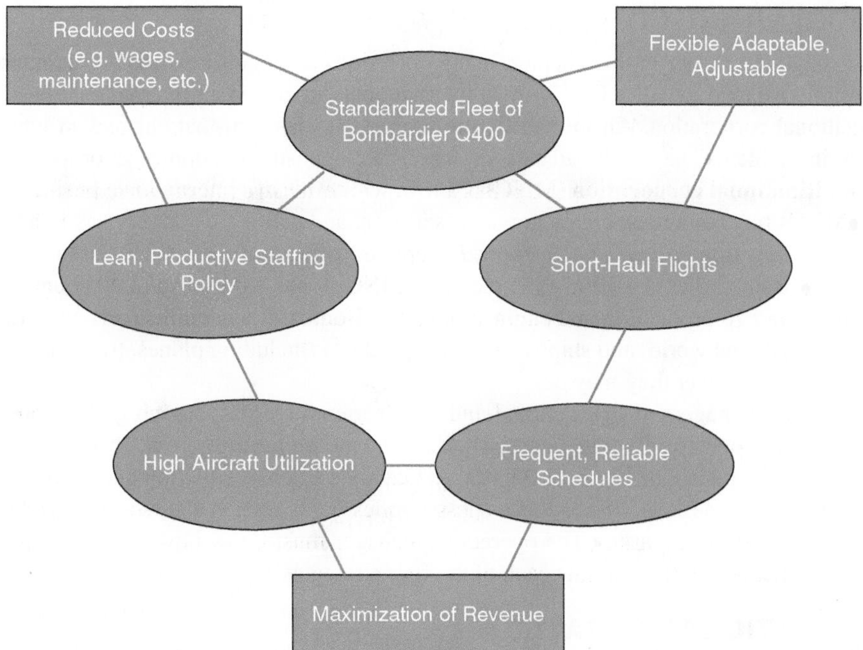

FIGURE 2.8 Activity Mapping of Porter Airline's Low-Cost Competitive Advantage
To achieve a low-cost competitive advantage, Porter Airlines addresses a number of key success factors. As the figure illustrates, a low-cost advantage is highly dependent on a very well-run operations function.

fit and reinforce each other, the more sustainable the competitive advantage. By focusing on enhancing its core competence and KSFs with a supporting set of activities, Porter Airlines has become one of the great airline success stories.

BUILD AND STAFF THE ORGANIZATION

The operations manager's job is a three-step process. Once a strategy and key success factors have been identified, the second step is to group the necessary activities into an organizational structure. The third step is to staff it with personnel who will get the job done. The manager works with subordinate managers to build plans, budgets, and programs that will successfully implement strategies that achieve missions. Firms tackle this organization of the operations function in a variety of ways. The organization charts shown in Chapter 1 (Figure 1.1) indicate the way some firms have organized to perform the required activities.

INTEGRATE OM WITH OTHER ACTIVITIES

The organization of the operations function and its relationship to other parts of the organization vary with the OM mission. Moreover, the operations function is most likely to be successful when the operations strategy is integrated with other functional areas of the firm, such as marketing, finance, information technology, and human resources. In this way, all of the areas support the company's objectives. For example, short-term scheduling in the airline industry is dominated by volatile customer travel patterns. Day-of-week preference, holidays, seasonality, school schedules, and so on all play a role in changing flight schedules. Consequently, airline scheduling, although an OM activity, can be a part of marketing. Effective scheduling in the trucking industry is reflected in the amount of time trucks travel loaded. However, scheduling of trucks requires information from delivery and pickup points, drivers, and other parts of the organization. When the OM function results in effective scheduling in the air passenger and commercial trucking industries, a competitive advantage can exist.

The operations manager transforms inputs into outputs. The transformations may be in terms of storage, transportation, manufacturing, dissemination of information, and utility of the product or service. *The operations manager's job is to implement an OM strategy, provide competitive advantage, and increase productivity.*

AUTHOR COMMENT
Firms that ignore the global economy will not survive.

Global Operations Strategy Options

International business
A firm that engages in cross-border transactions.

Multinational corporation (MNC)
A firm that has extensive involvement in international business, owning or controlling facilities in more than one country.

As we suggested earlier in this chapter, many operations strategies now require an international dimension. We tend to call a firm with an international dimension an international business or a multinational corporation. An **international business** is any firm that engages in international trade or investment. This is a broad category and is the opposite of a domestic, or local, firm.

A **multinational corporation (MNC)** is a firm with *extensive* international business involvement. MNCs buy resources, create goods or services, and sell goods or services in a variety of countries. The term *multinational corporation* applies to most of the world's large, well-known businesses. Bombardier is a good example of an MNC. It has a presence in 60 countries worldwide, including 76 production and engineering sites. Bombardier acquires parts and raw materials from around the world, and ships its finished products (including planes, trains, and buses) to its customers wherever they may be.

Operations managers of international and multinational firms approach global opportunities with one of four operations strategies: *international*, *multidomestic*, *global*, or *transnational* (see Figure 2.9). The matrix of Figure 2.9 has a vertical axis of cost reduction and a horizontal axis of local responsiveness. Local responsiveness implies quick response and/or the differentiation necessary for the local market. The operations manager must know how to position the firm in this matrix. Let us briefly examine each of the four strategies.

INTERNATIONAL STRATEGY

International strategy
A strategy in which global markets are penetrated using exports and licences.

An **international strategy** uses exports and licences to penetrate the global arena. As Figure 2.9 suggests, the international strategy is the least advantageous, with little local responsiveness and little cost advantage. There is little responsiveness because we are exporting or licensing goods from the home country. And the cost advantages may be few because we are using the existing production process at some distance from the new market. However, an international strategy is often the easiest, as exports can require little change in existing operations, and licensing agreements often leave much of the risk to the licensee.

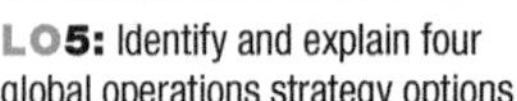

LO5: Identify and explain four global operations strategy options

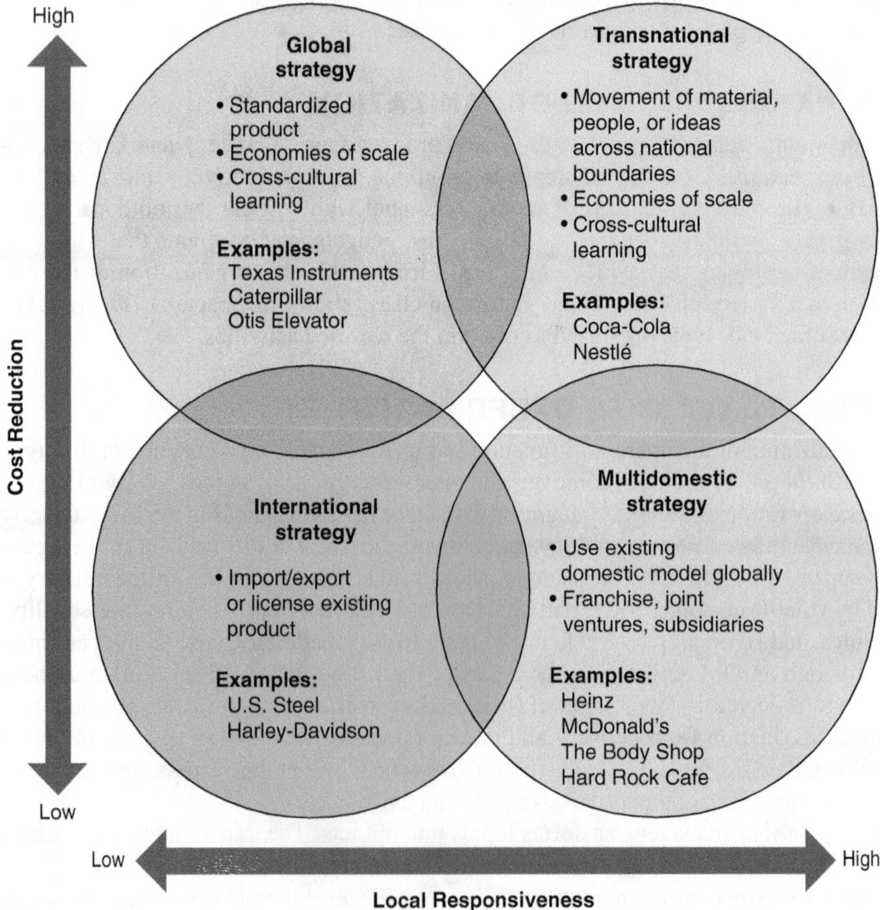

FIGURE 2.9
Four International Operations Strategies

Source: See a similar presentation in M. Hitt, R. D. Ireland, and R. E. Hoskisson, *Strategic Management, Competitiveness and Globalization*, 7th ed. (Cincinnati: Southwestern College Publishing, 2009).

MULTIDOMESTIC STRATEGY

The **multidomestic strategy** has decentralized authority with substantial autonomy at each business. Organizationally, these are typically subsidiaries, franchises, or joint ventures with substantial independence. The advantage of this strategy is maximizing a competitive response for the local market; however, the strategy has little or no cost advantage. Many food producers, such as Heinz, use a multidomestic strategy to accommodate local tastes because global integration of the production process is not critical. The concept is one of "we were successful in the home market; let's export the management talent and processes, not necessarily the product, to accommodate another market." McDonald's is operating primarily as a multidomestic, which gives it the local responsiveness needed to modify its menu country by country. McDonald's can then serve beer in Germany, wine in France, McHuevo (poached egg hamburger) in Uruguay, and hamburgers without beef in India. With over 2000 restaurants in Japan and a presence for more than a generation, the average Japanese family thinks Japan invented McDonald's. Interestingly, McDonald's prefers to call itself *multilocal*.[4]

Multidomestic strategy
A strategy in which operating decisions are decentralized to each country to enhance local responsiveness.

GLOBAL STRATEGY

A **global strategy** has a high degree of centralization, with headquarters coordinating the organization to seek out standardization and learning between plants, thus generating economies of scale. This strategy is appropriate when the strategic focus is cost reduction but has little to recommend it when the demand for local responsiveness is high. Caterpillar, the world leader in earth-moving equipment, and Texas Instruments, a world leader in semiconductors, pursue global strategies. Caterpillar and Texas Instruments find this strategy advantageous because the end products are similar throughout the world. Earth-moving equipment is the same in Nigeria as in Prince Edward Island, which allows Caterpillar to have individual factories focus on a limited line of products to be shipped worldwide. This results in economies of scale and learning within each facility. A global strategy also allows Texas Instruments to build optimum-size plants with similar processes and to then maximize learning by aggressive communication between plants. The result is an effective cost reduction advantage for Texas Instruments.

Global strategy
A strategy in which operating decisions are centralized and headquarters coordinates the standardization and learning between facilities.

TRANSNATIONAL STRATEGY

A **transnational strategy** exploits the economies of scale and learning, as well as pressure for responsiveness, by recognizing that core competence does not reside in just the "home" country but can exist anywhere in the organization. *Transnational* describes a condition in which material,

Transnational strategy
A strategy that combines the benefits of global-scale efficiencies with the benefits of local responsiveness.

In a continuing fierce worldwide battle, both Komatsu and Caterpillar seek global advantage in the heavy equipment market. As Komatsu (left) moved west to the U.K., Caterpillar (right) moved east, with 13 facilities and joint ventures in China. Both firms are building equipment throughout the world as cost and logistics dictate. Their global strategies allow production to move as markets, risk, and exchange rates dictate.

[4]James L. Watson, ed., *Golden Arches East: McDonald's in East Asia* (Stanford University Press, 1997): 12.
Note: McDonald's also operates with some of the advantages of a global organization. By using very similar product lines throughout the world, McDonald's obtains some of the standardization advantages of a global strategy. However, it manages to retain the advantages of a multidomestic strategy.

people, and ideas cross—or *transgress*—national boundaries. These firms have the potential to pursue all three operations strategies (i.e., differentiation, low cost, and response). Such firms can be thought of as "world companies" whose country identity is not as important as its interdependent network of worldwide operations. Key activities in a transnational company are neither centralized in the parent company nor decentralized so that each subsidiary can carry out its own tasks on a local basis. Instead, the resources and activities are dispersed, but specialized, so as to be both efficient and flexible in an interdependent network. Nestlé is a good example of such a company. Although it is legally Swiss, 95% of its assets are held and 98% of its sales are made outside Switzerland. Fewer than 10% of its workers are Swiss. Similarly, service firms such as Asea Brown Boveri (an engineering firm that is Swedish but headquartered in Switzerland), Reuters (a news agency), Bertelsmann (a publisher), and Citicorp (a banking corporation) can be viewed as transnationals. We can expect the national identities of these transnationals to continue to fade.

CHAPTER SUMMARY

Global operations provide an increase in both the challenges and opportunities for operations managers. Although the task is challenging, operations managers can and do improve productivity. They can build and manage OM functions that contribute in a significant way to competitiveness. Organizations identify their strengths and weaknesses. They then develop effective missions and strategies that account for these strengths and weaknesses and complement the opportunities and threats in the environment. If this procedure is performed well, the organization can have competitive advantage through some combination of product differentiation, low cost, and response. This competitive advantage is often achieved via a move to international, multidomestic, global, or transnational strategies.

Effective use of resources, whether domestic or international, is the responsibility of the professional manager, and professional managers are among the few in our society who *can* achieve this performance. The challenge is great, and the rewards to the manager and to society substantial.

Key Terms

Maquiladoras (p. 36)
World Trade Organization (WTO) (p. 37)
North American Free Trade Agreement (NAFTA) (p. 37)
European Union (EU) (p. 37)
Mission (p. 39)
Strategy (p. 40)
Competitive advantage (p. 40)
Differentiation (p. 42)
Experience differentiation (p. 42)
Low-cost leadership (p. 42)
Response (p. 42)
Operations decisions (p. 45)
Resources view (p. 46)
Value-chain analysis (p. 48)
Five forces model (p. 48)
SWOT analysis (p. 49)
Key success factors (KSFs) (p. 49)
Core competencies (p. 49)
Activity map (p. 50)
International business (p. 52)
Multinational corporation (MNC) (p. 52)
International strategy (p. 52)
Multidomestic strategy (p. 53)
Global strategy (p. 53)
Transnational strategy (p. 53)

Ethical Dilemma

As a manufacturer of athletic shoes whose image, indeed performance, is widely regarded as socially responsible, you find your costs increasing. Traditionally, your athletic shoes have been made in Indonesia and South Korea. Although the ease of doing business in those countries has been improving, wage rates have also been increasing. The labour-cost differential between your present suppliers and a contractor who will get the shoes made in China now exceeds $1 per pair. Your sales next year are projected to be 10 million pairs, and your analysis suggests that this cost differential is not offset by any other tangible costs; you face only the political risk and potential damage to your commitment to social responsibility. Thus, this $1 per pair savings should flow directly to your bottom line. There is no doubt that the Chinese government engages in censorship, remains repressive, and is a long way from a democracy. Moreover, you will have little or no control over working conditions, sexual harassment, and pollution. What do you do and on what basis do you make your decision?

Discussion Questions

1. Based on the descriptions and analyses in this chapter, would Boeing be better described as a global firm or a transnational firm? Discuss.
2. List six reasons to internationalize operations.
3. Coca-Cola is called a global product. Does this mean that it is formulated in the same way throughout the world? Discuss.
4. Define *mission*.
5. Define *strategy*.
6. Describe how an organization's *mission* and *strategy* have different purposes.
7. Identify the mission and strategy of your automobile repair garage. What are the manifestations of the 10 OM decisions at the garage? That is, how is each of the 10 decisions accomplished?
8. As a library or internet assignment, identify the mission of a firm and the strategy that supports that mission.
9. How does an OM strategy change during a product's life cycle?
10. There are three primary ways to achieve competitive advantage. Provide an example, not included in the text, of each. Support your choices.
11. Given the discussion of Porter Airlines in the text, define an *operations* strategy for that firm.
12. How must an operations strategy integrate with marketing and accounting?

Solved Problem **Virtual Office Hours help is available at MyOMLab.**

▼ SOLVED PROBLEM 2.1

The global tire industry continues to consolidate. Michelin buys Goodrich and Uniroyal and builds plants throughout the world. Bridgestone buys Firestone, expands its research budget, and focuses on world markets. Goodyear spends almost 4% of its sales revenue on research. These three aggressive firms have come to dominate the world tire market, with total market share approaching 60%. And the German tire maker Continental AG has strengthened its position as fourth in the world, with a dominant presence in Germany. Against this formidable array, the old-line Italian tire company Pirelli SpA found it difficult to respond effectively. Although Pirelli still had 5% of the market, it was losing millions a year while the competition was getting stronger. Tires are a tough, competitive business that rewards companies having strong market shares and long production runs. Pirelli has some strengths: an outstanding reputation for excellent high-performance tires and an innovative manufacturing function.

Use a SWOT analysis to establish a feasible strategy for Pirelli.

▼ SOLUTION

First, find an opportunity in the world tire market that avoids the threat of the mass-market onslaught by the big three tire makers. Second, utilize the internal marketing strength represented by Pirelli's strong brand name and history of winning World Rally Championships. Third, maximize the internal innovative capabilities of the operations function.

To achieve these goals, Pirelli made a strategic shift out of low-margin standard tires and into higher-margin performance tires. Pirelli established deals with luxury brands Jaguar, BMW, Maserati, Ferrari, Bentley, and Lotus Elise and established itself as a provider of a large share of tires on new Porsches, S-class Mercedes, and Saabs. As a result, more than 70% of the company's tire production is now high-performance tires. People are willing to pay a premium for Pirellis.

The operations function continued to focus its design efforts on performance tires and developing a system of modular tire manufacture that allows much faster switching between models. This modular system, combined with investments in new manufacturing flexibility, has driven batch sizes down to as small as 150 to 200, making small-lot performance tires economically feasible. Manufacturing innovations at Pirelli have streamlined the production process, moving it from a 14-step process to a 3-step process. A threat from the big three going after the performance market remains, but Pirelli has bypassed its weakness of having a small market share. The firm now has 24 plants in 12 countries and a presence in more than 160 countries, with sales exceeding $4.5 billion.

Sources: Just Auto (February 2009): 14–15 and (December 2008): 14–15; *Hoover's Company Records* (October 15, 2005): 41369; and www.pirelli.com/corporate/en/investors/pirelli_at_glance/default.html.

Problems

• **2.1** The text provides three primary ways—strategic approaches (differentiation, cost, and response)—for achieving competitive advantage. Provide an example of each not given in the text. Support your choices. (*Hint:* Note the examples provided in the text.)

•• **2.2** Within the food service industry (restaurants that serve meals to customers, but not just fast food), find examples of firms that have sustained competitive advantage by competing on the basis of (1) cost leadership, (2) response, and (3) differentiation. Cite one example in each category; provide a sentence or two in support of each choice. Do not use fast-food chains for all categories. (*Hint:* A "99¢ menu" is very easily copied and is not a good source of sustained advantage.)

•• **2.3** Browse through the financial section of a daily paper or read business news online. Seek articles that constrain manufacturing innovation and productivity—workers aren't allowed to do this, workers are not or cannot be trained to do that, this technology is not allowed, this material cannot be handled by workers, and so forth. Be prepared to share your articles in class discussion.

•• **2.4** Match the product with the proper parent company and country in the table below:

Product	Parent Company	Country
Arrow Shirts	a. Volkswagen	1. France
Braun Household Appliances	b. Bidermann International	2. Great Britain
Lotus Autos	c. Bridgestone	3. Germany
Firestone Tires	d. Campbell Soup	4. Japan
BlackBerry	e. Credit Lyonnais	5. Canada
Godiva Chocolate	f. Tata	6. United States
Häagen-Dazs Ice Cream (USA)	g. Procter & Gamble	7. Switzerland
Jaguar Autos	h. Michelin	8. Malaysia
MGM Movies	i. Nestlé	9. India
Lamborghini Autos	j. Research in Motion	
Goodrich Tires	k. Proton	
Alpo Pet Foods		

••• **2.5** Identify how changes within an organization affect the OM strategy for a company. For instance, discuss what impact the following internal factors might have on OM strategy:

a) Maturing of a product.
b) Technology innovation in the manufacturing process.
c) Changes in laptop computer design that builds in wireless technology.

••• **2.6** Identify how changes in the external environment affect the OM strategy for a company. For instance, discuss what impact the following external factors might have on OM strategy:

a) Major increases in oil prices.
b) Water- and air-quality legislation.
c) Fewer young prospective employees entering the labour market.
d) Inflation versus stable prices.
e) Legislation moving health insurance from a pretax benefit to taxable income.

••• **2.7** Develop a ranking for corruption in the following countries: Mexico, Turkey, Canada, Denmark, Taiwan, Brazil, and another country of your choice. (*Hint:* See sources such as *Transparency International*, *Asia Pacific Management News*, and *The Economist*.)

•• **2.8** Develop a ranking for competitiveness and/or business environment for Britain, Canada, Singapore, Hong Kong, and Italy. (*Hint:* See the *Global Competitive Report, World Economic Forum*, Geneva, and *The Economist*.)

Case Studies

Mr. Lube

A substantial market exists for automobile tune-ups, oil changes, and lubrication service for the more than 12 million cars on Canadian roads. Some of this demand is filled by full-service auto dealerships, some by Canadian Tire, and some by other tire/service dealers. However, Mr. Lube, Great Canadian Oil Change, Jiffy Lube, and others have also developed strategies to accommodate this opportunity.

Mr. Lube stations perform oil changes, lubrication, and interior cleaning in a spotless environment. The buildings are clean, freshly painted, and often surrounded by neatly trimmed landscaping and clean parking areas. To facilitate fast service, cars can be driven though the facility. At Mr. Lube, the customer is greeted by service representatives who take their order, which typically includes fluid checks (oil, water, brake fluid, transmission fluid, and differential grease) and the necessary lubrication, as well as filter changes for air and oil. Service personnel in neat uniforms then move into action. The standard team has one person checking fluid levels under the hood, another in the garage pit removing the oil filter, draining the oil, checking the differential and transmission, and lubricating as necessary. Precise task assignments and good training are designed to move the car into and out of the bay in minutes. The idea is to charge no more, and hopefully less, than gas stations, automotive repair chains, and auto dealers. While doing so, Mr. Lube strives to provide better service than their competitors.

Discussion Questions

1. What constitutes the mission of Mr. Lube?
2. How does the Mr. Lube operations strategy provide competitive advantage? (*Hint:* Evaluate how Mr. Lube's traditional competitors perform the 10 decisions of operations management compared to how Mr. Lube performs them.)
3. Is it likely that Mr. Lube has increased productivity over its more traditional competitors? Why? How would we measure productivity in this industry?

Operations Strategy at Regal Marine

Regal Marine, one of the U.S.'s 10 largest power-boat manufacturers, achieves its mission—providing luxury performance boats to customers worldwide—using the strategy of differentiation. It differentiates its products through constant innovation, unique features, and high quality. Increasing sales at the Orlando, Florida, family-owned firm suggest that the strategy is working.

As a quality boat manufacturer, Regal Marine starts with continuous innovation, as reflected in computer-aided design (CAD), high-quality moulds, and close tolerances that are controlled through both defect charts and rigorous visual inspection. In-house quality is not enough, however. Because a product is only as good as the parts put into it, Regal has established close ties with a large number of its suppliers to ensure both flexibility and perfect parts. With the help of these suppliers, Regal can profitably produce a product line of 22 boats, ranging from the $14 000 19-foot boat to the $500 000 44-foot Commodore yacht.

"We build boats," says VP Tim Kuck, "but we're really in the 'fun' business. Our competition includes not only 300 other boat, canoe, and yacht manufacturers in our $17 billion industry, but home theatres, the internet, and all kinds of alternative family entertainment." Fortunately, Regal has been paying down debt and increasing market share.

Regal has also joined with scores of other independent boat makers in the American Boat Builders Association. Through economies of scale in procurement, Regal is able to navigate against billion-dollar competitor Brunswick (makers of the Sea Ray and Bayliner brands). The *Global Company Profile* featuring Regal Marine provides further background on Regal and its strategy.

Discussion Questions*

1. State Regal Marine's mission in your own words.
2. Identify the strengths, weaknesses, opportunities, and threats that are relevant to the strategy of Regal Marine.
3. How would you define Regal's strategy?
4. How would each of the 10 operations management decisions apply to operations decision making at Regal Marine?

*You may wish to view the video that accompanies this case before addressing these questions.

Hard Rock Cafe's Global Strategy

Hard Rock brings the concept of the "experience economy" to its cafe operation. The strategy incorporates a unique "experience" into its operations. This innovation is somewhat akin to mass customization in manufacturing. At Hard Rock, the experience concept is to provide not only a custom meal from the menu but also a dining event that includes a unique visual and sound experience not duplicated anywhere else in the world. This strategy is succeeding. Other theme restaurants have come and gone while Hard Rock continues to grow. As Professor C. Markides of the London Business School says, "The trick is not to play the game better than the competition, but to develop and play an altogether different game."* At Hard Rock, the different game is the experience game.

From the opening of its first cafe in London in 1971, during the British rock music explosion, Hard Rock has been serving food and rock music with equal enthusiasm. Hard Rock Cafe has 40 U.S. locations, about a dozen in Europe, and the remainder scattered throughout the world, from Bangkok and Beijing to Beirut. New construction, leases, and investment in remodelling are long term; a global strategy means special consideration of political risk, currency risk, and social norms in a context of a brand fit. Although Hard Rock is one of the most recognized brands in the world, this does not mean its cafe is a natural everywhere. Special consideration must be given to the supply chain for the restaurant and its accompanying retail store. About 48% of a typical cafe's sales are from merchandise.

The Hard Rock Cafe business model is well defined, but because of various risk factors and differences in business practices and employment law, Hard Rock elects to franchise about half of its cafes. Social norms and preferences often suggest some tweaking of menus for local taste. For instance, Hard Rock focuses less on hamburgers and beef and more on fish and lobster in its British cafes.

Because 70% of Hard Rock's guests are tourists, recent years have found it expanding to "destination" cities. While this has been a winning strategy for decades, allowing the firm to grow from 1 London cafe to 157 facilities in 57 countries, it has made Hard Rock susceptible to economic fluctuations that hit the tourist business hardest. So Hard Rock is signing a long-term lease for a new location in Nottingham, England, to join recently opened cafes in Manchester and Birmingham—cities that are not standard tourist destinations. At the same time, menus are being upgraded. Hopefully, repeat business from locals in these cities will smooth demand and make Hard Rock less dependent on tourists.

Discussion Questions†

1. Identify the strategy changes that have taken place at Hard Rock Cafe since its founding in 1971.
2. As Hard Rock Cafe has changed its strategy, how has its responses to some of the 10 decisions of OM changed?
3. Where does Hard Rock fit in the four international operations strategies outlined in Figure 2.9? Explain your answer.

*Constantinos Markides, "Strategic Innovation," *MIT Sloan Management Review* 38, no. 3 (spring 1997): 9.

†You may wish to view the video that accompanies the case before addressing these questions.

▶ **Additional Case Study:** Visit **MyOMLab** for this free case study:
Motorola's Global Strategy: Focuses on Motorola's international strategy.

Bibliography

Beckman, S. L., and D. B. Rosenfield. *Operations Strategy: Competing in the 21st Century*. New York: McGraw-Hill, 2008.

Crotts, J. C., D. R. Dickson, and R. C. Ford. "Aligning Organizational Processes with Mission." *Academy of Management Executive* 19, no. 3 (August 2005): 54–68.

Flynn, B. B., R. G. Schroeder, and E. J. Flynn. "World Class Manufacturing." *Journal of Operations Management* 17, no. 3 (March 1999): 249–269.

Friedman, Thomas. *The World Is Flat: A Brief History of the Twenty-First Century*. New York: Farrar, Straus, and Giroux, 2005.

Greenwald, Bruce, and Judd Kahn. "All Strategy Is Local." *Harvard Business Review* 83, no. 9 (September 2005): 94–104.

Kaplan, Robert S., and David P. Norton. *Strategy Maps*. Boston: Harvard Business School Publishing, 2003.

Kathuria, R., M. P. Joshi, and S. Dellande. "International Growth Strategies of Service and Manufacturing Firms: The Case of Banking and Chemical Industries." *International Journal of Operations and Production Management* 28, no. 10 (2008): 968–990.

Porter, Michael, and Nicolaj Siggelkow. "Contextuality within Activity Systems and Sustainability of Competitive Advantage." *Academy of Management Perspectives* 22, no. 2 (May 2008): 34–36.

Rudberg, Martin, and B. M. West. "Global Operations Strategy." *Omega* 36, no. 1 (February 2008): 91.

Skinner, Wickham. "Manufacturing Strategy: The Story of Its Evolution." *Journal of Operations Management* 25, no. 2 (March 2007): 328–334.

Slack, Nigel, and Mike Lewis. *Operation Strategy*, 2nd ed. Upper Saddle River, NJ: Prentice Hall, 2008.

Wolf, Martin. *Why Globalization Works*. London: Yale University Press, 2004.

Zakaria, Fareed. *The Post American World*. New York: W.W. Norton, 2008.

CHAPTER 2 Rapid Review

<table>
<tr><th>Main Heading</th><th>Review Material</th><th>MyOMLab</th></tr>
<tr><td>A GLOBAL VIEW OF OPERATIONS
(pp. 35–39)</td><td>Domestic business operations decide to change to some form of international operations for six main reasons:
1. Reduce costs (labour, taxes, tariffs, etc.)
2. Improve supply chain
3. Provide better goods and services
4. Understand markets
5. Learn to improve operations
6. Attract and retain global talent
• NAFTA—A free trade agreement between Canada, Mexico, and the United States.
• Maquiladoras—Mexican factories located along the U.S.–Mexico border that receive preferential tariff treatment.
• World Trade Organization (WTO)—An international organization that promotes world trade by lowering barriers to the free flow of goods across borders.
• European Union (EU)—A European trade group that has 27 member states.
Other trade agreements include APEC (the Pacific Rim countries), SEATO (Australia, New Zealand, Japan, Hong Kong, South Korea, New Guinea, and Chile), MERCOSUR (Argentina, Brazil, Paraguay, and Uruguay), and CAFTA (Central America, the Dominican Republic, and the United States).
The World Trade Organization helps to make uniform the protection of both governments and industries from foreign firms that engage in unethical conduct.</td><td></td></tr>
<tr><td>DEVELOPING MISSIONS AND STRATEGIES
(pp. 39–40)</td><td>An effective operations management effort must have a mission so it knows where it is going and a strategy so it knows how to get there.
• Mission—The purpose or rationale for an organization's existence.
• Strategy—How an organization expects to achieve its missions and goals.
The three strategic approaches to competitive advantage are:
1. Differentiation
2. Cost leadership
3. Response</td><td>VIDEO 2.1
Operations Strategy at Regal Marine</td></tr>
<tr><td>ACHIEVING COMPETITIVE ADVANTAGE THROUGH OPERATIONS
(pp. 40–44)</td><td>• Competitive advantage—The creation of a unique advantage over competitors.
• Differentiation—Distinguishing the offerings of an organization in a way that the customer perceives as adding value.
• Experience differentiation—Engaging the customer with a product through imaginative use of the five senses, so the customer "experiences" the product.
• Low-cost leadership—Achieving maximum value, as perceived by the customer.
• Response—A set of values related to rapid, flexible, and reliable performance.
Differentiation can be attained, for example, through innovative design, by providing a broad product line, by offering excellent after-sale service, or through adding a sensory experience to the product or service offering.
Cost leadership can be attained, for example, via low overhead, effective capacity use, or efficient inventory management.
Response can be attained, for example, by offering a flexible product line, reliable scheduling, or speedy delivery.</td><td>VIDEO 2.2
Hard Rock's Global Strategy</td></tr>
<tr><td>TEN STRATEGIC OM DECISIONS
(pp. 45–46)</td><td>• Operations decisions—The strategic decisions of OM are goods and service design, quality, process and capacity design, location selection, layout design, human resources and job design, supply-chain management, inventory, scheduling, and maintenance.</td><td></td></tr>
<tr><td>ISSUES IN OPERATIONS STRATEGY
(pp. 46–49)</td><td>• Resources view—A view in which managers evaluate the resources at their disposal and manage or alter them to achieve competitive advantage.
• Value-chain analysis—A way to identify the elements in the product/service chain that uniquely add value.
• Five-forces model—A way to analyze the five forces in the competitive environment.
The potential competing forces in Porter's five-forces model are (1) immediate rivals, (2) potential entrants, (3) customers, (4) suppliers, and (5) substitute products.
Different issues are emphasized during different stages of the product life cycle:
• Introduction—Company strategy: Best period to increase market share, R&D engineering is critical. OM strategy: Product design and development critical, frequent product and process design changes, short production runs, high production costs, limited models, attention to quality.
• Growth—Company strategy: Practical to change price or quality image, strengthen niche. OM strategy: Forecasting critical, product and process reliability, competetive product improvements and options, increase capacity, shift toward product focus, enhance distribution.</td><td></td></tr>
</table>

Main Heading	Review Material	MyOMLab
	• **Maturity**—Company strategy: Poor time to change image or price or quality, competitive costs become critical, defend market position. OM strategy: Standardization, less rapid product changes (more minor changes), optimum capacity, increasing stability of process, long production runs, product improvement and cost cutting. • **Decline**—Company strategy: Cost control critical. OM strategy: Little product differentiation, cost minimization, overcapacity in the industry, prune line to eliminate items not returning good margin, reduce capacity.	
STRATEGY DEVELOPMENT AND IMPLEMENTATION (pp. 49–51)	• **SWOT analysis**—A method of determining internal strengths and weaknesses and external opportunities and threats. The strategy development process first involves performing environmental analysis, followed by determining the corporate mission, and finally forming a strategy. • **Key success factors (KSFs)**—Activities or factors that are key to achieving competitive advantage. • **Core competencies**—A set of skills, talents, and activities that a firm does particularly well. A core competence may be a subset of, or a combination of, KSFs. • **Activity map**—A graphical link of competitive advantage, KSFs, and supporting activities. An operations manager's job is to implement an OM strategy, provide competitive advantage, and increase productivity.	Virtual Office Hours for Solved Problem: 2.1
GLOBAL OPERATIONS STRATEGY OPTIONS (pp. 52–54)	• **International business**—A firm that engages in cross-border transactions. • **Multinational corporation (MNC)**—A firm that has extensive involvement in international business, owning or controlling facilities in more than one country. • **International strategy**—A strategy in which global markets are penetrated using exports and licences. • **Multidomestic strategy**—A strategy in which operating decisions are decentralized to each country to enhance local responsiveness. • **Global strategy**—A strategy in which operating decisions are centralized and headquarters coordinates the standardization and learning between facilities. • **Transnational strategy**—A strategy that combines the benefits of global-scale efficiencies with the benefits of local responsiveness. These firms transgress national boundaries. The four operations strategies for approaching global opportunities can be classified according to local responsiveness and cost reduction: 1. **International**—Little local responsiveness and little cost advantage 2. **Multidomestic**—Significant local responsiveness but little cost advantage 3. **Global**—Little local responsiveness but significant cost advantage 4. **Transnational**—Significant local responsiveness and significant cost advantage	

Self Test

■ **Before taking the self-test,** refer to the learning objectives listed at the beginning of the chapter and the key terms listed at the end of the chapter.

LO1. A mission statement is beneficial to an organization because it:
- **a)** is a statement of the organization's purpose.
- **b)** provides a basis for the organization's culture.
- **c)** identifies important constituencies.
- **d)** details specific income goals.
- **e)** ensures profitability.

LO2. The three strategic approaches to competitive advantage are ________, ________, and ________.

LO3. The 10 decisions of OM:
- **a)** are functional areas of the firm.
- **b)** apply to both service and manufacturing organizations.
- **c)** are the goals that are to be achieved.
- **d)** form an action plan to achieve a mission.
- **e)** are key success factors.

LO4. The relatively few activities that make a difference between a firm having and not having a competitive advantage are known as:
- **a)** activity maps.
- **b)** SWOT.
- **c)** key success factors.
- **d)** global profile.
- **e)** response strategy.

LO5. A company that is organized across international boundaries, with decentralized authority and substantial autonomy at each business via subsidiaries, franchises, or joint ventures has:
- **a)** a global strategy.
- **b)** a transnational strategy.
- **c)** an international strategy.
- **d)** a multidomestic strategy.
- **e)** a regional strategy.

Answers: LO1. a; LO2. differentiation, cost leadership, response; LO3. b; LO4. c; LO5. d.

MyOMLab

Visit MyOMLab to access cases, videos, downloadable software, and much more. MyOMLab also features a personalized Study Plan that helps you identify which chapter concepts you've mastered and guides you towards study tools for additional practice.

Student Profile

Kyle Leslie, BBA, MBA Candidate
Quality Improvement Consultant, Grand River Hospital
Senior Buyer, Grand River Hospital until 2013
Business Administration Materials and Operations Management Program 2008
Preston High school 2005

In my professional career, I continuously call upon the skills and knowledge I learned from the Materials and Operations Management program at Conestoga College. Every aspect of the program has proven to be useful. Projects that I have been directly involved with showcase the skills I learned at Conestoga College including: strategic sourcing, generation and management of RFPs, and facilitation of lean process improvement initiatives among others. Since graduating, I have completed a BBA and I am currently pursuing an MBA. The opportunities this program offers are endless if you apply the knowledge and skills learned within it.

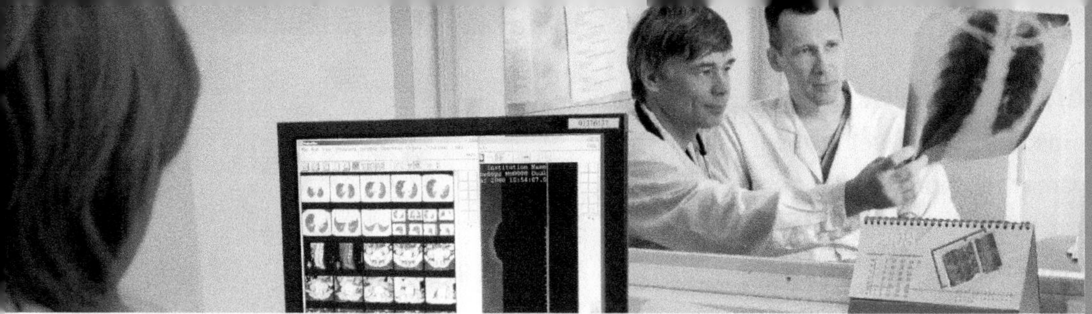

3

Business Processes

Chapter Outline

AP Photo/Wilfredo Lee

PROCTER & GAMBLE (P&G) is one of the world's largest consumer goods firms, with such well-known brands as Tide detergent, Crest toothpaste, and Pampers disposable diapers. In the mid-1990s, P&G was organized around five business sectors: laundry and cleaning, paper goods, beauty care, food and beverages, and health care. To the folks within P&G, this made a lot of sense. Dividing such a large organization along product lines allowed each business sector to develop product, pricing, and promotion policies, as well as supply chain strategies, independent of one another.

But to the distributors and retailers who were P&G's direct customers, the view was quite different. Each of these customers had to deal with five separate billing and logistics processes—one for each business sector (Figure 3.1). As Ralph Drayer, vice president of Efficient Consumer Response for Procter & Gamble, noted, this created a wide range of problems:

[P&G] did not allow customers to purchase all P&G brands together for delivery on the same truck. Some customers might go several days without receiving an order, only to have several trucks with P&G orders arrive at the receiving dock at the same time on the same morning. Different product categories were shipped on different trucks with different invoices. The trade promotions process was so complex that more than 27,000 orders a month required manual corrections. . . . The separate pricing and promotion policies, coupled with noncoordinated management of logistics activities across the five business sectors, resulted in as many as nine prices per item and order quantities of less-than-full truckload.

In response, P&G launched its Streamlined Logistics initiative. Among many other things, it drastically reduced the number of new products being introduced (many of which only served to

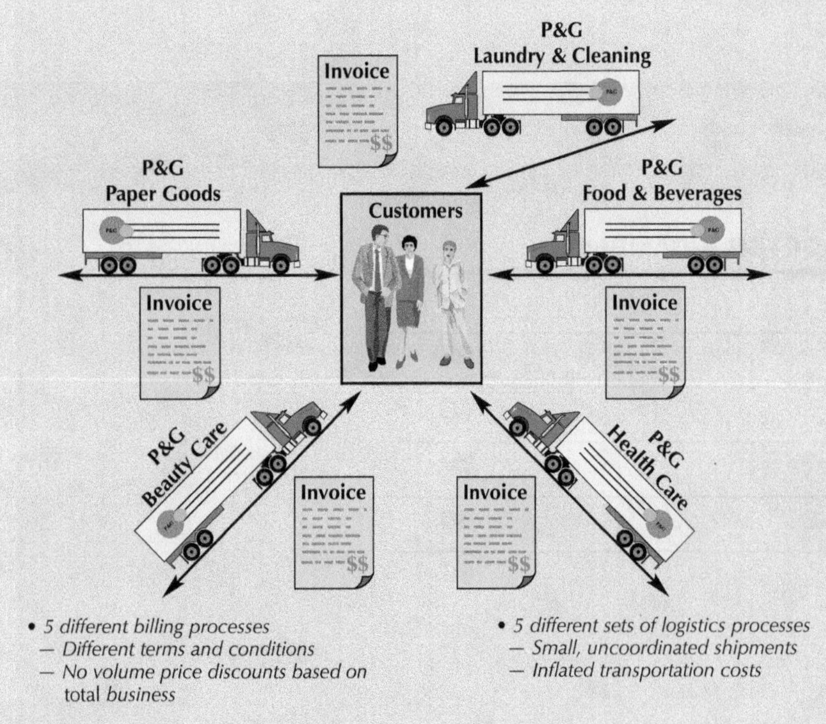

FIGURE 3.1
Procter & Gamble before the Streamlined Logistics Initiative

[1]Adapted from R. Drayer, "Procter & Gamble's Streamlined Logistics Initiative," *Supply Chain Management Review* 3, no. 2 (Summer 1999): 32–43. Reprinted with permission of Supply Chain Management Review.

• *One integrated billing process*
  – *Administrative cost savings passed on to customers*
  – *Volume discounts applied across all purchases*
• *One set of logistics processes*
  – *Full-truckload quantities shipped 98% of the time, resulting in substantial transportation cost savings*

FIGURE 3.2
Procter & Gamble after the Streamlined Logistics Initiative

confuse consumers) and simplified the pricing and promotion structure. But, more importantly, P&G redesigned the information and physical flows across the business sectors so that customers had to deal with only *one* P&G billing process and *one* set of logistics processes (Figure 3.2). The results were dramatic:

- **Full truckloads were shipped 98% of the time, resulting in dramatically lower transportation costs.**
- **The number of invoices the typical P&G customer had to handle fell anywhere from 25% to 75%. At a processing cost of $35 to $75 for each invoice, this represented substantial savings to P&G's customers.**
- **Customers were able to get volume discounts from P&G based on their *total* purchase volume. Under the previous system, this had been difficult, if not impossible, to do.**

Procter & Gamble's Streamlined Logistics initiative not only improved profitability for P&G and its customers but also served as a model for other manufacturers in the industry who have made similar efforts to simplify and streamline their own business processes.

Chapter 3 Learning Objectives

1: Explain what a business process is and how the business perspective differs from a traditional, functional perspective.

2: Create process maps for a business process and use them to understand and diagnose a process.

3: Calculate and interpret some common measures of process performance.

4: Discuss the importance of benchmarking and distinguish between competitive benchmarking and process benchmarking.

5: Describe the Six Sigma methodology, including the steps of the DMAIC process.

6: Use and interpret some common continuous improvement tools.

7: Explain what the Supply Chain Operations Reference (SCOR) model is and why it is important to businesses.

Introduction

In recent years, corporate executives and management theorists have recognized the importance of putting in place business processes that effectively manage the flow of information, products, and money across the supply chain. One reason is the dollars involved: Experts estimate that total supply chain costs represent the majority of the total operating budget for most organizations; in some cases, they may be as high as 75%.[2]

[2] F. Quinn, "What's the Buzz? Supply Chain Management: Part 1," *Logistics Management* 36, no. 2 (February 1997): 43. Reprinted with permission

Another reason is the increased emphasis on providing value to the customer. Look again at Procter & Gamble's Streamlined Logistics initiative. P&G used the *customer* as a focal point for reinventing and simplifying its billing and logistics processes. Because of these efforts, customers found their relationship with P&G to be more rewarding.

The purpose of this chapter is to give you a solid understanding of what business processes are and how the business process perspective differs from more traditional perspectives. We will describe various tools and techniques companies use to manage and improve business processes. In particular, we will introduce you to the Six Sigma methodology, including the DMAIC (Define–Measure–Analyze–Improve–Control) approach to business process improvement. We end the chapter with a discussion of the Supply Chain Operations Reference (SCOR) model, which gives companies a common language and model for designing, implementing, and evaluating supply chain business processes.

Business Processes

Process
According to APICS, "A set of logically related tasks or activities performed to achieve a defined business outcome."

So, just what do we mean by the term *business process*? APICS defines a **process** as "a set of logically related tasks or activities performed to achieve a defined business outcome."[3] For our purposes, these outcomes can be physical, informational, or even monetary in nature. Physical outcomes might include the manufacture and delivery of goods to a customer; an informational outcome might be registering for college courses; and a monetary outcome might include payment to a supply chain partner for services rendered. Of course, many business processes have elements of all three.

TABLE 3.1
Examples of Business Processes

Primary Processes	Support Processes	Development Processes
Providing a service	Evaluating suppliers	Developing new products
Educating customers	Recruiting new workers	Performing basic research
Manufacturing	Developing a sales and operations plan (S&OP)	Training new workers

Primary process
A process that addresses the main value-added activities of an organization.

Support process
A process that performs necessary, albeit not value-added, activities.

Development process
A process that seeks to improve the performance of primary and support processes.

Primary processes address the main value-added activities of an organization. They include activities such as delivering a service and manufacturing a product. These processes are considered "value-added" because some customer is willing to pay for the resulting outputs. In contrast, **support processes** perform necessary, albeit not value-added, activities. An example is tuition billing. No student wants to pay tuition, and the university would rather not spend the overhead required to collect it, but the university would not be able to sustain itself for very long without monetary flows from the students. Finally, **development processes** are processes that improve the performance of primary and support processes.[4] Table 3.1 gives examples of primary, support, and development processes.

As with our discussion of supply chains, you may be saying to yourself that "business processes aren't new," and, once again, you'd be right. What *is* new is the level of attention these processes have attracted in recent years. Prior to the 1990s, most managerial attention was on the activities within specific business *functions*, such as marketing, operations, logistics, and finance. The assumption was that if companies concentrated on how these functions were organized, how individuals were trained, and how the individual functional strategies lined up with the overall business strategy, then everything would be fine.

The problem was, however, that managing functions is not the same as managing what a business *does*. Look again at the business processes listed in Table 3.1. Nearly every one of these processes spans multiple functional areas and even multiple supply chain partners.

Figure 3.3 shows three of the business processes we will discuss in this book and how they cut across both functions and organizations. There are other processes that we have not shown here, but our point is this: For many business processes, no single function or supply chain partner has a

[3] J. H. Blackstone, ed., *APICS Dictionary*, 13th ed. (Chicago, IL: APICS, 2010).

[4] B. Andersen, *Business Process Improvement Toolbox* (Milwaukee, WI: ASQ Quality Press, 1999).

Suppliers | Purchasing | Engineering | Operations | Finance | Marketing | Customers

Developing new products

Evaluating suppliers (Chapter 7)

Developing sales and operations plans

FIGURE 3.3

Examples of Business Processes that Cut across Functions and Organizations

complete view or complete control of the situation. Developing superior business processes, therefore, requires a cross-functional and cross-organizational perspective that actively looks at the logical flow of activities that make up a business process. We will expand on this idea below.

IMPROVING BUSINESS PROCESSES

Let's illustrate the idea of improving business processes with an example many college students are familiar with: enrolling in classes each semester. Not too long ago, students had to interact with three distinct functional areas in order to register: the individual colleges or departments (which granted permission to take classes), the registrar's office (which managed the actual enrollment process), and the cashier's office (which handled tuition payments). A student would visit his home college or department to pick up the proper permission forms, schedule his classes, and finally pay tuition. Of course, any problem in the system could force the student to revisit one or more of these areas.

This process was convenient for everyone except the students. Now many colleges and universities have reorganized these activities into a single process, with a focus on speed, accuracy, and convenience to the students. Students can now register and pay tuition all with one phone call or visit to a Web site. In some cases, students can even purchase their books and have them automatically delivered to them. The key point is this: Improving the enrollment process required the different functional areas to look beyond their own activities and see the process through the *customers'* (i.e., students') eyes.

Improving business process is at the very core of operations and supply chain management. For one thing, the performance level of most processes tends to decrease over time unless forces are exerted to maintain it. In addition, even if an organization does not feel a need to improve its business processes, it may be forced to due to competitive pressures. Procter & Gamble's Streamlined Logistics initiative forced competitors, such as Kraft Foods, to undertake similar

Bill Aron/PhotoEdit

Many universities have already combined course registration with tuition payments into a single, integrated process. How long do you think it will be until all course and textbook information is integrated electronically into this process?

process involvement efforts.[5] Finally, today's customers are becoming more and more demanding; what a customer might have considered quite satisfactory a few years ago might not meet his or her requirements today.

Mapping Business Processes

Mapping
The process of developing graphic representations of the organizational relationships and/or activities that make up a business process

Before a firm can effectively manage and improve a business process, it must understand the process. One way to improve understanding is by developing graphic representations of the organizational relationships and/or activities that make up a business process. This is known as **mapping**. Done properly, mapping serves several purposes

- It creates a common understanding of the content of the process: its activities, its results, and who performs the various steps.
- It defines the boundaries of the process.
- It provides a baseline against which to measure the impact of improvement efforts.

PROCESS MAPS

Process map
A detailed map that identifies the specific activities that make up the informational, physical, and/or monetary flow of a process.

A **process map** identifies the specific activities that make up the information, physical, or monetary flow of a process. Process maps often give managers their first complete picture of how a process works. Experts have developed a set of graphical symbols to represent different aspects of the process. Figure 3.4 shows some of the most common symbols used.

Because of the level of detail required, process flowcharts can quickly become overly complex or wander off the track unless a conscious effort is made to maintain focus. Some useful rules for maintaining this focus include:

1. **Identify the entity that will serve as the focal point.** This may be a customer, an order, a raw material, or the like. The mapping effort should focus on the activities and flows associated with the movement of that entity through the process.
2. **Identify clear boundaries and starting and ending points.** Consider a manufacturer who wants to better understand how it processes customer orders. To develop the process map, the manufacturer must decide on the starting and ending points. Will the starting point be when the customer places the order or when the manufacturer receives it? Similarly, will the flowchart end when the order is shipped out of the plant or when the order is actually delivered to the customer? The manufacturer might also decide to focus only on the physical and information flows associated with the order and not the monetary flows.
3. **Keep it simple.** Most people developing process maps for the first time tend to put in *too* much detail. They develop overly complex maps, often subdividing major activities into several smaller ones that don't provide any additional insight or including logical branches to deal with every conceivable occurrence, even ones that very rarely occur. There are no simple rules of thumb for avoiding this trap, other than to ask whether the additional detail is important to understanding the process and whether it is worth the added complexity.

Let's illustrate these ideas with an example we are all familiar with: a customer visiting a restaurant. The customer is greeted by a host, who then seats the customer. A waitress takes the customer's order, delivers the drinks and food, and writes up and delivers the check. Finally, a cashier takes the customer's money.

Figure 3.5 shows a simplified map of the Bluebird Café. In this example, the focal point is the customer: The process begins when the customer enters the Bluebird Café and ends when she leaves. Notice, too, that there are many activities that occur in the restaurant that are *not* included in this particular map—scheduling employee work hours, planning deliveries from suppliers, prepping food, etc. This is because our current focus is on the customer's interactions with the restaurant. Even so, our "simplified" map still has 11 distinct steps.

With the major customer interaction points laid out, we can start to see how important each of the steps is to the customer's overall satisfaction with her dining experience. We might also start to ask how the Bluebird Café can measure and perhaps improve its performance. Example 3.1

[5]S. Tibey, "How Kraft Built a 'One-Company' Supply Chain," *Supply Chain Management Review* 3, no. 3 (Fall 1999): 34–42.

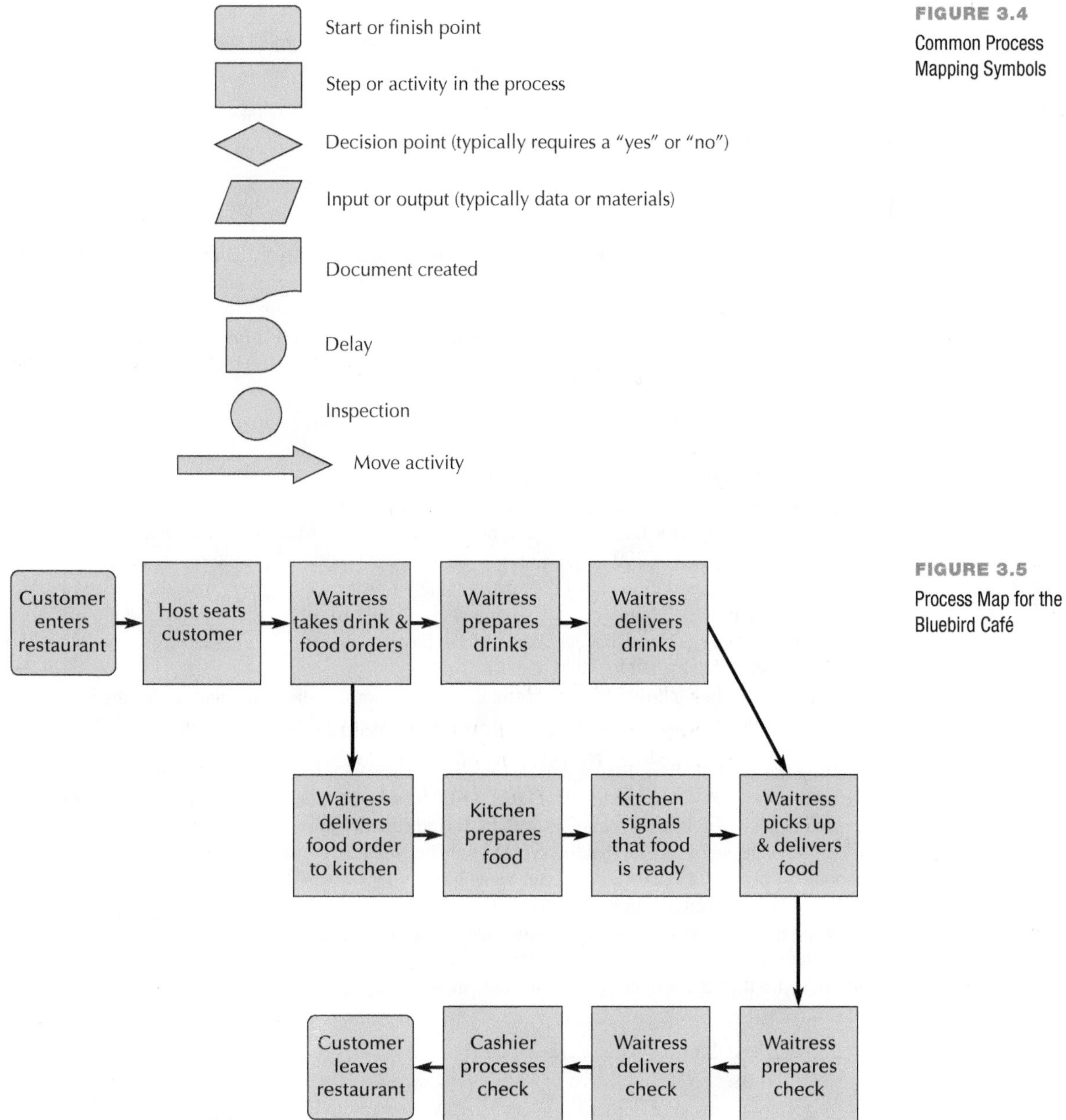

FIGURE 3.4
Common Process Mapping Symbols

FIGURE 3.5
Process Map for the Bluebird Café

illustrates a somewhat more complex process map for a fictional distribution center. As you read through the example, ask yourself the following questions:

- What is the focal point of the process mapping effort?
- What are the boundaries and the starting and stopping points for the process map?
- What detail is not included in this example?

Keep in mind that the idea is to document the process *as it is*—not the way people remember it. In some cases, employees might need to physically walk through a process, "stapling themselves" to a document or a product. Second, management needs to decide which parts of the

EXAMPLE 3.1

Process Mapping at a Distribution Center

A San Diego distribution center (DC) has responsibility for supplying products to dealers located within a 30-mile radius. Lately, the DC has been receiving a lot of complaints from dealers regarding lost orders and the time required to process orders for items that are already in stock at the DC. A process improvement team has decided to study the process in more detail by tracing the flow of a dealer

(*Continued*)

order through the DC, starting from when the dealer faxes in the order and ending with the order's delivery to the dealer. The team has collected the following information:

- The dealer faxes an order to the DC. Sometimes the paper gets jammed in the fax machine or an order gets thrown away accidentally. Employees estimate that about 1 in 25 orders is "lost" in this manner.
- The fax sits in an inbox anywhere from 0 to 4 hours, with an average of 2 hours, before the fax is picked up by the DC's internal mail service.
- It takes the internal mail service 1 hour, on average, to deliver the order to the picking area (where the desired items are picked off the shelves). In addition, 1 out of 100 orders is accidentally delivered to the wrong area of the DC, resulting in additional "lost" orders.
- Once an order is delivered to the picking area, it sits in the clerk's inbox until the clerk has time to process it. The order might wait in the inbox anywhere from 0 to 2 hours, with an average time of 1 hour.
- Once the clerk starts processing the order, it takes her about 5 minutes to determine whether the item is in stock.
- If the requested product is in stock, a worker picks the order and puts it into a box. Average picking time is 20 minutes, with a range of 10 minutes to 45 minutes.
- Next, an inspector takes about 2 minutes to check the order for correctness. Even with this inspection, 1 out of 200 orders shipped has the wrong items or quantities.
- A local transportation firm takes the completed order and delivers it to the dealer (average delivery time is 2 hours but can be anywhere from 1 to 3 hours). The transportation firm has an exemplary performance record: Over the past 5 years, the firm has never lost or damaged a shipment or delivered to the wrong dealer.
- If the item being ordered is out of stock, the clerk notifies the dealer and passes the order on to the plant, which will arrange a special shipment directly to the dealer, usually within a week.

Using the symbols from Figure 3.5, the process improvement team draws the process map for the order-filling process of in-stock items (Figure 3.6). The map includes detailed information on the times required at each step in the process, as well as various quality problems. Adding up the times at each process step, the team can see that the average time between ordering and delivery for an in-stock item is about 6.4 hours (387 minutes) and can be as long as 11.3 hours (682 minutes). If an item is not in stock, it will take even longer to be delivered.

Of the 6.4 hours an order spends on average in the process, a full 3 hours is waiting time. Finally, 5% of the orders are "lost" before they even get to the picking area. For the orders that do survive to this point, 1 out of 200 will be shipped with the incorrect items or quantities. Clearly, there is room for improvement.

FIGURE 3.6
Order-Filling Process for In-stock Items

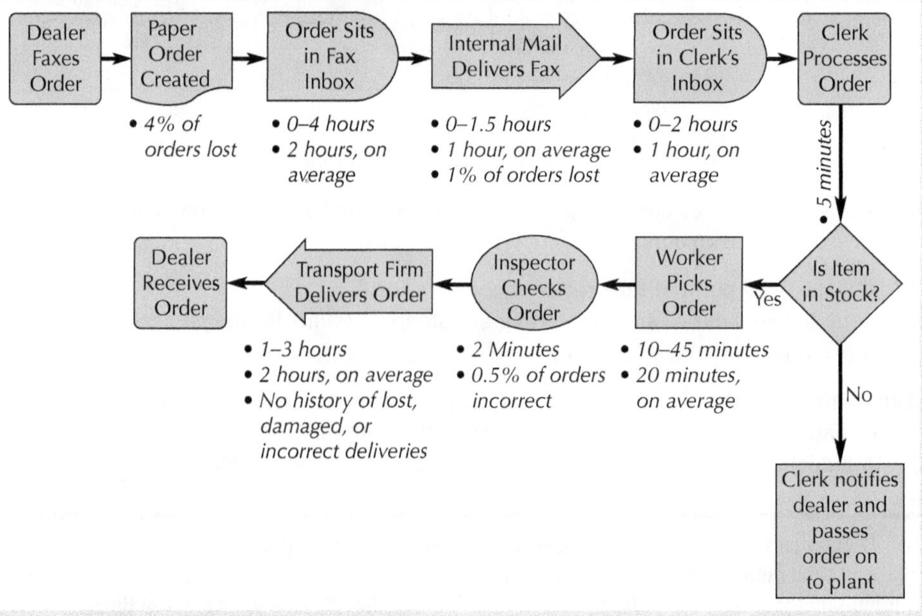

(*Continued*)

Once the process has been mapped, the team considers ways to improve the process. It is clear that the order-filling process is hampered by unnecessary delays, "lost" paperwork, and an inspection process that yields less-than-perfect results. One potential improvement is to have dealers place orders electronically, with this information sent directly to the picking area. Not only would this cut down on the delays associated with moving the fax through the DC, but also it would cut down on the number of "lost" orders. Errors in the picking and inspection process will require additional changes.

TABLE 3.2
Guidelines for Improvinga Process

1. Examine each delay symbol
   What causes the delay? How long is it?
   How could we reduce the delay or its impact?

2. Examine each activity symbol
   Is this an unnecessary or redundant activity?
   What is the value of this activity relative to its cost?
   How can we prevent errors in this activity?

3. Examine each decision symbol
   Does this step require an actual decision (e.g., "Do we want to accept this customer's order?"), or is it a simple checking activity (e.g., "Is the inventory in stock?")? If it is a checking activity, can it be automated or eliminated? Is itredundant?

4. Look for any loops (arrows that go back to a previous point in the process).

   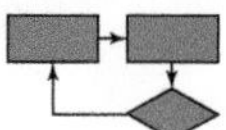

   Would we need to repeat these activities if we had no failures (e.g., cooking a new steak for a customer because the first one was cooked incorrectly)? What are the costs associated with this loop (additional time, resources cosumed, etc.)? Can this loop be eliminated? If so, how?

process to look at. Areas that are beyond a manager's control or are not directly related to the problem at hand can be omitted from the process mapping effort. In Example 3.1, the focus was on *in-stock* items, so the flowchart did not go into detail regarding what happens if the product is out of stock.

Table 3.2 lists some guidelines to use in identifying opportunities to improve a process. In general, personnel should critically examine each step in the process. In many cases, steps can be improved dramatically or even eliminated.

SWIM LANE PROCESS MAPS

Sometimes we are interested in understanding not only the steps in a process but *who* is involved and how these parties interact with one another. In the restaurant example, at least four people were involved in serving the customer—the host, the waitress, the cook, and the cashier. **Swim lane process maps** graphically arrange the process steps so that the user can see who is responsible for each step. As John Grout of Berry College puts it, "The advantage of this mapping approach is that process flows that change 'lanes' indicate hand-offs. This is where lack of coordination and communication can cause process problems. It also shows who sees each part of the process."[6]

Swim lane process map
A process map that graphically arranges the process steps so that the user can see who is responsible for each step.

Figure 3.7 shows a swim lane process map for the San Diego DC order-filling process described in Example 3.1. In setting up a swim lane map, the first "lane" is usually reserved for the customer of the process. This customer can be an internal (i.e., within the company) or external customer. As Figure 3.7 shows, the order-filling process involves seven different parties, including the dealer who places the order. Furthermore, there are three parties—the sales office, internal mail, and picking clerk—that handle the order before it gets to the workers who

[6]J. Grout, "Swim Lane," **http://csob.berry.edu/faculty/jgrout/processmapping/Swim_Lane/swim_lane.html.**

FIGURE 3.7
Swim Lane Process Map for Order-Filling Process

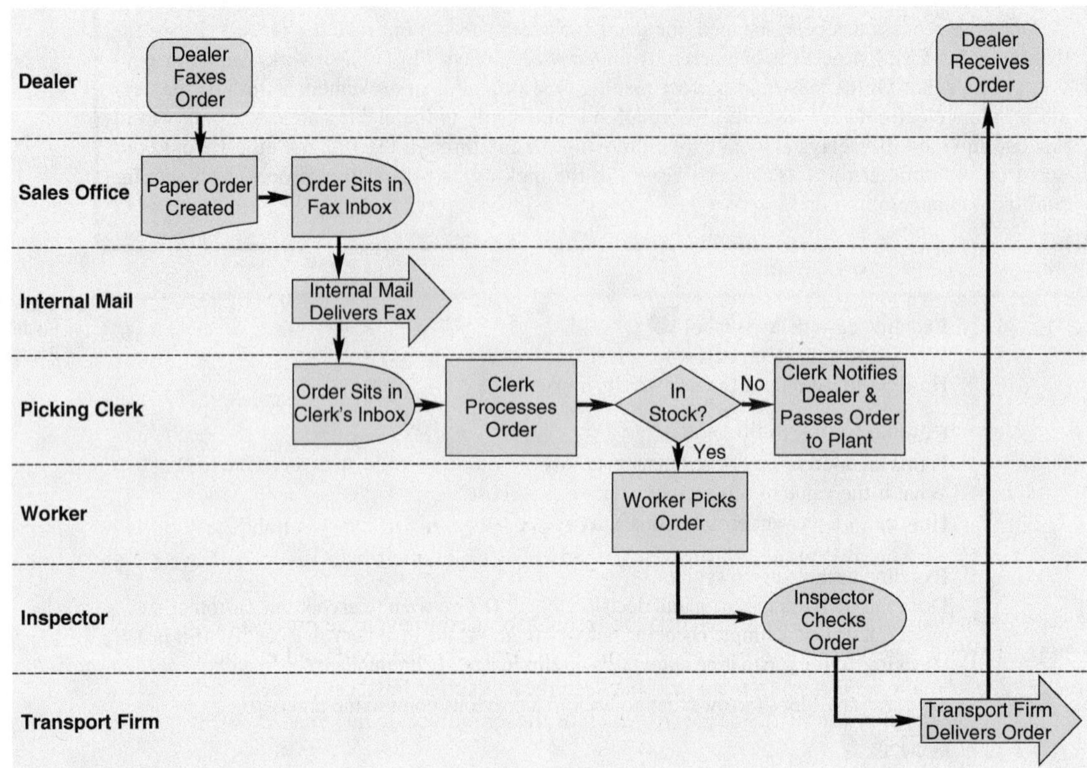

actually do the picking. All these hand-offs and delays clearly add time and potential errors to the order-filling process.

Managing and Improving Business Processes

By now, you should appreciate how critical business processes are to the success of an organization. But you still might wonder how businesses should go about managing and improving these processes. For instance:

- How do we know if a business process is meeting customers' needs? Even if customers' needs are being met, how do we know whether the business process is being run efficiently and effectively?
- How should we organize for business process improvement? What steps should we follow? What roles should people play?
- What types of tools and analytical techniques can we use to rigorously evaluate business processes? How can we make sure we manage based on fact and not opinion?

Organizations have been asking these questions for years. As a result, experts have developed various measures, methodologies, and tools for managing business processes. In fact, the body of knowledge continues to evolve as more is learned about what works and what doesn't. In this section, we will introduce you to current thinking in the area.

MEASURING BUSINESS PROCESS PERFORMANCE

Before we can answer the question "How is the process performing?" we must first understand what it is the customer wants and calculate objective performance information for the process. Let's reconsider the process mapping exercise in Example 3.1 for a moment. Suppose one of the San Diego DC's key customers has told DC management that:

1. All deliveries for in-stock items must be made within 8 hours from when the order was placed.

2. Order conformance quality must be 99% or higher. That is, 99% of the orders must be delivered with the right items in the right quantities.

Furthermore, the customer has told DC management that these are *order qualifiers*: If the DC cannot meet these minimum requirements, then the customer will take his business elsewhere. In Example 3.1, the DC managers determined that the time between ordering and delivery for an in-stock item could be as long as 11.3 hours and that fewer than 95% of the orders were processed properly. Clearly, there is a gap between what the customer needs and what the process is currently able to provide.

There are countless possible measures of process performance, many of which are derived from the four core measures:

1. **Quality**—Quality can be further divided into dimensions such as performance quality, conformance quality, and reliability.
2. **Cost**—Cost can include such categories as labor, material, and quality-related costs, to name just a few.
3. **Time**—Time includes such dimensions as delivery speed and delivery reliability.
4. **Flexibility**—Flexibility includes mix, changeover, and volume flexibility.

In addition, some specific measures that are frequently used to evaluate process performance are productivity, efficiency, and cycle (or throughput) time. Productivity and efficiency measures are particularly important to managers because they evaluate business process performance from the perspective of the firm. We discuss each of these in more detail.

PRODUCTIVITY

One measure that often comes up in discussions is **productivity**. Productivity is a ratio measure, defined as follows:

Productivity
A measure of process performance; the ratio of outputs to inputs.

$$\text{Productivity} = \text{outputs}/\text{inputs} \tag{3-1}$$

Productivity measures are always expressed in terms of units of output per unit of input. The outputs and inputs can be expressed in monetary terms or in some other unit of measure. In general, organizations seek to improve productivity by raising outputs, decreasing inputs, or both. Some examples of productivity measures include the following:

(Number of customer calls handled)/(support staff hours)

(Number of items produced)/(machine hours)

(Sales dollars generated)/(labor, material, and machine costs)

The first two examples represent single-factor productivity measures. **Single-factor productivity** measures output levels relative to a single input. In the first example, we are interested in the number of calls handled per support staff hour, while the second measure looks at the number of items produced per machine hour. The assumption is that there is a one-to-one relationship between the output and input of interest that can be managed. In contrast, when it's hard to separate out the effects of various inputs, **multifactor productivity** measures should be used. Look at the last example. "Sales dollars generated" is an output that depends on multiple factors, including labor, material, and machine costs. Considering just labor costs may be inappropriate, especially if labor costs could be driven down by driving up some other cost (e.g., machine costs). In situations like this, multifactor productivity measures may be preferable.

Single-factor productivty
A productivity score that measures output levels relative to single input.

Multifactor productivity
A productivity score that measures output levels relative to more than one input.

While there are some common productivity measures used by many firms, often organizations develop productivity measures that are tailored to their particular needs. Firms use productivity measures to compare their performance to that of other organizations, as well as to compare performance against historic levels or set targets.

EXAMPLE 3.2

Measuring Productivity at BMA Software

For the past 15 weeks, a project team at BMA Software has been working on developing a new software package. Table 3.3 shows the number of programmers assigned to the project each week, as well as the resulting total lines of computer code generated.

TABLE 3.3
Programming Results for the First 15 Weeks of the Project

Week	Lines of Code	No. of Programmers
1	8,101	4
2	7,423	4
3	8,872	4
4	8,483	4
5	8,455	5
6	10,100	5
7	11,013	5
8	8,746	5
9	13,710	7
10	13,928	7
11	13,160	7
12	13,897	7
13	12,588	6
14	12,192	6
15	12,386	6

Susan Clarke, the project manager, has heard rumblings from other managers that her programmers aren't being as productive as they were a few weeks earlier. In order to determine whether this is true, Susan develops a measure of programmer productivity, defined as (lines of code)/(total number of programmers). Using this measure, Susan calculates the productivity numbers in Table 3.4 for the first 15 weeks of the project.

The results indicate that the programmers have actually been *more* productive over the past few weeks (weeks 13–15) than they were in the weeks just prior. In fact, the weekly productivity results for weeks 13–15 are higher than the average weekly productivity for all 15 weeks (1,992.70). Of course, Susan recognizes that there are other performance measures to consider, including the quality of the lines coded (whether they are bug-free) and the difficulty of the lines being coded (which would tend to hold down the number of lines generated).

TABLE 3.4
Programming Results for the First 15 Weeks of the Project

Week	Lines of Code	No. of Programmers	Productivity (Lines of Code Per Programmer)
1	8,101	4	2,025.25
2	7,423	4	1,855.75
3	8,872	4	2,218.00
4	8,483	4	2,120.75
5	8,455	5	1,691.00
6	10,100	5	2,020.00
7	11,013	5	2,202.60
8	8,746	5	1,749.20
9	13,710	7	1,958.57
10	13,928	7	1,989.71
11	13,160	7	1,880.00
12	13,897	7	1,985.29
13	12,588	6	2,098.00
14	12,192	6	2,032.00
15	12,386	6	2,064.33
	Average Productivity:		1,992.70

EFFICIENCY

While measures of productivity compare outputs to inputs, measures of **efficiency** compare *actual* outputs to some standard—specifically:

Efficiency
A measure of process performance; the ratio of actual outputs to standard outputs. Usually expressed in percentage terms.

$$\text{Efficiency} = 100\% \text{ (actual outputs / standard outputs)} \quad (3\text{-}2)$$

The **standard output** is an estimate of what should be produced, given a certain level of resources. This standard might be based on detailed studies or even historical results. The efficiency measure, then, indicates actual output as a percentage of the standard. An efficiency score of less than 100% suggests that a process is not producing up to its potential.

Standard output
An estimate of what should be produced, given a certain level of resources.

To illustrate, suppose each painter on an assembly line is expected to paint 30 units an hour. Bob actually paints 25 units an hour, while Casey paints 32. The efficiency of each painter is, therefore, calculated as follows:

$$\text{Efficiency}_{\text{Bob}} = 100\%\frac{25}{30} = 83\% \qquad \text{Efficiency}_{\text{Casey}} = 100\%\frac{32}{30} = 107\%$$

Currently, Bob is performing below the standard. If his efficiency were to remain at this level, management might either intervene with additional training to raise his hourly output level or reassign Bob to another area.

EXAMPLE 3.3

Measuring Efficiency at BMA Software

Based on the results of her productivity study, Susan Clarke decides to set a standard for her programmers of 1,800 lines of code per programmer per week. Susan consciously set the standard slightly below the average productivity figure shown in Table 3.4. Her reasoning is that she wants her programmers to be able to meet the standard, even when they are dealing with particularly difficult code.

In week 16, Susan hires a new programmer, Charles Turner. After five weeks on the job, Charles has recorded the results in Table 3.5.

Susan calculates Charles's efficiency by dividing the actual lines of code produced each week by the standard value of 1,800. Therefore, Charles's efficiency for week 16 is calculated as:

$$\text{Efficiency}_{\text{Week16}} = 100\%(1{,}322/1{,}800) = 73.4\%$$

Results for all five weeks are shown in Table 3.6.

TABLE 3.5
Programming Results for Charles Turner

Week	Lines of Code
16	1,322
17	1,605
18	1,770
19	1,760
20	1,820

TABLE 3.6
Efficiency Results for Charles Turner

Week	Lines of Code	Efficiency
16	1,322	73.4%
17	1,605	89.2%
18	1,770	98.3%
19	1,760	97.8%
20	1,820	101.1%

Although Charles started off slowly, his efficiency has steadily improved over the five-week period. Susan is pleased with the results and recognizes that Charles needs some time to become familiar with the project. Nonetheless, she will continue to track Charles's efficiency performance.

CYCLE TIME

Cycle time
The total elapsed time needed to complete a business process. Also called throughput time.

The last measure of process performance we will discuss is cycle time. **Cycle time** (also called throughput time) is the total elapsed time needed to complete a business process. Many authors have noted that cycle time is a highly useful measure of process performance.[7] For one thing, in order to reduce cycle times, organizations and supply chains typically must perform well on other dimensions, such as quality, delivery, productivity, and efficiency.

Consider the order-filling process in Figures 3.6 and 3.7. In this case, cycle time is the time that elapses from when the dealer faxes the order until she receives the product. Notice how the process suffers from delays due to waiting, lost orders, and incorrect orders. Therefore, in order to reduce cycle time, the San Diego DC must address these other problems as well. Notice, too, that reducing cycle times does not mean "fast and sloppy." The process cannot be considered "complete" until the dealer receives a *correctly filled* order.

A second advantage of cycle time is that it is a straightforward measure. In comparison to cost data, quality levels, or productivity measures—all of which may be calculated and interpreted differently by various process participants—the time it takes to complete a business process is unambiguous.

Percent value-added time
A measure of process performance; the percentage of total cycle time that is spent on activities that actually provide value.

In addition to measuring cycle time in absolute terms, it is often useful to look at the **percent value-added time**, which is simply the percentage of total cycle time that is spent on activities that actually provide value:

$$\text{Percent value-added time} = 100\%(\text{value-added time})/(\text{total cycle time}) \qquad (3\text{-}3)$$

For example, what is the percent value-added time for the typical "quick change" oil center? Even though the customer may spend an hour in the process, it usually takes only about 10 minutes to actually perform the work. According to Equation (3.3), then:

$$\text{Percent value-added time} = 100\%(10 \text{ minutes})/(60 \text{ minutes}) = 16.7\%$$

Of course, cycle time is not a perfect measure. Our discussion of trade-offs between performance measures applies here as well. It might not be cost-effective, for example, to drive down cycle times at the drivers' license bureau by quadrupling the number of officers (but don't you wish they would?). Therefore, organizations that use cycle time to measure process performance should also use other measures to make sure cycle time is not being reduced at the expense of some other key performance dimension.

BENCHMARKING

Benchmarking
According to Cook, "The process of identifying, understanding, and adapting outstanding practices from within the same organization or from other businesses to help improve performance."

Competitive bench marking
The comparison of an organization's processes with those of competing organizations.

Process bench marking
The comparison of an organization's processes with those of noncompetitors that have been identified as superior processes.

Organizations often find it helpful to compare their business processes against those of competitors or even other firms with similar processes. This activity is known as **benchmarking**. Sarah Cook defines benchmarking as "the process of identifying, understanding, and adapting outstanding practices from within the same organization or from other businesses to help improve performance."[8] Benchmarking involves comparing an organization's practices and procedures to those of the "best" in order to identify ways in which the organization or its supply chain can make improvements.

Some experts make a further distinction between competitive benchmarking and process benchmarking. **Competitive benchmarking** is the comparison of an organization's processes with those of competing organizations. In contrast, **process benchmarking** refers to the comparison of an organization's processes with those of noncompetitors that have been identified as having superior processes. As an example of the latter, many organizations have carefully studied Walmart's supply chain practices, even though Walmart might not be a direct competitor.

---

[7] J. Blackburn, *Time-Based Competition: The Next Battle Ground in American Manufacturing* (Homewood, IL: Irwin, 1991); G. Stalk and T. Hout, *Competing against Time: How Time-Based Competition Is Reshaping Global Markets* (New York: Free Press, 1990); C. Meyer, *Fast Cycle Time: How to Align Purpose, Strategy, and Structure for Speed* (New York: Free Press, 1993).

[8] S. Cook, *Practical Benchmarking: A Manager's Guide to Creating a Competitive Advantage* (London: Kogan Page, 1995), p. 13.

TABLE 3.7
Competitive Benchmarking Date for Selected U.S. Airline Carriers, January–December 2010

Airline Carrier	Percentage Of Flights Arriving On Time	Percentage Of Flights Cancelled	Mishandled Baggage Reports Per 1,000 Passengers
American	79.6%	2.7%	3.82
Continental	81.4%	3.3%	2.65
Delta	77.4%	4.9%	3.49
Frontier	81.4%	0.6%	2.58
Hawaiian	92.5%	0.0%	2.23
JetBlue	75.7%	8.7%	2.48
Pinnacle	78.5%	8.2%	6.30
Southwest	79.5%	2.3%	3.43
United	85.2%	2.2%	3.40
US Airways	83.0%	2.5%	2.56

Source: U.S. Department of Transportation, "Air Travel Consumer Report," February 2011. **http://airconsumer.dot.gov/reports/2011/February/2011FebruaryATCR.PDF**

TABLE 3.8
2008 Competitive Benchmarking Results for North American Automakers

Manufacturer	Total Assembly Hours Per Vehicle	Hours Per Engine	Pretax Profit Per Vehicle
Chrysler	21.31	3.35	–$142
Ford	22.65	4.32	–$1,467
GM	22.19	3.44	–$729
Honda	20.90	4.93	$1,641
Toyota	22.35	3.13	$922
Nissan	23.45	n/a	$1,641

Source: Selected data from Harbour Consulting, "Harbour Report North America 2008," **www.harbourinc.com.**

To give you an idea of the power of benchmarking, let's look at some competitive benchmarking results for the U.S. airline industry. The U.S. Department of Transportation (DOT) tracks and reports the performance of various U.S. carriers across several measures of interest to consumers, including the percentage of flights that arrive on time (within 15 minutes of schedule), the percentage of flights cancelled, and mis-handled baggage reports filed per 1,000 passengers, and it reports these results at regular intervals. Table 3.7 shows 2010 results for a subset of U.S. carriers.

While some of these results might be due to conditions beyond the companies' control (e.g., weather), the hard-nosed nature of these data still gives carriers a clear idea of where they stand relative to the competition. Whose management team do you think is happy with the 2010 results? Whose management team is not?

On the manufacturing side, Table 3.8 looks at some 2008 competitive benchmarking data put out by Harbour Consulting that compares North American automotive plant performance across different manufacturers. The results suggest that while the productivity gap has closed between U.S. and Japanese-based manufacturers, the latter still enjoy a significant per-vehicle profit advantage.

THE SIX SIGMA METHODOLOGY

Of all the various approaches to organizing for business process improvement, the Six Sigma methodology arguably best represents current thinking. It certainly is popular, with many top companies, such as GE, Motorola, and Bank of America, citing it as a key element of their business strategy. Six Sigma has its roots in the quality management discipline. (Quality management is such an important topic to operations and supply chain managers.)

The term *Six Sigma* refers to both a quality metric and a methodology. In *statistical terms*, a process that achieves Six Sigma quality will generate just 3.4 defects per 1 million opportunities (DPMO). As a *methodology* for process improvement, Six Sigma has a much broader meaning. Motorola describes the **Six Sigma methodology** as:

Six Sigma methodolgy
According to Motorola, "A business improvement methodology that focuses an organization on understanding and managing customer requirements, aligning key business processes to achieve those requirements, utilizing rigorous data analysis to understand and ultimately minimize variation in those processes, and driving rapid and sustainable improvement to business processes."

A business improvement methodology that focuses an organization on:

- Understanding and managing customer requirements
- Aligning key business processes to achieve those requirements
- Utilizing rigorous data analysis to understand and ultimately minimize variation in those processes
- Driving rapid and sustainable improvement to business processes[9]

Let's consider this definition for a moment. The first two points reinforce the idea that business process improvement efforts need to be driven by the needs of the customer. In this case, the "customer" can be someone inside the organization as well as someone from outside the organization. The third point emphasizes the use of rigorous data analysis tools to ensure that any diagnoses or recommendations are based on *fact* and not just opinion. Finally, there must an organizational mechanism in place for carrying out these efforts in a timely and efficient manner.

SIX SIGMA PEOPLE. Six Sigma process improvement efforts are carried out by project teams consisting of people serving specialized roles. In the lexicon of Six Sigma, the teams consist of champions, master black belts, black belts, green belts, and team members. **Champions** are typically senior-level executives who "own" the projects and have the authority and resources needed to carry them out. This can be particularly important if a Six Sigma effort requires large investments of time or money, or if multiple functional areas or supply chain partners are affected. **Master black belts** are "fulltime Six Sigma experts who are responsible for Six Sigma strategy, training, mentoring, deployment and results."[10] These individuals often work across organizations and consult with projects on an as-needed basis, but are not permanently assigned to the projects.

Black belts are "fully-trained Six Sigma experts with up to 160 hours of training who perform much of the technical analyses required of Six Sigma projects, usually on a full-time basis."[11] **Green belts** have some basic training in Six Sigma methodologies and tools and are assigned to projects on a part-time basis. Finally, **team members** are individuals with knowledge or direct interest in a process. While they may be included on a Six Sigma project team they are usually not trained in Six Sigma.

Champion
A senior-level executive who "owns" a Six Sigma project and has the authority and resources needed to carry it out.

Master black belt
A full-time Six Sigma expert who is "responsible for Six Sigma strategy, training, mentoring, deployment and results."

Black belt
A fully trained Six Sigma expert "with up to 160 hours of training who perform[s] much of the technical analyses required of Six Sigma projects, usually on a full-time basis."

Green belt
An individual who has some basic training in Six Sigma methodologies and tools and is assigned to a project on a part-time basis.

Team members
Individuals who are not trained in Six Sigma but are included on a Six Sigma project team due to their knowledge or direct interest in a process.

SIX SIGMA PROCESSES. The Six Sigma methodology has its own specialized business processes that project teams follow. The first of these is the **DMAIC (Define–Measure–Analyze–Improve–Control)** process, which outlines the steps that should be followed to improve an *existing* business process. The steps are as follows:

DMAIC (Define-Measure-Analyze-Improve-Control)
A Six Sigma process that outlines the steps that should be followed to improve an *existing* business process.

Step 1: *Define* the goals of the improvement activity. The Six Sigma team must first clarify how improving the process will support the business, and establish performance targets. This ensures that the team doesn't waste time on efforts that will not see a pay-off to either the customer or the business.

Step 2: *Measure* the existing process. The second step requires the team members to develop a basic understanding of how the process works. What are the process steps? Who are the parties who carry out or are otherwise touched by the process? How is the process currently performing? What data do we need to analyze the process and evaluate the impact of any changes?

Step 3: *Analyze* the process. Next, the Six Sigma team identifies the relationships and factors that cause the process to perform the way it does. In doing so, the team must make sure to identify the true underlying causes of the process's performance. We will talk later about two approaches for accomplishing this: cause-and-effect diagrams and the "Five Whys" approach.

---

[9]Motorola University, **www.motorola.com/motorolauniversity.jsp**

[10]J. Evans and W. Lindsay, *The Management and Control of Quality* (Mason, OH: Thomson South-Western, 2005).

[11]Ibid.

Step 4: ***Improve*** **the process.** During this step, the team identifies ways to eliminate the gap between the current performance level and the performance targets established in step 1.

Step 5: ***Control*** **the new process.** The Six Sigma team must work with the individuals affected to maintain the process improvements. This may involve such activities as developing process control charts, training workers in any new procedures, and updating information systems to monitor ongoing performance.

The second Six Sigma process **DMADV (Define–Measure–Analyze–Design–Verify)**, outlines the steps needed to create *completely new* business processes or products.

DMADV (Define-Measure-Analyze-Design-Verify)
A Six Sigma process that outlines the steps needed to create *completely new* business processes or products.

CONTINUOUS IMPROVEMENT TOOLS

Organizations interested in process improvement have a broad collection of data analysis tools to help guide their efforts. Many of these tools, which first appeared in the engineering and quality management disciplines, were specifically designed to help users apply logical thinking and statistical concepts to process improvement efforts. The term **continuous improvement** refers to a managerial philosophy that small, incremental improvements can add up to significant performance improvements over time.

Continuous improvement
The philosophy that small, incremental improvements can add up to significant performance improvements over time.

Already in this chapter we have talked about one continuous improvement tool: process mapping. This section highlights some additional tools: root cause analysis, cause-and-effect diagrams, scatter plots, check sheets, and Pareto charts. As the DMAIC steps suggest, firms need to follow a more formal process to make sure that they have indeed diagnosed problem(s) correctly. **Root cause analysis** is a process by which organizations brainstorm about possible causes of problems (referred to as "effects") and then, through structured analyses and datagathering efforts, gradually narrow the focus to a few root causes. Root cause analysis fills the gap between the realization that a problem exists and the proposal and implementation of solutions to the problem.

Root cause analysis
A process by which organizations brainstorm about possible causes of problems (referred to as "effects") and then, through structured analyses and data-gathering efforts, gradually narrow the focus to a few root causes.

Organizations often divide root cause analysis into three distinct phases: open, narrow, and closed. The ***open phase*** is devoted to brainstorming. All team members should be free to make suggestions, no matter how far-fetched they might seem at the time. Teams often use a **cause-and-effect diagram** (also known as a fishbone diagram or Ishikawa diagram) to organize their thoughts at this stage. Figure 3.8 shows a generic format for a cause-and-effect diagram.

Cause-and-effect diagram
A graphical tool used to categorize the possible causes for a particular result.

To construct such a diagram, the team members must first describe the "effect" for which they are seeking a cause, such as late deliveries, high defect rates, or lost orders. This effect is written on a large poster or chalkboard, at the end of a long arrow. Next, the team categorizes the possible causes and places them at the ends of branches drawn along the shaft of the arrow. These branches are often organized around five categories known as the **Five Ms:**

Five Ms
The five main branches of a typical cause-and-effect diagram: manpower, methods, materials, machines, and measurement.

- **Manpower**—People who do not have the right skills, authority, or responsibility
- **Methods**—Poor business practices; poor process, product, or service designs
- **Materials**—Poor-quality inputs
- **Machines**—Equipment that is not capable of doing the job
- **Measurements**—Performance measurements that are not geared toward eliminating the problem

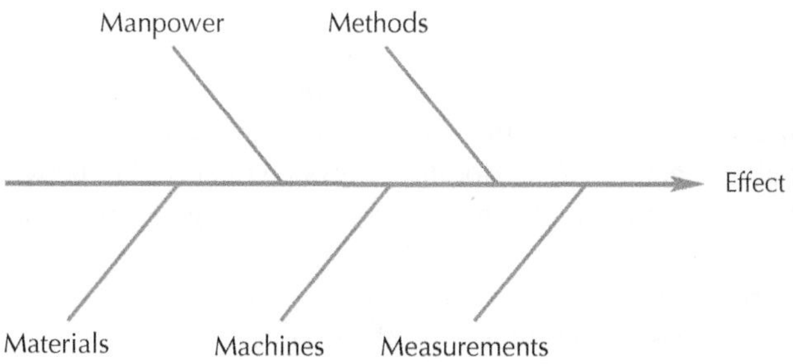

FIGURE 3.8
Cause-and Effect diagram

EXAMPLE 3.4

Cause-and-Effect Diagram for a Pump Manufacturer

A Six Sigma team investigating variations in pump shaft dimensions at a pump manufacturer decided to develop a cause-and-effect diagram to identify the possible causes. The resulting diagram is shown in Figure 3.9. The team did not identify any potential causes along the "Measurements" branch; hence, it was left off). Notice that some of the branches are further subdivided in an effort to get to the true underlying causes. For example, "Low motivation" is listed as a possible cause under "Manpower." But why are employees unmotivated? One possible cause, "Low pay," is shown as a branch off of "Low motivation."

FIGURE 3.8
Cause-and Effect Diagram for a Pump Manufacturer

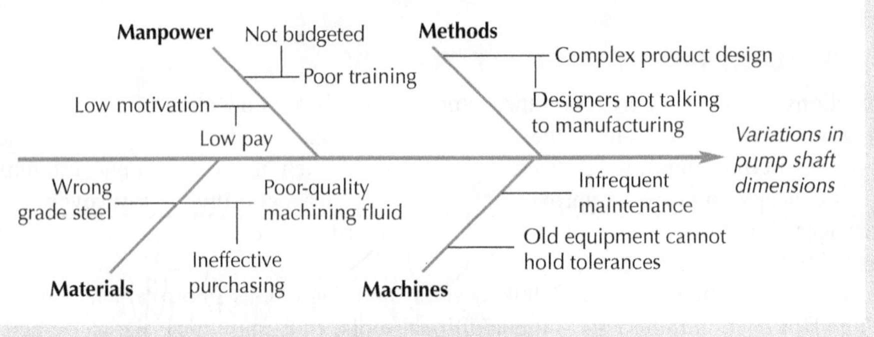

The second phase of root cause analysis is known as the narrow phase. Here participants pare down the list of possible causes to a manageable number. Some teams formalize this process by using an approach called the **Five Whys.** With this approach, the team members brainstorm successive answers to the question "Why is this a cause of the original problem?" For each new answer, they repeat the question until they can think of no new answers. The last answer will probably be one root cause of the problem. The name comes from the general observation that the questioning process can require up to five rounds.

Five Whys
An approach used during the narrow phase of root cause analysis, in which teams brainstorm successive answers to the question "Why is this a cause of the original problem?" The name comes from the general observation that the questioning process can require up to five rounds.

To illustrate, suppose a business is trying to understand why a major customer won't pay its bills on time. One possible explanation generated during the open phase is that, by delaying payment, the customer is getting a free loan at the business's expense ("Methods"). Using the Five Whys approach, the team members might ask the following series of questions:

Q1: WHY does the customer use our credit as a free loan?
A1: Because there are no penalties for doing so.
Q2: WHY are there no penalties for late payment of our invoices?
A2: Because we charge no penalty fees.
Q3: WHY don't we charge penalty fees?
A3: Because we have never encountered this problem before.

Process improvement efforts must be based on facts, not opinions. Although team members may think they have discovered the root cause of a problem, they must verify it before moving on to a solution. In the ***closed phase*** of root cause analysis, the team validates the suspected root cause(s) through the analysis of available data. Three commonly used data analysis tools are scatter plots, check sheets, and Pareto charts. A **scatter plot** is a graphic representation of the relationship between two variables, typically the potential root cause and the effect of interest.

Scatter plot
A graphical representation of the relationship between two variables.

To illustrate, the scatter plot in Figure 3.10 shows how the defect rate at a manufacturer seems to increase as the amount of monthly overtime increases.

Figure 3.10 shows a strong relationship between the two variables of interest. But does the lack of a pattern in a scatter plot mean that a Six Sigma team has failed in its effort to identify a root cause? Not at all. In fact, a scatter plot that shows no relationship between a particular root cause and the effect of interest simply shortens the list of potential root causes that need to be investigated.

Check sheet
A sheet used to record how frequently a certain event occurs.

Pareto chart
A special form of bar chart that shows frequency counts from highest to lowest.

Whereas scatter plots highlight the relationship between two variables, check sheets and Pareto charts are used to assess the frequency of certain events. Specifically, **check sheets** are used to record how frequently certain events occur, and **Pareto charts** plot out the resulting frequency counts in bar graph form, from highest to lowest.

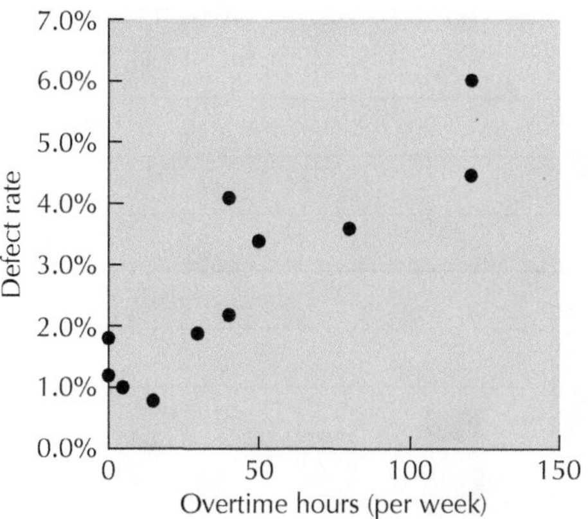

FIGURE 3.10
Example Scatter Plot Showing the Relationship between Overtime Hours (Cause) and Defect Rate (Effect)

EXAMPLE 3.5

Check Sheets and Pareto Charts at Healthy Foods

Sasha Davas/Shutterstock.com

The Healthy Foods grocery store is attempting to isolate the root causes of unexpected delays at checkout counters. The open and narrow phases have resulted in a long list of possible causes, including the register being out of change, price checks, and customers going back to get items they forgot. In the closed phase, the quality team at Healthy Foods sets up check sheets at each checkout counter. Each time an unexpected delay occurs, the clerk records the reason for the delay. This process continues until the managers feel they have enough data to draw some conclusions. Table 3.9 shows summary results for 391 delays occurring over a one-week period.

TABLE 3.9
Check Sheet Results for Healthy Foods

Cause	Frequency
Price check	142
Register out of money	14
Bagger unavailable	33
Register out of tape	44
Customer forgot item	12
Management override needed due to incorrect entry	86
Wrong item	52
Other	8
Total Delays	391

FIGURE 3.11
Pareto Chart Ranking Causes of Unexpected Delays at Checkout Counter

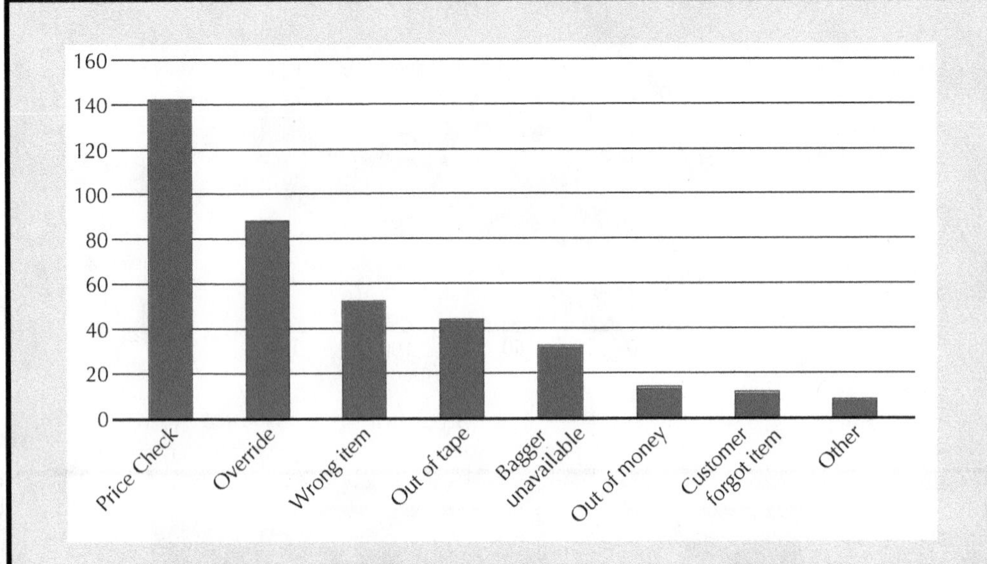

To create the Pareto chart, the Six Sigma team ranks the causes in Table 3.9 from most frequent to least frequent and graphs the resulting data in bar graph form. The Pareto chart for Healthy Foods is shown in Figure 3.11.

The check sheets and Pareto chart provide the process improvement team with some powerful information. Rather than complaining about customers who forget items (a small problem), the results suggest that Healthy Foods should instead concentrate on creating more comprehensive and accurate price lists and training clerks to properly use the cash registers. In fact, these two causes alone account for nearly 60%of the delays.

Bar graph
A graphical representation of data that places observations into specific categories.

Histogram
A special form of bar chart that tracks the number of observations that fall within a certain interval.

Run chart
A graphical representation that tracks changes in a key measure over time.

To complete our discussion of visual tools, Figure 3.12 contains examples and brief descriptions of run charts, **bar graphs,** and **histograms.** A **run chart** tracks changes in a key measure over time.

In Example 3.6, we return to the Bluebird Café. The example demonstrates how the DMAIC process and continuous improvement tools can be used to address customer satisfaction problem.

FIGURE 3.12
Edditional Date Analysis Tools

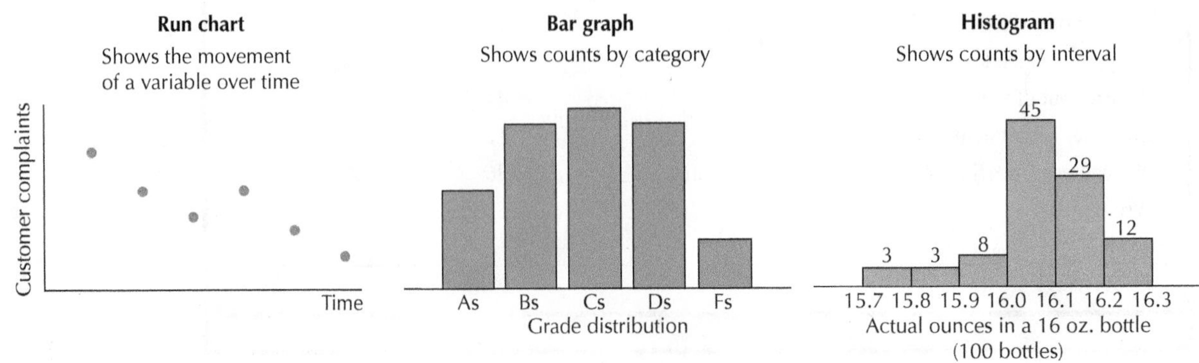

EXAMPLE 3.6

Applying DMAIC and Continuous Improvement Tools at the Bluebird Café

Katie Favre, owner of the Bluebird Café, is browsing a Web site that allows individuals to rate restaurants on a 1-to-5 scale, with 1 = "Highly Dissatisfied" and 5 = "Highly Satisfied." Katie is disappointed to learned that, based on several hundred responses, the average rating for the Bluebird Café is only 3.83 and that 12% of respondents actually rated their dining experience as a 1 or 2. Unfortunately, the Web site does not provide any specific information about why the customers rated the café as they did. Katie takes great pride in the reputation of the Bluebird Café, and she decides to use the DMAIC process and continuous improvement tools to tackle the customer satisfaction issue.

Step 1: *Define* the Goals of the Improvement Activity

At a meeting with the management team, Katie emphasizes the importance of customer satisfaction to the ongoing success of the business. The Bluebird Café is located in a college town and has plenty of competition; local customers can go elsewhere if they are dissatisfied, and out-of-town visitors often depend on Internet-based ratings to decide where they will dine. With this in mind, Katie and the management team set a target average rating of 4.5 or greater for any future Internet ratings, with no more than 2% of respondents giving a rating of 1 or 2.

Step 2: *Measure* the Existing Process

Katie already has a process map that identifies the major steps required to serve a customer (Figure 3.5). While this is a good start, the team feels that more data is needed. Katie spends a week measuring the time it takes to perform various activities, as well as the percentage of time certain process steps are completed correctly. Figure 3.13 shows the updated process map.

The management team also wants to know what process characteristics lead customers to rate the restaurant as satisfactory or unsatisfactory. To get this information, Katie puts together a survey card (see Figure 3.14) that is given out to a random sample of customers over several weeks. The survey cards are similar to check sheets, in that they allow the customer to identify particular areas of the café's performance that they are uncomfortable with. A total of 50 customers fill out the cards.

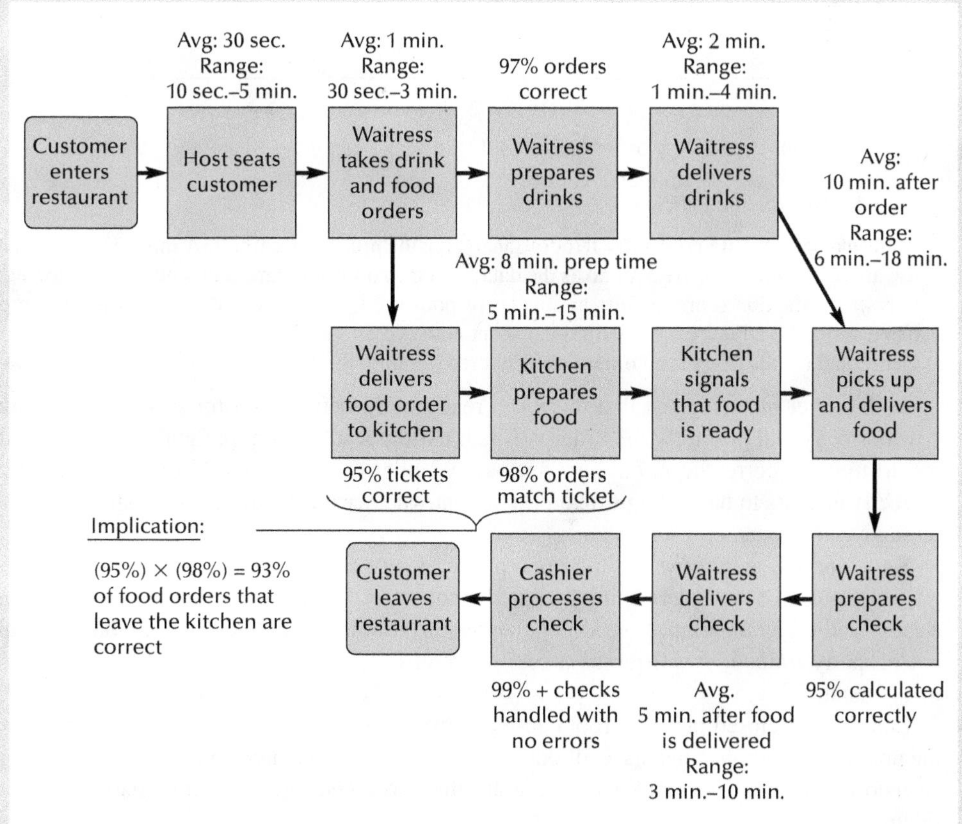

FIGURE 3.13

Process Map for Bluebird Café, Updated to Show Performance Results for Various Steps

FIGURE 3.14
Customer Survey Card for the Bluebird Café

GIVE US YOUR FEEDBACK, GET A FREE CUP OF JOE!

The Bluebird Café is always looking for ways to improve your dining experience. Please take a few moments to let us know how we are doing, and **your coffee (or tea or soda) will be on us!**

	Strongly Disagree				Strongly Agree
1. I was seated quickly.	1	2	3	4	5
2. My drink order was prepared correctly.	1	2	3	4	5
3. My drink order was delivered promptly.	1	2	3	4	5
4. My food order was prepared correctly.	1	2	3	4	5
5. My food order was delivered promptly.	1	2	3	4	5
6. The menu selection was excellent.	1	2	3	4	5
7. The prices represent a good value.	1	2	3	4	5
8. The café was clean and tidy.	1	2	3	4	5
9. The café has a pleasant ambiance.	1	2	3	4	5

On a scale of 0–100, how would you rate your **overall satisfaction** with your dining experience?

____

Are there any other ideas or comments you'd like to share with us?

____

____

____

Step 3: *Analyze* the Process

Katie and her team are now ready to begin analyzing the process in earnest. A mong the tools they use are scatter plots. Figure 3.15 takes the data from the 50 survey cards and plots each customer's overall satisfaction score against his or her response to Question 4 ("My food order was prepared correctly"). Figure 3.16 is similar, except now overall satisfaction scores are plotted against Question 5 results ("My food order was delivered promptly").

Both scatter plots suggest that there is a relationship between customer satisfaction and how correctly and promptly the order is filled, but the results seem particularly strong with regard to order correctness. Put another way, whether or not the food order was prepared correctly appears to have a significant impact on whether the customer is satisfied with the dining experience.

Katie and the team now use the open phase of root cause analysis to brainstorm about possible causes of the orders being prepared incorrectly. The team documents their ideas on a cause-and-effect diagram, from which they identify some potential causes, including "cook not properly trained," "waitresses takes incorrect order information," and "food doesn't match menu."

Entering the closed phase of root cause analysis, Katie develops a check sheet and, over the next few weeks, has the staff fill out these sheets each time a customer complains about an incorrect order. The check sheet data are than arranged into a Pareto Chart, shown in Figure 3.17.

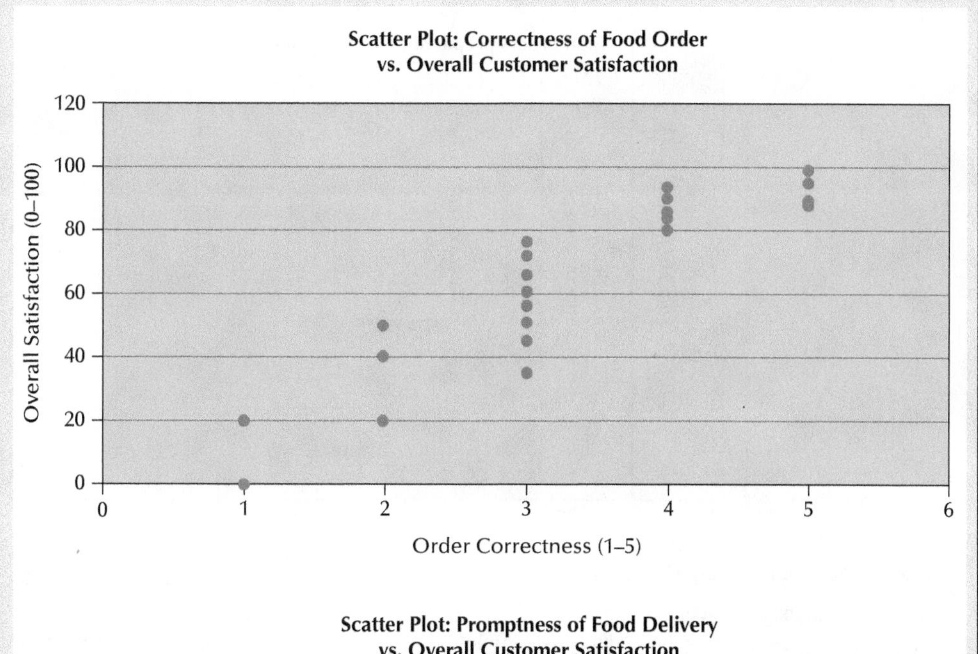

FIGURE 3.15

Scatter Plot Showing the Relationship between Survey Question 4 ("My food order was prepared correctly") and Customer's Overall Satisfaction Score

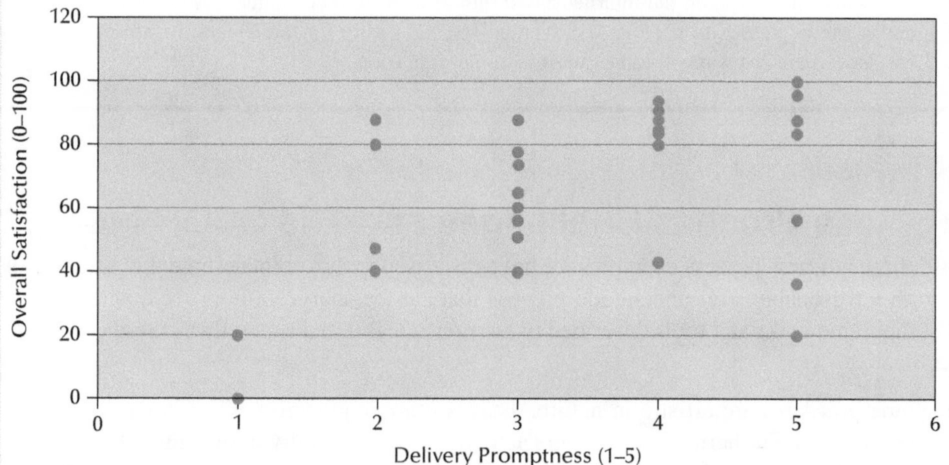

FIGURE 3.16

Scatter Plot Showing the Relationship between Survey Question 5 ("My food order was delivered promptly") and Customer's Overall Satisfaction Score

Step 4: *Improve* the Process

In looking at the Pareto chart, the team quickly realizes that the two highest-ranked items are really communications problems: The waitress gets the order wrong and the cook hears it incorrectly. Together, these problems account for roughly 60% of the incidences recorded. The third- and fourth-ranked items make up another 30% of the total and are tied to the failure of the kitchen staff to cook the food properly and match what's put on the plates to what's on the menu.

Armed with this information, the team makes some simple improvements aimed at bringing down the number of order prepared incorrectly:

1. Waitresses no longer take orders orally but write them down on an order ticket. The waitresses also repeat the orders back to the customers to verify that they have them right.
2. Cooks are given a written copy of the order ticket.
3. Waitresses compare the prepared dishes against the order ticket prior to taking it to the customer.
4. Cooks now refer to printed posters hanging on the wall that highlight important cooking steps and show pictures of how each dish should look.

FIGURE 3.17
Pareto Chart Ranking Causes of Incorrect Food Orders at Bluebird Café

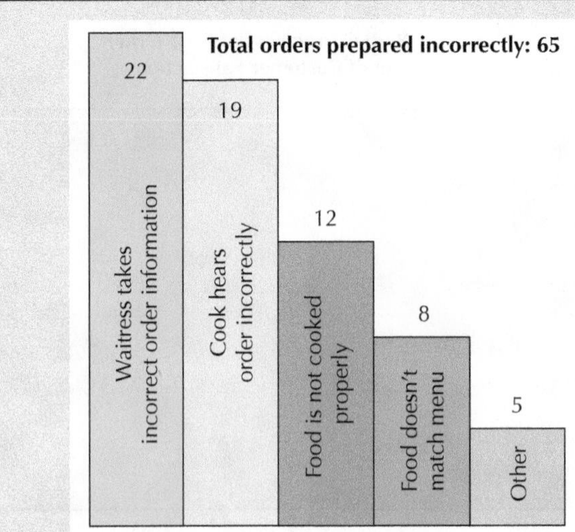

Step 5: *Control* the New Process

With the changes in place, the café staff make sure that all employees are familiar with the changes and follow the new procedures. Meanwhile, Katie continues to monitor the performance of the Bluebird Café using the Internet-based ratings as well as customer survey cards A fter four months, she is pleased to see that the average Internet rating for the Bluebird Café has risen to 3.25—not where she wants it to be, but it's on the right track.

Business Process Challenges and The SCOR Model

Most of the business process examples we have discussed to this point assume that we are working with a reasonably well-understood process that can be analyzed, improved, and controlled using the frameworks and tools described in Section 3.3. But this is not always true. Specifically:

- Some processes are artistic in nature. That is, they require flexibility in carrying out the various steps. Furthermore, customers actually *value* variability in the outcomes.
- Some processes may be so broken or so mismatched to the organization's strategy that only a total redesign of the process will do.
- Some processes cross organizational boundaries, which introduces additional challenges.

We talk about each of these challenges in turn.

HOW STANDARDIZED SHOULD PROCESSES BE?

According to some business experts, tools such as process mapping and the DMAIC cycle have become so popular that they have been *overused*—applied to process environments in which flexibility in the process and variability in outcomes are valued by the business and customers. For example, while it certainly makes sense to standardize and control the process for administering intravenous drugs to a hospital patient, it makes less sense to control every step of a doctor's diagnosis process, especially when a patient has unique or unusual symptoms. To help managers understand when they should and shouldn't try to standardize processes, Joseph Hall and M. Eric Johnson developed a framework that divides processes into four main types based on (1) how much variability there is in the process and (2) whether customers actually value variability in outputs.[12]

Mass processes are perhaps the easiest to understand. Here, the goal of the process is to provide exactly the same output each time. The key to *mass customization is controlled* variation.

[12] J. Hall and E. Johnson, "When Should a Process Be Art, Not Science?" *Harvard Business Review* (March 2009): 58–65.

For instance, when a customer orders a laptop computer from Dell, he or she can choose from a predetermined set of options. The goal is to provide some variability in output without undermining the stability of Dell's assembly operations.

At the other extreme from mass processes are *artistic processes* where both variability in the process and outputs are valued. A prime example would be a research and development (R&D) lab where employees are expected to use their creativity to identify new product or service opportunities. In fact, efforts to standardize R&D activities may actually interfere with the ability of a lab to generate breakthrough products or services.

The last type of process is a what Hall and Johnson refer to as a *nascent, or broken* process. Unlike the other three types, processes that fall into this group have a fundamental mismatch between what the customer wants (standardized output) and what the process is currently capable of providing. Managers have two choices here: Reduce the variability of the process or switch to customers or markets that value output variability.

BUSINESS PROCESS REENGINEERING (BPR)

An alternative approach to Six Sigma and the DMAIC process is **business process reengineering (BPR).** As APICS notes, BPR is "a procedure that involves the fundamental rethinking and radical redesign of business processes to achieve dramatic organizational improvements in such critical measures of performance as cost, quality, service, and speed."[13] Proponents of BPR suggest that organizations start the BPR process with a "blank sheet" of paper rather than try to understand and modify processes that may be severely outdated or dysfunctional. Which approach a firm uses—Six Sigma or BPR—depends on several factors, including how severe the problems are with the current business process and the ability of process participants to make radical changes.

Business process reengineering (BPR)
According to APICS, "A procedure that involves the fundamental rethinking and radical redesign of business processes to achieve dramatic organizational improvements in such critical measures of performance as cost, quality, service, and speed."

COORDINATING PROCESS MANAGEMENT EFFORTS ACROSS THE SUPPLY CHAIN

In Example 3.6, the Six Sigma process improvement effort was focused on the activities within a single organization, in this case a café. But many times, firms must extend their efforts to include external supply chain partners. Extending process management to include external partners is an important step, as significant opportunities for improvement often lie at the interfaces between various partners. But doing so adds greater complexity, given that multiple organizations and their representatives are now participating in the effort. The SCOR model, described next, provides one framework for understanding and managing cross-organizational supply chain processes.

THE SCOR MODEL

We end this chapter with a discussion of the **Supply Chain Operations Reference (SCOR) model.**[14] The SCOR model is a comprehensive model of high-level business processes and detailed individual processes that together define the scope of supply chain management activity. The SCOR model is supported by the Supply Chain Council, an industry group consisting of hundreds of companies and academics.

Supply Chain Operations Reference (SCOR)
A comprehensive model of the core management processes and individual process types that, together, define the domain of supply chain management.

Why would companies spend time and money to develop a reference model such as SCOR? Actually, there are several good reasons. First, a reference model gives individuals a common language for discussing and comparing supply chain business processes. This can be especially important when benchmarking performance or coordinating with other firms to build a supply chain. Second, a reference model provides a template to guide the design and implementation of an organization's own supply chain processes. Third, seeing the processes laid out in a single, comprehensive model helps some managers better understand what supply chain management is all about.

[13] J. H. Blackstone, ed., *APICS Dictionary*, 13th ed. (Chicago, IL: APICS, 2010).

[14] The Supply Chain Council, "Supply Chain Operations Reference (SCOR) Model Overview: Version 10.0". **http://supply-chain.org/f/Web-Scor-Overview.pdf**

The SCOR model looks at a firm's supply chain activities in three levels of increasing detail. Level 1 of the views SCM activities as being structured around five core management processes (Figure 3.18):

1. **Source**—Processes that procure goods and services to meet planned or actual demand.
2. **Make**—Processes that transform product to a finished state to meet planned or actual demand.
3. **Deliver**—Processes that provide finished goods and services to meet planned or actual demand. These processes include order management as well as logistics and distribution activities.
4. **Return**—Processes associated with returning or receiving returned products for any reason.
5. **Plan**—Processes that balance aggregate resources with requirements.

Level 2 processes break down level 1 activities into more detail. For example, SCOR differentiates between three types of "make" processes: make-to-stock, make-to-order, and engineerto-order. Make-to-stock, make-to-order, and engineer-to-order manufacturing processes differ with regard to the level of product customization and therefore require very different solutions.

Finally, SCOR level 3 processes describes in detail the actual steps required to execute level 2 processes. Companies can use these maps as a rough guide for developing their own unique processes or for identifying gaps. Consider the example in Figure 3.19, which shows the level 3 process map for one particular process type, "Make E ngineer-to-Order Product."

The process map suggests that manufacturing an engineer-to-order product should consist of seven sequential process "elements," labeled in SCOR nomenclature as M3.1–M3.7. The map also shows the prescribed information inflows and outflows to these elements. For example, the second element, "Schedule Production A ctivities," should take place in response to information inflows, including the production plan, scheduled receipts, feedback from downstream "make" elements, and equipment and facilities schedules and plans. In turn, the information outflow of this element should be an updated production schedule used by the production, sourcing, and distribution areas. Note too that the entire "make engineer-toorder" process, as prescribed by the SCOR model, should contain information links to all five of the core management processes.

FIGURE 3.18

Overview of the SCOR Model Showing the Five Level 1 Processes

Source: Supply Chain Operations, (Supply-Chain Council, 2011).

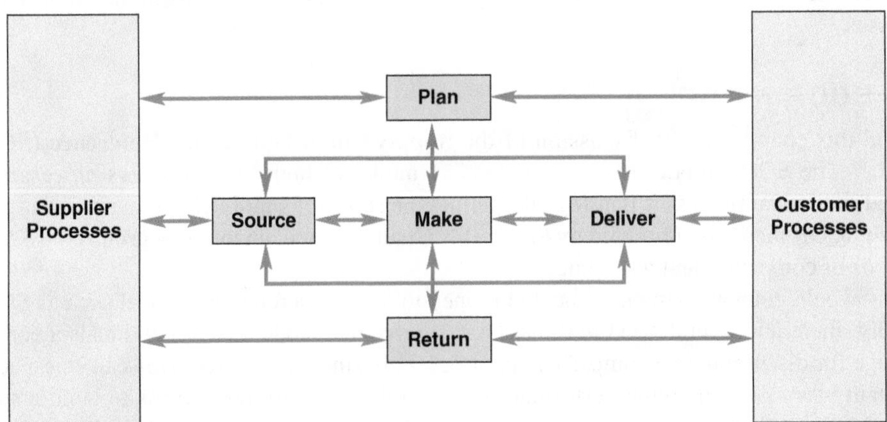

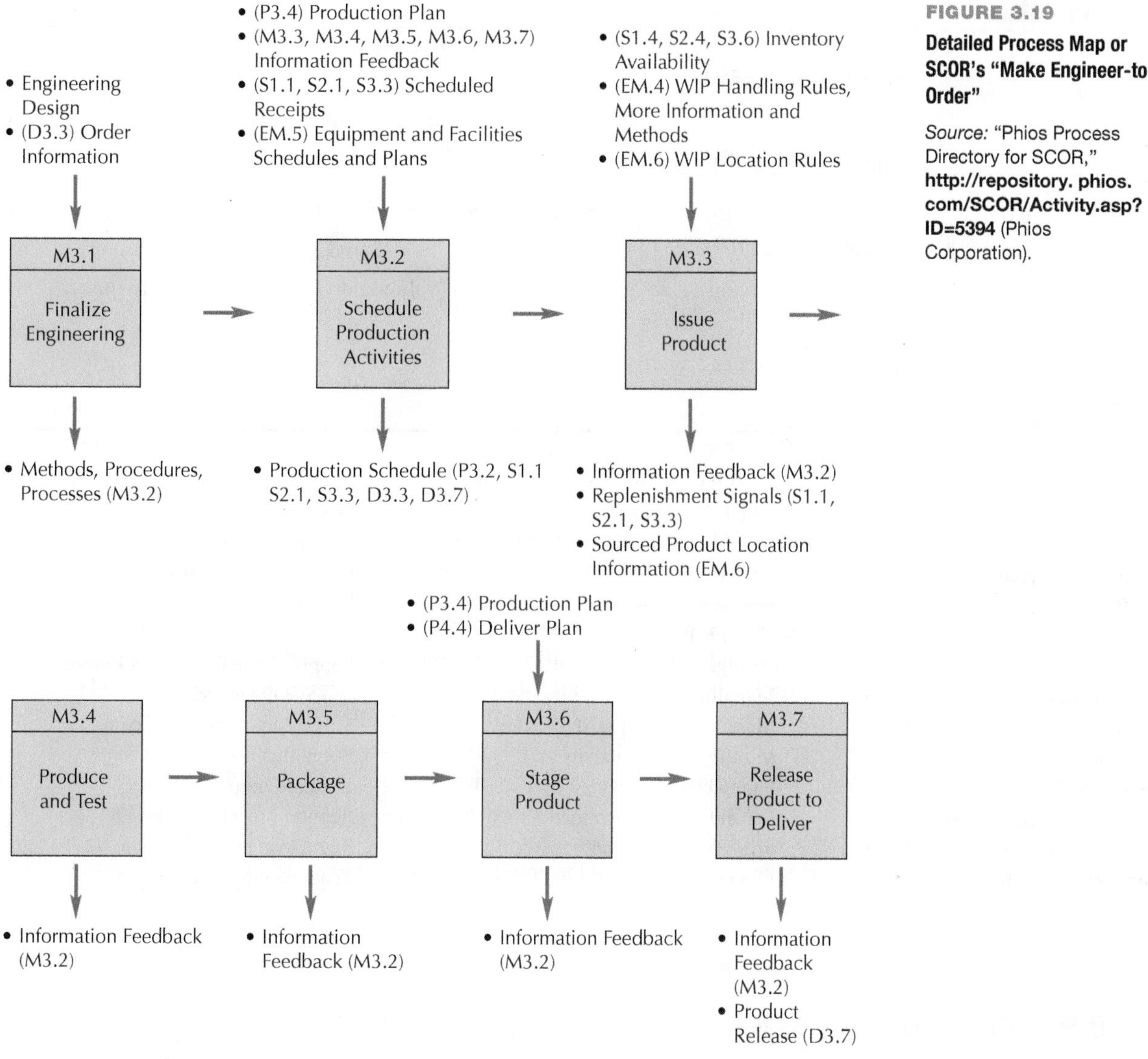

FIGURE 3.19

Detailed Process Map or SCOR's "Make Engineer-to-Order"

Source: "Phios Process Directory for SCOR," **http://repository.phios.com/SCOR/Activity.asp?ID=5394** (Phios Corporation).

CHAPTER SUMMARY

Although the term *business processes* has been in the management lexicon for years, not all organizations clearly understand the importance of business processes and their effects on operations and supply chain performance. In this chapter, we defined the concept of business processes and showed how the business process perspective is different from the traditional, functionally oriented view of business. Business processes change the focus from "How is the business organized?" to "What does the business do?"

Fortunately, practitioners and theorists continue to develop various tools and approaches for managing business processes. In this chapter, we described two process mapping approaches and demonstrated how they can be used. We also spent considerable time talking about various approaches to managing and improving business processes, including performance measurement and benchmarking, the Six Sigma methodology, and continuous improvement tools. We concluded the chapter with a discussion of the SCOR model, which represents an attempt by industry partners to develop a comprehensive model of the various business processes that define supply chain management.

Key Formulas

Productivity (page 73):

Productivity = outputs>inputs (3.1)

Efficiency (page 75):

Efficiency = 100%(actual outputs>standard outputs) (3.2)

Percent value-added time (page 76):

Percent value-added time = 100%(value-added time0//(total cycle time) (3.3)

Key Terms

Bar graph (p. 82)
Benchmarking (p. 76)
Black belt (p. 78)
Business process reengineering (BPR) (p. 87)
Cause-and-effect diagram (p. 79)
Champion (p. 78)
Check sheet (p. 80)
Competitive benchmarking (p. 76)
Continuous improvement (p. 79)
Cycle time (p. 76)
Development process (p. 66)
DMAIC (Define–Measure–Analyze–Improve–Control) (p. 78)
DMADV (Define–Measure–Analyze–Design–Verify) (p. 79)
Efficiency (p. 75)
Five Ms (p. 79)
Five Whys (p. 80)
Green belt (p. 78)
Histogram (p. 82)
Mapping (p. 68)
Master black belt (p. 78)
Multifactor productivity (p. 73)
Pareto chart (p. 80)
Percent value-added time (p. 76)
Primary process (p. 66)
Process (p. 66)
Process benchmarking (p. 76)
Process map (p. 68)
Productivity (p. 73)
Root cause analysis (p. 79)
Run chart (p. 82)
Scatter plot (p. 80)
Supply Chain Operations Reference (SCOR) model (p. 87)
Single-factor productivity (p. 73)
Six Sigma methodology (p. 78)
Standard output (p. 75)
Support process (p. 66)
Swim lane process map (p. 71)
Team members (p. 78)

Solved Problems **The repair at Biosphere.**

SOLVED PROBLEM 3.1

Biosphere Products makes and sells environmental monitoring devices for use in industry. These devices monitor and record air quality levels and issue an alarm whenever conditions warrant.

If a monitoring device fails, Biosphere will repair the device as part of the customer's service agreement. The repair process consists of the following steps:

1. Once the device arrives at Biosphere's repair center, a work order is immediately entered into the computer system. This step takes 5 minutes.
2. A device will then wait, on average, 24 hours before a technician has a chance to run diagnostics and disassemble the device. The diagnostics procedure usually takes about 30 minutes, while disassembly takes around 1 hour.
3. Next the technician orders replacements for any broken/worn parts from the main plant. While it takes only 5 minutes to order the parts, it usually takes 48 hours for them to arrive from the main plant.
4. After the parts come in, the device will usually wait another 24 hours until a technician has time to reassemble and test the device. The reassembly and testing process takes, on average, 3 hours.
5. If the device still fails to work, the technician will repeat the process, starting with diagnostics and disassembly. The first time through, 10% of the devices aren't fixed; however, virtually all of them work by the time a second pass has been completed.
6. Once the device has been tested and passed, it is immediately boxed up (10 minutes)and a call is made to UPS, which picks up the package, usually within 1 hour.

Map Biosphere's current process. How long will it take, on average, to move a device through the system, assuming that everything "works" the first time? How long will it take if the device has to be repaired a second time? What is the percent value-added time under each scenario?

▼ SOLUTION

Figure 3.20 shows the process map, starting with the arrival of the device at the repair facility and ending when UPS picks it up. If the device has to be repaired only once, the total cycle time is 101 hours and 50 minutes. However, if the device has to be "repaired again," we must add another 76 hours and 35 minutes, resulting in a total cycle time of 178 hours and 25 minutes.

It gets worse. One could argue that the only value-added activities are running the diagnostics, disassembling and reassembling the device, and testing. These activities total 4.5 hours. Therefore, if Biosphere correctly repairs the device the first time:

Percent value-added time = 100%(4.5 hours/101.83 hours) = 4.4%

If the device has to be repaired a second time:

Percent value-added time = 100%(4.5 hours/178.42 hours) = 2.5%

In other words, over 95% of the time is spent on non-value-added activities. A careful reader will notice that, in the second calculation, we didn't add in any more time for diagnostics, disassembling and reassembling the device, and testing. This was intentional: Our argument is that if these activities did not fix the device the first time, then the first pass through was wasted time, not value-added time.

So what should Biosphere do? Looking at the process map, it becomes clear that the vast majority of the time is spent waiting on a technician or on parts or looping through activities because a device wasn't fixed right the first time. If, for example, Biosphere could keep spare parts at the repair center, it could chop 48 hours off the cycle time. Management might also investigate why it takes technicians so long to get around to working on a device. Are they busy working on other devices, or are they involved in other activities that can wait? Management might even decide that more technicians are needed.

With regard to the relatively high failure rate of "repaired" devices, Biosphere might have to do some more detailed analysis: Are the technicians being trained properly? Are they making the same mistakes over and over again? If so, why? Clearly, Biosphere is an ideal candidate for a DMAIC improvement efforts.

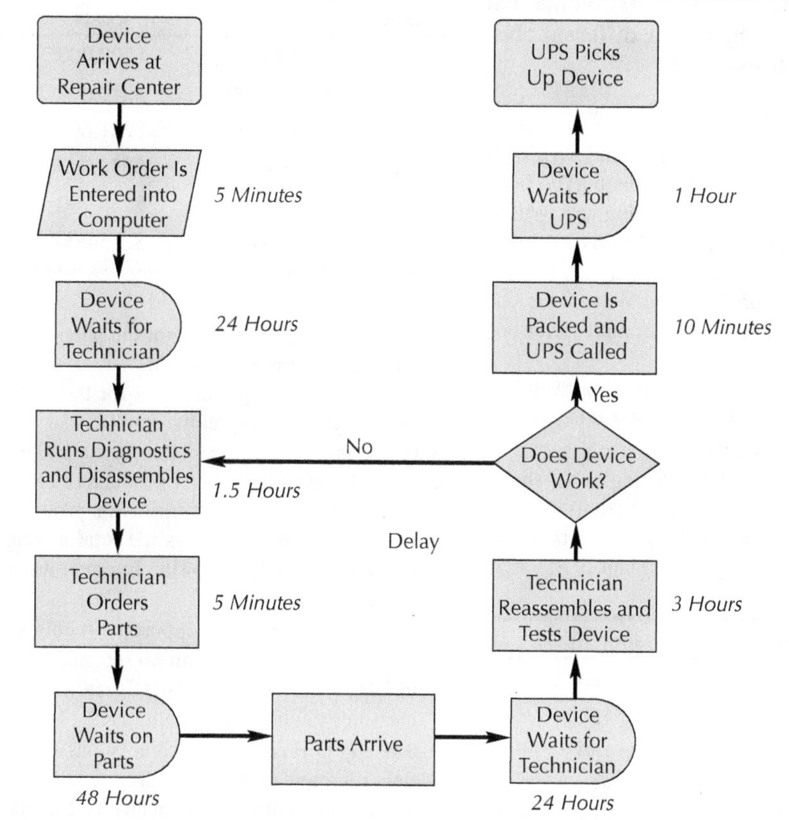

FIGURE 3.20

Process Map for Biosphere Products—Device Repair Process

Discussion Questions

1. Use the P&G example at the beginning of the chapter to explain the benefits to the customer of adopting a business processes perspective. Why might a traditional functional perspective have "blinded" P&G to the problems with the old system?
2. We noted that cycle time, while an important measure of process performance, is not the only measure to be considered. Give an example where focusing exclusively on reducing cycle times might hurt other, equally important, measures of process performance.
3. Consider the course registration process at your college. Is this a mass process, mass customization, artistic, or nascent/ broken process? Justify your answer.
4. In the chapter, we stated that "there are countless possible measures of process performance, many of which are derived from the four core measures" quality, cost, time, and flexibility. In the following table, identify how you think the three measures we described (productivity, efficiency, and cycle time) relate to the four core measures. Specifically:
   - If you think the measure always has a positive impact on a core measure, mark the square with a "+".
   - If you think the measure always has a negative impact, mark the square with "-".
   - If you think the measure can have either a positive or a negative impact, depending on the circumstances, mark the square with "+/-".

   Be ready to justify your answers. What are the implications for using performance measures to evaluate processes?

	Quality	Cost	Time	Flexibility
Productivity				
Efficiency				
Cycle time				

Problems

Additional homework problems are available at www. pearsonhighered. com/bozarth. These problems use Excel to generate customized problems for different class sections or even different students.

(* = easy; ** = moderate; *** = advanced)

•• **3.1** Marci spends 15 hours researching and writing a 20-page report for her philosophy class. Jack brags thaThe has a "streamlined process" for performing the researching and writing. Jack takes just 8 hours to research and write the paper, but his report is only 15 pages long.

a) (*) Calculate Marci's and Jack's productivity. What is the output? What is the input? Is this a single-factor or multifactor productivity measure?

b) (**) What are the limitations of using productivity measures to evaluate Marci's and Jack's performance? What other performance measures might the instructor use?

•• **3.2** (**) Consider the output and labor hour figures shown in the following table. Calculate the labor productivity for each week, as well as the average labor productivity for all six weeks. Do any of the weeks seem unusual to you? Explain.

Week	Output (In Units)	Labor Hours
1	1,850	200
2	1,361	150
3	2,122	150
4	2,638	250
5	2,599	250
6	2,867	300

•• **3.3** Smarmy Sales, Inc. (SSI), sells herbal remedies through its Web site and through phone reps. Over the past six years, SSI has started to depend more and more on its Web site to generate sales. The figures below show total sales, phone rep costs, and Web site costs for the past six years:.

Year	Total Sales	Phone Rep Costs	Web Site Costs
2008	$4,790,000	$200,000	$50,000
2009	$5,750,000	$210,000	$65,000
2010	$6,900,000	$221,000	$85,000
2011	$8,280,000	$230,000	$110,000
2012	$9,930,000	$245,000	$145,000
2013	$11,920,000	$255,000	$190,000

a) (*) Calculate productivity for the phone reps for each of the past six years. Interpret the results.

b) (*) Calculate the productivity for the Web site for each of the past six years. Interpret the results.

c) (**) Compare your results in parts a and b. What are the limitations of these single-factor productivity measures?

d) (**) Now calculate a multifactor productivity score for each year, where the "input" is the total amount spent on both the phone reps and the Web site. Interpret the results. What can you conclude?.

•• **3.4** (*) A customer support job requires workers to complete a particular online form in 60 seconds. L es can finish the form in 70 seconds. What is his efficiency? What other performance measures might be important here?

•• **3.5** (**) Precision Machinery has set standard times for its field representatives to perform certain jobs. The standard time allowed for routine maintenance is 2 hours (i.e., "standard output" = 0.5 jobs per hour). One of Precision's field representatives records the results below. Calculate the rep's efficiency for each customer and her average efficiency. Interpret the results.

Customer	Actual Time Required to Perform Routine Maintenance
ABC Company	1.8 hours
Preztel	2.4 hours
SCR Industries	1.9 hours
BeetleBob	1.8 hours

•• **3.6** Gibson's Bodywork does automotive collision work. A n insurance agency has determined that the standard time to replace a fender is 2.5 hours (i.e., "standard output" = 0.4 fenders per hour) and is willing to pay Gibson $50 per hour for labor (parts and supplies are billed separately). Gibson pays its workers $35 per hour.

a) (**) Suppose Gibson's workers take 4 hours to replace a fender. What is Gibson's labor hour efficiency? Given Gibson's labor costs, will the company make money on the job?

b) (***) What does Gibson's labor hour efficiency have to be for Gibson to break even on the job? Show your work.

•• **3.7** (**) When a driver enters the license bureau to have his license renewed, he spends, on average, 45 minutes in line, 2 minutes having his eyes tested, and 3 minutes to have his photograph taken. What is the percent value-added time? Explain any assumptions you made in coming up with your answer.

•• **3.8** Average waiting times and ride times for two of DizzyWorld's rides are as follows:

Ride	Average Waiting Time	Length of Ride	Total Process Time
Magical Mushroom	30 minutes	10 minutes	40 minutes
Haunted Roller Coaster	40 minutes	5 minutes	45 minutes

a) (*) Calculate the percent value-added time for each ride.

b) (**) Now suppose DizzyWorld puts in place a reservation system for the Haunted Roller Coaster ride. Here's how it works: The customer receives a coupon that allows him to come back in 40 minutes and immediately go to the front of the line. In the meantime, the customer can wait in line and then ride the Magical Mushroom. Under this new system, what is the customer's total time waiting? T otal time riding? What is the new percent-value added time?

•• **3.9** A(**) Consider Example 3.1 and the accompanying Figure 3.6. Calculate the percent value-added time for the current process. Which activities do you consider to be value added? Why?

•• **3.10** Returning to Example 3.1 and Figure 3.6, suppose management actually does put a system in place that lets customers enter orders electronically, with this information sent directly to the picking area.

a) (***) Redraw the process map to illustrate the changes. What is the new cycle time for the process? What is the new percent value-added time?

b) (**) What do you think the impact would be on the number of lost orders? On customer satisfaction?

•• **3.11** (**) Billy's Hamburger Barn has a single drive-up window. Currently, there is one attendant at the window who takes the order (30–40 seconds), gathers up the food and bags it (30–120 seconds), and then takes the customer's money (30–40 seconds) before handing the food to the customer. Map the current process. What is the minimum cycle time? The longest cycle time?

•• **3.12** (***) Suppose Billy's Hamburger Barn redesigns the process described in problem 11 so there are now two attendants. The first attendant takes the order. Once this step is finished, the first attendant then takes the money, and the second one gathers up and bags the food. If two of the process steps can now run in parallel (gathering the food and taking the money), what is the new minimum cycle time? What is the longest cycle time? What potential problems could arise by splitting the process across two individuals?

•• **3.13** Faircloth Financial specializes in home equity loans, loans that customers can take out against the equity they have in their homes. ("Equity" represents the difference between the home's value and the amount a customer owns on any other loans.) The current process is as follows:

- The customer downloads the loan application forms from the Web, fills them in, and mails them to Faircloth (3–5 days).
- If there are any problems with the forms (and there usually are), a customer sales representative calls up the customer and reviews these problems. It may take 1 to 2 days to contact the customer. After reaching the customer, resolving the problem can take anywhere from 5 minutes to 30 minutes. If the customer needs to initial or sign some new forms, it takes 5–7 days to mail the forms to the customer and have her send them back.
- Every Monday morning, the customer sales representatives take a batch of completed, correct application forms to the loan officers. This means that if a correct loan application comes in on Tuesday, the soonest it can get to a loan officer is the following Monday. The loan officers then take 2 to 3 days to process the batch of loans, based on information on the forms and information available from credit rating bureaus. Customers are advised by e-mail and regular mail regarding the final decision.
- (***) Map out the current process. Identify any rework loops and delays in the process. What causes these? What is the impact on cycle times? How might this affect customers' willingness to do business with Faircloth?
- (***) What changes might you recommend to redesign this process with the needs of the customer in mind? You might start by imagining how the "perfect" process would look to the customer and base your recommendations on that.

Case Studies

Swim Lane Process Map for a Medical Procedure

Figure 3.21 shows the swim lane process map for a patient undergoing a lumpectomy (the surgical removal of a small tumor from the breast). Nine parties, including the patient, were involved in the process. For many of the steps in Figure 3.21, a box has been drawn around multiple parties, indicating that two or more parties were involved in the step. For example, the "surgery" step involved three parties: the patient, the surgeon, and the hospital.

During the treatment process, the patient (who was a registered nurse) detected two errors. Error 1 occurred when the surgeon intended to employ a needle locator to identify the location of the tumor, but failed to forward an order to that effect to the hospital. The patient identified the omission prior to surgery. No harm occurred. Error 2 was a typographic error on the pathology report indicating that the tumor was 1.6 *millimeters* diameter when in fact it was 1.6 *centimeters*. This could have been a more serious mistake, but a phone call to confirm the correction avoided any harm.

Questions

1. Who or what organization is responsible for this process from start to finish? What are the implications for managing and improving the treatment process?
2. Which process steps should be standardized? Which process steps should be more artistic? Explain.
3. Consider the errors that occurred during the treatment process. How might you use the Six Sigma methodology and continuous improvement tools to keep these errors from reoccurring? Looking ahead, what kinds of solutions might you see coming out of such an analysis?

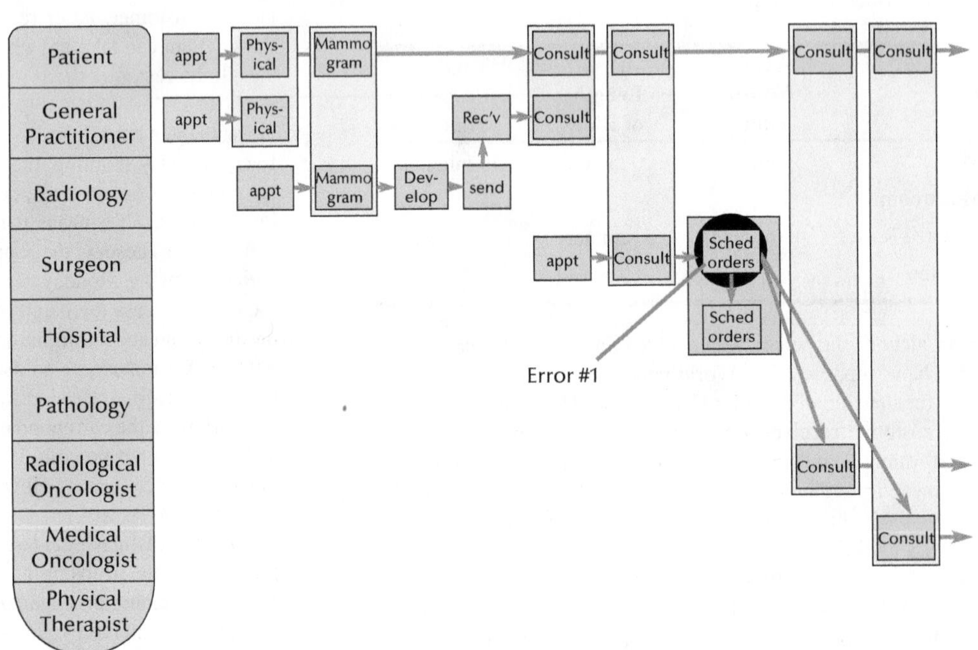

FIGURE 3.21
Swim Lane Process Map for a Surgical Procedure
Source: John Grout, "Swim Lane,"
http://csob.berry.edu/faculty/ jgrout/process-mapping/ Swim_Lane/swim_lane.html.

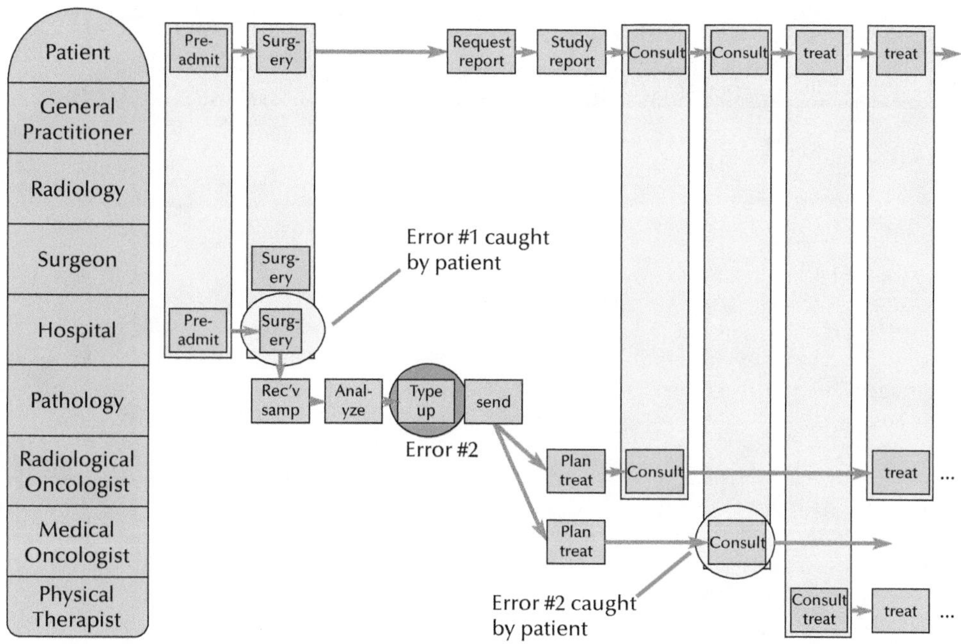

FIGURE 3.21 *(Continued)*

References

Books and Articles

Andersen, B., *Business Process Improvement Toolbox* (Milwaukee, WI: ASQ Quality Press, 1999).

Blackburn, J., *Time-Based Competition: The Next Battle Ground in American Manufacturing* (Homewood, IL: Irwin, 1991).

Blackstone, J. H., ed., *APICS Dictionary*, 13th ed. (Chicago, IL: APICS, 2010).

Cook, S., *Practical Benchmarking: A Manager's Guide to Creating a Competitive Advantage* (London: Kogan Page, 1995).

Drayer, R., "Procter & Gamble's Streamlined Logistics Initiative," *Supply Chain Management Review* 3, no. 2 (Summer 1999): 32–43.

Evans, J., and Lindsay, W., *The Management and Control of Quality* (Mason, OH: Thomson South-Western, 2005).

Hall, J., and Johnson, M.E., "When Should a Process Be Art, Not Science?" *Harvard Business Review* (March 2009): 58–65.

Meyer, C., Fast Cycle Time: *How to Align Purpose, Strategy, and Structure for Speed* (New York: Free Press, 1993).

Quinn, F. "What's the Buzz? Supply Chain Management: Part 1," *Logistics Management* 36, no. 2 (February 1997): 43.

Stalk, G., and T . Hout, *Competing against Time: How Time- Based Competition Is Reshaping Global Markets* (New York: Free Press, 1990).

Tibey, S., "How Kraft Built a 'One-Company' Supply Chain," *Supply Chain Management Review* 3, no. 3 (Fall 1999): 34–42.

Internet

Grout, J., "Swim L ane," **http://csob.berry.edu/faculty/jgrout/processmapping/Swim_Lane/swim_lane.html.**

Harbour Consulting, "Harbour Report North A merica 2006," **www.harbourinc.com**

Motorola University, **www.motorola.com/motorolauniversity.jsp**

The Supply Chain Council, "Supply Chain Operations Reference (SCOR) Model Overview: Version 10.0," **http:// supply-chain.org/f/Web-Scor-Overview.pdf.**

U.S. Department of T ransportation, "Air T ravel Consumer Report," February 2011, **http://airconsumer.dot.gov/reports/2011/February/2011FebruaryATCR.PD**

Student Profile

Roxanne Asher System Administrator, QCSolver Inc.
Business Analyst, Cambridge Solutions Inc.
Owner, The Urban Farmers Company
Graduate of Materials and Operations Management Co op Program at Conestoga College, 2010

Graduating from Conestoga College in 2010 has allowed me to expand into many different opportunities – from pursuing my passion for urban farming and starting my own company, as well as solidifying my job in the supply chain industry. On a regular basis, I utilize various theoretical and practical skills to develop professionally and personally.

I work as the system administrator for QCSolver, a software product focused on increasing transparency through the supply chain, as well as being a business analyst for consulting projects with Cambridge Solutions Inc.

The opportunities are endless when taking this comprehensive college program. With the knowledge attained from each course, I am prepared to work in any type of business industry or environment.

As a young entrepreneur I am pleased with the skills and the knowledge obtained this program at Conestoga. All the best to success in the future!

4

Developing Products and Services

Chapter Outline

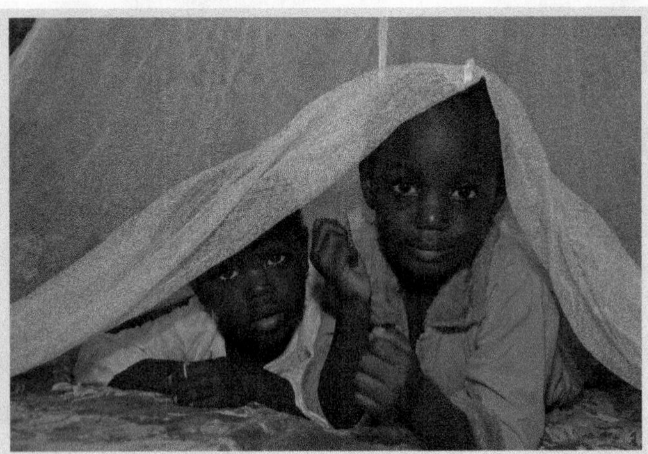

© Irene Abdou / Alamy

Henry Kimuyu, 3, and his brother Vincent, 8, rest after school under an insecticide-treated mosquito net at their home in Nairobi, Kenya.

Since its symptoms were first reported in Chinese medical writings more than 4,000 years ago,[1] malaria has presented an enormous health challenge. Recent efforts to eradicate the mosquito-borne parasitic disease have met with some success: In 2010, the World Health Organization (WHO) reported that the number of cases fell from 244 million in 2005 to 225 million in 2009, while the number of deaths due to malaria decreased from 985,000 in 2000 to 781,000 in 2009.[2] Malaria has had a disproportionately large impact in Sub-Saharan Africa, where approximately 40% of public health expenditures can be traced back to the disease.

One relatively new product that has been used to fight the spread of malaria combines an old idea with state-of-the-art textiles and chemistry: bed nets impregnated with insecticides. One of the companies producing such bed nets is Vestergaard Frandsen, a European company specializing in complex emergency response and disease control products. Recently, Vestergaard Frandsen introduced the PermaNet 3.0 Combination Net, which slowly releases insecticide embedded in the yarn onto the surface of the netting. The result is a bed net that is effective at killing mosquitoes, even after multiple washings.[3]

While the PermaNet product concept is a good one, producing and then distributing the bed nets to where they are needed presents some significant operations and supply chain challenges for Vestergaard Frandsen. For one thing, the prevailing price for similar bed nets is $5 to $7 a unit. Such a low price target puts significant cost pressure on operations and supply chain activities. Second, Vestergaard Frandsen must build and maintain a network of suppliers and manufacturers capable of providing the needed volumes of specialized insecticides and textiles required to produce the PermaNet bed nets. A third challenge is effectively and efficiently distributing the bed nets in countries with limited transportation infrastructures and scattered populations.

While overcoming these operations and supply chain challenges is not easy, the payoff is much more than financial. As United Nations Secretary General Ban Ki-Moon wrote in the introduction to the *2010 World Malaria Report*:[4]

---

[1]Centers for Disease Control and Prevention, *The History of Malaria, an Ancient Disease*, **www.cdc.gov/malaria/about/history/**.
[2]World Health Organization, *World Malaria Report 2010*, **www.who.int/malaria/world_malaria_report_2010/en/index.html**.
[3]Vestergaard Frandsen, *What Is PermaNet 3.0, and How Is It Different from Other Bed Nets?* **www.vestergaard-frandsen.com/permanet/permanet-3/49-what-is-permanet-3-and-how-is-it-different-from-other-bed-nets.**
[4]World Health Organization, *World Malaria Report 2010*, **www.who.int/malaria/world_malaria_report_2010/en/index.html**.

Two years ago, I called for universal coverage of malaria-control interventions by the end of 2010, in order to bring an end to malaria deaths by 2015. The response was impressive. Enough insecticide-treated mosquito nets have been delivered to Sub-Saharan Africa to protect nearly 580 million people. . . . An additional 54 million nets are slated for delivery in the coming months, bringing the goal of universal coverage within reach. . . . The World *Malaria Report 2010 shows what is possible when we join forces and embrace the mission of saving lives.*

Chapter 4 Learning Objectives

1: Explain why product design is important to the success of a business.

2: Describe the six dimensions of product design that are of particular interest to operations and supply chain managers.

3: Describe the five phases of product and service development and explain the difference between sequential development and concurrent engineering.

4: Discuss the different roles played by areas such as engineering and accounting during the development process.

5: Describe some of the most common approaches to improving product and service designs, including the Define–Measure–Analyze–Design–Verify (DMADV) process, quality function deployment (QFD), design for manufacturability (DFM), and target costing.

Introduction

Vestergaard Frandsen's experiences highlight some of the issues companies face when developing new products and services. But how do companies go about managing the development process, and what roles do various parties within and outside the firm play? These questions are the subject of this chapter. First, we discuss the role of product and service development in today's businesses, emphasizing the impact new and enhanced products and services have on a firm's ability to compete.

We then turn our attention to the actual process by which companies develop new products and services or modify existing ones. We pay special attention to operations and supply chain perspectives on product and service design: What are the important considerations? What role do the purchasing function and suppliers play? What tools and techniques are companies using to enhance the product development effort?

PRODUCT DESIGN AND THE DEVELOPMENT PROCESS

It's important for us to distinguish between product design and the product development process. **Product design** can be thought of as the characteristics or features of a product or service that determine its ability to meet the needs of the user. In contrast, according to the Product Development and Management Association (PDMA), the **product development process** is "the overall process of strategy, organization, concept generation, product and marketing plan creation and evaluation, and commercialization of a new product."[5] In this chapter, we focus on how product and service design affects operations and supply chain activities and what role operations and supply chains play in the development process. We use the term *product design* to refer to the development of both intangible services and physical products. As you can probably guess, product development is by necessity a cross-functional effort affecting operations and supply chain activities, as well as marketing, human resources, and finance.

Product design
The characteristics or features of a product or service that determine its ability to meet the needs of the user.

Product development process
According to the PDMA, "the overall process of strategy, organization, concept generation, product and marketing plan creation and evaluation, and commercialization of a new product."

[5]Product Development and Management Association, *The PDMA Glossary for New Product Development*, **http://www.pdma.org/npd_glossary.cfm**.

FOUR REASONS FOR DEVELOPING NEW PRODUCTS AND SERVICES

There are least four reasons why a company might develop new products or services or update its existing ones. The first is straightforward: *New products or services can give firms a competitive advantage in the marketplace.* Consider the problem facing H&R Block a few years ago: How do you attract customers when faced with increasing competition from other tax preparation firms as well as PC-based software packages that can help people do their tax returns on their own? You do it by providing new and distinctive services such as PC-based will kits, refund anticipation loans (RALs), and a Web page that provides customers free and for-fee tax preparation software, as well as valuable information in multiple languages.

Not all product development efforts *directly* benefit the customer, however. This leads to our second reason for developing new products or services: *New products or services provide benefits to the firm.* Motorola might redesign one of its smartphones so it has fewer parts and is easier to assemble. Even though the smartphone might look and function exactly as before, the result is improved assembly productivity and lower purchasing and production costs. Motorola might or might not share these savings with the customer.

Third, *companies develop new products or services to exploit existing capabilities.* An excellent example is Honda. Honda progressed from making and selling motorcycles, to automobiles, and, most recently, to lawn equipment and jet skis. In retrospect, it is easy to see that Honda has built on its core competencies in the design and production of gas-powered vehicles. It will be interesting to see how Honda maintains its advantage as more products shift to alternative fuels.

Fourth, *companies can use new product development to block out competitors.* Consider the case of Gillette.[6] By the early 1990s, Gillette had grown tired of spending millions to develop a new razor blade, only to have competitors introduce cheaper (and poorer-quality) replacement blades within a few months. Gillette now makes a point of designing new razors so that they not only provide customers with a superior shave but are also difficult for competitors to copy. Developing new products like this requires a great deal of coordination with the manufacturing arm of the firm. Of course, a firm might have multiple reasons for developing a new product or service or for updating existing ones. But regardless of the underlying reasons, the development effort must be consistent with the strategy of a firm.

Just how important are new products and services to firms? Consider the following figures[7]:

- On average, about 30% of revenues and profits come from products introduced in the past five years.
- Over 84% of the most innovative development projects use cross-functional development teams.
- Average product development lead times have dropped from 31 months to under 24 months. Despite this, the percentage of new product development efforts deemed successful by the firms has held steady, at around 60%.

© Cherkas | Dreamstime.com

© Valleysnow | Dreamstime.com

Honda is a leader in the design and manufacture of gas-powered engines. These strengths have allowed the company to enter a wide range of markets, including automobiles, motorcycles, jetskis, and portable generators.

[6] L. Ingrassia, "Taming the Monster: How Big Companies Can Change: Keeping Sharp: Gillette Holds Its Edge by Endlessly Searching for a Better Shave," *Wall Street Journal*, December 10, 1992.

[7] A. Griffin, "PDMA Research on New Product Development Practices: Updating Trends and Benchmarking Best Practices," *Journal of Product Innovation Management* 14 (1997): 429–458.

Operations and Supply Chain Perspectives on Design

If someone were to ask you, as a consumer, what the important dimensions of product design are, you might mention such aspects as functionality, aesthetics, ease of use, and cost. Operations and supply chain managers also have an interest in product design because ultimately these managers will be responsible for providing the products or services on a day-to-day basis. To understand the operations and supply chain perspective, think about a new electronic device. It is one thing for a team of highly trained engineers to build a working prototype in a lab. It's quite another thing to make millions of devices each year, using skilled and semiskilled labor, coordinate the flow of parts coming from all over the world, and ship the devices so that they arrive on time, undamaged, and at the lowest possible cost. Yet, this is exactly what the operations and supply chain managers at companies such as Apple are doing.

The interest of operations and supply chain management in *service* design is even greater. This is because the service design is often the operations process itself. To take an example from physical distribution, when a transportation firm agrees to provide global transportation services to a large customer, it has to make decisions regarding the number of trucks, ships, or airplanes required; the size and location of any warehousing facilities; and the information systems and personnel needed to support the new service.

With this in mind, the operations and supply chain perspective on product design usually focuses on six dimensions:

1. Repeatability,
2. Testability,
3. Serviceability,
4. Product volumes,
5. Product costs, and
6. Match between the design and existing capabilities.

REPEATABILITY, TESTABILITY, AND SERVICEABILITY

Repeatability, testability, and serviceability are dimensions of product design that affect the ability of operations to deliver the product in the first place and to provide ongoing support afterward. *Repeatability* deals with the question, Are we capable of making the product over and over again, in the volumes needed? This is addressed through robust design. The PDMA describes **robust design** as "the design of products to be less sensitive to variations, including manufacturing variation and misuse, increasing the probability that they will perform as intended."[8] Product designs that are robust are better able to meet tolerance limits, making it easier for the operations and supply chain functions to provide good products on an ongoing basis.

Robust design
According to the PDMA, "the design of products to be less sensitive to variations, including manufacturing variation and misuse, increasing the probability that they will perform as intended."

Testability refers to the ease with which critical components or functions can be tested during production. Suppose for a moment that your company manufactures expensive electronics equipment. The manufacturing process consists of a series of steps, each of which adds parts, costs, and value to the product. If a $5 circuit board has gone bad, you want to find this out before you assemble it with some other component or put together the final product.

Testability
The ease with which critical components or functions can be tested during production.

Serviceability is similar to testability. In this case, serviceability refers to the ease with which parts can be replaced, serviced, or evaluated. Many modern automobiles require that the engine be unbolted from the car frame and tilted forward before the spark plugs can be changed—hardly a plus for shade-tree mechanics! On the other hand, all new cars have computer diagnostics systems that allow mechanics to quickly troubleshoot problems.

Serviceability
The ease with which parts can be replaced, serviced, or evaluated.

Serviceability is of particular interest to organizations that are responsible for supporting products in the field. When products are easy to service, costs can be contained, and service times become more predictable, resulting in higher productivity and greater customer satisfaction.

---

[8]Product Development and Management Association, *The PDMA Glossary for New Product Development*, **http://www.pdma.org/npd_glossary.cfm**.

PRODUCT VOLUMES

Once a company decides to go forward with a new product or service, it becomes the job of operations and supply chain managers to make sure that the company can handle the resulting volumes. This responsibility might mean expanding the firm's own operations by building new facilities, hiring additional workers, and buying new equipment. It might also require joint planning with key suppliers.

The expected volume levels for a product or service also affect the *types* of equipment, people, or facilities needed. Highly automated processes that are too expensive and inflexible for low-volume custom products can be very cost-effective when millions of units will be made.

PRODUCT COSTS

A study conducted by Computer-Aided Manufacturing International (CAM–I) concluded that 80% of the cost for a typical product is "locked in" at the design stage. In other words, any effort to "tweak" costs later on will be limited by decisions that were made early in a product's life. Given the importance of costs in operations and supply chain activities, it is not surprising that operations and supply chain managers have a vested interest in addressing cost before the product design has been finalized.

For our purposes, we can think of products and services as having obvious and hidden costs. Obvious costs include such things as the materials required, the labor hours needed, and even the equipment costs needed to provide a particular service or product. These costs are usually the easiest ones to see and manage (i.e., we can track material usage, machine time, and the amount of direct labor that goes into our products or services).

Hidden costs are not as easy to track, but can have a major impact nonetheless. Hidden costs are typically associated with the overhead and support activities driven by some aspect of design. There are numerous drivers of hidden costs, but we will talk about three to make the point:

1. The number of parts in a product,
2. Engineering changes, and
3. Transportation costs.

Think about the activities that are driven by the number of parts used in a product, such as a washing machine. Engineering specifications must be developed for each part. The manufacturer must identify a supplier for each part and then place and track orders. Furthermore, the manufacturer must monitor the inventory levels of each part in its manufacturing plants and service support centers. Even if the manufacturer stops selling the washing machine after five years, it must continue to stock each part for years to come. All these activities represent hidden costs driven by the number of parts. Clearly, the manufacturer has an incentive to reduce the number of parts in a washing machine and to share parts across as many products as possible.

Engineering change
A revision to a drawing or design released by engineering to modify or correct a part.

There are also hidden costs associated with engineering changes to a product. An **engineering change** is a revision to a drawing or design released by engineering to modify or correct a part.[9] Returning to our washing machine example, suppose the manufacturer decides to make improvements to a part once the washing machine has been on the market for a few years. Suppliers, plants, and service support centers have to be notified of the change, and inventories have to be switched over from the old part to the new one. Yet the manufacturer will still have to keep track of information on both parts for years to come. Clearly, the manufacturer has a real financial incentive to design the part right the first time.

Products can also be designed to minimize transportation costs. Oddly shaped or fragile products can quickly drive up transportation costs. In contrast, products that can be shipped in standardized containers to take advantage of lower transportation rates can hold down the costs of distribution. NordicTrack engineers designed the Walk-Fit treadmill so that the electronics could be shipped to the customer separately from the treadmill. This was important because these components were made in different facilities. By separating the electronics from the treadmill,

[9]J. H. Blackstone, ed., *APICS Dictionary*, 13th ed. (Chicago, IL: APICS, 2010).

engineers allowed the bulky treadmill to be shipped at a lower per-pound rate. If the relatively fragile electronics had been included with the bulkier treadmill, the entire product would have had to be shipped at a much higher rate.

MATCH WITH EXISTING CAPABILITIES

Finally, operations and supply chain managers are always concerned with how well new products or services match up with existing products or capabilities. A new product or service that allows a manufacturer to use existing parts and manufacturing facilities is usually easier to support than one that requires new ones. Similarly, services that exploit existing capabilities are especially attractive. An excellent example is the online tracking service that FedEx provides to its customers. In fact, this service was built on an existing capability supported by FedEx's internal tracking software.

SUPPLY CHAIN *Connection* How Hard is it to Make a Cookie?

Nabisco Biscuit Co. makes cake and snack products that have become American classics, like Oreo's, Chips Ahoy, and Barnum's Animal Crackers. Another Nabisco classic is the story of the debut of its SnackWell's line of cookies and cakes. More than a year after launching the fat-free chocolate-and-marshmallow Devil's Food Cookie Cake in the early 1990s, Nabisco still couldn't meet consumer demand, setting off rumors of store rationing and fights among frenzied customers in search of a "healthy" snack. How hard could it be to make a cookie?

It turns out that it can be very hard indeed. Nabisco's senior director of operations services at the time claimed "the Devil's Food Cookie Cake is the hardest one we make." Because the cookie's center, unlike simpler confections, is covered with marshmallow all around and then drenched in chocolate icing, it would get stuck to a conventional conveyor belt. The solution was a "pin trolley system," invented in the 1920s, which sets each cookie-cake center on a tiny upright pin mounted on a trolley. A chain pulls the trolley along, taking 4 hours to cover a mile-long track winding through the bakery while the centers are coated with marshmallow and chocolate and allowed to air-dry in between. (Because the cookie is fat-free, the company can't chill it to shorten the drying time.) In contrast, it takes only half an hour to make a Chips Ahoy cookie start to finish.

On top of having a painfully slow manufacturing process for its product, for a time Nabisco had pin-trolley equipment available in only one bakery in South Dakota. The initial shortage was so great that when it was first introduced, the cookie was sold only in the Northeast United States.

Nabisco has long since ramped up its production of the Devil's Food Cookie Cake, and over the years the product has had to prove itself against up-and-coming competitors in the low-calorie snack-food market. Nabisco's current marketing plans call for a renewed advertising campaign for the SnackWell brand, and it's a safe bet there will be plenty of Devil's Food Cookie Cakes on the shelves this time around.

Sources: Based on the company website, www.nabiscoworld.com, accessed September 26, 2011; Andrew Adam Newman, "Snackwell's Nudges Up the Portion Pack," *The New York Times*, April 20, 2011, http://www.nytimes.com/2011/04/21/business/media/21adco.html; K. Deveny, "Man Walked on the Moon but Man Can't Make Enough Devil's Food Cookie Cakes," *Wall Street Journal*, September 28, 1993.

It may *seem* obvious that companies should consider such factors as production volumes and existing capabilities when designing new products or services. But what happens if they don't? Well, Nabisco ran into exactly this problem in 1993, when it introduced SnackWell's Devil's Food Cookie Cakes. The Supply Chain Connections box reveals a classic example of what can happen when the operations and supply chain perspective is not adequately considered when designing a new product.

The Development Process

In the previous section, we talked about some product design dimensions of particular interest to operations and supply chain managers. But there are other perspectives to consider, including those of the final customer, marketing, engineering, and finance, to list just a few. How do firms go about designing products and services that incorporate all these perspectives? And how do they move from the idea stage to the actual launch of a new product or service? This section describes a model of the product development process and discusses the organizational roles played by different functional areas and supply chain partners.

A MODEL OF THE DEVELOPMENT PROCESS

All of us have experienced products or services that for some reason stood out from the competition—a hand tool that was easier to use or more powerful than previous models, an airline seat that was more comfortable, or an online financial service that allowed us to check our portfolios and initiate trades 24 hours a day.

TABLE 4.1
Phases of Product and Service Development

Functional Activities	Concept Development	Planning	Design and Development	Commercial Preparation	Launch
Engineering	Propose new technologies; develop product ideas	Identify *general* performance characteristics for the product or service; identify underlying technologies	Develop *detailed* product specifications; build and test prototypes	Resolve remaining technical \problems	Evaluate field experience with product or service
Marketing	Provide market-based input; propose and investigate product or service concepts	Define target customers' needs; estimate sales and margins; include customers in development effort	Conduct customer tests; evaluate prototypes; plan marketing rollout	Train sales force; prepare sales procedures; select distribution channels	Fill downstream supply chain; sell and promote
Operations and supply chain functions	Scan suppliers for promising technologies/ capabilities	Develop initial cost estimates; identify key supply chain partners	Develop *detailed* process maps of the operations and supply chain flows; test new processes	Build pilot units using new operations; train personnel; verify that supply chain flows work as expected	Ramp up volumes; meet targets for quality, cost, and other performance goals

Based on S. Wheelwright and K. Clark, *Revolutionizing Product Development* (New York: Free Press, 1992).

Good design does not happen by accident. Rather, it requires a coordinated effort supported by many individuals, both within and outside a firm. Table 4.1 offers one view of the development process. The table divides the development process into five phases, paying particular attention to the roles played by the operations and supply chain functions, as well as by marketing and engineering.

Concept development phase
The first phase of a product development effort. Here a company identifies ideas for new or revised products and services.

In the **concept development phase**, a company identifies ideas for new or revised products and services. As Table 4.1 suggests, these ideas can come from a variety of sources, not just from customers. For example, engineering might identify a new material that can reduce the weight and cost of a product, even before marketing or the customer knows about it. The operations and supply chain functions have a role to play here as well: Purchasing personnel might look at potential suppliers to see if they have any promising new technologies or capabilities that could be turned into a new product or service.

Planning phase
The second phase of a product development effort. Here the company begins to address the feasibility of a product or service.

If a concept is approved, it will pass on to the **planning phase**, where the company begins to address the feasibility of a product or service. Customers are often brought in at this stage to evaluate ideas. Engineering might begin to identify the general performance characteristics of the product or service and the process technologies needed to produce it. Marketing will start to estimate sales volumes and expected profit margins. Operations and supply chain personnel might start identifying the key supply chain partners to be involved. Many ideas that look good in the concept development phase fail to pass the hurdles set at the planning phase. A product may be too costly to make, may not generate enough revenues, or may simply be impossible to produce in the volumes needed to support the market.

Design and development phase
The third phase of a product development effort. Here the company starts to invest heavily in the development effort and builds and evaluates prototypes.

Ideas that do clear the hurdles go on to the **design and development phase**, during which the company starts to invest heavily in the development effort. In this phase, the company builds and evaluates prototypes of the product or service. Product prototypes can range from simple Styrofoam mock-ups to fully functional units. Service prototypes can range from written descriptions to field tests using actual customers. At the same time, operations and physical distribution begin to develop detailed process maps of the physical, information, and monetary flows that will need to take place in order to provide the product or service on a regular basis (Chapter 3). They may even start to develop quality levels for key process steps. The design and development phase is complete when the company approves the final design for the product and related processes.

The **commercial preparation phase** is characterized by activities associated with the introduction of a new product or service. At this stage, firms start to invest heavily in the operations and supply chain resources needed to support the new product or service. This may mean new facilities, warehouses, personnel, and even information systems to handle production requirements. Obviously, this phase will go more smoothly if the new product or service can build on existing operations and supply chain systems. If new supply chain partners are required or if new technologies are needed, commercial preparation and launch can be much more difficult and expensive.

Commercial preparation phase
The fourth phase of a product development effort. At this stage, firms start to invest heavily in the operations and supply chain resources needed to support the new product or service.

The last phase is the **launch phase**. For physical products, this usually means "filling up" the supply chain with products. For services, it can mean making the service broadly available to the target marketplace, as in the case of cell phone service. In either case, operations and supply chain managers must closely monitor performance results to make sure that quality, cost, and delivery targets are being met and must take corrective action when necessary.

Launch phase
The final phase of a product development effort. For physical products, this usually means "filling up" the supply chain with products. For services, it can mean making the service broadly available to the target marketplace.

SEQUENTIAL DEVELOPMENT VERSUS CONCURRENT ENGINEERING

The development model in Table 4.1 outlines a sequential development process. A **sequential development process** is one in which a product or service idea must clear specific hurdles before it can go on to the next development phase. The result is that while many ideas may be considered at the relatively inexpensive concept development phase, few make it to the commercial development and launch phases, where significant resources have to be invested. Steven Wheelright and Kim Clark of the Harvard Business School describe this process as the *development funnel.*

Sequential development process
A process in which a product or service idea must clear specific hurdles before it can go on to the next development phase.

An alternative to sequential development is concurrent engineering. As the name implies, **concurrent engineering** allows activities in different development stages to overlap with one another, thereby shortening the total development time. For example, engineering may begin to build and test prototypes (design and development phase) even before the general product characteristics have been finalized (planning phase). In contrast to a sequential development process, in which there is a clear handoff from one stage to the next, concurrent engineering requires constant communication between participants at various stages in the development effort. Figure 4.1 illustrates the idea.

Concurrent engineering
An alternative to sequential development in which activities in different development stages are allowed to overlap with one another, thereby shortening the total development time.

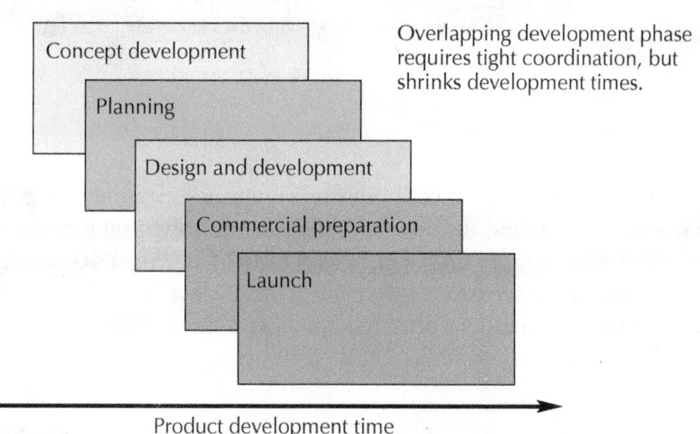

FIGURE 4.1
Concurrent Engineering

Concurrent engineering helps reduce development times by forcing development teams to agree on critical product and process characteristics *early* in the development process, usually in the concept through design and development phases. These broad characteristics—costs, size, materials, markets to be served, and so on—provide clear guidance and boundaries for later activities. Returning to our engineering example, the *only way* engineers can start to build prototypes before the product characteristics are finalized is if there is *general* agreement regarding the characteristics of the new product (size, basic features, etc.). When this isn't the case, firms will need to follow a more sequential approach.

Organizational Roles in Product and Service Development

Product or service development is almost always a cross-functional effort. Table 4.1 shows how various parties contribute to the development effort in different ways. How well the different functions coordinate their efforts goes a long way toward determining the success of any development effort. Marketing, for example, might need to work with engineering to know what product features are technologically feasible. Purchasing then might help identify outside sources for needed inputs or services. Let's take a moment to discuss how different functions contribute to the development effort.

ENGINEERING

Engineering provides the expertise needed to resolve many of the technological issues associated with a firm's products or services. Some of these issues center on the actual design of a product or service. A product engineer might be asked to design a lightweight yet durable outer casing for a new cell phone. Or a team of civil and electrical engineers might be asked to design a network of transmission towers for the relay of cell phone signals.

Other issues center on operational and supply chain considerations. Industrial engineers, for instance, might develop specifications for the manufacturing equipment needed to make the cell phone casings or transmission towers. Packaging engineers might be asked to develop shipping containers that strike a balance between cost and protection against damage.

MARKETING

In most firms, marketing has primary responsibility for understanding what goes on in the marketplace and applying that knowledge to the development process. Who buys our company's products or services, and how much will they pay? Who are our company's competitors, and how do their products and services stack up against ours? How large is the market for a particular product or service? Marketing professionals use a variety of research techniques to answer such questions, including surveys, focus groups, and detailed market studies. When it comes to really understanding what customers want, many companies would be lost without marketing's input.

But marketing's role goes beyond providing information in the early phases of the development process. Marketing also has to select distribution channels, train sales personnel, and develop selling and promotional strategies.

ACCOUNTING

Accounting plays the role of "scorekeeper" in many companies. Not only do accountants prepare reports for the government and outside investors, they are also responsible for developing the cost and performance information many companies need to make intelligent business decisions. How much will a new product or service cost? How many hours of labor or machine time will be needed? The answers to these types of questions often require input from the firm's accountants.

FINANCE

The role of finance in product and service development is twofold. First, finance establishes the criteria used to judge the financial impact of a development effort. How much time will pass before our company recoups its investment in a product or service? What is the expected rate of

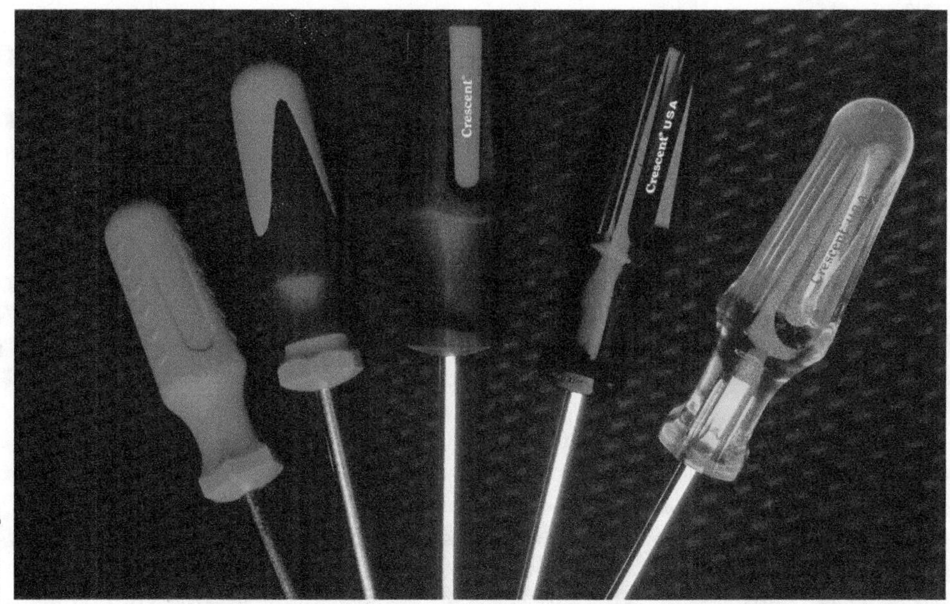

Forma Design

Forma Designs of Raleigh, North Carolina, improved the grips of screwdrivers. Even small changes such as this can make a big difference in the marketplace.

return? How risky is the project? Once a company decides to proceed with the development of a product or service, it is the responsibility of finance to determine exactly how the company will acquire the needed capital.

DESIGNERS

Designers can come from a variety of educational backgrounds—from engineering, design, and business schools, to name a few. Their role is one of the least understood aspects of the development process. One myth is that designers only do *product* design. But they do much more than that. They create identities for companies (logos, brochures, etc.), environments (such as buildings, interiors, and exhibits), and even service experiences. To make cell phone towers blend in with the environment, for example, designers have camouflaged the giant poles as trees or added decorative latticework.

A second myth is that designers simply make something "look good." This suggests that design is all form and no content. Yet consider an apparently simple handheld tape measure redesigned by Forma Design of Raleigh, North Carolina. As part of the redesign effort, Forma changed the tape measure so that the thumb presses against the index finger to work the tape measure's locking mechanism. Before that, users had to apply force between the thumb and *little* finger. If you try pushing your thumb against your little finger and then your index finger, you can see for yourself that the new design results in considerably less hand fatigue. Designers also work with schedules and constraints, just like other professionals. For example, in the redesign of the tape measure, Forma was not allowed to change any of the internal mechanisms.

PURCHASING

Purchasing deserves special mention because it plays several important roles in product development. As the main contact with suppliers, purchasing is in a unique position to identify the best suppliers and sign them up early in the development process. Many purchasing departments even have databases of preapproved suppliers. The process of preapproving suppliers for specific commodities or parts is known as **presourcing**.

Presourcing
The process of preapproving suppliers for specific commodities or parts.

Another role purchasing plays is that of a consultant with special knowledge of material supply markets. Purchasing personnel might recommend substitutes for high-cost or volatile materials or standard items instead of more expensive custom-made parts. Finally, purchasing plays the role of monitor, tracking forecasts of the prices and long-term supply of key materials or monitoring technological innovations that might affect purchasing decisions.

SUPPLIERS

Suppliers can bring a fresh perspective to the table, thereby helping organizations see opportunities for improvement they might otherwise miss. Teaming up with suppliers can also help organizations divide up the development effort, thereby saving time and reducing financial risks. Boeing, for instance, uses outside suppliers to develop many of the key components and subassemblies for its jets. If Boeing tried to develop a jet on its own, the project would cost considerably more money and take much longer.

Bringing suppliers into the development effort goes beyond just sharing information with them. Important suppliers should be included early in the development of a new product, perhaps even as part of the project team. The benefits of such early inclusion include gaining a supplier's insight into the development process, allowing comparisons of proposed production requirements with a supplier's existing capabilities, and allowing a supplier to begin preproduction work early.

Gray box design
A situation in which a supplier works with a customer to jointly design the product.

Black box design
A situation in which suppliers are provided with general requirements and are asked to fill in the technical specifications.

The degree of supplier participation can also vary. At one extreme, the supplier is given blueprints and told to produce to the specifications. In a hybrid arrangement, called **gray box design**, the supplier works with the customer to jointly design the product. At the highest level of supplier participation, known as **black box design**, suppliers are provided with general requirements and are asked to fill in the technical specifications.

Black box design is best when the supplier is the acknowledged "expert." For example, an automotive manufacturer may tell a key supplier that it wants an electric window motor that costs under $15, pulls no more than 5 amps, fits within a certain space, and weighs less than 2 pounds. Given these broad specifications, the supplier is free to develop the best motor that meets the automotive manufacturer's needs.

WHO LEADS?

Ultimately, someone or some group has to have primary responsibility for making sure the product development process is a success. But who? The answer depends largely on the nature of the development effort and the industrial setting. In high-tech firms, scientists and engineers typically take the lead. Their scientific and technological expertise is essential to developing safe, effective products that can be made in the volumes required. In contrast, at a toy producer, the technical questions usually aren't nearly as interesting as the consumers and markets themselves: What toys will be "hot" next December? How many will be sold? Marketing is, therefore, likely to have primary responsibility for managing the development effort.

Approaches to Improving Product and Service Designs

Coordinating a product development effort while ensuring that all dimensions of performance are adequately considered is not an easy task. As a result, organizations have developed useful approaches to help accomplish these goals. The purpose of this section is to introduce you to some of the most common approaches.

DMADV (DEFINE–MEASURE–ANALYZE–DESIGN–VERIFY)

DMAV (Define-Measure-Analyze-Design-Verify)
A Six Sigma process that outlines the steps needed to create *completely new* business processes or products

Chapter 3 introduced the Six Sigma methodology and the DMAIC (Define–Measure–Analyze–Improve–Control) approach to improving *existing* business processes. The Six Sigma methodology also includes a process called **DMADV (Define–Measure–Analyze–Design–Verify)**, which outlines the steps needed to create *completely new* business processes or products. As with DMAIC, the DMADV process places a premium on rigorous data analysis, and depends on teams of black belts, green belts, and champions to carry it out. The five steps of DMADV are:

Step 1. *Define* the project goals and customer deliverables. Since the focus is on a *new* process or product, the Six Sigma team must properly scope the project to ensure that the effort is carried out in a timely and efficient manner. What products or services do we want to provide and to whom? How will we know when we have completed the project successfully?

Step 2. ***Measure* and determine customer needs and specifications.** The second step requires the team to develop a clear picture of what the targeted customers want in terms of quality, delivery, cost or other measures of interest. Market research techniques as well as quality function deployment (QFD), which we describe shortly, are employed here.

Step 3. ***Analyze* the product or process options to meet the customer needs.** In this step, the Six Sigma team evaluates how the various options available stack up against the customers' requirements.

Step 4. ***Design* the product or process.** Here, the hard work of designing the product or process, as outlined in the "Design and Development" column of Table 4.1, takes place.

Step 5. ***Verify* the new product or process.** Finally, the team must verify the results. Does the product or process perform as intended? Does it meet the needs of the targeted customers?

QUALITY FUNCTION DEPLOYMENT (QFD)

One of the greatest challenges firms face when designing new products or services is moving from vague notions of what the customer wants to specific engineering or operational requirements. **Quality function deployment (QFD)** is one tool that has been developed to formalize this process. First introduced in Japan in the early 1970s, QFD became very popular in the late 1980s and continues to be used by companies.[10]

Quality Function Deployment (QFD)
A graphical tool used to help organizations move from vague notions of what customers want to specific engineering and operational requirements. Also called the "house of quality."

Figure 4.2 shows a simplified example of a QFD matrix for a cell phone. This matrix is sometimes called the "house of quality," due to its obvious resemblance. The left side of the matrix lists general customer requirements and their relative importance (1–10) to the target customers. Note that these requirements are stated in terms of how the product performs, not specific characteristics. Along the top is a list of specific product characteristics. The main body of the matrix shows how each of the product characteristics does or does not support the customer requirements. As you can see, there are some potential conflicts. For example, the off-the-shelf electronics characteristic is consistent with an inexpensive unit but conflicts with customers' desires for more functionality. Ultimately, a trade-off may need to be made. Finally, the "roof" of the matrix shows synergies between some of the features. Obviously, off-the-shelf electronics conflicts with customized ones. On the other hand, a molded plastic casing and a thicker casing are two product characteristics that can easily be combined.

Customer requirements	Importance	Thicker casing	Molded plastic casing	Off-the-shelf electronics	Custom electronics
Inexpensive	7	✗	✓	✓	
Good looking	4				
Rugged	5	✓			
Unique functions	3			✗	✓

FIGURE 4.2
QFD Matrix for a Cell Phone

Synergies (roof): Thicker casing / Molded plastic casing ✓; Off-the-shelf electronics / Custom electronics ✗
Product characteristics

[10]J. Hauser and D. Clausing, "The House of Quality," *Harvard Business Review*, 66, no. 3 (May–June 1988): 63–73.

FIGURE 4.3
Using QFD Matrices to Move from Customer Requirements to Process Specifications

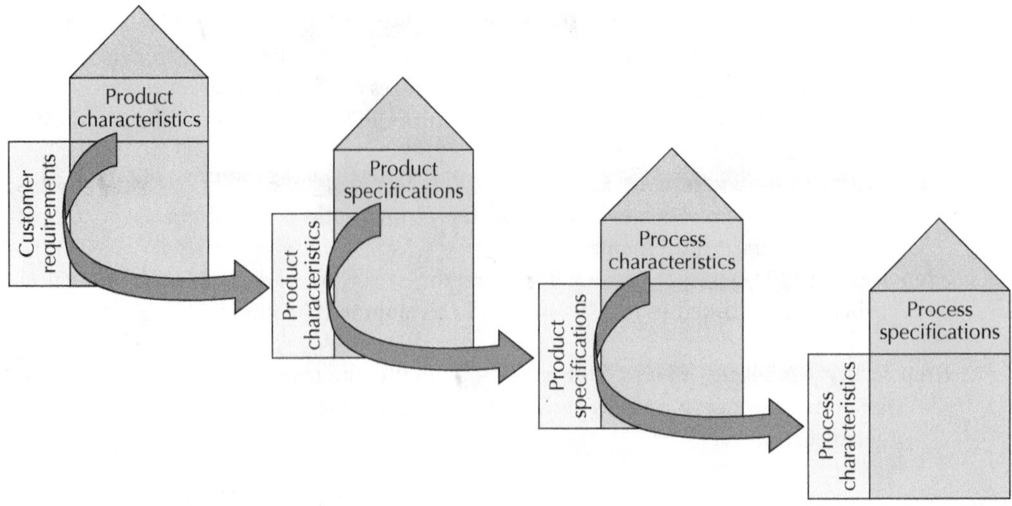

The matrix in Figure 4.3 moves the organization from customer requirements to broad product characteristics. But the process doesn't end here. The ultimate goal is to identify the specific manufacturing and service process steps needed to meet the customers' requirements. As a result, an organization may develop a series of QFD matrices that make the following logical linkages:

First matrix:	Customer requirements → Product characteristics
Second matrix:	Product characteristics → Product specifications
Third matrix:	Product specifications → Process characteristics
Fourth matrix:	Process characteristics → Process specifications

Figure 4.3 illustrates this idea.

In Figure 4.2, we identified "Rugged" as an important customer requirement and "Thicker Casing" as one product characteristic that would support this need. To move to *product specifications*, we need to translate "Thicker Casing" into more detailed information regarding the materials needed and the actual thickness value. Next, we have to describe the *process characteristics* needed to meet these product specifications regularly. This might include information on tolerance limits and acceptable process variability. Finally, we need to identify the specific manufacturing resources needed (e.g., "an injection molding device with computer controls") to support the process characteristics.

COMPUTER-AIDED DESIGN (CAD) AND COMPUTER-AIDED DESIGN/COMPUTER-AIDED MANUFACTURING (CAD/CAM)

Computer-aided design (CAD) system
An information system that allows engineers to develop, modify, share, and even test designs in a virtual world. CAD systems help organizations avoid the time and expense of paper-based drawings and physical prototypes.

Computer-aided design/computer-aided manufactoring (CAD/CAM) system
An extension of CAD. Here, CAD-based designs are translated into machine instructions, which are then fed automatically into computer-controlled manufacturing equipment.

Advancements in information systems have also transformed the development process. In particular, **computer-aided design (CAD) systems** allow engineers to develop, modify, share, and even test designs in a virtual world. By doing so, CAD systems help organizations avoid the time and expense of paper-based drawings and physical prototypes.

Computer-aided design/computer-aided manufacturing (CAD/CAM) systems take the process a step further. Here CAD-based designs are translated into machine instructions, which are then fed automatically into computer-controlled manufacturing equipment. Such systems allow for rapid prototyping and reduce the time and costs associated with producing one-of-a-kind pieces.

THE "DESIGN FOR … " APPROACHES

At a minimum, products and services must be designed to meet the needs of customers. But beyond this, organizations also want products and services to be easy to make, easy to maintain, virtually defect free (to reduce their costs as well as improve customer satisfaction), and environmentally sound. This has led to what can be called the "design for … " approaches to product and service design. Four critical approaches are design for manufacturability (DFM), design for maintainability (DFMt), Design for Six Sigma (DFSS) and design for the environment (DFE).

Design for manufacturability (DFM) is "the systematic consideration of manufacturing issues in the design and development process, facilitating the fabrication of the product's components and their assembly into the overall product."[11] In general, the goal of DFM is to design a product that can be produced at consistently high quality levels, at the lowest cost, and, when possible, with existing processes.

Two ways in which organizations accomplish DFM are parts standardization and modularity. **Parts standardization** refers to the planned elimination of superficial, accidental, and deliberate differences between similar parts in the interest of reducing part and supplier proliferation. By standardizing and sharing parts across various products, companies can reduce the time and cost of developing new products and reduce the cost of the final product.

Modular architecture is another way in which organizations implement DFM. A **modular architecture** is a "product architecture in which each functional element maps into its own physical chunk. Different chunks perform different f unctions; the interactions between the chunks are minimal, and they are generally well defined."[12] To illustrate, consider the typical IBM-compatible PC. Suppose a PC retailer sells PCs that are assembled from the following module options:

- Four different system units,
- Two different graphics cards,
- Five different displays, and
- Three different printers.

The visual functionality of the PC is contained within the graphics cards and displays, while the print functionality is contained within the printer. The remainder of the PC's functionality is within the system unit itself. What makes this product truly "modular" is the fact that the PC retailer can easily swap modules to make a different final configuration, as PCs use standard interfaces for plugging in displays, printers, and the like. In fact, the 14 modules above can theoretically be configured into 4 × 2 × 5 × 3 = 120 different combinations.

In contrast to DFM, **design for maintainability (DFMt)** is "the systematic consideration of maintainability issues over a product's projected life cycle in the design and development process."[13] Here the focus is on how easy it is to maintain and service a product after it has reached the customer. DFMt directly supports an organization's efforts to improve the serviceability of its products and services.

Design for Six Sigma (DFSS), as the name implies, seeks to ensure that the organization is capable of providing products or services that meet Six Sigma quality levels—in general, no more than 3.4 defects per million opportunities. DFSS is often mentioned in conjunction with DMADV, with DMADV serving as the process for achieving DFSS.

Finally, **design for the environment (DFE)** addresses "environmental, safety, and health issues over the product's projected life cycle in the design and development process."[14] DFE is becoming increasingly important for companies seeking to respond to both market pressures and regulatory requirements. To illustrate how companies are implementing DFE, consider some examples recently reported by Apple:[15]

- Between 2007 and 2011, Apple reduced the packaging for the iPhone by 42%.
- Even though it has a much larger screen than its 15-inch predecessor, the new 21.5-inch iMac is produced using 50% less material.
- Computer displays are now manufactured with mercury-free LED backlighting and arsenic-free glass.

Design for manufacturability (DFM)
The systematic consideration of manufacturing issues in the design and development process, facilitating the fabrication of the product's components and their assembly into the overall product.

Parts standardization
The planned elimination of superficial, accidental, and deliberate differences between similar parts in the interest of reducing part and supplier proliferation.

Modular architecture
A product architecture in which each functional element maps into its own physical chunk. Different chunks perform different functions; the interactions between the chunks are minimal, and they are generally well defined.

Design for maintainability (DFMt)
The systematic consideration of maintainability issues over a product's projected life cycle in the design and development process.

Design for Six Sigma (DFSS)
An approach to product and process design which seeks to ensure that the organization is capable of providing products or services that meet Six Sigma quality levels—in general, no more than 3.4 defects per million opportunities.

Design for the environment (DFE)
An approach to new product design that addresses environmental, safety, and health issues over the product's projected life cycle in the design and development process.

---

[11] Product Development and Management Association, *The PDMA Glossary for New Product Development*, **http://www.pdma.org/npd_glossary.cfm**.

[12] ibid.

[13] ibid.

[14] ibid.

[15] Apple, *The story behind Apple's environmental footprint*, **http://www.apple.com/environment/**.

TARGET COSTING AND VALUE ANALYSIS

Target costing (or design to cost)
The process of designing a product to meet a specific cost objective. Target costing involves setting the planned selling price and subtracting the desired profit, as well as marketing and distribution costs, thus leaving the required target cost. Also known as *design to cost.*

Value analysis (VA)
A process that involves examining all elements of a component, an assembly, an end product, or a service to make sure it fulfills its intended function at the lowest total cost.

Cost is such an important aspect of product and service design that organizations have developed approaches specifically focused on this dimension. In this section, we talk about two of them: target costing and value analysis. In general, target costing is done during the initial design effort, while value analysis is applied to both new and existing products and services. **Target costing**, also called **design to cost**, is the process of designing a product to meet a specific cost objective. Target costing involves setting the planned selling price and subtracting the desired profit, as well as marketing and distribution costs, thus leaving the required target cost.

Value analysis (VA) is a process that involves examining all elements of a component, an assembly, an end product, or a service to make sure it fulfills its intended function at the lowest total cost. The primary objective of value analysis is to increase the value of an item or a service at the lowest cost without sacrificing quality. In equation form, value is the relationship between the function of a product or service and its cost:

$$\text{Value} = \text{function}/\text{cost} \tag{4-1}$$

There are many variations of function and cost that will increase the value of a product or service. The most obvious ways to increase value include increasing the functionality or use of a product or service while holding cost constant, reducing cost while not reducing functionality, and increasing functionality more than cost (e.g., offering a five-year warranty versus a two-year warranty with no price increase raises the value of a product to the customer).

A common approach for implementing value analysis is to create a VA team composed of professionals with knowledge about a product or service. Many functional groups can contribute to the value analysis team, including engineering, marketing, purchasing, production, and key suppliers. Value analysis teams ask a number of questions to determine if opportunities exist for item, product, or service improvement. Some typical questions include the following:

1. Is the cost of the final product proportionate to its usefulness?
2. Does the product need all its features or internal parts?
3. Is there a better production method to produce the item or product?
4. Can a lower-cost standard part replace a customized part?
5. Are we using the proper tooling, considering the quantities required?
6. Will another dependable supplier provide material, components, or subassemblies for less?
7. Are there equally effective but lower-cost materials available?
8. Are packaging cost reductions possible?
9. Is the item properly classified for shipping purposes to receive the lowest transportation rates?
10. Are design or quality specifications too tight, given customer requirements?
11. If we are making an item now, can we buy it for less (and vice versa)?

CHAPTER SUMMARY

Product and service development is critical to the success of many firms. Points to take away from this chapter include the following:

- Having a well-managed development process, whether it is a sequential process or one based on concurrent engineering, is crucial.
- It is important to consider operations and supply chain perspectives when developing new products and services, including repeatability, testability, and serviceability of the design; volumes; costs; and the match with a company's existing capabilities.

As the last section of this chapter made clear, organizations have developed various tools and techniques for ensuring that the development process not only goes smoothly but also results in "good" designs.

Key Terms

Discussion Questions

1. In this chapter, we described several approaches to product design, including parts standardization and modularity. How do these two approaches relate to the dimensions of product design described earlier in the chapter?
2. We talked about concurrent engineering as an alternative to sequential development. What are the advantages of concurrent engineering? Under what circumstances might sequential development be preferable?
3. Consider some of the dimensions of product design that we listed as important to operations and supply chain managers. Are these dimensions more or less important than whether the product or service meets the customers' needs? Can you think of situations in which there might be conflict between these different perspectives?
4. Consider the phases of product and service development shown in Table 4.1. Why is it important to include customers early in the development process?
5. Which type of product development effort would be better suited to concurrent engineering: a radically new product involving cutting-edge technologies or the latest version of an existing product? Why?
6. What are some of the benefits of including suppliers in the product development process? Can you think of any risks?

Case Studies

Design for Supply Chain Programs

Design for Supply Chain (DfSC) is a systematic method of ensuring the best fit between the design of a product throughout its lifetime and its supply chain members' resources and capabilities. Even something as simple as flattening the tops of soda cans, as beverage makers did in the 1950s, can revolutionize product development, transform transportation and inventory processes, and generate huge cost savings and increased customer satisfaction. Hewlett-Packard (HP) has been in the forefront of adopting DfSC principles, and IBM is another staunch proponent.

IBM developed a short list of DfSC principles that have helped it create products that are both competitive and supply-chain-efficient throughout their life cycles. Briefly stated, these principles are:

1. Integrate products parts and components as much as possible to reduce product assembly time.
2. Use industry-standard parts whenever possible to lower costs and simplify sourcing efforts.
3. Reduce lead times on critical components to avoid paying premium shipping fees on rush orders.
4. Design products for supply-chain friendliness throughout their life cycle, planning for and minimizing the cost and disruption of design and technology changes as products mature.
5. Build supply chains based on the company's strategic plan, not around the idiosyncratic requirements of specific products.
6. Use common components and modular design, thereby reducing product variability.
7. Minimize inventory costs and reduce the risk of obsolescence by building to order from common components and subassemblies, rather than building to stock.
8. Design products to give customers flexibility when ordering while keeping costs in line.

9.Use high quality parts and parts which can be quickly diagnosed to minimize warranty costs and improve after sales service.

HP similarly uses DfSC to consider the impact of its design decisions over product lifetimes, from pre-launch through production to end of life cycle, in all its business units and regions. The DfSC strategy—essentially looking back in order to see ahead—helps improve HP's relationships with suppliers, manufacturers, logistics service firms, retailers, and consumers.

To use DfSC, which it adopted in the early 1990s, HP first asks four questions about its products:

1. What makes the product a good fit for a particular supply chain?
2. Which design decisions produce that result? For example, does the product have unique parts?
3. When and why are design decisions being made, and who is making them?

4. How can the company deliver great products at higher profit margins?

Since adopting DfSC and successfully propagating its use throughout the company, HP has been able to introduce more new products faster and at lower cost. It has increased its revenues and kept customers happy. At the same time, the company has found ways to improve its inventory efficiency without offsetting risks onto its suppliers (which would damage its supply-chain relationships) or reducing the quality of product inputs (which would increase the cost of honoring product warranties as well as damaging customer relationships).

HP's six DfSC techniques are:

1. **Variety control.** Having fewer SKUs allowed the company to reduce inventory 42% and increase product availability in its PC division.
2. **Logistics enhancement.** Making an InkJet printer 45% smaller saved more than $1 per unit in logistics costs.
3. **Commonality and reuse.** While unique parts make products distinctive, they increase inventory costs and, often, time to market.
4. **Postponement.** Designing products to remain generic as long as possible during the production process, until it's known how the end user wants to customize them, saves costs.
5. **Tax and duty reduction.** These costs can be higher or lower based on the country of origin.
6. **Take-back facilitation.** Design and packaging changes can reduce both manufacturing and environmental costs.

HP estimates that DfSC techniques have saved it about $200 million per year.

Questions

1. What is the relationship between design for manufacturability (DFM) and design for supply chain (DfSC)?
2. In the chapter, we discussed parts standardization and modular architecture. How do these two approaches support DfSC?
3. You hear someone say, "DfSC sounds fine in theory, but I think it will have two negative effects. First, it will slow down the product development process because now all the areas that make up supply chain management—procurement, manufacturing, and logistics—will need to be involved. Second, it gives too much power to the supply chain functions. After all, if supply chain managers think something is too difficult to ship or too expensive to make, they may say no." What do you think? Are these legitimate concerns? How should operations managers address them?

Sources: Based on Heather E. Domin, James Wisner, and Matthew Marks, "Design for Supply Chain," *Supply and Demand Chain Executive,* December 2, 2007, **http://www.sdcexec.com/article/10289661/design-for-supply-chain?page=3**; Brian Cargille and Chris Fry, "Design for Supply Chain: Spreading the Word Across HP," *Supply Chain Management Review,* July-August 2006, **http://www.strategicmgmtsolutions.com/DfSC-HP.PDF;** "Hewlett Packard's Design for Supply Chain Program," *Supply Chain Brain,* **www.supplychainbrain.com/content/industry-verticals/high-techelectronics/single-article-page/article/hewlett-packards-design-for-supply-chain-program/**, December 1, 2005.

References

Books and Articles

Blackstone, J. H., ed., *APICS Dictionary*, 13th ed. (Chicago, IL: APICS, 2010).

Deveny, K., "Man Walked on the Moon but Man Can't Make Enough Devil's Food Cookie Cakes," *Wall Street Journal*, September 28, 1993.

Griffin, A., "PDMA Research on New Product Development Practices: Updating Trends and Benchmarking Best Practices," *Journal of Product Innovation Management* 14 (1997): 429–458

Hauser, J., and D. Clausing, "The House of Quality," *Harvard Business Review* 66, no. 3 (May–June 1988): 63–73.

Ingrassia, L., "Taming the Monster: How Big Companies Can Change: Keeping Sharp: Gillette Holds Its Edge by Endlessly Searching for a Better Shave," *Wall Street Journal*, December 10, 1992.

Wheelwright, S., and K. Clark, *Revolutionizing Product Development* (New York: Free Press, 1992).

Internet

Apple, *The story behind Apple's environmental footprint*, **http://www.apple.com/environment/**.

Cargille, B., and C. Fry, "Design for Supply Chain: Spreading the Word Across HP," *Supply Chain Management Review*, July-August 2006, **http://www.strategicmgmtsolutions.com/DfSC-HP.PDF**

Centers for Disease Control and Prevention, *The History of Malaria, an Ancient Disease*, **www.cdc.gov/malaria/about/history/**.

Domin, H. E., J. Wisner, and M. Marks, "Design for Supply Chain," *Supply and Demand Chain Executive*, December 2, 2007, **http://www.sdcexec.com/article/10289661/design-for-supply-chain?page=3**

"Hewlett Packard's Design for Supply Chain Program," *Supply Chain Brain*, **http://www.supplychainbrain.com/content/industry-verticals/high-techelectronics/single-article-page/article/hewlett-packards-design-for-supply-chain-program/**, December 1, 2005.

Newman, A. A., "Snackwell's Nudges Up the Portion Pack," *The New York Times*, April 20, 2011, **http://www.nytimes.com/2011/04/21/business/media/21adco.html**

Product Development and Management Association, *The PDMA Glossary for New Product Development*, **http://www.pdma.org/npd_glossary.cfm**.

Vestergaard Frandsen, *What Is PermaNet 3.0, and How Is It Different from Other Bed Nets*? **www.vestergaard-frandsen.com/permanet/permanet-3/49-what-is-permanet-3-and-how-is-it-different-from-other-bed-nets**.

World Health Organization, *World Malaria Report 2010*, **www.who.int/malaria/world_malaria_report_2010/en/index.html.Nabisco, www.nabiscoworld.com**.

Student Profile

Victor Bernardo, CSCMP
Strategic Supply Manager, Teledyne DALSA
Business Administration Materials Management Program, 1988

As I reflect on my 25 years working in the Supply Chain Management field, I am very thankful to Conestoga College for giving me a solid educational foundation in which to build upon a diverse and rewarding career, one which still continues to open up so many doors for me.

Since graduating from the program in 1988, I have been fortunate to have held job roles of increasing responsibility including positions such as Planner, Buyer, Lean Facilitator, Team Manager and Operations Manager. I have discovered, along with many others who have graduated from the program, that a career in Supply Chain and Operations Management offers so many job opportunities and allows you to expand your horizons. It's an exciting and fast paced career that brings new challenges every day where you can have a global impact.

It's for this reason that I've been actively involved in the Supply Chain & Operations Management Program Advisory Council at Conestoga College for the past 14 years. One of the highlights of being part of this council is the opportunity to go to the local grade schools and high schools to talk with them about this rewarding career path. It's a great way for me to give back to a career which has given me so much more in return.

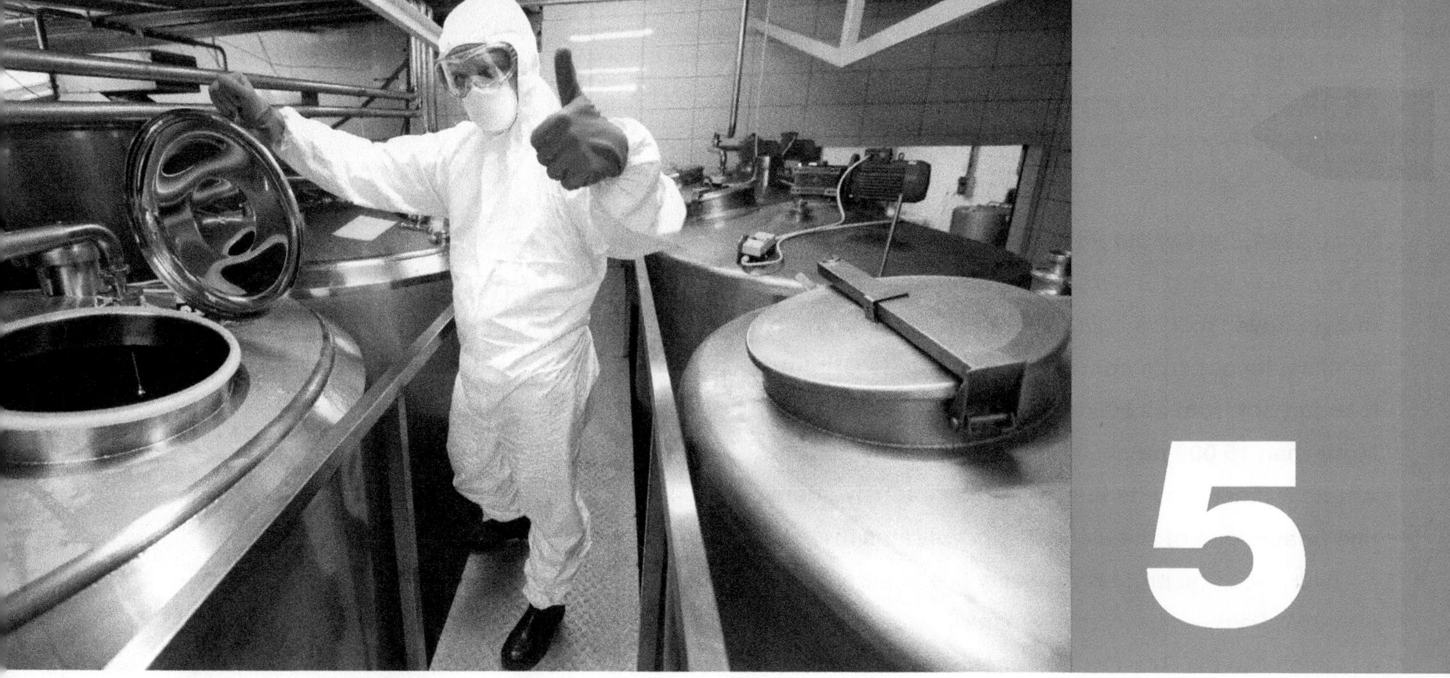

5

Managing Quality

Chapter Outline

10 OM Strategy Decisions

- Design of Goods and Services
- Managing Quality
- Process Strategy
- Location Strategies
- Layout Strategies
- Human Resources
- Supply-Chain Management
- Inventory Management
- Scheduling
- Maintenance

Managing Quality Provides a Competitive Advantage at Arnold Palmer Hospital

Since 1989, the Arnold Palmer Hospital, named after its famous golfing benefactor, has touched the lives of over seven million children and women and their families. Its patients come not only from its Orlando location but from all 50 states and around the world. More than 16 000 babies are delivered every year at Arnold Palmer, and its huge neonatal intensive care unit boasts one of the highest survival rates in the U.S.

Every hospital professes quality health care, but at Arnold Palmer quality is the mantra—practised in a fashion like the Ritz-Carlton practises it in the hotel industry. The hospital typically scores in the top 10% of national benchmark studies in terms of patient satisfaction. And its managers follow patient questionnaire results daily. If anything is amiss, corrective action takes place immediately.

Virtually every quality management technique we present in this chapter is employed at Arnold Palmer Hospital:

- *Continuous improvement:* The hospital constantly seeks new ways to lower infection rates, readmission rates, deaths, costs, and hospital stay times.
- *Employee empowerment:* When employees see a problem, they are trained to take care of it; staff are empowered to give gifts to patients displeased with some aspect of service.
- *Benchmarking:* The hospital belongs to a 2000-member organization that monitors standards in many areas and provides monthly feedback to the hospital.
- *Just-in-time:* Supplies are delivered to Arnold Palmer on a JIT basis. This keeps inventory costs low and keeps quality problems from hiding.
- *Tools such as Pareto charts and flowcharts:* These tools monitor processes and help the staff graphically spot problem areas and suggest ways they can be improved.

From their first day of orientation, employees from janitors to nurses learn that the patient comes first. Staff standing in hallways will never be heard discussing their personal lives or commenting on confidential issues of health care. This culture of quality at Arnold Palmer Hospital makes a hospital visit, often traumatic to children and their parents, a warmer and more comforting experience.

The lobby of the Arnold Palmer Hospital is clearly intended as a bright and cheerful place for children and their families.

This PYXIS inventory station gives nurses quick access to medicines and supplies needed in their departments. When the nurse removes an item for patient use, the item is automatically billed to that account, and usage is noted at the main supply area.

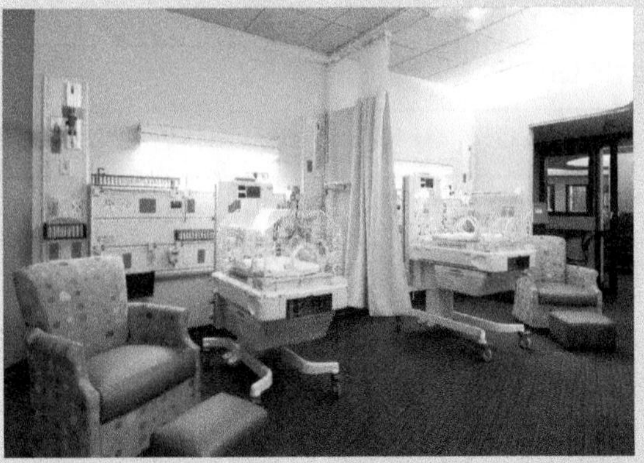

The hospital has redesigned its neonatal rooms. In the old system, there were 16 neonatal beds in an often noisy and large room. The new rooms are semiprivate, with a quiet simulated-night atmosphere. These rooms have proven to help babies develop and improve more quickly.

Chapter 5 Learning Objectives

Quality and Strategy

AUTHOR COMMENT
Quality is an issue that affects an entire organization.

As Arnold Palmer Hospital and many other organizations have found, quality is a wonderful tonic for improving operations. Managing quality helps build successful strategies of *differentiation, low cost*, and *response*. For instance, defining customer quality expectations has helped Bose Corp. successfully *differentiate* its stereo speakers as among the best in the world. Nucor has learned to produce quality steel at *low cost* by developing efficient processes that produce consistent quality. And Dell Computer rapidly *responds* to customer orders because quality systems, with little rework, have allowed it to achieve rapid throughput in its plants. Indeed, quality may be the critical success factor for these firms just as it is at Arnold Palmer Hospital.

VIDEO 5.1
The Culture of Quality at Arnold Palmer Hospital

As Figure 5.1 suggests, improvements in quality help firms increase sales and reduce costs, both of which can increase profitability. Increases in sales often occur as firms speed response, increase or lower selling prices, and improve their reputation for quality products. Similarly, improved quality allows costs to drop as firms increase productivity and lower rework, scrap, and warranty costs. One study found that companies with the highest quality were five times as productive (as measured by units produced per labour-hour) as companies with the poorest quality. Indeed, when the implications of an organization's long-term costs and the potential for increased sales are considered, total costs may well be at a minimum when 100% of the goods or services are perfect and defect free.

Quality, or the lack of quality, affects the entire organization from supplier to customer and from product design to maintenance. Perhaps more importantly, *building* an organization that can achieve quality is a demanding task. Figure 5.2 lays out the flow of activities for an organization to use to achieve total quality management (TQM). A successful quality strategy begins with an organizational culture that fosters quality, followed by an understanding of the principles of quality, and then engaging employees in the necessary activities to implement quality. When these things are done well, the organization typically satisfies its customers and obtains a competitive advantage. The ultimate goal is to win customers. Because quality causes so many other good things to happen, it is a great place to start.

Defining Quality

AUTHOR COMMENT
To create a quality good or service, operations managers need to know what the customer expects.

An operations manager's objective is to build a total quality management system that identifies and satisfies customer needs. Total quality management takes care of the customer. Consequently, we accept the definition of **quality** as adopted by the American Society for Quality (ASQ, at **www.asq.org**): "The totality of features and characteristics of a product or service that bears on its ability to satisfy stated or implied needs."

Quality
The ability of a product or service to meet customer needs.

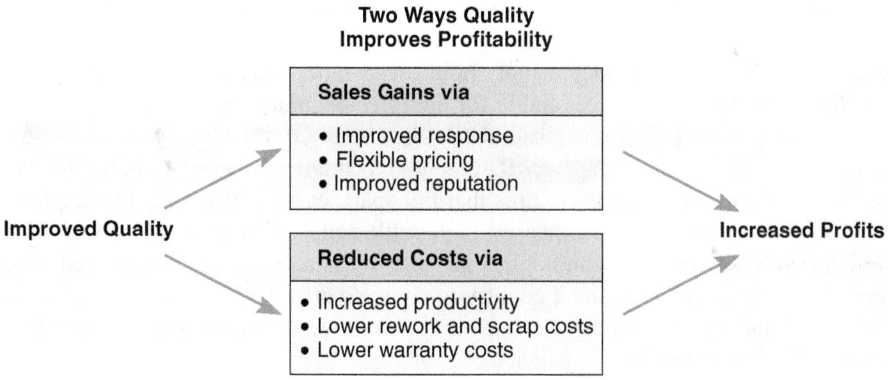

FIGURE 5.1
Two Ways Quality Improves Profitability

Two Ways Quality Improves Profitability

Improved Quality → **Sales Gains via**
- Improved response
- Flexible pricing
- Improved reputation

Improved Quality → **Reduced Costs via**
- Increased productivity
- Lower rework and scrap costs
- Lower warranty costs

→ Increased Profits

AUTHOR COMMENT
High-quality products and services are the most profitable.

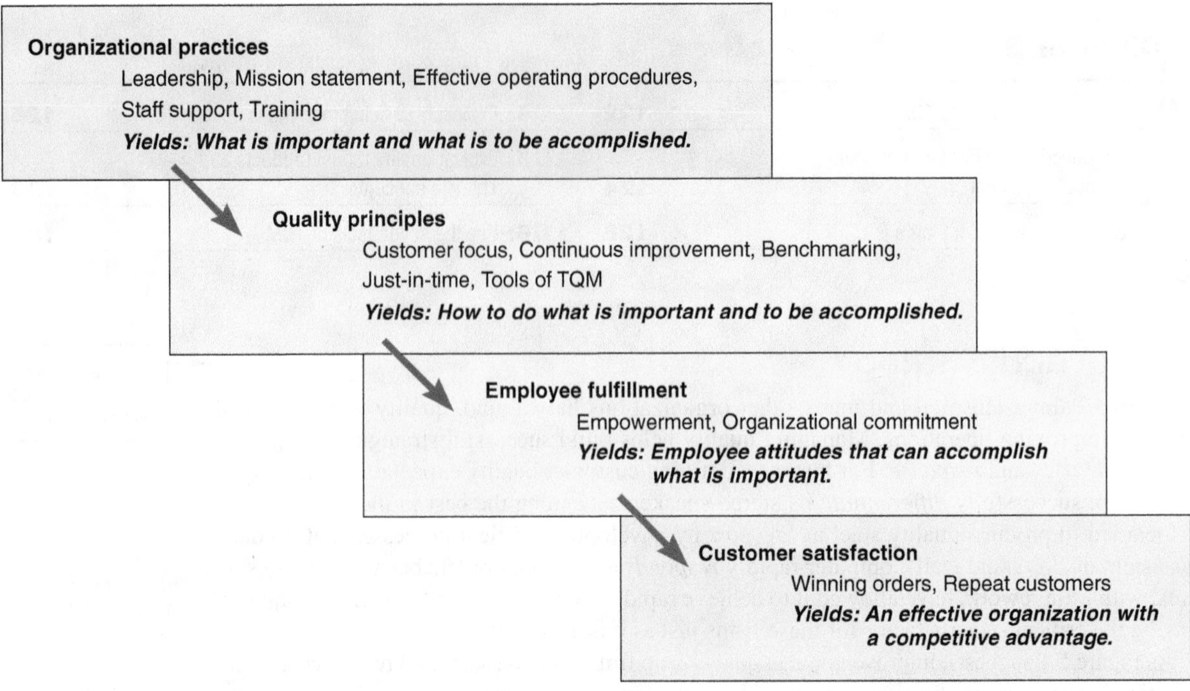

FIGURE 5.2 The Flow of Activities That Are Necessary to Achieve Total Quality Management

LO1: Define quality and TQM

Others, however, believe that definitions of quality fall into several categories. Some definitions are *user based*. They propose that quality "lies in the eyes of the beholder." Marketing people like this approach and so do customers. To them, higher quality means better performance, nicer features, and other (sometimes costly) improvements. To production managers, quality is *manufacturing based*. They believe that quality means conforming to standards and "making it right the first time." Yet a third approach is *product based*, which views quality as a precise and measurable variable. In this view, for example, really good ice cream has high butterfat levels.

This text develops approaches and techniques to address all three categories of quality. The characteristics that connote quality must first be identified through research (a user-based approach to quality). These characteristics are then translated into specific product attributes (a product-based approach to quality). Then, the manufacturing process is organized to ensure that products are made precisely to specifications (a manufacturing-based approach to quality). A process that ignores any one of these steps will not result in a quality product.

IMPLICATIONS OF QUALITY

In addition to being a critical element in operations, quality has other implications. Here are three other reasons why quality is important:

1. *Company reputation:* An organization can expect its reputation for quality—be it good or bad—to follow it. Quality will show up in perceptions about the firm's new products, employment practices, and supplier relations. Self-promotion is not a substitute for quality products.
2. *Product liability:* The courts increasingly hold organizations that design, produce, or distribute faulty products or services liable for damages or injuries resulting from their use. Legislation such as the Canadian Consumer Product Safety Act (CCPSA) sets and enforces product standards by banning products that do not reach those standards. Impure foods that cause illness, nightgowns that burn, tires that fall apart, or auto fuel tanks that explode on impact can all lead to huge legal expenses, large settlements or losses, and terrible publicity.
3. *Global implications:* In this technological age, quality is an international, as well as OM, concern. For both a company and a country to compete effectively in the global economy, products must meet global quality, design, and price expectations. Inferior products harm a firm's profitability and a nation's balance of payments.

NATIONAL QUALITY AWARDS

The perpetual pursuit of quality improvement in Canadian business has led to the creation of the National Quality Institute (**www.nqi.ca**) in Canada. The purpose of this organization is to promote and recognize quality in both public and private firms. Recent award recipients include Mullen Trucking LP (Alberta), Histovet Surgical Pathology (Ontario), and Groupe Esprit de Corps Inc. (Quebec).

The U.S. has also established the Malcolm Baldridge National Quality Award for quality achievement. The award is named for former secretary of commerce Malcolm Baldridge. Winners include such firms as Motorola, Milliken, Xerox, FedEx, Ritz-Carlton Hotels, AT&T, Cadillac, and Texas Instruments. (For details about the Baldridge Award and its 1000-point scoring system, visit **www.quality.nist.gov**)

The Japanese have a similar award, the Deming Prize, named after an American, Dr. W. Edwards Deming.

> 匠
> Takumi is a Japanese character that symbolizes a broader dimension than quality, a deeper process than education, and a more perfect method than persistence.

COST OF QUALITY (COQ)

Four major categories of costs are associated with quality. Called the **cost of quality (COQ)**, they are:

Cost of quality (COQ)
The cost of doing things wrong—that is, the price of nonconformance.

- *Prevention costs:* costs associated with reducing the potential for defective parts or services (e.g., training, quality improvement programs).
- *Appraisal costs:* costs related to evaluating products, processes, parts, and services (e.g., testing, labs, inspectors).
- *Internal failure:* costs that result from production of defective parts or services before delivery to customers (e.g., rework, scrap, downtime).
- *External costs:* costs that occur after delivery of defective parts or services (e.g., rework, returned goods, liabilities, lost goodwill, costs to society).

The first three costs can be reasonably estimated, but external costs are very hard to quantify. When GE had to recall 3.1 million dishwashers recently (because of a defective switch alleged to have started seven fires), the cost of repairs exceeded the value of all the machines. This leads to the belief by many experts that the cost of poor quality is consistently underestimated.

Observers of quality management believe that, on balance, the cost of quality products is only a fraction of the benefits. They think the real losers are organizations that fail to work aggressively at quality. For instance, Philip Crosby stated that quality is free. "What costs money are the unquality things—all the actions that involve not doing it right the first time."[1]

LEADERS IN QUALITY Besides Crosby there are several other giants in the field of quality management, including Deming, Feigenbaum, and Juran. Table 5.1 summarizes their philosophies and contributions.

ETHICS AND QUALITY MANAGEMENT

For operations managers, one of the most important jobs is to deliver healthy, safe, and quality products and services to customers. The development of poor-quality products, because of inadequate design and production processes, results not only in higher production costs but also leads to injuries, lawsuits, and increased government regulation.

If a firm believes that it has introduced a questionable product, ethical conduct must dictate the responsible action. This may be a worldwide recall, as conducted by both Johnson & Johnson (for Tylenol) and Perrier (for sparkling water) when each of their products was found to be contaminated. A manufacturer must accept responsibility for any poor-quality product released to the public. In recent years, Ford (the Explorer SUV maker) and Firestone (the radial tire maker) have been accused of failing to issue product recalls, of withholding damaging information, and of handling complaints on an individual basis.[2]

---

[1]Philip B. Crosby, *Quality Is Free* (New York: McGraw-Hill, 1979). Further, J. M. Juran states, in his book *Juran on Quality by Design* (The Free Press 1992, p. 119), that costs of poor quality "are huge, but the amounts are not known with precision. In most companies the accounting system provides only a minority of the information needed to quantify this cost of poor quality. It takes a great deal of time and effort to extend the accounting system so as to provide full coverage."
[2]For further reading, see O. Fisscher and A. Nijhof, "Implications of Business Ethics for Quality Management," *TQM Magazine* 17 (2005): 150–161; and M. R. Nayebpour and D. Koehn, "The Ethics of Quality: Problems and Preconditions," *Journal of Business Ethics* 44 (April, 2003): 37–48.

TABLE 5.1 Leaders in the Field of Quality Management

Leader	Philosophy/Contribution
W. Edwards Deming	Deming insisted management accept responsibility for building good systems. The employee cannot produce products that on average exceed the quality of what the process is capable of producing. His 14 points for implementing quality improvement are presented in this chapter.
Joseph M. Juran	A pioneer in teaching the Japanese how to improve quality, Juran believed strongly in top-management commitment, support, and involvement in the quality effort. He was also a believer in teams that continually seek to raise quality standards. Juran varies from Deming somewhat in focusing on the customer and defining quality as fitness for use, not necessarily the written specifications.
Armand Feigenbaum	His 1961 book, *Total Quality Control*, laid out 40 steps to quality improvement processes. He viewed quality not as a set of tools but as a total field that integrated the processes of a company. His work in how people learn from each other's successes led to the field of cross-functional teamwork.
Philip B. Crosby	*Quality is Free* was Crosby's attention-getting book published in 1979. Crosby believed that in the traditional trade-off between the cost of improving quality and the cost of poor quality, the cost of poor quality is understated. The cost of poor quality should include all of the things that are involved in not doing the job right the first time. Crosby coined the term *zero defects* and stated, "There is absolutely no reason for having errors or defects in any product or service."

There are many stakeholders involved in the production and marketing of poor-quality products, including shareholders, employees, customers, suppliers, distributors, and creditors. As a matter of ethics, management must ask if any of these stakeholders are being wronged. Every company needs to develop core values that become day-to-day guidelines for everyone from the CEO to production-line employees.

AUTHOR COMMENT International quality standards grow in prominence every year. See **www.iso.ch** and **www.asq.org** to learn more about them.

International Quality Standards

ISO 9000

ISO 9000
A set of quality standards developed by the International Organization for Standardization (ISO).

Quality is so important globally that the world is uniting around a single quality standard, **ISO 9000**. It is the only quality standard with international recognition. In 1987, 91 member nations (including Canada) of the International Organization for Standardization published a series of quality assurance standards, known collectively as ISO 9000. The focus of the standards is to establish quality management procedures through leadership, detailed documentation, work instructions, and record keeping. These procedures, we should note, say nothing about the actual quality of the product—they deal entirely with standards to be followed.

To become ISO 9000 certified, organizations go through a 9- to 18-month process that involves documenting quality procedures, an onsite assessment, and an ongoing series of audits of their products or services. To do business globally, being listed in the ISO directory is critical. As of 2009, there were over 1 million certifications awarded to firms in 175 countries. About 40 000 U.S. firms are ISO 9000 certified. Over 200 000 Chinese firms have received certificates.

LO2: Describe the ISO international quality standards

ISO upgraded its standards in 2008 into more of a quality management system, which is detailed in its ISO 9001: 2008 component. Leadership by top management and customer requirements and satisfaction play a much larger role, while documented procedures receive less emphasis under ISO 9001: 2008.

ISO 14000

ISO 14000
A series of environmental management standards established by the International Organization for Standardization (ISO).

The continuing internationalization of quality is evident with the development of **ISO 14000**. ISO 14000 is a series of environmental management standards that contain five core elements: (1) environmental management, (2) auditing, (3) performance evaluation, (4) labelling, and (5) life cycle assessment. The new standard could have several advantages:

- Positive public image and reduced exposure to liability.
- Good systematic approach to pollution prevention through the minimization of ecological impact of products and activities.
- Compliance with regulatory requirements and opportunities for competitive advantage.
- Reduction in need for multiple audits.

OM *in Action* ISO 14001 Certification Cherished by Canada's Military Training Centre in Goose Bay

When people think of ISO 14001 certification, a nation's military does not often spring to mind. However, Canada's Department of National Defence (DND) takes matters involving their impact on the environment very seriously. The military training location in Goose Bay, Newfoundland, has achieved ISO 14001 certification due to its demonstrated commitment to safeguard the environment through an ongoing mitigation program. In this context, the environmental impact at this DND location is unlike other industrial or commercial ventures. Much of the impact is a short-lived noise event resulting from an ultra-low over-flight and is in the range of 114–118 decibels, typically lasting only a few brief seconds. At a worst case, acoustic startle may result, with potential effects to sensitive wildlife ranging from:

- Abandonment of an animal's prime habitat.
- Auditory damage.
- Breaking the cow/calf bond.
- Breaking or chilling of eggs.

The mitigation program is funded in large part by the revenues derived from the training that is offered for foreign air forces at Goose Bay. It relies on extensive observation and monitoring of the training area to identify sensitive human or wildlife locations on the ground and to restrict aircraft activity from those areas. Working closely with federal and provincial wildlife managers and the scientific community, the DND makes use of satellite telemetry and aerial surveys to detect and monitor caribou herds and bird nest sites. In addition, they sponsor field studies of migrating waterfowl and other species. Also, in order to independently conduct "effects research," the DND funds the operation of the Institute for Environmental Monitoring and Research (IEMR), a group whose board of directors includes a majority of aboriginal voting members.

The DND has demonstrated a solid commitment to environmental "stewardship" and every reasonable effort is made to ensure they remain a "good neighbour."

Source: www.forces.gc.ca; http://www.rcaf-arc.forces.gc.ca/itp-pfi/goosebay/page-eng.asp?id=985.

This standard is being accepted worldwide, with ISO 14001, which addresses environmental impacts of activities systematically, receiving great attention. The *OM in Action* box, "ISO 14001 Certification Cherished by Canada's Military Training Centre in Goose Bay," illustrates the growing application of the ISO 14000 series.

As a follow-on to ISO 14000, ISO 24700 reflects the business world's current approach to reusing recovered components from many products. These components must be "qualified as good as new" and meet all safety and environmental criteria. Xerox was one of the companies that helped write ISO 24700 and an early applicant for certification.

Total Quality Management

AUTHOR COMMENT The seven concepts that make up TQM are part of the lexicon of business.

Total quality management (TQM) refers to a quality emphasis that encompasses the entire organization, from supplier to customer. TQM stresses a commitment by management to have a continuing companywide drive toward excellence in all aspects of products and services that are important to the customer. Each of the 10 decisions made by operations managers deals with some aspect of identifying and meeting customer expectations. Meeting those expectations requires an emphasis on TQM if a firm is to compete as a leader in world markets.

Total quality management (TQM)
Management of an entire organization so that it excels in all aspects of products and services that are important to the customer.

Quality expert W. Edwards Deming used 14 points (see Table 5.2) to indicate how he implemented TQM. We develop these into seven concepts for an effective TQM program: (1) continuous improvement, (2) Six Sigma, (3) employee empowerment, (4) benchmarking, (5) just-in-time (JIT), (6) Taguchi concepts, and (7) knowledge of TQM tools.

CONTINUOUS IMPROVEMENT

Total quality management requires a never-ending process of continuous improvement that covers people, equipment, suppliers, materials, and procedures. The basis of the philosophy is that every aspect of an operation can be improved. The end goal is perfection, which is never achieved but always sought.

PLAN–DO–CHECK–ACT Walter Shewhart, another pioneer in quality management, developed a circular model known as **PDCA** (plan, do, check, act) as his version of continuous improvement.

PDCA
A continuous improvement model of plan, do, check. act.

TABLE 5.2
Deming's 14 Points for Implementing Quality Improvement

1. Create consistency of purpose.
2. Lead to promote change.
3. Build quality into the product; stop depending on inspections to catch problems.
4. Build long-term relationships based on performance instead of awarding business on the basis of price.
5. Continuously improve product, quality, and service.
6. Start training.
7. Emphasize leadership.
8. Drive out fear.
9. Break down barriers between departments.
10. Stop haranguing workers.
11. Support, help, and improve.
12. Remove barriers to pride in work.
13. Institute a vigorous program of education and self-improvement.
14. Put everybody in the company to work on the transformation.

Source: Deming, W. Edwards. *Out of the Crisis*, pp. 23–24, © 2000 Massachusetts Institute of Technology, by permission of The MIT Press.

Deming later took this concept to Japan during his work there after the Second World War.[3] The PDCA cycle is shown in Figure 5.3 as a circle to stress the continuous nature of the improvement process.

The Japanese use the word *kaizen* to describe this ongoing process of unending improvement—the setting and achieving of ever-higher goals. In Canada and the U.S., *TQM* and *zero defects* are also used to describe continuous improvement efforts. But whether it's PDCA, kaizen, TQM, or zero defects, the operations manager is a key player in building a work culture that endorses continuous improvement.

SIX SIGMA

Six Sigma
A program to save time, improve quality, and lower costs.

The term **Six Sigma**, popularized by Motorola, Honeywell, and General Electric, has two meanings in TQM. In a *statistical* sense, it describes a process, product, or service with an extremely high capability (99.9997% accuracy). For example, if 1 million passengers pass through the Kelowna International Airport with checked baggage each year, a Six Sigma program for baggage handling will result in only 3.4 passengers with misplaced luggage. The more common *three-sigma* program (which we address in the supplement to this chapter) would result in 2700 passengers with misplaced bags every year (see Figure 5.4).

The second TQM definition of Six Sigma is a program designed to reduce defects to help lower costs, save time, and improve customer satisfaction. Six Sigma is a comprehensive system—a strategy, a discipline, and a set of tools—for achieving and sustaining business success:

LO3: Explain what Six Sigma is

- It is a *strategy* because it focuses on total customer satisfaction.
- It is a *discipline* because it follows the formal Six Sigma Improvement Model known as *DMAIC*. This five-step process improvement model (1) *D*efines the project's purpose, scope, and outputs and then identifies the required process information, keeping in mind the customer's definition of quality; (2) *M*easures the process and collects data; (3) *A*nalyzes the data, ensuring repeatability (the results can be duplicated), and reproducibility (others get the

FIGURE 5.3
PDCA Cycle

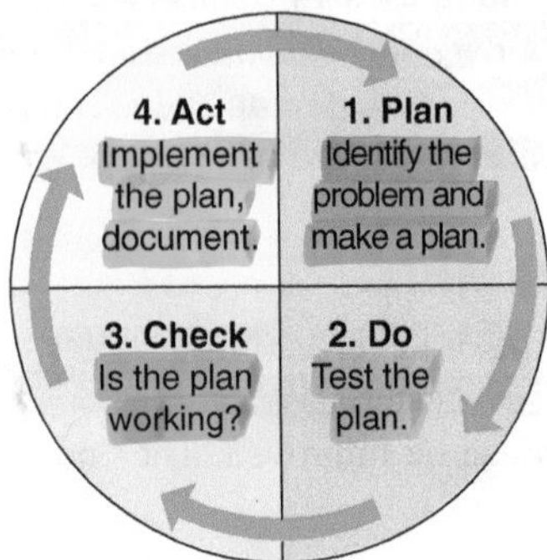

[3]As a result, the Japanese refer to the PDCA cycle as a Deming circle, while others call it a Shewhart circle.

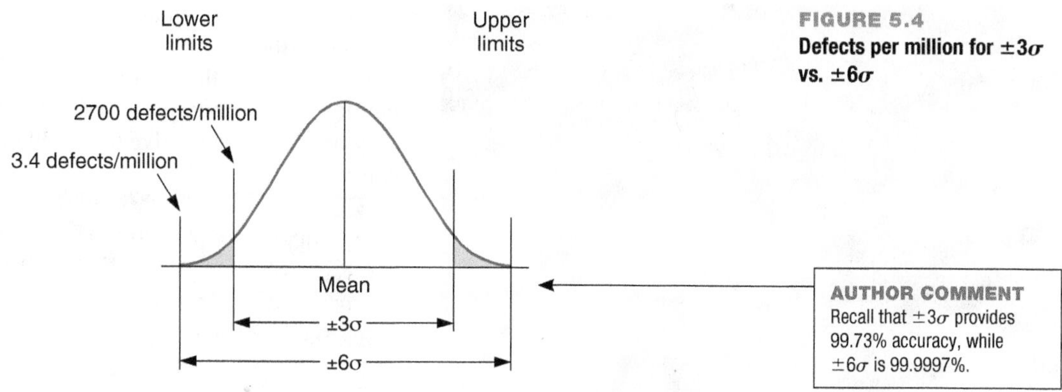

FIGURE 5.4
Defects per million for $\pm 3\sigma$ vs. $\pm 6\sigma$

AUTHOR COMMENT
Recall that $\pm 3\sigma$ provides 99.73% accuracy, while $\pm 6\sigma$ is 99.9997%.

same result); (4) *I*mproves, by modifying or redesigning, existing processes and procedures; and (5) *C*ontrols the new process to make sure performance levels are maintained.

- It is a *set of seven tools* that we introduce shortly in this chapter: check sheets, scatter diagrams, cause-and-effect diagrams, Pareto charts, flowcharts, histograms, and statistical process control.

Motorola developed Six Sigma in the 1980s in response to customer complaints about its products, and to stiff competition. The company first set a goal of reducing defects by 90%. Within one year, it had achieved such impressive results—through benchmarking competitors, soliciting new ideas from employees, changing reward plans, adding training, and revamping critical processes—that it documented the procedures into what it called Six Sigma. Although the concept was rooted in manufacturing, GE later expanded Six Sigma into services, including human resources, sales, customer services, and financial/credit services. The concept of wiping out defects turns out to be the same in both manufacturing and services.

IMPLEMENTING SIX SIGMA Implementing Six Sigma "is a big commitment," says the head of that program at Praxair, a major industrial gas company. "We're asking our executives to spend upward of 15% of their time on Six Sigma. If you don't spend the time, you don't get the results." Indeed, successful Six Sigma programs in every firm, from GE to Motorola to DuPont to Texas Instruments, require a major time commitment, especially from top management. These leaders have to formulate the plan, communicate their buy-in and the firm's objectives, and take a visible role in setting the example for others.

Successful Six Sigma projects are clearly related to the strategic direction of a company. It is a management-directed, team-based, and expert-led approach.[4]

EMPLOYEE EMPOWERMENT

Employee empowerment means involving employees in every step of the production process. Consistently, business literature suggests that some 85% of quality problems have to do with materials and processes, not with employee performance. Therefore, the task is to design equipment and processes that produce the desired quality. This is best done with a high degree of involvement by those who understand the shortcomings of the system. Those dealing with the system on a daily basis understand it better than anyone else. One study indicated that TQM programs that delegate responsibility for quality to shop-floor employees tend to be twice as likely to succeed as those implemented with "top-down" directives.[5]

Employee empowerment
Enlarging employee jobs so that the added responsibility and authority is moved to the lowest level possible in the organization.

[4]To train employees in quality improvement and its relationship to customers, there are three other key players in the Six Sigma program: Master Black Belts, Black Belts, and Green Belts. Master Black Belts are full-time teachers who have extensive training in statistics, quality tools, and leadership. They mentor Black Belts, who in turn are project team leaders, directing perhaps a half-dozen projects per year. Dow Chemical and DuPont have more than 1000 Black Belts each in their global operations. DuPont also has 160 Master Black Belts and introduces over 2000 Green Belts per year into its ranks.

[5]"The Straining of Quality," *The Economist* (January 14, 1995): 55. We also see that this is one of the strengths of Southwest Airlines, which offers bare-bones domestic service but whose friendly and humorous employees help it obtain number one ranking for quality. (See *Fortune* [March 6, 2006]: 65–69.)

A production employee examines a sample product in order to ensure quality.

When nonconformance occurs, the worker is seldom wrong. Either the product was designed wrong, the system that makes the product was designed wrong, or the employee was improperly trained. Although the employee may be able to help solve the problem, the employee rarely causes it.

Techniques for building employee empowerment include (1) building communication networks that involve employees; (2) developing open, supportive supervisors; (3) moving responsibility from both managers and staff to production employees; (4) building high-morale organizations; and (5) creating such formal organization structures as teams and quality circles.

Teams can be built to address a variety of issues. One popular focus of teams is quality. Such teams are often known as quality circles. A **quality circle** is a group of employees who meet regularly to solve work-related problems. The members receive training in group planning, problem solving, and statistical quality control. They generally meet once a week (usually after work but sometimes on company time). Although the members are not rewarded financially, they do receive recognition from the firm. A specially trained team member, called the *facilitator*, usually helps train the members and keeps the meetings running smoothly. Teams with a quality focus have proven to be a cost-effective way to increase productivity as well as quality.

BENCHMARKING

Benchmarking is another ingredient in an organization's TQM program. **Benchmarking** involves selecting a demonstrated standard of products, services, costs, or practices that represent the very best performance for processes or activities very similar to your own. The idea is to develop a target at which to shoot and then to develop a standard or benchmark against which to compare your performance. The steps for developing benchmarks are:

Quality circle
A group of employees meeting regularly with a facilitator to solve work-related problems in their work area.

Benchmarking
Selecting a demonstrated standard of performance that represents the very best performance for a process or an activity.

LO4: Explain how benchmarking is used in TQM

1. Determine what to benchmark.
2. Form a benchmark team.
3. Identify benchmarking partners.
4. Collect and analyze benchmarking information.
5. Take action to match or exceed the benchmark.

Typical performance measures used in benchmarking include percentage of defects, cost per unit or per order, processing time per unit, service response time, return on investment, customer satisfaction rates, and customer retention rates.

In the ideal situation, you find one or more similar organizations that are leaders in the particular areas you want to study. Then you compare yourself (benchmark yourself) against them. The company need not be in your industry. Indeed, to establish world-class standards, it may be best to look outside your industry. If one industry has learned how to compete via rapid product development while yours has not, it does no good to study your industry.

This is exactly what Xerox and Mercedes Benz did when they went to L.L. Bean for order-filling and warehousing benchmarks. Xerox noticed that L.L. Bean was able to "pick" orders three times as fast as it could. After benchmarking, it was immediately able to pare warehouse costs by 10%. Mercedes Benz observed that L.L. Bean warehouse employees used flowcharts to spot wasted motions. The auto giant followed suit and now relies more on problem solving at the worker level.

TABLE 5.3
Best Practices for Resolving Customer Complaints

Best Practice	Justification
Make it easy for clients to complain.	It is free market research.
Respond quickly to complaints.	It adds customers and loyalty.
Resolve complaints on the first contact.	It reduces cost.
Use computers to manage complaints.	Discover trends, share them, and align your services.
Recruit the best for customer service jobs.	It should be part of formal training and career advancement.

Source: Canadian Government Guide on Complaint Mechanism.

Benchmarks often take the form of "best practices" found in other firms or in other divisions. Table 5.3 illustrates best practices for resolving customer complaints.

Likewise, Britain's Great Ormond Street Hospital benchmarked the Ferrari Racing Team's pit stops to improve one aspect of medical care. (See the *OM in Action* box, "A Hospital Benchmarks against the Ferrari Racing Team?")

INTERNAL BENCHMARKING When an organization is large enough to have many divisions or business units, a natural approach is the internal benchmark. Data are usually much more accessible than from outside firms. Typically, one internal unit has superior performance worth learning from.

Xerox's almost religious belief in benchmarking has paid off not only by looking outward to L.L. Bean but also by examining the operations of its various country divisions. For example, Xerox Europe, a $6-billion subsidiary of Xerox Corp., formed teams to see how better sales

OM *in Action* A Hospital Benchmarks against the Ferrari Racing Team?

After surgeons successfully completed a six-hour operation to fix a hole in a three-year-old boy's heart, Dr. Angus McEwan supervised one of the most dangerous phases of the procedure: the boy's transfer from surgery to the intensive care unit.

Thousands of such "handoffs" occur in hospitals every day, and devastating mistakes can happen during them. In fact, at least 35% of preventable hospital mishaps take place because of handoff problems. Risks come from many sources: using temporary nursing staff, frequent shift changes for interns, surgeons working in larger teams, and an ever-growing tangle of wires and tubes connected to patients.

In one of the most unlikely benchmarks in modern medicine, Britain's largest children's hospital turned to Italy's Formula One Ferrari racing team for help in revamping patient-handoff techniques. Armed with videos and slides, the racing team described how they analyze pit crew performance. It also explained how its system for recording errors stressed the small ones that go unnoticed in pit-stop handoffs.

To move forward, Ferrari invited a team of doctors to attend practice sessions at the British Grand Prix in order to get closer looks at pit stops. Ferrari's technical director, Nigel Stepney, then watched a video of a hospital handoff. Stepney was not impressed. "In fact, he was amazed at how clumsy, chaotic, and informal the process appeared," said one hospital official. At that meeting, Stepney described how each Ferrari crew member is required to do a specific job, in a specific sequence, and in silence. The hospital handoff, in contrast, had several conversations going on at once, while different members of its team disconnected or reconnected patient equipment, but in no particular order.

Results of the benchmarking process: handoff errors fell 42% to 49%, with a bonus of faster handoff time.

Sources: The Wall Street Journal (December 3, 2007): B11 and (November 14, 2006): A1, A8.

could result through internal benchmarking. Somehow, France sold five times as many colour copiers as did other divisions in Europe. By copying France's approach, namely, better sales training and use of dealer channels to supplement direct sales, Norway increased sales by 152%, the Netherlands by 300%, and Switzerland by 328%!

Benchmarks can and should be established in a variety of areas. Total quality management requires no less.[6]

JUST-IN-TIME (JIT)

The philosophy behind just-in-time (JIT) is one of continuing improvement and enforced problem solving. JIT systems are designed to produce or deliver goods just as they are needed. JIT is related to quality in three ways:

- *JIT cuts the cost of quality:* This occurs because scrap, rework, inventory investment, and damage costs are directly related to inventory on hand. Because there is less inventory on hand with JIT, costs are lower. In addition, inventory hides bad quality, whereas JIT immediately *exposes* bad quality.
- *JIT improves quality:* As JIT shrinks lead time, it keeps evidence of errors fresh and limits the number of potential sources of error. JIT creates, in effect, an early warning system for quality problems, both within the firm and with vendors.
- *Better quality means less inventory and a better, easier-to-employ JIT system:* Often, the purpose of keeping inventory is to protect against poor production performance resulting from unreliable quality. If consistent quality exists, JIT allows firms to reduce all the costs associated with inventory.

TAGUCHI CONCEPTS

Most quality problems are the result of poor product and process design. Genichi Taguchi has provided us with three concepts aimed at improving both product and process quality: *quality robustness*, *quality loss function*, and *target-oriented quality*.[7]

Quality robust
Products that are consistently built to meet customer needs in spite of adverse conditions in the production process.

Quality robust products are ones that can be produced uniformly and consistently in adverse manufacturing and environmental conditions. Taguchi's idea is to remove the *effects* of adverse conditions instead of removing the causes. Taguchi suggests that removing the effects is often cheaper than removing the causes and more effective in producing a robust product. In this way, small variations in materials and process do not destroy product quality.

Quality loss function (QLF)
A mathematical function that identifies all costs connected with poor quality and shows how these costs increase as product quality moves from what the customer wants.

A **quality loss function (QLF)** identifies all costs connected with poor quality and shows how these costs increase as the product moves away from being exactly what the customer wants. These costs include not only customer dissatisfaction but also warranty and service costs; internal inspection, repair, and scrap costs; and costs that can best be described as costs to society. Notice that Figure 5.5(a) shows the quality loss function as a curve that increases at an increasing rate. It takes the general form of a simple quadratic formula:

$$L = D^2C$$

where L = loss to society
D^2 = square of the distance from the target value
C = cost of the deviation at the specification limit

LO5: Explain quality robust products and Taguchi concepts

All the losses to society due to poor performance are included in the loss function. The smaller the loss, the more desirable the product. The farther the product is from the target value, the more severe the loss.

Taguchi observed that traditional conformance-oriented specifications (i.e., the product is good as long as it falls within the tolerance limits) are too simplistic. As shown in Figure 5.5(b), conformance-oriented quality accepts all products that fall within the tolerance limits, producing more units farther from the target. Therefore, the loss (cost) is higher in terms of customer

[6]Note that benchmarking is good for evaluating how well you are doing the thing you are doing compared with the industry, but the more imaginative approach to process improvement is to ask, "Should we be doing this at all?" Comparing your warehousing operations to the marvellous job that L.L. Bean does is fine, but maybe you should be outsourcing the warehousing function (see Supplement 11).

[7]G. Taguchi, S. Chowdhury, and Y. Wu, *Taguchi's Quality Engineering Handbook* (New York: Wiley, 2004).

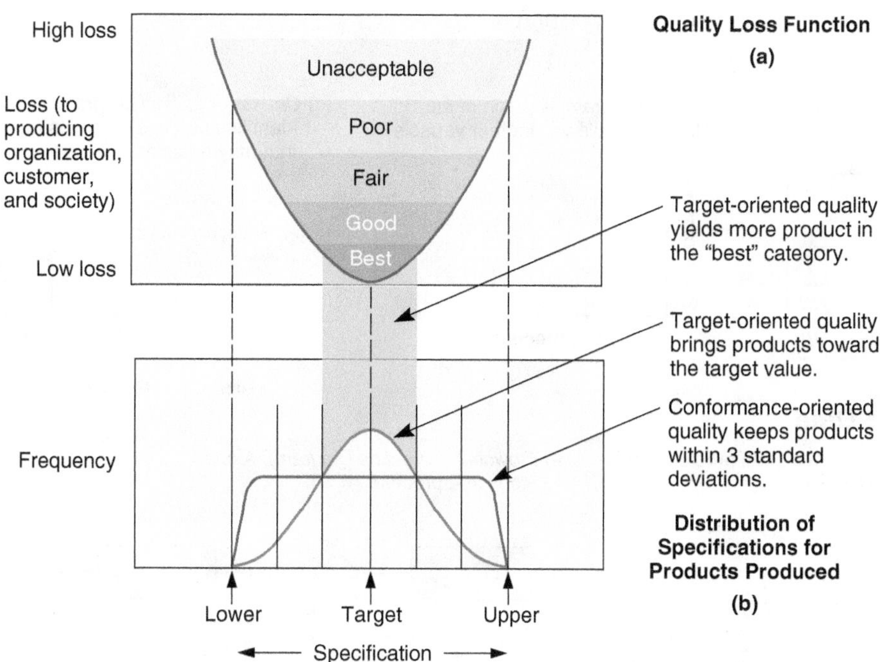

FIGURE 5.5
(a) Quality Loss Function and (b) Distribution of Products Produced
Taguchi aims for the target because products produced near the upper and lower acceptable specifications result in higher quality loss function.

satisfaction and benefits to society. Target-oriented quality, on the other hand, strives to keep the product at the desired specification, producing more (and better) units near the target. **Target-oriented quality** is a philosophy of continuous improvement to bring the product exactly on target.

Target-oriented quality
A philosophy of continuous improvement to bring a product exactly on target.

KNOWLEDGE OF TQM TOOLS

To empower employees and implement TQM as a continuing effort, everyone in the organization must be trained in the techniques of TQM. In the following section, we focus on some of the diverse and expanding tools that are used in the TQM crusade.

Tools of TQM

Seven tools that are particularly helpful in the TQM effort are shown in Figure 5.6. We will now introduce these tools.

AUTHOR COMMENT
These seven tools will prove useful in many of your courses and throughout your career.

CHECK SHEETS

A check sheet is any kind of a form that is designed for recording data. In many cases, the recording is done so the patterns are easily seen while the data are being taken (see Figure 5.6[a]). Check sheets help analysts find the facts or patterns that may aid subsequent analysis. An example might be a drawing that shows a tally of the areas where defects are occurring or a check sheet showing the type of customer complaints.

LO6: Use the seven tools of TQM

SCATTER DIAGRAMS

Scatter diagrams show the relationship between two measurements. An example is the positive relationship between length of a service call and the number of trips a repair person makes back to the truck for parts. Another example might be a plot of productivity and absenteeism, as shown in Figure 5.6(b). If the two items are closely related, the data points will form a tight band. If a random pattern results, the items are unrelated.

CAUSE-AND-EFFECT DIAGRAMS

Another tool for identifying quality issues and inspection points is the **cause-and-effect diagram**, also known as an **Ishikawa diagram** or a **fish-bone chart**. Figure 5.7 on page 133 illustrates a chart (note the shape resembling the bones of a fish) for a basketball quality control problem—missed free throws. Each "bone" represents a possible source of error.

Cause-and-effect diagram
A schematic technique used to discover possible locations of quality problems.

FIGURE 5.6 Seven Tools of TQM

Tools for Generating Ideas

(a) *Check Sheet:* An organized method of recording data

	Hour							
Defect	1	2	3	4	5	6	7	8
A	///	/		/	/	/	///	/
B	//	/	/	/			//	///
C	/	//					//	////

(b) *Scatter Diagram:* A graph of the value of one variable vs. another variable

(c) *Cause-and-Effect Diagram:* A tool that identifies process elements (causes) that may affect an outcome

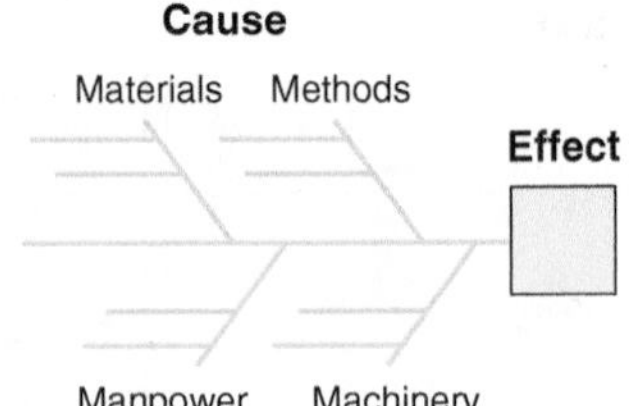

Tools for Organizing the Data

(d) *Pareto Chart:* A graph that identifies and plots problems or defects in descending order of frequency

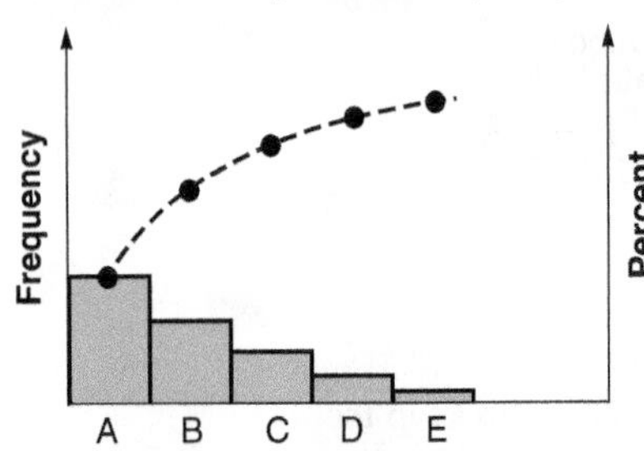

(e) *Flowchart (Process Diagram):* A chart that describes the steps in a process

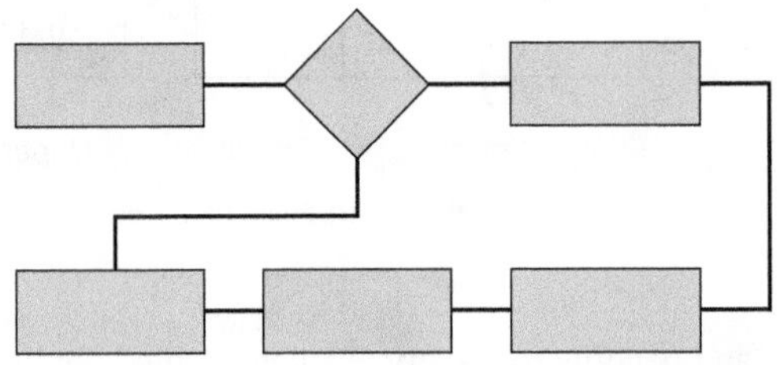

Tools for Identifying Problems

(f) *Histogram:* A distribution that shows the frequency of occurrences of a variable

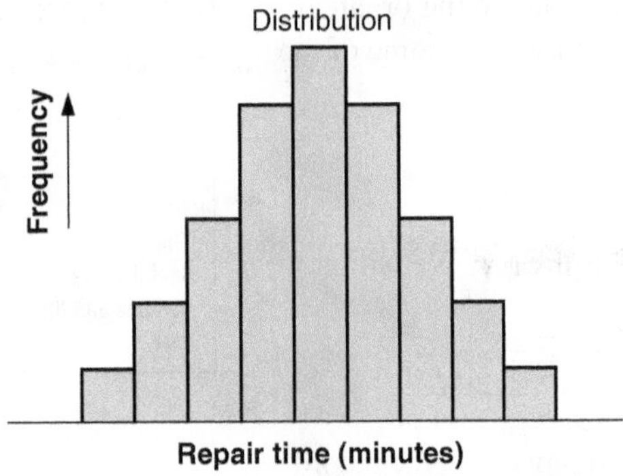

(g) *Statistical Process Control Chart:* A chart with time on the horizontal axis for plotting values of a statistic

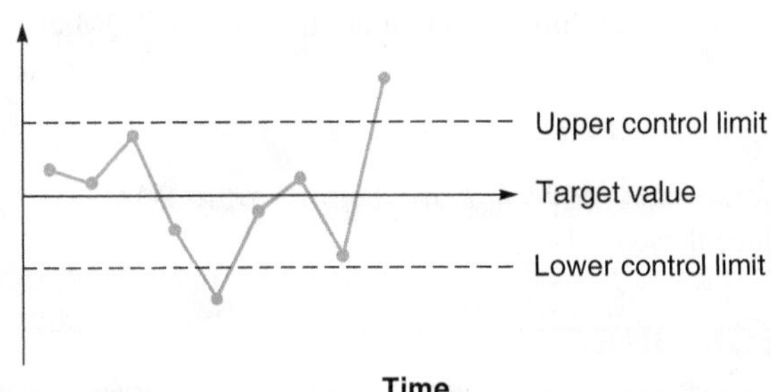

The operations manager starts with four categories: material, machinery/equipment, manpower, and methods. These four *M*s are the "causes." They provide a good checklist for initial analysis. Individual causes associated with each category are tied in as separate bones along that branch, often through a brainstorming process. For example, the method branch in Figure 5.7 has problems caused by hand position, follow-through, aiming point, bent knees, and balance. When a fish-bone chart is systematically developed, possible quality problems and inspection points are highlighted.

PARETO CHARTS

Pareto charts
Graphics that identify the few critical items as opposed to many less important ones.

Pareto charts are a method of organizing errors, problems, or defects to help focus on problem-solving efforts. They are based on the work of Vilfredo Pareto, a 19th-century economist. Joseph M. Juran popularized Pareto's work when he suggested that 80% of a firm's problems are a result of only 20% of the causes.

Example 1 indicates that of the five types of complaints identified, the vast majority were of one type—poor room service.

FIGURE 5.7 Fish-Bone Chart (or Cause-and-Effect Diagram) for Problems with Missed Free Throws

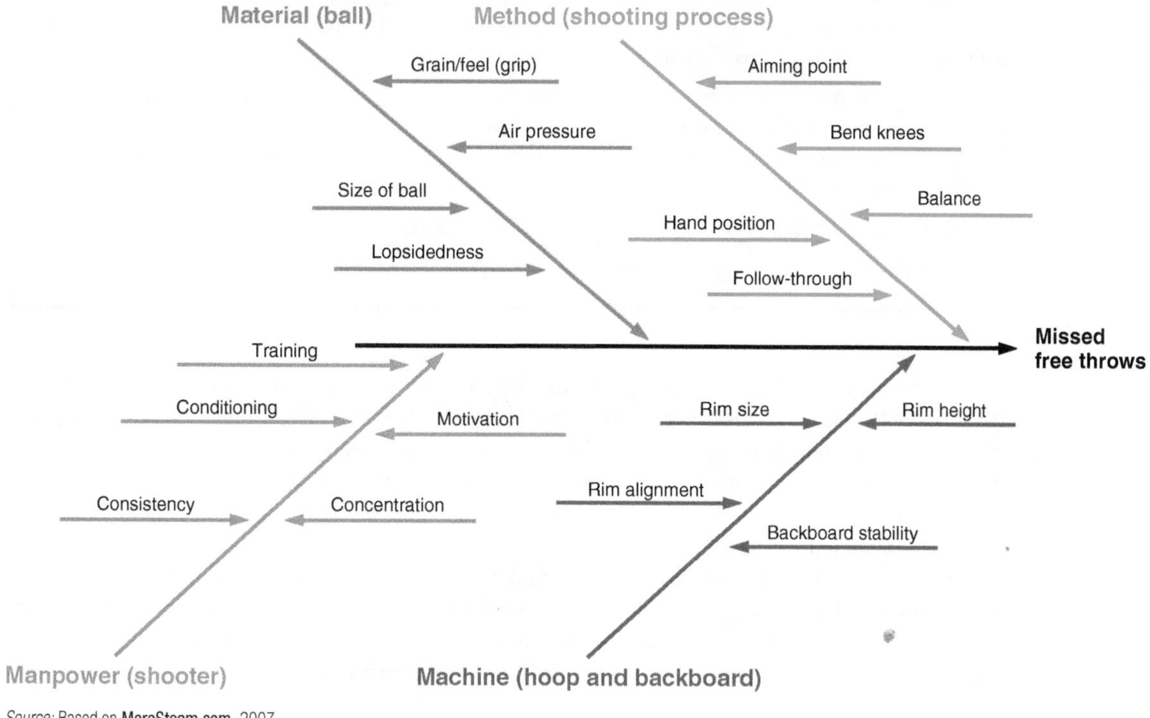

Source: Based on MoreSteam.com, 2007.

EXAMPLE 1

A Pareto chart at the Hard Rock Hotel

The Hard Rock Hotel in Bali has just collected the data from 75 complaint calls to the general manager during the month of October. The manager wants to prepare an analysis of the complaints. The data provided are room service, 54; check-in delays, 12; hours the pool is open, 4; minibar prices, 3; and miscellaneous, 2.

APPROACH ▶ A Pareto chart is an excellent choice for this analysis.

SOLUTION ▶ The Pareto chart shown below indicates that 72% of the calls were the result of one cause: room service. The majority of complaints will be eliminated when this one cause is corrected.

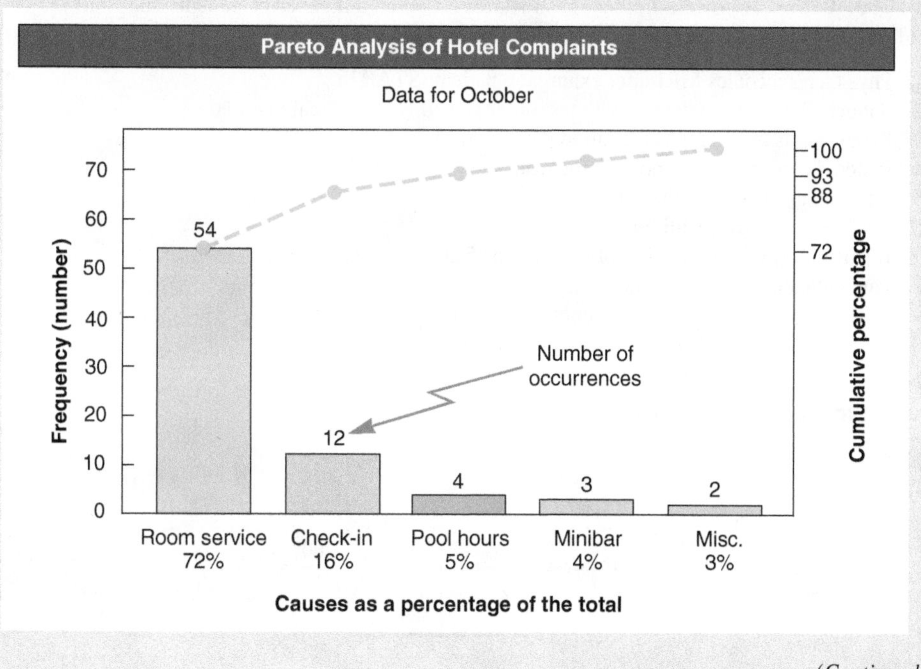

(Continued)

INSIGHT ▶ This visual means of summarizing data is very helpful—particularly with large amounts of data, as in the Fast Creek Lightning case study at the end of this chapter. We can immediately spot the top problems and prepare a plan to address them.

LEARNING EXERCISE ▶ Hard Rock's bar manager decides to do a similar analysis on complaints she has collected over the past year: too expensive, 22; weak drinks, 15; slow service, 65; short hours, 8; unfriendly bartender, 12. Prepare a Pareto chart. [Answer: slow service, 53%; too expensive, 18%; weak drinks, 12%; unfriendly bartender, 10%; short hours, 7%.]

RELATED PROBLEMS ▶ 5.1, 5.3, 5.7b, 5.12, 5.13, 5.16c

ACTIVE MODEL 5.1 This example is further illustrated in Active Model 5.1 at **MyOMLab.**

Pareto analysis indicates which problems may yield the greatest payoff. A regional service division at Bell Canada discovered this when it tried to find a way to reduce damage to buried phone cable, the number-one cause of phone outages. Pareto analysis showed that 69% of cable damage was caused by human error. Armed with this information, the regional service division at Bell Canada was able to devise a plan to reduce cable cuts by 28% in one year, saving millions of dollars on an annual basis.

Likewise, Japan's Ricoh Corp., a copier maker, used the Pareto principle to tackle the "callback" problem. Callbacks meant the job was not done right the first time and that a second visit, at Ricoh's expense, was needed. Identifying and retraining only the 11% of the customer engineers with the most callbacks resulted in a 19% drop in return visits.

FLOWCHARTS

Flowcharts
Block diagrams that graphically describe a process or system.

Flowcharts graphically present a process or system using annotated boxes and interconnected lines (see Figure 5.6[e]). They are a simple but great tool for trying to make sense of a process or explain a process. Example 2 uses a flowchart to show the process of completing an MRI at a hospital.

EXAMPLE 2

A flowchart for hospital MRI service

Port Owen Hospital has undertaken a series of process improvement initiatives. One of these is to make the MRI service efficient for patient, doctor, and hospital. The first step, the administrator believes, is to develop a flowchart for this process.

APPROACH ▶ A process improvement staffer observed a number of patients and followed them (and information flow) from start to end. Here are the 11 steps:

1. Physician schedules MRI after examining patient (START).
2. Patient taken to the MRI lab with test order and copy of medical records.
3. Patient signs in, completes required paperwork.
4. Patient is prepped by technician for scan.
5. Technician carries out the MRI scan.
6. Technician inspects film for clarity.
7. If MRI not satisfactory (20% of time), steps 5 and 6 are repeated.
8. Patient taken back to hospital room.
9. MRI is read by radiologist and report is prepared.
10. MRI and report are transferred electronically to physician.
11. Patient and physician discuss report (END).

SOLUTION ▶ Here is the flowchart:

AUTHOR COMMENT
Flowcharting any process is an excellent way to understand and then try to improve that process.

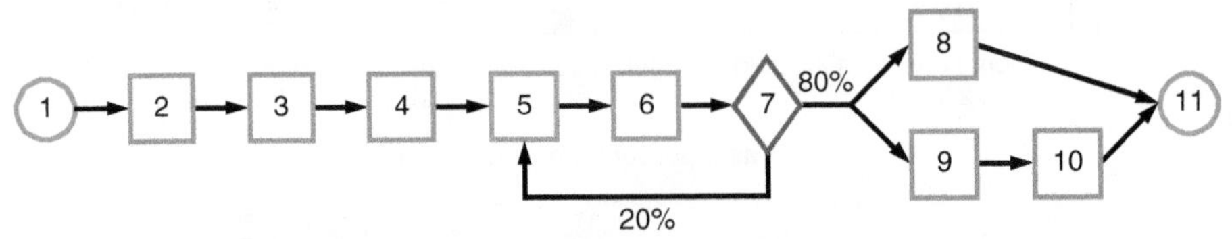

INSIGHT ▶ With the flowchart in hand, the hospital can analyze each step and identify value-added activities and activities that can be improved or eliminated.

LEARNING EXERCISE ▶ If the patient's blood pressure is over 200/120 when being prepped for the MRI, she is taken back to her room for two hours and the process returns to Step 2. How does the flowchart change? Answer:

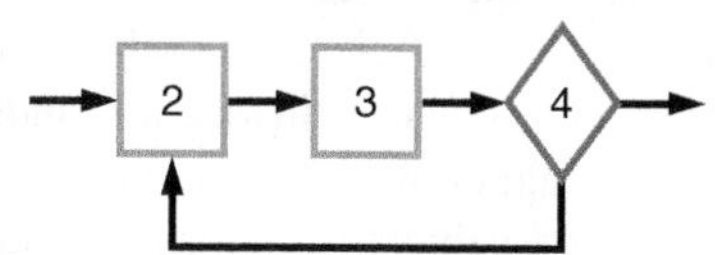

RELATED PROBLEMS ▶ 5.6, 5.15

HISTOGRAMS

Histograms show the range of values of a measurement and the frequency with which each value occurs (see Figure 5.6[f]). They show the most frequently occurring readings as well as the variations in the measurements. Descriptive statistics, such as the average and standard deviation, may be calculated to describe the distribution. However, the data should always be plotted so the shape of the distribution can be "seen." A visual presentation of the distribution may also provide insight into the cause of the variation.

STATISTICAL PROCESS CONTROL (SPC)

Statistical process control (SPC)
A process used to monitor standards, make measurements, and take corrective action as a product or service is being produced.

Statistical process control monitors standards, makes measurements, and takes corrective action as a product or service is being produced. Samples of process outputs are examined; if they are within acceptable limits, the process is permitted to continue. If they fall outside certain specific ranges, the process is stopped and, typically, the assignable cause located and removed.

Control charts
Graphic presentations of process data over time, with predetermined control limits.

Control charts are graphic presentations of data over time that show upper and lower limits for the process we want to control (see Figure 5.6[g]). Control charts are constructed in such a way that new data can be quickly compared with past performance data. We take samples of the process output and plot the average of each of these samples on a chart that has the limits on it. The upper and lower limits in a control chart can be in units of temperature, pressure, weight, length, and so on.

Figure 5.8 shows the plot of the average percentages of samples in a control chart. When the average of the samples falls within the upper and lower control limits and no discernible pattern is present, the process is said to be in control with only natural variation present. Otherwise, the process is out of control or out of adjustment.

The supplement to this chapter details how control charts of different types are developed. It also deals with the statistical foundation underlying the use of this important tool.

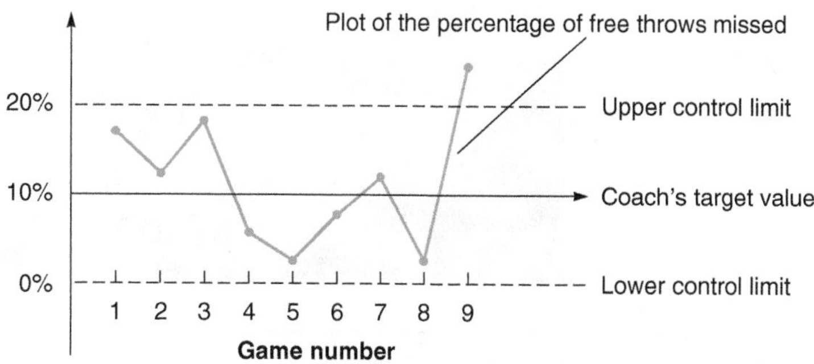

FIGURE 5.8
Control Chart for Percentage of Free Throws Missed by the Chicago Bulls in Their First Nine Games of the New Season

AUTHOR COMMENT
One of the themes of quality is that "quality cannot be inspected into a product."

The Role of Inspection

Inspection
A means of ensuring that an operation is producing at the quality level expected.

To make sure a system is producing at the expected quality level, control of the process is needed. The best processes have little variation from the standard expected. The operations manager's task is to build such systems and to verify, often by inspection, that they are performing to standard. This **inspection** can involve measurement, tasting, touching, weighing, or testing of the product (sometimes even destroying it when doing so). Its goal is to detect a bad process immediately. Inspection does not correct deficiencies in the system or defects in the products; nor does it change a product or increase its value. Inspection finds only deficiencies and defects. Moreover, inspections are expensive and do not add value to the product.

Inspection should be thought of as a vehicle for improving the system. Operations managers need to know critical points in the system: (1) *when to inspect* and (2) *where to inspect.*

WHEN AND WHERE TO INSPECT

Deciding when and where to inspect depends on the type of process and the value added at each stage. Inspections can take place at any of the following points:

1. At your supplier's plant while the supplier is producing.
2. At your facility upon receipt of goods from your supplier.
3. Before costly or irreversible processes.
4. During the step-by-step production process.
5. When production or service is complete.
6. Before delivery to your customer.
7. At the point of customer contact.

The seven tools of TQM discussed in the previous section aid in this "when and where to inspect" decision. However, inspection is not a substitute for a robust product produced by well-trained employees in a good process. In one well-known experiment conducted by an independent research firm, 100 defective pieces were added to a "perfect" lot of items and then subjected to 100% inspection.[8] The inspectors found only 68 of the defective pieces in their first inspection. It took another three passes by the inspectors to find the next 30 defects. The last two defects were never found. So the bottom line is that there is variability in the inspection process. Additionally, inspectors are only human: They become bored, they become tired, and the inspection equipment itself has variability. Even with 100% inspection, inspectors cannot guarantee perfection. Therefore, good processes, employee empowerment, and source control are a better solution than trying to find defects by inspection. You cannot inspect quality into the product.

For example, at Velcro Industries, as in many organizations, quality was viewed by machine operators as the job of "those quality people." Inspections were based on random sampling, and if a part showed up bad, it was thrown out. The company decided to pay more attention to

Good methods analysis and the proper tools can result in poka-yokes that improve both quality and speed. Here, two poka-yokes are demonstrated. First, the aluminum scoop automatically positions the french fries vertically, and second, the properly sized container ensures that the portion served is correct. McDonald's thrives by bringing rigour and consistency to the restaurant business.

[8] *Statistical Quality Control* (Springfield, MA: Monsanto Chemical Company, n.d.): 19.

OM *in Action* Maple Leaf Foods Inc.

After many years with an excellent reputation for quality, Canada was shocked to learn of a listeriosis outbreak originating in a food processing location operated by Maple Leaf Foods in 2008. Regrettably, 22 Canadians died and many more became sick because of this. Because their meat products were linked to these deaths, the company stated they were committed to "becoming a global leader in food safety to prevent this kind of a tragedy from ever happening again." They took out full-page ads in a number of Canadian newspapers to mark the one-year anniversary of the listeriosis outbreak. "On behalf of our 24 000 employees, we promise to never forget," said Michael McCain, Maple Leaf's chief executive officer, in a letter-style advertisement.

To prevent the situation from recurring, Maple Leaf recalled the meat, closed and cleaned the plant where it was packaged, and stepped up company-wide sanitary procedures. Moreover, the company hired a chief food safety officer whose role is to improve inspection procedures and policies within Maple Leaf to ensure there is no repeat of such an outbreak. Maple Leaf has since stated it has "zero tolerance" for listeria contamination, which occurs once in every 200 meat packages, a company spokesperson said. So, more testing—twice the level the company did previously—means that the company will be recalling more meat under the new quality-control regime.

Quality control is important in most, if not all, aspects of business. But when it comes to the food industry, it is vital.

Source: http://www.cbc.ca/news/story/2009/08/24/maple-leaf-anniversary-listeriosis.html.

the system (operators, machine repair and design, measurement methods, communications, and responsibilities), and to invest more money in training. Over time as defects declined, Velcro was able to pull half its quality control people out of the process.

SOURCE INSPECTION

The best inspection can be thought of as no inspection at all; this "inspection" is always done at the source—it is just doing the job properly with the operator ensuring that this is so. This may be called **source inspection** (or source control) and is consistent with the concept of employee empowerment, where individual employees self-check their own work. The idea is that each supplier, process, and employee *treats the next step in the process as the customer*, ensuring perfect product to the next "customer." This inspection may be assisted by the use of checklists and controls such as a fail-safe device called a *poka-yoke*, a name borrowed from the Japanese.

Source inspection
Controlling or monitoring at the point of production or purchase—at the source.

A **poka-yoke** is a foolproof device or technique that ensures production of good units every time. These special devices avoid errors and provide quick feedback of problems. A simple example of a poka-yoke device is the diesel gas pump nozzle that will not fit into the "unleaded" gas tank opening on your car. In McDonald's, the french fry scoop and standard-size bag used to measure the correct quantity are poka-yokes. Similarly, in a hospital, the prepackaged surgical coverings that contain exactly the items needed for a medical procedure are poka-yokes. Checklists are another type of poka-yoke. The idea of source inspection and poka-yokes is to ensure that 100% good product or service is provided at each step in the process.

Poka-yoke
Literally translated, "foolproof"; it has come to mean a device or technique that ensures the production of a good unit every time.

SERVICE INDUSTRY INSPECTION

In *service*-oriented organizations, inspection points can be assigned at a wide range of locations, as illustrated in Table 5.4. Again, the operations manager must decide where inspections are justified and may find the seven tools of TQM useful when making these judgments.

INSPECTION OF ATTRIBUTES VERSUS VARIABLES

When inspections take place, quality characteristics may be measured as either *attributes* or *variables*. **Attribute inspection** classifies items as being either good or defective. It does not address the *degree* of failure. For example, the lightbulb burns or it does not. **Variable inspection** measures such dimensions as weight, speed, size, or strength to see if an item falls within an acceptable range. If a piece of electrical wire is supposed to be 0.01 inch in diameter, a micrometer can be used to see if the product is close enough to pass inspection.

Attribute inspection
An inspection that classifies items as being either good or defective.

Variable inspection
Classifications of inspected items as falling on a continuum scale, such as dimension or strength.

TABLE 5.4
Examples of Inspection in Services

Organization	What Is Inspected	Standard
Torys Law Firm	Receptionist performance	Phone answered by the second ring
	Billing	Accurate, timely, and correct format
	Lawyer	Promptness in returning calls
Holiday Inn Express	Reception desk	Use customer's name
	Doorman	Greet guest in less than 30 seconds
	Room	All lights working, spotless bathroom
	Minibar	Restocked and charges accurately posted to bill
Mt. Sinai Hospital	Pharmacy	Prescription accuracy, inventory accuracy
	Lab	Audit for lab-test accuracy
	Nurses	Charts immediately updated
	Admissions	Data entered correctly and completely
Boston Pizza	Busboy	Serves water within one minute
	Busboy	Clears all entrée items and crumbs prior to dessert
	Server	Knows and suggests specials, desserts
Real Canadian Superstore	Display areas	Attractive, well organized, stocked, good lighting
	Stockrooms	Rotation of goods, organized, clean
	Salesclerks	Neat, courteous, very knowledgable

Knowing whether attributes or variables are being inspected helps us decide which statistical quality control approach to take, as we will see in the supplement to this chapter.

AUTHOR COMMENT
The personal component of a service can make quality measurement difficult.

TQM in Services

The personal component of services is more difficult to measure than the quality of the tangible component. Generally, the user of a service, like the user of a good, has features in mind that form a basis for comparison among alternatives. Lack of any one feature may eliminate the service from further consideration. Quality also may be perceived as a bundle of attributes in which many lesser characteristics are superior to those of competitors. This approach to product comparison differs little between goods and services. However, what is very different about the selection of services is the poor definition of the (1) *intangible differences between products* and (2) *the intangible expectations customers have of those products*. Indeed, the intangible attributes may not be defined at all. They are often unspoken images in the purchaser's mind. This is why all of those marketing issues such as advertising, image, and promotion can make a difference (see the photo of the UPS driver).

The operations manager plays a significant role in addressing several major aspects of service quality. First, the *tangible component of many services is important*. How well the service is designed and produced does make a difference. This might be how accurate, clear, and complete your checkout bill at the hotel is, how warm the food is at Boston Pizza, or how well your car runs after you pick it up at the repair shop.

Second, another aspect of service and service quality is the process. Notice in Table 5.5 that 9 out of 10 of the determinants of service quality are related to *the service process*. Such things

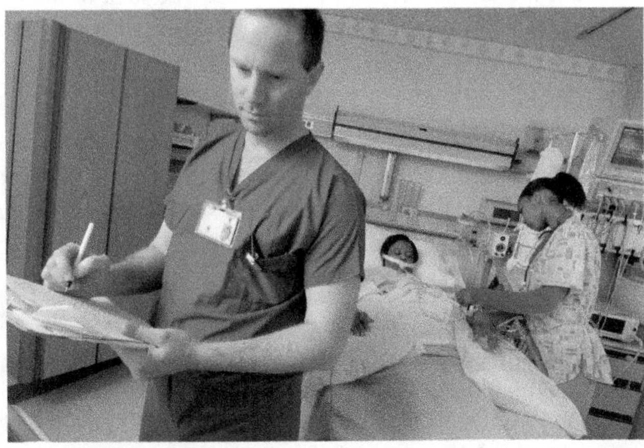

Checklists, simple as they are, provide a powerful way to improve quality. Everyone from airline pilots to physicians use them.

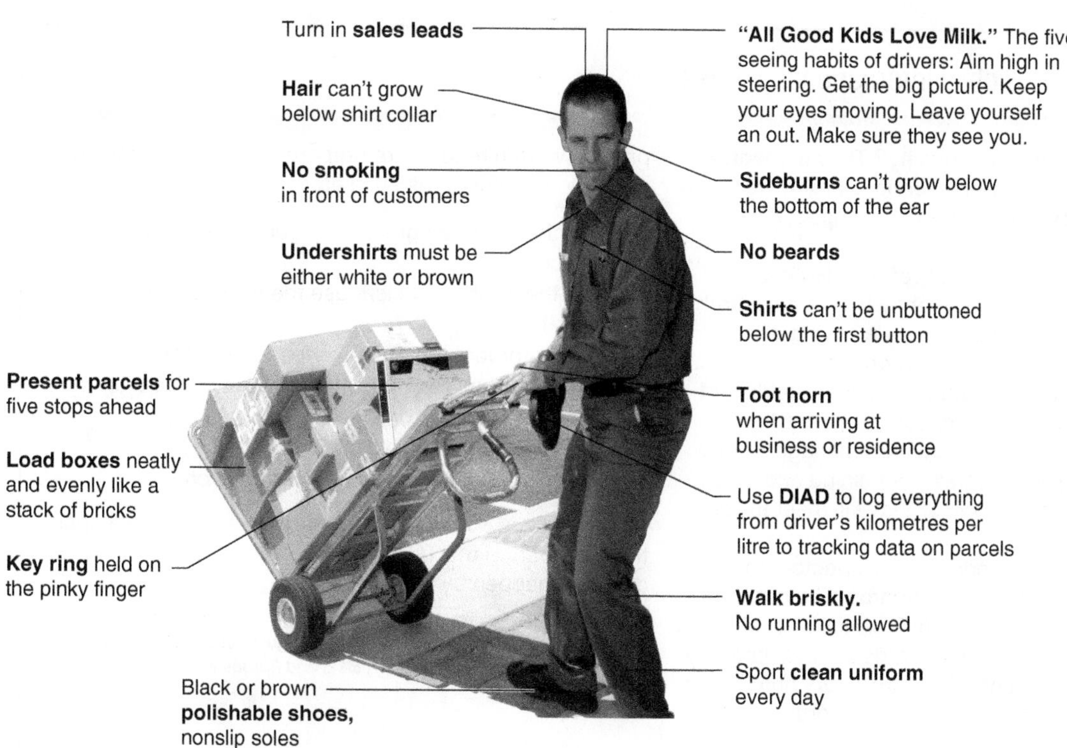

UPS drivers are taught 340 precise methods of how to correctly deliver a package. Regimented? Absolutely. But UPS credits its uniformity and efficiency with laying the foundation for its high-quality service.

as reliability and courtesy are part of the process. An operations manager can *design processes (service products) that have these attributes* and can ensure their quality through the TQM techniques discussed in this chapter.

Third, the operations manager should realize that the customer's expectations are the standard against which the service is judged. Customers' perceptions of service quality result from a comparison of their before-service expectations with their actual-service experience. In other words, service quality is judged on the basis of whether it meets expectations. The *manager may*

VIDEO 5.2
TQM at Ritz-Carlton Hotels

TABLE 5.5
Determinants of Service Quality

Reliability involves consistency of performance and dependability. It means that the firm performs the service right the first time and that the firm honours its promises.

Responsiveness concerns the willingness or readiness of employees to provide service. It involves timeliness of service.

Competence means possession of the required skills and knowledge to perform the service.

Access involves approachability and ease of contact.

Courtesy involves politeness, respect, consideration, and friendliness of contact personnel (including receptionists, telephone operators, etc.).

Communication means keeping customers informed in language they can understand and listening to them. It may mean that the company has to adjust its language for different consumers—increasing the level of sophistication with a well-educated customer and speaking simply and plainly with a novice.

Credibility involves trustworthiness, believability, and honesty. It involves having the customer's best interests at heart.

Security is the freedom from danger, risk, or doubt.

Understanding/knowing the customer involves making the effort to understand the customer's needs.

Tangibles include the physical evidence of the service.

Source: Adapted from A. Parasuranam, Valarie A. Zeithaml, and Leonard L. Berry, "A Conceptual Model of Service Quality and its Implications for Future Research," *Journal of Marketing* (Fall 1985): 44; *Journal of Marketing*, 58, no. 1 (January 1994): 111–125; *Journal of Retailing* 70 (Fall 1994): 201–230.

OM *in Action* Richey International's Spies

How do luxury hotels maintain quality? They inspect. But when the product is one-on-one service, largely dependent on personal behaviour, how do you inspect? You hire spies!

Richey International is the spy. Preferred Hotels and Resorts Worldwide and Intercontinental Hotels have both hired Richey to do quality evaluations via spying. Richey employees posing as customers perform the inspections. However, even then management must have established what the customer expects and specific services that yield customer satisfaction. Only then do managers know where and how to inspect. Aggressive training and objective inspections reinforce behaviour that will meet those customer expectations.

The hotels use Richey's undercover inspectors to ensure performance to exacting standards. The hotels do not know when the evaluators will arrive. Nor what aliases they will use. Over 50 different standards are evaluated before the inspectors even check in at a luxury hotel. Over the next 24 hours, using checklists, tape recordings, and photos, written reports are prepared. The reports include evaluation of standards such as:

- Does the doorman greet each guest in less than 30 seconds?
- Does the front-desk clerk use the guest's name during check-in?
- Is the bathroom tub and shower spotlessly clean?
- How many minutes does it take to get coffee after the guest sits down for breakfast?
- Did the waiter make eye contact?
- Were minibar charges posted correctly on the bill?

Established standards, aggressive training, and inspections are part of the TQM effort at these hotels. Quality does not happen by accident.

Sources: Hotel and Motel Management (August 2002): 128; *The Wall Street Journal* (May 12, 1999): B1, B12; and *Forbes* (October 5, 1998): 88–89.

be able to influence both the quality of the service and the expectation. Don't promise more than you can deliver.

Fourth, the manager must expect exceptions. There is a standard quality level at which the regular service is delivered, such as the bank teller's handling of a transaction. However, there are "exceptions" or "problems" initiated by the customer or by less-than-optimal operating conditions (e.g., the computer "crashed"). This implies that the quality control system must recognize and *have a set of alternative plans for less-than-optimal operating conditions.*

Service recovery
Training and empowering frontline workers to solve a problem immediately.

Well-run companies have **service recovery** strategies. This means they train and empower frontline employees to immediately solve a problem. For instance, staff at Marriott Hotels are drilled in the LEARN routine—*L*isten, *E*mpathize, *A*pologize, *R*eact, *N*otify—with the final step ensuring that the complaint is fed back into the system. And at the Ritz-Carlton, staff members are trained not to say merely "sorry" but "please accept my apology." The Ritz gives them a budget for reimbursing upset guests.

Designing the product, managing the service process, matching customer expectations to the product, and preparing for the exceptions are keys to quality services. The *OM in Action* box, "Richey International's Spies," provides another glimpse of how OM managers improve quality in services.

CHAPTER SUMMARY

Quality is a term that means different things to different people. We define quality as "the totality of features and characteristics of a product or service that bears on its ability to satisfy stated or implied needs." Defining quality expectations is critical to effective and efficient operations.

Quality requires building a total quality management (TQM) environment because quality cannot be inspected into a product. The chapter also addresses seven TQM *concepts*: continuous improvement, Six Sigma, employee empowerment, benchmarking, just-in-time, Taguchi concepts, and knowledge of TQM tools. The seven TQM *tools* introduced in this chapter are check sheets, scatter diagrams, cause-and-effect diagrams, Pareto charts, flowcharts, histograms, and statistical process control (SPC).

Key Terms

Quality (p. 121)
Cost of quality (COQ) (p. 123)
ISO 9000 (p. 124)
ISO 14000 (p. 124)
Total quality management (TQM) (p. 125)
PDCA (p. 125)
Six Sigma (p. 126)
Employee empowerment (p. 127)
Quality circle (p. 128)
Benchmarking (p. 128)
Quality robust (p. 130)
Quality loss function (QLF) (p. 130)
Target-oriented quality (p. 131)
Cause-and-effect diagram, Ishikawa diagram, or fish-bone chart (p. 131)
Pareto charts (p. 132)
Flowcharts (p. 134)
Statistical process control (SPC) (p. 135)
Control charts (p. 135)
Inspection (p. 136)
Source inspection (p. 137)
Poka-yoke (p. 137)
Attribute inspection (p. 137)
Variable inspection (p. 137)
Service recovery (p. 140)

Ethical Dilemma

A lawsuit a few years ago made headlines worldwide when a McDonald's drive-thru customer spilled a cup of scalding hot coffee on herself. Claiming the coffee was too hot to be safely consumed in a car, the badly burned 80-year-old woman won $2.9 million (USD) in court. (The judge later reduced the award to $640 000 (USD).) McDonald's claimed the product was served to the correct specifications and was of proper quality. Further, the cup read "Caution—Contents May Be Hot." McDonald's coffee, at 31.5°C, is substantially hotter (by corporate rule) than typical restaurant coffee, despite hundreds of coffee-scalding complaints in the past 10 years. Similar court cases, incidentally, resulted in smaller verdicts, but again in favour of the plaintiffs. For example, Motor City Bagel Shop was sued for a spilled cup of coffee by a drive-thru patron, and Starbucks by a customer who spilled coffee on her own ankle.

Are McDonald's, Motor City, and Starbucks at fault in situations such as these? How do quality and ethics enter into these cases?

Discussion Questions

1. Explain how improving quality can lead to reduced costs.
2. As an internet exercise, determine the Baldrige Award Criteria. See the website **www.quality.nist.gov**.
3. Which three of Deming's 14 points do you think are most critical to the success of a TQM program? Why?
4. List the seven concepts that are necessary for an effective TQM program. How are these related to Deming's 14 points?
5. Name three of the important people associated with the quality concepts of this chapter. In each case, write a short sentence about each one summarizing their primary contribution to the field of quality management.
6. What are seven tools of TQM?
7. How does fear in the workplace (and in the classroom) inhibit learning?
8. How can a university control the quality of its output (that is, its graduates)?
9. Philip Crosby said that quality is free. Why?
10. List the three concepts central to Taguchi's approach.
11. What is the purpose of using a Pareto chart for a given problem?
12. What are the four broad categories of "causes" to help initially structure an Ishikawa diagram or cause-and-effect diagram?
13. Of the several points where inspection may be necessary, which apply especially well to manufacturing?
14. What roles do operations managers play in addressing the major aspects of service quality?
15. Explain, in your own words, what is meant by *source inspection*.
16. What are 10 determinants of service quality?
17. Name several products that do not require high quality.
18. What does the formula $L = D^2C$ mean?
19. In this chapter, we have suggested that building quality into a process and its people is difficult. Inspections are also difficult. To indicate just how difficult inspections are, count the number of *E*s (both capital *E* and lowercase *e*) in the *OM in Action* box, "Richey International's Spies" on page 210 (include the title but not the footnote). How many did you find? If each student does this individually, you are very likely to find a distribution rather than a single number!

Problems

• **5.1** An avant-garde clothing manufacturer runs a series of high-profile, risqué ads on a billboard on the Trans Canada Highway and regularly collects protest calls from people who are offended by them. The company has no idea how many people in total see the ads, but it has been collecting statistics on the number of phone calls from irate viewers:

Type	Description	Number of Complaints
R	Offensive racially/ethnically	10
M	Demeaning to men	4
W	Demeaning to women	14
I	Ad(s) is/are incomprehensible	6
O	Other	2

a) Depict this data with a Pareto chart. Also depict the cumulative complaint line.
b) What percent of the total complaints can be attributed to the most prevalent complaint?

• **5.2** Develop a scatter diagram for two variables of interest (say pages in the newspaper by day of the week; see example in Figure 5.6b).

• **5.3** Develop a Pareto chart of the following causes of poor grades on an exam:

Reason for Poor Grade	Frequency
Insufficient time to complete	15
Late arrival to exam	7
Difficulty understanding material	25
Insufficient preparation time	2
Studied wrong material	2
Distractions in exam room	9
Calculator batteries died during exam	1
Forgot exam was scheduled	3
Felt ill during exam	4

• **5.4** Develop a histogram of the time it took for you or your friends to receive six recent orders at a fast-food restaurant.

•• **5.5** A small family restaurant in Saskatoon has recorded the following data for eight recent customers:

Customer Number, i	Minutes from Time Food Ordered Until Food Arrived (y_i)	No. of Trips to Kitchen by Waitress (x_i)
1	10.50	4
2	12.75	5
3	9.25	3
4	8.00	2
5	9.75	3
6	11.00	4
7	14.00	6
8	10.75	5

a) The owner wants you to graph the eight points (x_i, y_i), $i = 1, 2, \ldots 8$. She has been concerned because customers have been waiting too long for their food, and this graph is intended to help her find possible causes of the problem.
b) This is an example of what type of graph?

•• **5.6** Develop a flowchart (as in Figure 5.6[e] and Example 2) showing all the steps involved in planning a party.

•• **5.7** Consider the types of poor driving habits that might occur at a traffic light. Make a list of the 10 you consider most likely to happen. Add the category of "other" to that list.
a) Compose a check sheet (like that in Figure 5.6[a]) to collect the frequency of occurrence of these habits. Using your check sheet, visit a busy traffic light intersection at four different times of the day, with two of these times being during high-traffic periods (rush hour, lunch hour). For 15 to 20 minutes each visit, observe the frequency with which the habits you listed occurred.
b) Construct a Pareto chart showing the relative frequency of occurrence of each habit.

•• **5.8** Draw a fish-bone chart detailing reasons why an airline customer might be dissatisfied.

•• **5.9** Consider the everyday task of getting to work on time or arriving at your first class on time in the morning. Draw a fish-bone chart showing reasons why you might arrive late in the morning.

•• **5.10** Construct a cause-and-effect diagram to reflect "student dissatisfied with university registration process." Use the "four *M*s" or create your own organizing scheme. Include at least 12 causes.

•• **5.11** Draw a fish-bone chart depicting the reasons that might give rise to an incorrect fee statement at the time you go to pay for your registration at school.

••• **5.12** Mary Beth Marrs, the manager of an apartment complex, feels overwhelmed by the number of complaints she is receiving. Below is the check sheet she has kept for the past 12 weeks. Develop a Pareto chart using this information. What recommendations would you make?

Week	Grounds	Parking/ Drives	Pool	Tenant Issues	Electrical/ Plumbing
1	✓✓✓	✓✓	✓	✓✓✓	
2	✓	✓✓✓	✓✓	✓✓	✓
3	✓✓✓	✓✓✓	✓✓	✓	
4	✓	✓✓✓✓	✓	✓	✓✓
5	✓✓	✓✓✓	✓✓✓✓	✓✓	
6	✓	✓✓✓✓	✓✓		
7		✓✓✓	✓✓	✓✓	
8	✓	✓✓✓✓	✓✓	✓✓✓	✓
9	✓	✓✓	✓		
10	✓	✓✓✓✓	✓✓	✓✓	
11		✓✓✓	✓✓	✓	
12	✓✓	✓✓✓	✓✓✓	✓	

• **5.13** Use Pareto analysis to investigate the following data collected on a printed-circuit-board assembly line:

Defect	Number of Defect Occurrences
Components not adhering	143
Excess adhesive	71
Misplaced transistors	601
Defective board dimension	146
Mounting holes improperly positioned	12
Circuitry problems on final test	90
Wrong component	212

a) Prepare a graph of the data.
b) What conclusions do you reach?

•• **5.14** A list of 16 issues that led to incorrect formulations in Richard Dulski's jam manufacturing unit is provided below:

List of Issues

1. Incorrect measurement	9. Variability
2. Antiquated scales	10. Equipment in disrepair
3. Lack of clear instructions	11. Technician calculation off
4. Damaged raw material	12. Jars mislabelled
5. Operator misreads display	13. Temperature controls off
6. Inadequate cleanup	14. Incorrect weights
7. Incorrect maintenance	15. Priority miscommunication
8. Inadequate flow controls	16. Inadequate instructions

Create a fish-bone diagram and categorize each of these issues correctly, using the "four *M*s" method.

•• **5.15** Develop a flowchart for one of the following:

a) Filling up with gasoline at a self-serve station.
b) Determining your account balance and making a withdrawal at an ATM.
c) Getting a cone of yogurt or ice cream from an ice cream store.

•••• **5.16** Kenora Electric Generators has been getting many complaints from its major customer, Home Station, about the quality of its shipments of home generators. Daniel Magill, the plant manager, is alarmed that a customer is providing him with the only information the company has on shipment quality. He decides to collect information on defective shipments through a form he has asked his drivers to complete on arrival at customers' stores. The forms for the first 279 shipments have been turned in. They show the following over the past 8 weeks:

		No. of Shipments	*Reason for Defective Shipment*			
Week	**No. of Shipments**	**with Defects**	**Incorrect Bill of Lading**	**Incorrect Truckload**	**Damaged Product**	**Trucks Late**
1	23	5	2	2	1	
2	31	8	1	4	1	2
3	28	6	2	3	1	
4	37	11	4	4	1	2
5	35	10	3	4	2	1
6	40	14	5	6	3	
7	41	12	3	5	3	1
8	44	15	4	7	2	2

Even though Daniel increased his capacity by adding more workers to his normal contingent of 30, he knew that for many weeks he exceeded his regular output of 30 shipments per week. A review of his turnover over the past 8 weeks shows the following:

Week	No. of New Hires	No. of Terminations	Total No. of Workers
1	1	0	30
2	2	1	31
3	3	2	32
4	2	0	34
5	2	2	34
6	2	4	32
7	4	1	35
8	3	2	36

a) Develop a scatter diagram using total number of shipments and number of defective shipments. Does there appear to be any relationship?
b) Develop a scatter diagram using the variable "turnover" (number of new hires plus number of terminations) and the number of defective shipments. Does the diagram depict a relationship between the two variables?
c) Develop a Pareto chart for the type of defects that have occurred.
d) Draw a fish-bone chart showing the possible causes of the defective shipments.

••• **5.17** A Gallup poll of 519 adults who flew during a year (published in *The Economist*, June 16, 2007, p. 6) found the following their number one complaints about flying: cramped seats (45), cost (16), dislike or fear of flying (57), security measures (119), poor service (12), connecting flight problems (8), overcrowded planes (42), late planes/waits (57), food (7), lost luggage (7), and other (51).

a) What percentage of those surveyed found nothing they disliked?
b) Draw a Pareto chart summarizing these responses. Include the "no complaints" group.
c) Use the "four *Ms*" method to create a fish-bone diagram for the 10 specific categories of dislikes (exclude "other" and "no complaints").
d) If you were managing an airline, what two or three specific issues would you tackle to improve customer service? Why?

▶ **Refer to MyOMLab for these additional homework problems: 5.18–5.21**

Case Studies

Fast Creek Lightning: (C)*

The popularity of the Fast Creek Lightning hockey team under its new coach, Scotty Beauchamp, has surged in each of the five years since his arrival in town. (See Fast Creek Lightning (A) in Chapter 3 and (B) in Chapter 4.) With an arena close to maxing out at 10 800 seats and a vocal coach pushing for a new facility, Fast Creek Lightning owner Keith MacLennan faced some difficult decisions. After a phenomenal upset victory over its archrival, the Walkerford Wolves, at the Holiday Classic in December, MacLennan was not as happy as one would think. Instead of ecstatic fans, all MacLennan heard were complaints. "The lines at the concession stands were too long"; "Parking was harder to find and farther away than in the old days"; "Seats were shabby"; "Traffic was backed up halfway to Saskatoon"; and on and on. "I just can't win," muttered MacLennan.

At his staff meeting the following Monday, MacLennan turned to his VP of operations, Leslie Gardner. "I wish you would take on these complaints, Leslie," he said. "See what the real problems are—let me know how you've resolved them." Gardner wasn't surprised at the request. "I've already got a handle on it, Keith," she replied. "We've been randomly surveying 50 fans per game for the past 5 games to see what's on their minds. It's all part of the organization-wide TQM effort. Let me tally things up and I'll get back to you in a week."

When she returned to her office, Gardner pulled out the file her assistant had compiled (see Table 5.6). "There's a lot of information here," she thought.

TABLE 5.6 Fan Satisfaction Survey Results (N = 250)

		Overall Grade				
		A	B	C	D	E
Game Day	A. Parking	90	105	45	5	5
	B. Traffic	50	85	48	52	15
	C. Seating	45	30	115	35	25
	D. Entertainment	160	35	26	10	19
	E. Printed Program	66	34	98	22	30
Tickets	A. Pricing	105	104	16	15	10
	B. Season Ticket Plans	75	80	54	41	0
Concessions	A. Prices	16	116	58	58	2
	B. Selection of Foods	155	60	24	11	0
	C. Speed of Service	35	45	46	48	76
Respondents	250					

Open-Ended Comments on Survey Cards:

Parking a mess	More hot dog stands	Put in bigger seats	My company will buy a box—build it!
Add a luxury box	Seats are all metal	Friendly ushers	
	Need boxes	Need better seats	Programs overpriced
Double the parking attendants	Seats stink	Expand parking lots	Want softer seats
Everything is okay	Go Lightning!		Beat those Wolves!
Too crowded	Lines are awful	Hot dogs cold	I'll pay for a box
Seats too narrow	Seats are uncomfortable	$3 for a coffee? No way!	Seats too small
Great food	I will pay more for better view	Get some boxes	Music was terrific
Scotty B. for prime minister	Get a new arena	Love the new uniforms	Love Beauchamp
I smelled drugs being smoked		Took an hour to park	Everything is great
Stadium is ancient	I want cushioned seats	Coach is terrific	Build new arena
Seats are like rocks	Not enough police	More water fountains	Move games to Saskatoon
Not enough cops for traffic	Fans too rowdy	Better seats	No complaints
Game starts too late	Parking terrible	Seats not comfy	Dirty bathroom
Hire more traffic cops	Toilets weren't clean	Bigger parking lot	
Need new sound system	Not enough handicap spots in lot	I'm too old for these seats	
Great!	Well done	Cold coffee served at game	

Discussion Questions

1. Using at least two different quality tools, analyze the data and present your conclusions.
2. How could the survey have been more useful?
3. What is the next step?

*This integrated case study runs throughout the text. Other issues facing Fast Creek's new arena include: (A) Managing the renovation project; (B) Forecasting game attendance; (D) Break-even analysis of food services (Supplement 7 MyOMLab); (E) Locating the new arena (Chapter 8 MyOMLab); (F) Inventory planning of hockey programs (Chapter 12 MyOMLab); and (G) Scheduling of security officers/staff for game days.

The Culture of Quality at Arnold Palmer Hospital

Founded in 1989, Arnold Palmer Hospital is one of the largest hospitals for women and children in the U.S., with 431 beds in two facilities totalling 62 800 square metres. Located in downtown Orlando, Florida, and named after its famed golf benefactor, the hospital, with more than 2000 employees, serves an 18-county area in central Florida and is the only Level 1 trauma centre for children in that region. Arnold Palmer Hospital provides a broad range of medical services including neonatal and paediatric intensive care, paediatric oncology and cardiology, care for high-risk pregnancies, and maternal intensive care.

The Issue of Assessing Quality Health Care

Quality health care is a goal all hospitals profess, but Arnold Palmer Hospital has actually developed comprehensive and scientific means of asking customers to judge the quality of care they receive. Participating in a national benchmark comparison against other hospitals, Arnold Palmer Hospital consistently scores in the top 10% in overall patient satisfaction. Executive Director Kathy Swanson states, "Hospitals in this area will be distinguished largely on the basis of their customer satisfaction. We must have accurate information about how our patients and their families judge the quality of our care, so I follow the questionnaire results daily. The in-depth survey helps me and others on my team to gain quick knowledge from patient feedback." Arnold Palmer Hospital employees are empowered to provide gifts in value up to $200 to patients who find reason to complain about any hospital service such as food, courtesy, responsiveness, or cleanliness.

Swanson doesn't focus just on the customer surveys, which are mailed to patients one week after discharge, but also on a variety of internal measures. These measures usually start at the grassroots level, where the staff sees a problem and develops ways to track performance. The hospital's longstanding philosophy supports the concept that each patient is important and respected as a person. That patient has the right to comprehensive, compassionate family-centred health care provided by a knowledgable physician-directed team.

Some of the measures Swanson carefully monitors for continuous improvement are morbidity, infection rates, readmission rates, costs per case, and length of stays. The tools she uses daily include Pareto charts, flowcharts, and process charts, in addition to benchmarking against hospitals both nationally and in the southeast region.

The result of all of these efforts has been a quality culture as manifested in Arnold Palmer's high ranking in patient satisfaction and one of the highest survival rates of critically ill babies.

Discussion Questions*

1. Why is it important for Arnold Palmer Hospital to get a patient's assessment of health care quality? Does the patient have the expertise to judge the health care she or he receives?
2. How would you build a culture of quality in an organization, such as Arnold Palmer Hospital?
3. What techniques does Arnold Palmer Hospital practise in its drive for quality and continuous improvement?
4. Develop a fish-bone diagram illustrating the quality variables for a patient who just gave birth at Arnold Palmer Hospital (or any other hospital).

*You may wish to view the video that accompanies this case before answering these questions.

Quality at the Ritz-Carlton Hotel Company

Ritz-Carlton. The name alone evokes images of luxury and quality. As the first hotel company to win the Malcolm Baldrige National Quality Award, the Ritz treats quality as if it is the heartbeat of the company. This means a daily commitment to meeting customer expectations and making sure that each hotel is free of any deficiency.

In the hotel industry, quality can be hard to quantify. Guests do not purchase a product when they stay at the Ritz: They buy an experience. Thus, creating the right combination of elements to make the experience stand out is the challenge and goal of every employee, from maintenance to management.

Before applying for the Baldrige Award, company management undertook a rigorous self-examination of its operations in an attempt to measure and quantify quality. Nineteen processes were studied, including room service delivery, guest reservation and registration, message delivery, and breakfast service. This period of self-study included statistical measurement of process work flows and cycle times for areas ranging from room service delivery times and reservations to valet parking and housekeeping efficiency. The results were used to develop performance benchmarks against which future activity could be measured.

With specific, quantifiable targets in place, Ritz-Carlton managers and employees now focus on continuous improvement. The goal is 100% customer satisfaction: If a guest's experience does not meet expectations, the Ritz-Carlton risks losing that guest to competition.

One way the company has put more meaning behind its quality efforts is to organize its employees into "self-directed" work teams. Employee teams determine work scheduling, what work needs to be done, and what to do about quality problems in their own areas. In order that they can see the relationship of their specific area to the overall goals, employees are also given the opportunity to take additional training in hotel operations. Ritz-Carlton believes that a more educated and informed employee is in a better position to make decisions in the best interest of the organization.

Discussion Questions*

1. In what ways could the Ritz-Carlton monitor its success in achieving quality?
2. Many companies say that their goal is to provide quality products or services. What actions might you expect from a company that intends quality to be more than a slogan or buzzword?
3. Why might it cost the Ritz-Carlton less to "do things right" the first time?
4. How could control charts, Pareto diagrams, and cause-and-effect diagrams be used to identify quality problems at a hotel?
5. What are some nonfinancial measures of customer satisfaction that might be used by the Ritz-Carlton?

*You may wish to view the video that accompanies this case before addressing these questions.

▶ **Additional Case Study:** Visit **MyOMLab** for this case study:
Westover Electrical, Inc: This electric motor manufacturer has a large log of defects in its wiring process.

Bibliography

Besterfield, Dale H. *Quality Control*, 8th ed. Upper Saddle River, NJ: Prentice Hall, 2009.

Brown, Mark G. *Baldrige Award Winning Quality*, 19th ed. University Park, IL: Productivity Press, 2010.

Crosby, P. B. *Quality Is Still Free*. New York: McGraw-Hill, 1996.

Evans, J. R., and W. M. Lindsay. *Managing for Quality and Performance Excellence*, 7th ed. Mason, OH: Thompson-Southwestern, 2008.

Feigenbaum, A. V. "Raising the Bar." *Quality Progress* 41, no. 7 (July 2008): 22–28.

Gitlow, Howard S. A *Guide to Lean Six Sigma Management Skills*. University Park, IL: Productivity Press, 2009.

Gonzalez-Benito, J., and O. Gonzalez-Benito. "Operations Management Practices Linked to the Adoption of ISO 14001." *International Journal of Production Economics* 113, no. 1 (May 2008): 60.

Gryna, F. M., R. C. H. Chua, and J. A. DeFeo. *Juran's Quality Planning and Analysis for Enterprise Quality*, 5th ed. New York: McGraw-Hill, 2007.

Harrington, D. R., M. Khanna, and G. Deltas. "Striving to Be Green: The Adoption of Total Quality Environmental Management." *Applied Economics* 40, no. 23 (December 2008): 2995.

Mitra, Amit. *Fundamentals of Quality Control and Improvement*. New York: Wiley, 2009.

Pande, P. S., R. P. Neuman, R. R. Cavanagh. *What Is Design for Six Sigma?* New York: McGraw-Hill, 2005.

Schroeder, Roger G., et al. "Six Sigma: Definition and Underlying Theory." *Journal of Operations Management* 26, no. 4 (2008): 536–554.

Soltani, E., P. Lai, and P. Phillips. "A New Look at Factors Influencing Total Quality Management Failure." *New Technology, Work, and Employment* 23, no. 1–2 (March 2008): 125.

Stewart, D. M. "Piecing Together Service Quality: A Framework for Robust Service." *Production and Operations Management* (Summer 2003): 246–265.

Summers, Donna. *Quality Management*, 2nd ed. Upper Saddle River, NJ: Prentice Hall, 2009.

CHAPTER 5 Rapid Review

Main Heading | **Review Material** | MyOMLab

QUALITY AND STRATEGY
(p. 121)

Managing quality helps build successful strategies of differentiation, low cost, and *response*.

Two ways that quality improves profitability are:

- Sales gains via improved response, price flexibility, increased market share, and/or improved reputation
- Reduced costs via increased productivity, lower rework and scrap costs, and/or lower warranty costs

VIDEO 5.1
The Culture of Quality at Arnold Palmer Hospital

DEFINING QUALITY
(pp. 121–124)

An operations manager's objective is to build a total quality management system that identifies and satisfies customer need.

- **Quality**—The ability of a product or service to meet customer needs.

The American Society for Quality (ASQ) defines quality as "the totality of features and characteristics of a product or service that bears on its ability to satisfy stated or implied needs."

The two most well-known quality awards are:

- *U.S.*: Malcolm Baldrige National Quality Award, named after a former secretary of commerce
- *Japan*: Deming Prize, named after an American, Dr. W. Edwards Deming

- **Cost of quality (COQ)**—The cost of doing things wrong; that is, the price of nonconformance.

The four major categories of costs associated with quality are: *prevention costs, appraisal costs, internal failure*, and *external costs.*

Four leaders in the field of quality management are W. Edwards Deming, Joseph M. Juran, Armand Feigenbaum, and Philip B. Crosby.

INTERNATIONAL QUALITY STANDARDS
(pp. 124–125)

- **ISO 9000**—A set of quality standards developed by the International Organization for Standardization (ISO).

ISO 9000 is the only quality standard with international recognition. To do business globally, being listed in the ISO directory is critical.

- **ISO 14000**—A series of environmental management standards established by the ISO.

ISO 14000 contains five core elements: (1) environmental management, (2) auditing, (3) performance evaluation, (4) labelling, and (5) life cycle assessment.

As a follow-on to ISO 14000, ISO 24700 reflects the business world's current approach to reuse recovered components from many products.

Problem: 5.17

TOTAL QUALITY MANAGEMENT
(pp. 125–131)

- **Total quality management (TQM)**—Management of an entire organization so that it excels in all aspects of products and services that are important to the customer.

Seven concepts for an effective TQM program are (1) continuous improvement, (2) Six Sigma, (3) employee empowerment, (4) benchmarking, (5) just-in-time (JIT), (6) Taguchi concepts, and (7) knowledge of TQM tools.

- **PDCA**—A continuous improvement model that involves four stages: plan, do, check, and act.

The Japanese use the word *kaizen* to describe the ongoing process of unending improvement—the setting and achieving of ever-higher goals.

- **Six Sigma**—A program to save time, improve quality, and lower costs.

In a statistical sense, Six Sigma describes a process, product, or service with an extremely high capability—99.9997% accuracy, or 3.4 defects per million.

- **Employee empowerment**—Enlarging employee jobs so that the added responsibility and authority is moved to the lowest level possible in the organization.

Business literature suggests that some 85% of quality problems have to do with materials and processes, not with employee performance.

- **Quality circle**—A group of employees meeting regularly with a facilitator to solve work-related problems in their work area.
- **Benchmarking**—Selecting a demonstrated standard of performance that represents the very best performance for a process or an activity.

The philosophy behind just-in-time (JIT) involves continuing improvement and enforced problem solving. JIT systems are designed to produce or deliver goods just as they are needed.

- **Quality robust**—Products that are consistently built to meet customer needs, in spite of adverse conditions in the production process.

Main Heading	Review Material	MyOMLab
	• **Quality loss function (QLF)**—A mathematical function that identifies all costs connected with poor quality and shows how these costs increase as product quality moves from what the customer wants: $L = D^2C$. • **Target-oriented quality**—A philosophy of continuous improvement to bring the product exactly on target.	Problems: 5.1, 5.3, 5.5, 5.13, 5.14, 5.16, and 5.17
TOOLS OF TQM (pp. 131–135)	TQM tools that generate ideas include the *check sheet* (organized method of recording data), *scatter diagram* (graph of the value of one variable vs. another variable), and *cause-and-effect diagram.* Tools for organizing the data are the *Pareto chart* and *flowchart.* Tools for identifying problems are the *histogram* (distribution showing the frequency of occurrences of a variable) and *statistical process control chart.* • **Cause-and-effect diagram**—A schematic technique used to discover possible locations of quality problems. (Also called an Ishikawa diagram or a fish-bone chart.) The 4 *Ms* (material, machinery/equipment, manpower, and methods) may be broad "causes." • **Pareto chart**—A graphic that identifies the few critical items as opposed to many less important ones. • **Flowchart**—A block diagram that graphically describes a process or system. • **Statistical process control (SPC)**—A process used to monitor standards, make measurements, and take corrective action as a product or service is being produced. • **Control chart**—A graphic presentation of process data over time, with predetermined control limits.	ACTIVE MODEL 5.1
THE ROLE OF INSPECTION (pp. 136–138)	• **Inspection**—A means of ensuring that an operation is producing at the quality level expected. • **Source inspection**—Controlling or monitoring at the point of production or purchase: at the source. • **Poka-yoke**—Literally translated, "foolproof"; it has come to mean a device or technique that ensures the production of a good unit every time. • **Attribute inspection**—An inspection that classifies items as being either good or defective. • **Variable inspection**—Classifications of inspected items as falling on a continuum scale, such as dimension, size, or strength.	
TQM IN SERVICES (pp. 138–140)	Determinants of service quality: reliability, responsiveness, competence, access, courtesy, communication, credibility, security, understanding/knowing the customer, and tangibles. • **Service recovery**—Training and empowering frontline workers to solve a problem immediately.	VIDEO 5.2 TQM at Ritz-Carlton Hotels

Self Test

■ **Before taking the self-test,** refer to the learning objectives listed at the beginning of the chapter and the key terms listed at the end of the chapter.

LO**1.** In this chapter, *quality* is defined as:
- **a)** the degree of excellence at an acceptable price and the control of variability at an acceptable cost.
- **b)** how well a product fits patterns of consumer preferences.
- **c)** the totality of features and characteristics of a product or service that bears on its ability to satisfy stated or implied needs.
- **d)** being impossible to define, but you know what it is.

LO**2.** ISO 14000 is an international standard that addresses ______.

LO**3.** If 1 million passengers pass through the Jacksonville Airport with checked baggage each year, a successful Six Sigma program for baggage handling would result in how many passengers with misplaced luggage?
- **a)** 3.4 **b)** 6.0
- **c)** 34 **d)** 2700
- **e)** 6 times the monthly standard deviation of passengers

LO**4.** The process of identifying other organizations that are best at some facet of your operations and then modelling your organization after them is known as:
- **a)** continuous improvement. **b)** employee empowerment.
- **c)** benchmarking. **d)** copycatting.
- **e)** patent infringement.

LO**5.** The Taguchi method includes all except which of the following major concepts?
- **a)** Employee involvement
- **b)** Remove the effects of adverse conditions
- **c)** Quality loss function
- **d)** Target specifications

LO**6.** The seven tools of total quality management are ______, ______, ______, ______, ______, ______, and ______.

Answers: LO1. c; LO2. environmental management; LO3. a; LO4. c; LO5. a; LO6. check sheets, scatter diagrams, cause-and-effect diagrams, Pareto charts, flowcharts, histograms, SPC charts.

The problems marked in red can be found on MyOMLab. Visit MyOMLab to access cases, videos, downloadable software, and much more. MyOMLab also features a personalized Study Plan that helps you identify which chapter concepts you've mastered and guides you towards study tools for additional practice.

Student Profile

Graydon Peppler International Traffic Specialist-LOGIKOR Inc.
Business Administration Materials & Operations Management (Co-op) Program Graduate 2012

Upon graduating from Bluevale Collegiate Institute in 2008, I took a year off to consider my education and career options. After carefully weighing all my options I chose to attend Conestoga College.

I recently graduated from the Materials & Operations Management (now Supply Chain & Operations Management) Co-op program in December 2012, complete with one year of direct Co-op work experience gained while in the program. Furthermore, as part of graduating from this program I also earned a Lean Six Sigma Yellow Belt certificate, highly regarded by business and industry. During my final Co-op work term I accepted an offer of employment from LOGIKOR Inc. as an International Traffic Specialist, and I am enjoying every minute of my new career! I give full credit to the Materials and Operations Management program for helping me launch my career with an excellent company like LOGIKOR Inc. Successful completion of the program provides graduates like me with a wide range of career opportunities in a number of different sectors of the economy.

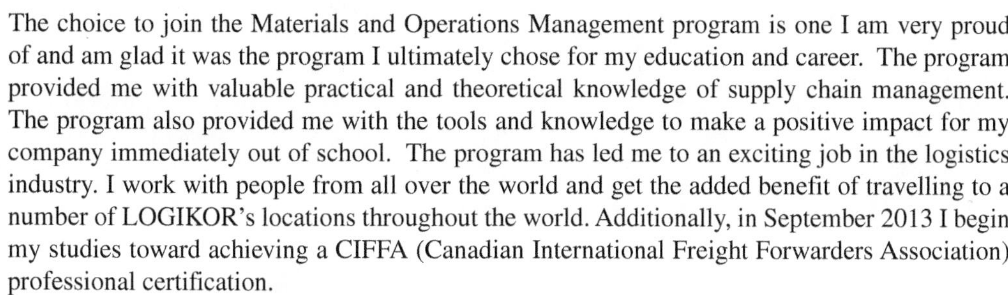

The choice to join the Materials and Operations Management program is one I am very proud of and am glad it was the program I ultimately chose for my education and career. The program provided me with valuable practical and theoretical knowledge of supply chain management. The program also provided me with the tools and knowledge to make a positive impact for my company immediately out of school. The program has led me to an exciting job in the logistics industry. I work with people from all over the world and get the added benefit of travelling to a number of LOGIKOR's locations throughout the world. Additionally, in September 2013 I begin my studies toward achieving a CIFFA (Canadian International Freight Forwarders Association) professional certification.

To all business students currently unsure of their career choice, know that all businesses compete within supply chains. As such, they need professionals with the skills and knowledge you will develop in the (now) Supply Chain and Operations Management program at Conestoga College. You will be able to make a meaningful impact with your firm right out of school in an exciting and challenging career. You will be glad you chose Supply Chain and Operations Management program at Conestoga College. I am!

6

Supply-Chain Management

Chapter Outline

10 OM Strategy Decisions

- Design of Goods and Services
- Managing Quality
- Process Strategy
- Location Strategies
- Layout Strategies
- Human Resources
- Supply-Chain Management
- Inventory Management
- Scheduling
- Maintenance

GLOBAL COMPANY PROFILE | DARDEN RESTAURANTS

Darden's Supply Chain Yields a Competitive Edge

Darden Restaurants Inc. is the largest publicly traded casual dining restaurant company in the world. It serves over 400 million meals annually from more than 1700 restaurants in the U.S. and Canada. Each of its well-known flagship brands—Olive Garden and Red Lobster—generates sales of $2 billion (USD) annually. Darden's other brands include Bahama Breeze, Seasons 52, Capital Grille, and LongHorn Steakhouse. The firm employs more than 150 000 people and is the 29th largest employer in the U.S.

"Operations is typically thought of as an execution of strategy. For us it is the strategy," Darden's former chairman, Joe R. Lee, stated.

In the restaurant business, a winning strategy requires a winning supply chain. Nothing is more important than sourcing and delivering healthy, high-quality food; and there are very few other industries where supplier performance is so closely tied to the customer.

Darden sources its food from five continents and thousands of suppliers. To meet Darden's needs for fresh ingredients, the company has developed four distinct supply chains: one for seafood; one for dairy/produce/other refrigerated foods; a third for other food items, like baked goods; and a fourth for restaurant supplies (everything from dishes to ovens to uniforms). Over $1.5 billion (USD) is spent in these supply chains annually. (See the *Video Case Study* at the end of this chapter for details.)

Darden's four supply channels have some common characteristics. They all require *supplier qualification*, have *product tracking*, are subject to *independent audits*, and employ *just-in-time delivery*. With best-in-class techniques and processes, Darden creates worldwide supply-chain partnerships and alliances that are rapid, transparent, and efficient. Darden achieves competitive advantage through its superior supply chain.

Qualifying Worldwide Sources: Part of Darden's supply chain begins with a crab harvest in the frigid waters off the coast of Alaska. But long before a supplier is qualified to sell to Darden, a total quality team is appointed. The team provides guidance, assistance, support, and training to the suppliers to ensure that overall objectives are understood and desired results accomplished.

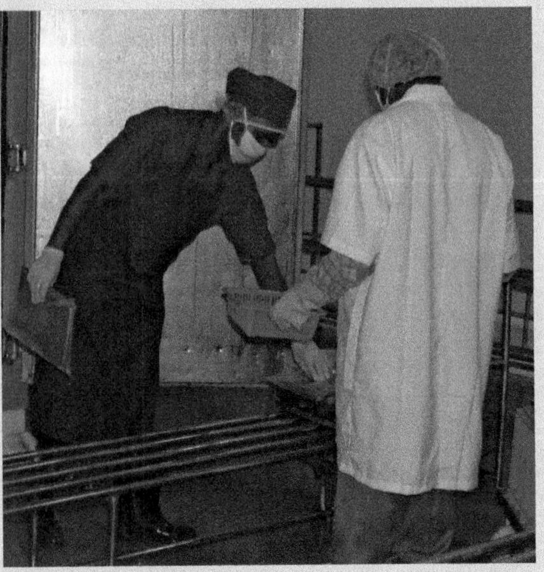

Independent Audits of Suppliers: To provide fair and accurate assessment, Darden's Total Quality Supplier Program includes an independent verification program. Each supplier is evaluated regularly by independent auditors on a risk-based schedule to determine the supplier's effectiveness.

Product Tracking: Darden's seafood inspection team developed an integral system that uses a lot ID to track seafood from its origin through shipping and receiving. Darden uses a modified atmosphere packaging (MAP) process to extend the shelf life and preserve the quality of its fresh fish. The tracking includes time temperature monitoring.

Chapter 6 Learning Objectives

The Supply Chain's Strategic Importance

AUTHOR COMMENT Competition today is not between companies; it is between supply chains.

Most firms, like Darden, spend a huge portion of their sales dollars on purchases. Because an increasing percentage of an organization's costs are determined by purchasing, relationships with suppliers are increasingly integrated and long term. Joint efforts that improve innovation, speed design, and reduce costs are common. Such efforts, when part of a corporate-wide strategy, can dramatically improve both partners' competitiveness. This integrated focus places added emphasis on managing supplier relationships.

Supply-chain management is the integration of the activities that procure materials and services, transform them into intermediate goods and final products, and deliver them to customers. These activities include purchasing and outsourcing activities, plus many other functions that are important to the relationship with suppliers and distributors. As Figure 6.1 suggests, supply-chain management includes determining (1) transportation vendors, (2) credit and cash transfers, (3) suppliers, (4) distributors, (5) accounts payable and receivable, (6) warehousing and inventory, (7) order fulfillment, and (8) sharing customer, forecasting, and production information. The *objective is to build a chain of suppliers that focuses on maximizing value to the ultimate customer.*

Supply-chain management Management of activities that procure materials and services, transform them into intermediate goods and final products, and deliver them through a distribution system.

As firms strive to increase their competitiveness via product customization, high quality, cost reductions, and speed to market, added emphasis is placed on the supply chain. Effective supply

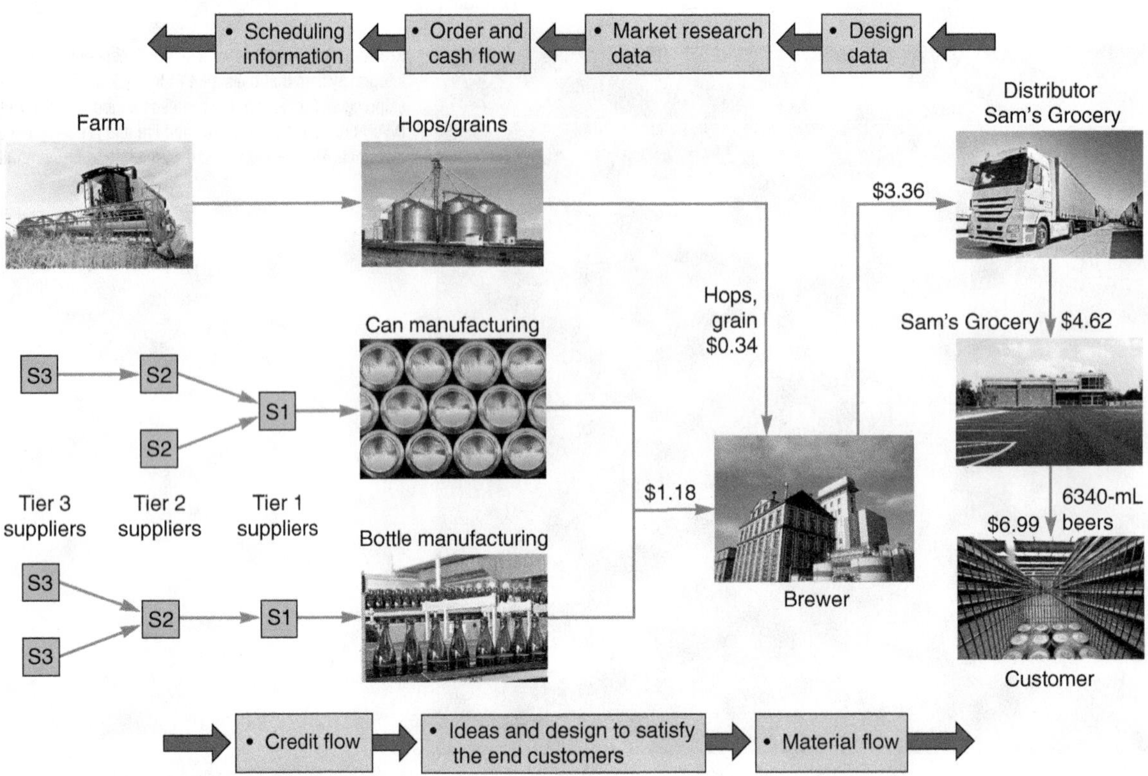

FIGURE 6.1 A Supply Chain for Beer

The supply chain includes all the interactions among suppliers, manufacturers, distributors, and customers. The chain includes transportation, scheduling information, cash and credit transfers, as well as ideas, designs, and material transfers. Even can and bottle manufacturers have their own tiers of suppliers providing components such as lids, labels, packing containers, etc. (Costs are approximate and include substantial taxes.)

chain management makes suppliers "partners" in the firm's strategy to satisfy an ever-changing marketplace. A competitive advantage may depend on a close long-term strategic relationship with a few suppliers.

LO 1: Explain the strategic importance of the supply chain

To ensure that the supply chain supports the firm's strategy, managers need to consider the supply chain issues shown in Table 6.1. Activities of supply chain managers cut across accounting, finance, marketing, and the operations discipline. Just as the OM function supports the firm's overall strategy, the supply chain must support the OM strategy. Strategies of low cost or rapid response demand different things from a supply chain than a strategy of differentiation. For instance, a low-cost strategy, as Table 6.1 indicates, requires suppliers be selected based primarily on cost. Such suppliers should have the ability to design low-cost products that meet the functional requirements, minimize inventory, and drive down lead times. However, if you want roses that are fresh, build a supply chain that focuses on response (see the *OM in Action* box, "A Rose Is a Rose, but Only if It Is Fresh").

VIDEO 6.1 Darden's Global Supply Chain

Firms must achieve integration of strategy up and down the supply chain, and must expect that strategy to be different for different products and to change as products move through their life cycle. Darden Restaurants, as noted in the opening *Global Company Profile*, has mastered worldwide product and service complexity by segmenting its supply chain and at the same time integrating four unique supply chains into its overall strategy.

AUTHOR COMMENT
The environment, controls, and process performance all affect supply-chain risk.

SUPPLY-CHAIN RISK

In this age of increasing specialization, low communication cost, and fast transportation, companies are making less and buying more. This means more reliance on supply chains and more risk. Managing the new integrated supply chain is a strategic challenge. Having fewer suppliers makes the supplier and customer more dependent on each other, increasing risk for both. This risk is compounded by globalization and logistical complexity. In any supply chain, vendor reliability and quality may be challenging, but the new paradigm of a tight, fast,

TABLE 6.1 How Supply-Chain Decisions Affect Strategy*

	Low-Cost Strategy	Response Strategy	Differentiation Strategy
Supplier's goal	Supply demand at lowest possible cost (e.g., Emerson Electric, Taco Bell)	Respond quickly to changing requirements and demand to minimize stockouts (e.g., Dell Computer)	Share market research; jointly develop products and options (e.g., Benetton)
Primary selection criteria	Select primarily for cost	Select primarily for capacity, speed, and flexibility	Select primarily for product development skills
Process characteristics	Maintain high average utilization	Invest in excess capacity and flexible processes	Use modular processes that lend themselves to mass customization
Inventory characteristics	Minimize inventory throughout the chain to hold down costs	Develop responsive system, with buffer stocks positioned to ensure supply	Minimize inventory in the chain to avoid obsolescence
Lead-time characteristics	Shorten lead time as long as it does not increase costs	Invest aggressively to reduce production lead time	Invest aggressively to reduce development lead time
Product-design characteristics	Maximize performance and minimize cost	Use product designs that lead to low setup time and rapid production ramp-up	Use modular design to postpone product differentiation for as long as possible

*See related table and discussion in Marshall L. Fisher, "What Is the Right Supply Chain for Your Product?" *Harvard Business Review* (March–April 1997): 105.

low-inventory supply chain, operating across political and cultural boundaries, adds a new dimension to risk. As organizations go global, shipping time may increase, logistics may be less reliable, and tariffs and quotas may block companies from doing business. In addition, international supply chains complicate information flows and increase political and currency risks.

Thus, the development of a successful strategic plan for supply-chain management requires careful research, an understanding of the risk involved, and innovative planning. Reducing risk

OM *in Action* A Rose Is a Rose, but Only if It Is Fresh

Supply chains for food and flowers must be fast, and they must be good. When the food supply chain has a problem, the best that can happen is the customer does not get fed on time; the worst that happens is the customer gets food poisoning and dies. In the floral industry, the timing and temperature are also critical. Indeed, flowers are the most perishable agricultural item—even more so than fish. Flowers not only need to move fast, but they must also be kept cool, at a constant temperature of 1 to 3 degrees Celcius. And they must be provided preservative-treated water while in transit. Roses are especially delicate, fragile, and perishable.

Roughly three-quarters of the roses sold in the Canadian market arrive by air from rural Colombia and Ecuador. Roses move through this supply chain via an intricate but fast transportation network. This network stretches from growers who cut, grade, bundle, pack, and ship, to importers who make the deal, to the Agriculture and Agri-Food Canada personnel who quarantine and inspect for insects, diseases, and parasites, to Canada Border

Services Agency staff who inspect and approve, to facilitators who provide clearance and labelling, to wholesalers who distribute, to retailers who arrange and sell, and finally to the customer. Each and every minute the product is deteriorating. The time and temperature sensitivity of perishables like roses requires sophistication and refined standards in the supply chain. Success yields quality and low losses. After all, when it's Valentine's Day, what good is a shipment of roses that arrives wilted or late? This is a difficult supply chain; only an excellent one will get the job done.

Sources: IIE Solutions (February 2002): 26–32; and *World Trade* (June 2004): 22–25.

in this increasingly global environment suggests that management must be able to mitigate and react to disruptions in:

1. *Processes* (raw material and component availability, quality, and logistics)
2. *Controls* (management metrics and reliable secure communication for financial transactions, product designs, and logistics scheduling)
3. *Environment* (customs duties, tariffs, security screening, natural disaster, currency fluctuations, terrorist attacks, and political issues)

Let's look at how several organizations address these risks in their supply chains:

- To reduce *process risk*, McDonald's planned its supply chain six years in advance of its opening in Russia. Creating a $60 million "food town," it developed independently owned supply plants in Moscow to keep its transportation costs and handling times low and its quality and customer-service levels high. Every component in this food chain—meat plant, chicken plant, bakery, fish plant, and lettuce plant—is closely monitored to make sure that all the system's links are strong.
- Ford's *process risk* reduction strategy is to develop a global network of *few but exceptional* suppliers who will provide the lowest cost and highest quality. This has driven one division's supplier base down to only 227 suppliers worldwide, compared with 700 previously.
- Darden Restaurants has placed extensive *controls*, including third-party audits, on supplier processes and logistics to ensure constant monitoring and reduction of risk.
- Boeing is reducing *control* risk through its state-of-the-art international communication system that transmits engineering, scheduling, and logistics data not only to Boeing facilities but to the suppliers of the 75% to 80% of the 787 Dreamliner that is built by non-Boeing companies.
- Hard Rock Cafe is reducing *environmental* (political) risk by franchising and licensing, rather than owning, when the political and cultural barriers seem significant.
- Toyota, after its experience with both fire and earthquakes, has moved to reduce *environmental* (natural disaster) risk with a policy of having at least two suppliers for each component.

Tight integration of the supply chain can have significant benefits, but the risks can and must be managed.

AUTHOR COMMENT
Because so much money passes through the supply chain, the opportunity for ethical lapses is significant.

Ethics and Sustainability

Let's look at three aspects of ethics in the supply chain: personal ethics, ethics within the supply chain, and ethical behaviour regarding the environment.

PERSONAL ETHICS Ethical decisions are critical to the long-term success of any organization. However, the supply chain is particularly susceptible to ethical lapses, as the opportunities for unethical behaviour are enormous. With sales personnel anxious to sell and purchasing agents spending huge sums, temptations abound. Many salespeople become friends with customers, do favours for them, take them to lunch, or present small (or large) gifts. Determining when tokens of friendship become bribes can be challenging. Many companies have strict rules and codes of conduct that limit what is acceptable. Recognizing these issues, the Institute for Supply Management—Canada has developed principles and standards to be used as guidelines for ethical behaviour (as shown in Table 6.2). As the supply chain becomes international, operations managers need to expect an additional set of ethical issues to manifest themselves as they deal with new cultural values.

ETHICS WITHIN THE SUPPLY CHAIN In this age of hyper-specialization, much of any organization's resources are purchased, putting great stress on ethics in the supply chain. Managers may be tempted to ignore ethical lapses by suppliers or offload pollution to suppliers. But firms must establish standards for their suppliers, just as they have established standards for themselves. Society expects ethical performance throughout the supply chain. For instance, Gap Inc. reported that of its 3000-plus factories worldwide, about 90% failed their initial evaluation.[1] The report indicated that 10% to 25% of its Chinese factories engaged in psychological or verbal abuse,

[1]Amy Merrick, "Gap Offers Unusual Look at Factory Conditions," *The Wall Street Journal* (May 12, 2004): A1, A12.

TABLE 6.2 Principles and Standards of Ethical Supply Management Conduct

INTEGRITY IN YOUR DECISIONS AND ACTIONS; VALUE FOR YOUR EMPLOYER; LOYALTY TO YOUR PROFESSION

1. **PERCEIVED IMPROPRIETY** Prevent the intent and appearance of unethical or compromising conduct in relationships, actions and communications.
2. **CONFLICTS OF INTEREST** Ensure that any personal, business, or other activity does not conflict with the lawful interests of your employer.
3. **ISSUES OF INFLUENCE** Avoid behaviours or actions that may negatively influence, or appear to influence, supply management decisions.
4. **RESPONSIBILITIES TO YOUR EMPLOYER** Uphold fiduciary and other responsibilities using reasonable care and granted authority to deliver value to your employer.
5. **SUPPLIER AND CUSTOMER RELATIONSHIPS** Promote positive supplier and customer relationships.
6. **SUSTAINABILITY AND SOCIAL RESPONSIBILITY** Champion social responsibility and sustainability practices in supply management.
7. **CONFIDENTIAL AND PROPRIETARY INFORMATION** Protect confidential and proprietary information.
8. **RECIPROCITY** Avoid improper reciprocal agreements.
9. **APPLICABLE LAWS, REGULATIONS, AND TRADE AGREEMENTS** Know and obey the letter and spirit of laws, regulations, and trade agreements applicable to supply management.
10. **PROFESSIONAL COMPETENCE** Develop skills, expand knowledge, and conduct business that demonstrate competence and promote the supply management profession.

Source: www.ism.ws.

and more than 50% of the factories visited in sub-Saharan Africa operate without proper safety devices. The challenge of enforcing ethical standards is significant, but responsible firms such as Gap are finding ways to deal with this difficult issue.

ETHICAL BEHAVIOUR REGARDING THE ENVIRONMENT While ethics on both a personal basis and in the supply chain are important, so is ethical behaviour in regard to the environment. Good ethics extends to doing business in a way that supports conservation and renewal of resources. This requires evaluation of the entire environmental impact, from raw material, to manufacture, through use, and final disposal. For instance, Darden and Walmart require their shrimp and fish suppliers in Southeast Asia to abide by the standards of the Global Aquaculture Alliance. These standards must be met if suppliers want to maintain the business relationship. Operations managers also ensure that sustainability is reflected in the performance of second- and third-tier suppliers. Enforcement can be done by in-house inspectors, third-party auditors, governmental agencies, or nongovernmental watchdog organizations. All four approaches are used.

The incoming supply chain garners most of the attention, but it is only part of the ethical challenge of sustainability. The "return" supply chain is also significant. Returned products can only be burned, buried, or reused. And the first two options have adverse consequences. Once viewed in this manner, the need for operations managers to evaluate the entire product life cycle is apparent.

While 84% of an automobile and 90% of an airplane are recycled, these levels are not easily achieved. Recycling efforts began at product and process design. Then special end-of-product-life processes were developed. Oil, lead, gasoline, explosives in air bags, acid in batteries, and the many components (axles, differentials, jet engines, hydraulic valves) that still have many years of service all demand their own unique recovery, remanufacturing, or recycling process. This complexity places significant demands on the producer as well as return and reuse supply chains in the quest for sustainability. But pursuing this quest is the ethical thing to do. Saving the earth is a challenging task.

AUTHOR COMMENT
A huge part of a firm's revenue is typically spent on purchases, so this is a good place to look for savings.

TABLE 6.3
Supply-Chain Costs as a Percentage of Sales

Industry	% Purchased
Automobile	67
Beverages	52
Chemical	62
Food	60
Lumber	61
Metals	65
Paper	55
Petroleum	79
Transportation	62

Supply-Chain Economics

The supply chain receives such attention because it is an integral part of a firm's strategy and the most costly activity in most firms. For both goods and services, supply chain costs as a percentage of sales are often substantial (see Table 6.3). Because such a huge portion of revenue is devoted to the supply chain, an effective strategy is vital. The supply chain provides a major opportunity to reduce costs and increase contribution margins.

Table 6.4 and Example 1 illustrate the amount of leverage available to the operations manager through the supply chain.

These numbers indicate the strong role that supply chains play in profitability.

EXAMPLE 1

Profit potential in the supply chain

Hau Lee Furniture Inc. spends 50% of its sales dollar in the supply chain and has a net profit of 4%. Hau wants to know how many dollars of sales is equivalent to supply-chain savings of $1.

APPROACH ▶ Table 6.4 (given Hau's assumptions) can be used to make the analysis.

SOLUTION ▶ Table 6.4 indicates that every $1 Hau can save in the supply chain results in the same profit that would be generated by $3.70 in sales.

TABLE 6.4
Dollars of Additional Sales Needed to Equal $1 Saved through the Supply Chain[a]

Percentage Net Profit of Firm	*Percentage of Sales Spent in the Supply Chain* 30%	40%	50%	60%	70%	80%	90%
2	$2.78	$3.23	$3.85	$4.76	$6.25	$9.09	$16.67
4	$2.70	$3.13	$3.70	$4.55	$5.88	$8.33	$14.29
6	$2.63	$3.03	$3.57	$4.35	$5.56	$7.69	$12.50
8	$2.56	$2.94	$3.45	$4.17	$5.26	$7.14	$11.11
10	$2.50	$2.86	$3.33	$4.00	$5.00	$6.67	$10.00

[a]The required increase in sales assumes that 50% of the costs other than purchases are variable and that half the remaining costs (less profit) are fixed. Therefore, at sales of $100 (50% purchases and 2% margin), $50 are purchases, $24 are other variable costs, $24 are fixed costs, and $2 profit. Increasing sales by $3.85 yields the following:

Purchases at 50%	$ 51.93 (50% of $103.85)
Other Variable Costs	24.92 (24% of $103.85)
Fixed Cost	24.00 (fixed)
Profit	3.00 (from $2 to $3 profit)
	$103.85

Through $3.85 of additional sales, we have increased profit by $1, from $2 to $3. The same increase in margin could have been obtained by reducing supply-chain costs by $1.

INSIGHT ▶ Effective management of the supply chain can generate substantial benefits.

LEARNING EXERCISE ▶ If Hau increases his profit to 6%, how much of an increase in sales is necessary to equal $1 savings? [Answer: $3.57.]

RELATED PROBLEMS ▶ 6.6, 6.7

MAKE-OR-BUY DECISIONS

A wholesaler or retailer buys everything that it sells; a manufacturing operation hardly ever does. Manufacturers, restaurants, and assemblers of products buy components and subassemblies that go into final products. Choosing products and services that can be advantageously obtained *externally* as opposed to produced *internally* is known as the **make-or-buy decision.** Supply-chain personnel evaluate alternative suppliers and provide current, accurate, and complete data relevant to the buy alternative. Increasingly, firms focus not on an analytical make-or-buy decision but on identifying their core competencies.

Make-or-buy decision
A choice between producing a component or service in-house or purchasing it from an outside source.

OUTSOURCING

Outsourcing transfers some of what are traditional internal activities and resources of a firm to outside vendors, making it slightly different from the traditional make-or-buy decision. Outsourcing is part of the continuing trend toward utilizing the efficiency that comes with specialization. The vendor performing the outsourced service is an expert in that particular specialty.

Outsourcing
Transferring a firm's activities that have traditionally been internal to external suppliers.

This leaves the outsourcing firm to focus on its critical success factors, that is, its core competencies that yield a competitive advantage. Outsourcing is the focus of the supplement to this chapter.

Supply-Chain Strategies

AUTHOR COMMENT
Supply-chain strategies come in many varieties; choosing the correct one is the trick.

For goods and services to be obtained from outside sources, the firm must decide on a supply chain strategy. One such strategy is the approach of *negotiating with many suppliers* and playing one supplier against another. A second strategy is to develop *long-term "partnering"* relationships with a few suppliers to satisfy the end customer. A third strategy is *vertical integration,* in which a firm decides to use vertical backward integration by actually buying the supplier. A fourth approach is some type of collaboration that allows two or more firms to combine resources—typically in what is called a *joint venture*—to produce a component. A fifth variation is a combination of few suppliers and vertical integration, known as a *keiretsu*. In a *keiretsu, suppliers become part of a company coalition.* Finally, a sixth strategy is to develop *virtual companies that use suppliers on an as-needed basis.* We will now discuss each of these strategies.

LO2: Identify six supply-chain strategies

MANY SUPPLIERS

With the many-suppliers strategy, a supplier responds to the demands and specifications of a "request for quotation," with the order usually going to the low bidder. This is a common strategy when products are commodities. This strategy plays one supplier against another and places the burden of meeting the buyer's demands on the supplier. Suppliers aggressively compete with one another. Although many approaches to negotiations can be used with this strategy, long-term "partnering" relationships are not the goal. This approach holds the supplier responsible for maintaining the necessary technology, expertise, and forecasting abilities, as well as cost, quality, and delivery competencies.

FEW SUPPLIERS

A strategy of few suppliers implies that rather than looking for short-term attributes, such as low cost, a buyer is better off forming a long-term relationship with a few dedicated suppliers. Long-term suppliers are more likely to understand the broad objectives of the procuring firm and the end customer. Using few suppliers can create value by allowing suppliers to have economies of scale and a learning curve that yields both lower transaction costs and lower production costs.

Few suppliers, each with a large commitment to the buyer, may also be more willing to participate in JIT systems as well as provide design innovations and technological expertise. Many firms have moved aggressively to incorporate suppliers into their supply systems. Ford, for one, now seeks to choose suppliers even before parts are designed. Motorola also evaluates suppliers on rigorous criteria, but in many instances has eliminated traditional supplier bidding, placing added emphasis on quality and reliability. On occasion, these relationships yield contracts that extend through the product's life cycle. The expectation is that both the purchaser and supplier collaborate, becoming more efficient and reducing prices over time. The natural outcome of such relationships is fewer suppliers, but those that remain have long-term relationships.

VIDEO 6.2
Supply-Chain Management at Regal Marine

Service companies like Marks & Spencer, a British retailer, have also demonstrated that cooperation with suppliers can yield cost savings for customers and suppliers alike. This strategy has resulted in suppliers that develop new products, winning customers for Marks & Spencer and the supplier. The move toward tight integration of the suppliers and purchasers is occurring in both manufacturing and services.

Like all strategies, a downside exists. With few suppliers, the cost of changing partners is huge, so both buyer and supplier run the risk of becoming captives of the other. Poor supplier performance is only one risk the purchaser faces. The purchaser must also be concerned about trade secrets and suppliers that make other alliances or venture out on their own. This happened when the Schwinn Bicycle Co., needing additional capacity, taught Taiwan's Giant Manufacturing Company to make and sell bicycles. Giant Manufacturing is now the largest bicycle manufacturer in the world, and Schwinn was acquired out of bankruptcy by Pacific Cycle LLC.

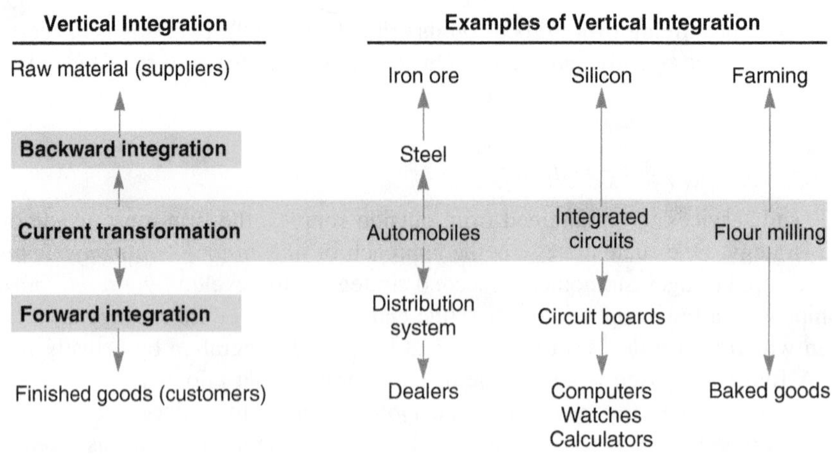

FIGURE 6.2
Vertical Integration Can Be Forward or Backward

VERTICAL INTEGRATION

Vertical integration
Developing the ability to produce goods or services previously purchased or actually buying a supplier or a distributor.

Purchasing can be extended to take the form of vertical integration. By **vertical integration**, we mean developing the ability to produce goods or services previously purchased or to actually buy a supplier or a distributor. As shown in Figure 6.2, vertical integration can take the form of *forward* or *backward integration*.

Backward integration suggests a firm purchase its suppliers, as in the case of Ford Motor Company deciding to manufacture its own car radios. Forward integration, on the other hand, suggests that a manufacturer of components make the finished product. An example is Texas Instruments, a manufacturer of integrated circuits that also makes calculators and flat-screens containing integrated circuits for TVs.

Vertical integration can offer a strategic opportunity for the operations manager. For firms with the capital, managerial talent, and required demand, vertical integration may provide substantial opportunities for cost reduction, quality adherence, and timely delivery. Other advantages, such as inventory reduction and scheduling, can accrue to the company that effectively manages vertical integration or close, mutually beneficial relationships with suppliers.

Because purchased items represent such a large part of the costs of sales, it is obvious why so many organizations find interest in vertical integration. Vertical integration appears to work best when the organization has large market share and the management talent to operate an acquired vendor successfully.

The relentless march of specialization continues, meaning that a model of "doing everything" or "vertical integration" is increasingly difficult. Backward integration may be particularly dangerous for firms in industries undergoing technological change if management cannot keep abreast of those changes or invest the financial resources necessary for the next wave of technology. The alternative, particularly in high-tech industries, is to establish close-relationship suppliers. This allows partners to focus on their specific contribution. Research and development costs are too high and technology changes too rapid for one company to sustain leadership in every component. Most organizations are better served concentrating on their specialty and leveraging the partners' contributions. Exceptions do exist. Where capital, management talent, and technology are available and the components are also highly integrated, vertical integration may make sense. On the other hand, it made no sense for Jaguar to make commodity components for its autos as it did until recently.

JOINT VENTURES

Because vertical integration is so dangerous, firms may opt for some form of formal collaboration. Firms may engage in collaboration to enhance their new product prowess or technological skills. But firms also engage in collaboration to secure supply or reduce costs. One version of a joint venture is the current Daimler–BMW effort to develop and produce standard automobile components. Given the global consolidation of the auto industry, these two rivals in the luxury segment of the automobile market are at a disadvantage in volume. Their relatively low volume means fewer units over which to spread fixed costs, hence the interest in consolidating to cut development and production costs. As in all other such collaborations, the trick is to co-operate without diluting the brand or conceding a competitive advantage.

KEIRETSU NETWORKS

Many large Japanese manufacturers have found another strategy; it is part collaboration, part purchasing from few suppliers, and part vertical integration. These manufacturers are often financial supporters of suppliers through ownership or loans. The supplier becomes part of a company coalition known as a ***keiretsu***. Members of the *keiretsu* are assured long-term relationships and are therefore expected to collaborate as partners, providing technical expertise and stable quality production to the manufacturer. Members of the *keiretsu* can also have suppliers farther down the chain, making second- and even third-tier suppliers part of the coalition.

Keiretsu
A Japanese term that describes suppliers who become part of a company coalition.

VIRTUAL COMPANIES

The limitations to vertical integration are severe. Our technological society continually demands more specialization, which complicates vertical integration. Moreover, a firm that has a department or division of its own for everything may be too bureaucratic to be world class. So rather than letting vertical integration lock an organization into businesses that it may not understand or be able to manage, another approach is to find good flexible suppliers. **Virtual companies** rely on a variety of supplier relationships to provide services on demand. Virtual companies have fluid, moving organizational boundaries that allow them to create a unique enterprise to meet changing market demands. Suppliers may provide a variety of services that include doing the payroll, hiring personnel, designing products, providing consulting services, manufacturing components, conducting tests, or distributing products. The relationships may be short or long term and may include true partners, collaborators, or simply able suppliers and subcontractors. Whatever the formal relationship, the result can be exceptionally lean performance. The advantages of virtual companies include specialized management expertise, low capital investment, flexibility, and speed. The result is efficiency.

Virtual companies
Companies that rely on a variety of supplier relationships to provide services on demand. Also known as hollow corporations or network companies.

The apparel business provides a *traditional* example of virtual organizations. The designers of clothes seldom manufacture their designs; rather, they license the manufacture. The manufacturer may then rent space, lease sewing machines, and contract for labour. The result is an organization that has low overhead, remains flexible, and can respond rapidly to the market.

A *contemporary* example is exemplified by Vizio, Inc., a North American producer of LCD TVs that has only 85 employees but huge sales. Vizio uses modules to assemble its own brand of TVs. Because the key components of TVs are now readily available and sold almost as commodities, innovative firms such as Vizio can specify the components, hire a contract manufacturer, and market the TVs with very little startup cost. In a virtual company, the supply chain is the company. Managing it is dynamic and demanding.

Managing the Supply Chain

AUTHOR COMMENT
Trust, agreed-upon goals, and compatible cultures make supply-chain management easier.

As managers move toward integration of the supply chain, substantial efficiencies are possible. The cycle of materials—as they flow from suppliers, to production, to warehousing, to distribution, to the customer—takes place among separate and often very independent organizations. Therefore, there are significant management issues that may result in serious inefficiencies. Success begins with mutual agreement on goals, followed by mutual trust, and continues with compatible organizational cultures.

VIDEO 6.3
Arnold Palmer Hospital's Supply Chain

MUTUAL AGREEMENT ON GOALS An integrated supply chain requires more than just agreement on the contractual terms of a buy/sell relationship. Partners in the chain must appreciate that the only entity that puts money into a supply chain is the end customer. Therefore, establishing a mutual understanding of the mission, strategy, and goals of participating organizations is essential. The integrated supply chain is about adding economic value and maximizing the total content of the product.

TRUST Trust is critical to an effective and efficient supply chain. Members of the chain must enter into a relationship that shares information. Visibility throughout the supply chain—what Darden Restaurants calls a *transparent supply chain*—is a requirement. Supplier relationships are more likely to be successful if risk and cost savings are shared—and activities such as end-customer research, sales analysis, forecasting, and production planning are joint activities. Such relationships are built on mutual trust.

COMPATIBLE ORGANIZATIONAL CULTURES A positive relationship between the purchasing and supplying organizations that comes with compatible organizational cultures can be a real advantage when making a supply chain hum. A champion within one of the two firms promotes both formal and informal contacts, and those contacts contribute to the alignment of the organizational cultures, further strengthening the relationship.

The operations manager is dealing with a supply chain that is made up of independent specialists, each trying to satisfy its own customers at a profit. This leads to actions that may not optimize the entire chain. On the other hand, the supply chain is replete with opportunities to reduce waste and enhance value. We now look at some of the significant issues and opportunities.

ISSUES IN AN INTEGRATED SUPPLY CHAIN

LO3: Explain issues and opportunities in the supply chain

Three issues complicate development of an efficient, integrated supply chain: local optimization, incentives, and large lots.

LOCAL OPTIMIZATION Members of the chain are inclined to focus on maximizing local profit or minimizing immediate cost based on their limited knowledge. Slight upturns in demand are overcompensated for because no one wants to be caught short. Similarly, slight downturns are overcompensated for because no one wants to be caught holding excess inventory. So fluctuations are magnified. For instance, a pasta distributor does not want to run out of pasta for its retail customers; the natural response to an extra large order from the retailer is to compensate with an even larger order to the manufacturer on the assumption that retail sales are picking up. Neither the distributor nor the manufacturer knows that the retailer had a major one-time promotion that moved a lot of pasta. This is exactly the issue that complicated the implementation of efficient distribution at the Italian pasta maker Barilla.

INCENTIVES (SALES INCENTIVES, QUANTITY DISCOUNTS, QUOTAS, AND PROMOTIONS) Incentives push merchandise into the chain for sales that have not occurred. This generates fluctuations that are ultimately expensive to all members of the chain.

LARGE LOTS There is often a bias toward large lots because large lots tend to reduce unit costs. A logistics manager wants to ship large lots, preferably in full trucks, and a production manager wants long production runs. Both actions drive down unit shipping and production costs, but fail to reflect actual sales and increased holding costs.

These three common occurrences—local optimization, incentives, and large lots—contribute to distortions of information about what is really occurring in the supply chain. A well-running supply system needs to be based on accurate information about how many products are truly being pulled through the chain. The inaccurate information is unintentional, but it results in distortions and fluctuations in the supply chain and causes what is known as the bullwhip effect.

Bullwhip effect
The increasing fluctuation in orders that often occurs as orders move through the supply chain.

The **bullwhip effect** occurs as orders are relayed from retailers, to distributors, to wholesalers, to manufacturers, with fluctuations increasing at each step in the sequence. The "bullwhip" fluctuations in the supply chain increase the costs associated with inventory, transportation, shipping, and receiving, while decreasing customer service and profitability. Procter & Gamble found that although the use of Pampers diapers was steady and the retail-store orders had little fluctuation, as orders moved through the supply chain, fluctuations increased. By the time orders were initiated for raw material, the variability was substantial. Similar behaviour has been observed and documented at many companies, including Cisco-Canada, Campbell Soup, Hewlett-Packard, and Applied Materials.

The bullwhip effect can occur when orders decrease as well as when they increase. A number of opportunities exist for reducing the bullwhip effect and improving opportunities in the supply chain. These are discussed in the following section.

OPPORTUNITIES IN AN INTEGRATED SUPPLY CHAIN

Opportunities for effective management in the supply chain include the following 11 items.

ACCURATE "PULL" DATA Accurate **pull data** are generated by sharing (1) point-of-sales (POS) information so that each member of the chain can schedule effectively and (2) computer-assisted ordering (CAO). This implies using POS systems that collect sales data and then adjusting that data for market factors, inventory on hand, and outstanding orders. Then a net order is sent directly to the supplier who is responsible for maintaining the finished-goods inventory.

Pull data
Accurate sales data that initiate transactions to "pull" product through the supply chain.

LOT SIZE REDUCTION Lot sizes are reduced through aggressive management. This may include (1) developing economical shipments of less than truckload lots; (2) providing discounts based on total annual volume rather than size of individual shipments; and (3) reducing the cost of ordering through techniques such as standing orders and various forms of electronic purchasing.

SINGLE-STAGE CONTROL OF REPLENISHMENT **Single-stage control of replenishment** means designating a member in the chain as responsible for monitoring and managing inventory in the supply chain based on the "pull" from the end user. This approach removes distorted information and multiple forecasts that create the bullwhip effect. Control may be in the hands of:

Single-stage control of replenishment
Fixing responsibility for monitoring and managing inventory for the retailer.

- A sophisticated *retailer* who understands demand patterns. Walmart does this for some of its inventory with radio frequency ID (RFID) tags as shown in the *OM in Action* box, "Radio Frequency Tags: Keeping the Shelves Stocked."
- A *distributor* who manages the inventory for a particular distribution area. Distributors who handle grocery items, beer, and soft drinks may do this. Where permissible by law, some Canadian brewers such as Labatt and Molson Coors manage beer inventory and delivery for many of its customers.
- A *manufacturer* such as Canadian auto parts leader Magna International that has a well-managed forecasting, manufacturing, and distribution system.

VENDOR-MANAGED INVENTORY **Vendor-managed inventory (VMI)** means the use of a local supplier (usually a distributor) to maintain inventory for the manufacturer or retailer. The supplier

Vendor-managed inventory (VMI)
A system in which a supplier maintains material for the buyer, often delivering directly to the buyer's using department.

OM *in Action* Radio Frequency Tags: Keeping the Shelves Stocked

Supply chains work smoothly when sales are steady, but often break down when confronted by a sudden surge or rapid drop in demand. Radio frequency ID (or RFID) tags can change that by providing real-time information about what's happening on store shelves. Here's how the system works for Procter & Gamble's (P&G's) Pampers.

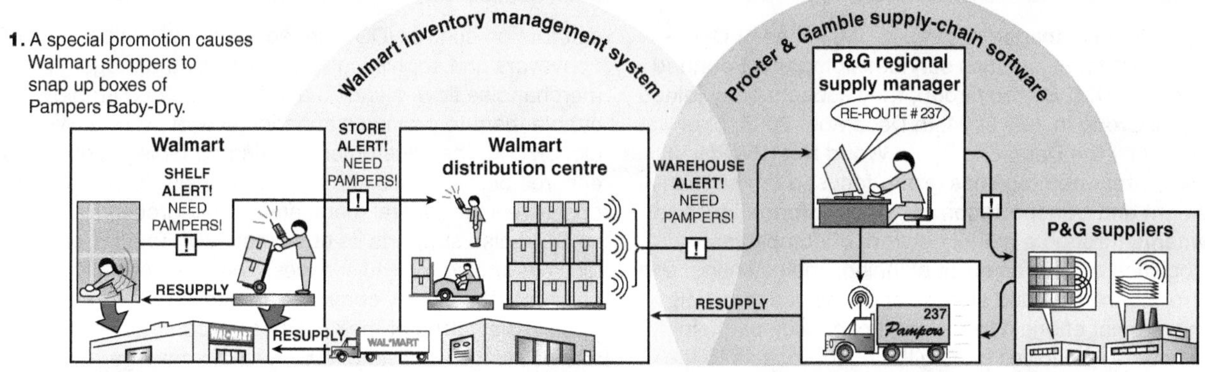

Sources: Financial Times (August 22, 2008): 12; *Business 2.0* (May 2002): 86; and *Knight Ridder Tribune Business News* (August 6, 2006): 1.

delivers directly to the purchaser's using department rather than to a receiving dock or stockroom. If the supplier can maintain the stock of inventory for a variety of customers who use the same product or whose differences are very minor (say, at the packaging stage), then there should be a net savings. These systems work without the immediate direction of the purchaser.

Collaborative planning, forecasting, and replenishment (CPFR)
A joint effort of members of a supply chain to share information in order to reduce supply-chain costs.

COLLABORATIVE PLANNING, FORECASTING, AND REPLENISHMENT (CPFR) Like single-stage control and vendor-managed inventory, **CPFR** is another effort to manage inventory in the supply chain. With CPFR, members of the supply chain share planning, forecasting, and inventory information. Partners in a CPFR effort begin with collaboration on product definition and a joint marketing plan. Promotion, advertising, forecasts, and timing of shipments are all included in the plan in a concerted effort to drive down inventory and related costs.

Blanket order
A long-term purchase commitment to a supplier for items that are to be delivered against short-term releases to ship.

BLANKET ORDERS Blanket orders are unfilled orders with a vendor.[2] A **blanket order** is a contract to purchase certain items from a vendor. It is not an authorization to ship anything. Shipment is made only on receipt of an agreed-on document, perhaps a shipping requisition or shipment release.

STANDARDIZATION The purchasing department should make special efforts to increase levels of standardization. That is, rather than obtaining a variety of similar components with labelling, colouring, packaging, or perhaps even slightly different engineering specifications, the purchasing agent should try to have those components standardized.

Postponement
Delaying any modifications or customization to a product as long as possible in the production process.

POSTPONEMENT **Postponement** withholds any modification or customization to the product (keeping it generic) as long as possible. The concept is to minimize internal variety while maximizing external variety. For instance, after analyzing the supply chain for its printers, Hewlett-Packard (HP) determined that if the printer's power supply was moved out of the printer itself and into a power cord, HP could ship the basic printer anywhere in the world. HP modified the printer, its power cord, its packaging, and its documentation so that only the power cord and documentation needed to be added at the final distribution point. This modification allowed the firm to manufacture and hold centralized inventories of the generic printer for shipment as demand changed. Only the unique power system and documentation had to be held in each country. This understanding of the entire supply chain reduced both risk and investment in inventory.

OM *in Action* Supply Chain Management Inc.

Supply Chain Management Inc. (SCM) is one of Canada's largest retail logistics services company. Founded by the Tibbett & Britten Group, they subsequently joined the Exel Group in July 2004. In December 2005, Exel was acquired by the Deutsche Poste World Net (DWPN), a leading integrated logistics group focused on the management and transportation of goods, information, and payments through a global network of companies.

Logistics is the process of planning, implementing, and controlling the flow and storage of goods and materials from the point of origin to the point of consumption. In other words, it involves getting the right products to the right place in the right quantity at the right time to satisfy customer demand.

SCM operates multiple state-of-the-art and very large distribution centres for a large international retailer in Cornwall, Calgary, and Mississauga. Their three largest distribution centres (DCs) are equipped with kilometres of conveyors and sophisticated technology that, together with merchandise flow–planning and highly trained employees, enable them to provide a superior level of service. Working closely with their customer's buying/replenishment teams ensures best-in-class store in stock/quality/supply chain cost levels for general merchandise and grocery lines.

SCM also supports its customers with fourth-party logistics provider (4PL) services. They successfully manage other third-party contracts on behalf of their customer. The nature of their business is continually growing and evolving. The field of supply-chain management is quickly becoming a key success factor for organizations, thus creating a demand for expertise and continuous improvement in this area.

Source: **www.scm3pl.com.**

[2]Unfilled orders are also referred to as "open" orders or "incomplete" orders.

DROP SHIPPING AND SPECIAL PACKAGING **Drop shipping** means the supplier will ship directly to the end consumer, rather than to the seller, saving both time and reshipping costs. Other cost-saving measures include the use of special packaging, labels, and optimal placement of labels and bar codes on containers. The final location down to the department and number of units in each shipping container can also be indicated. Substantial savings can be obtained through management techniques such as these. Some of these techniques can be of particular benefit to wholesalers and retailers by reducing shrinkage (lost, damaged, or stolen merchandise) and handling cost.

Drop shipping
Shipping directly from the supplier to the end consumer rather than from the seller, saving both time and reshipping costs.

For instance, Dell Computer has decided that its core competence is not in stocking peripherals, but in assembling PCs. So if you order a PC from Dell, with a printer and perhaps other components, the computer comes from Dell, but the printer and many of the other components will be drop shipped from the manufacturer.

PASS-THROUGH FACILITY A **pass-through facility** is a distribution centre where merchandise is held, but it functions less as a holding area and more as a shipping hub. These facilities, often run by logistics vendors, use the latest technology and automated systems to expedite orders. For instance, Purolator, a courier firm owned by Canada Post, offers assembly and distribution services in their facilities around Canada in order to assist companies in accelerating delivery times.

Pass-through facility
Expedites shipment by holding merchandise and delivering from shipping hubs.

CHANNEL ASSEMBLY **Channel assembly** is an extension of the pass-through facility. Channel assembly sends individual components and modules, rather than finished products, to the distributor. The distributor then assembles, tests, and ships. Channel assembly treats distributors more as manufacturing partners than as distributors. This technique has proven successful in industries where products are undergoing rapid change, such as personal computers. With this strategy, finished-goods inventory is reduced because units are built to a shorter, more accurate forecast. Consequently, market response is better, with lower investment—a nice combination.

Channel assembly
Postpones final assembly of a product so the distribution channel can assemble it.

E-procurement

AUTHOR COMMENT
The internet has revolutionized procurement.

E-procurement uses the internet to facilitate purchasing. E-procurement speeds purchasing, reduces costs, and integrates the supply chain, enhancing an organization's competitive advantage. The traditional supply chain is full of paper transactions, such as requisitions, requests for bids, bid evaluations, purchase orders, order releases, receiving documents, invoices, and the issuance of cheques. E-procurement reduces this barrage of paperwork and at the same time provides purchasing personnel with an extensive database of vendor, delivery, and quality data. With this history, vendor selection has improved.

E-procurement
Purchasing facilitated through the internet.

In this section, we discuss traditional techniques of electronic ordering and funds transfer and then move on to online catalogues, auctions, RFQs, and real-time inventory tracking.

ELECTRONIC ORDERING AND FUNDS TRANSFER Electronic ordering and bank transfers are traditional approaches to speeding transactions and reducing paperwork. Transactions between firms often use **electronic data interchange (EDI)**, which is a standardized data-transmittal format for computerized communications between organizations. EDI provides data transfer for virtually any business application, including purchasing. Under EDI, data for a purchase order, such as order date, due date, quantity, part number, purchase order number, address, and so forth, are fitted into the standard EDI format. EDI also provides for the use of **advanced shipping notice (ASN)**, which notifies the purchaser that the vendor is ready to ship. Although some firms are still moving to EDI and ASN, the internet's ease of use and lower cost is proving more popular.

Electronic data interchange (EDI)
A standardized data-transmittal format for computerized communications between organizations.

Advanced shipping notice (ASN)
A shipping notice delivered directly from vendor to purchaser.

ONLINE CATALOGUES

Purchase of standard items is often accomplished via online catalogues. Such catalogues provide current information about products in electronic form. Online catalogues support cost comparisons and incorporate voice and video clips, making the process efficient for both buyers and sellers. Online catalogues are available in three versions:

1. Typical of *catalogues provided by vendors* are those of IKEA Canada and Grand & Toy. Well-known for their clear and comprehensive catalogue, IKEA is a retailer of furniture and housewares, while Grand & Toy provides the same service for office supplies.

2. *Catalogues provided by intermediaries* are internet sites where business buyers and sellers can meet. These intermediaries typically create industry-specific catalogues with content from many suppliers.
3. One of the first online *exchanges provided by buyers* was Avendra (**www.avendra.com**). Avendra was created by Marriott and Hyatt (and subsequently joined by other large hotel firms) to economically purchase the huge range of goods needed by the 2800 hotels now in the exchange.

Such exchanges—and there are many—move companies from a multitude of individual phone calls, faxes, and emails to a centralized online system, and drive billions of dollars of waste out of the supply chain.

AUCTIONS

Online auction sites can be maintained by sellers, buyers, or intermediaries. Operations managers find online auctions a fertile area for disposing of excess raw material and discontinued or excess inventory. Online auctions lower entry barriers, encouraging sellers to join and simultaneously increase the potential number of buyers.

The key for auction firms is to find and build a huge base of potential bidders, improve client buying procedures, and qualify new suppliers.

RFQs

When purchasing requirements are nonstandard, time spent preparing requests for quotes (RFQs) and the related bid package can be substantial. Consequently, e-procurement has now moved these often expensive parts of the purchasing process online, allowing purchasing agents to inexpensively attach electronic copies of the necessary drawings to RFQs.

REAL-TIME INVENTORY TRACKING

FedEx's pioneering efforts at tracking packages from pickup to delivery has shown the way for operations managers to do the same for their shipments and inventory. Because tracking cars and trucks has been a chronic and embarrassingly inexact science, Ford has hired UPS to track millions of vehicles as they move from factory to dealers. Using bar codes and the internet, Ford dealers are now able to log onto a website and find out exactly where the ordered vehicles are in the distribution system. As operations managers move to an era of mass customization, with customers ordering exactly the cars they want, customers will expect to know where their cars are and exactly when they can be picked up. E-procurement, supported by bar codes and RFID, can provide economical inventory tracking on the shop floor, in warehouses, and in logistics.

Vendor Selection

LO4: Describe the steps in vendor selection

For those goods and services a firm buys, vendors must be selected. Vendor selection considers numerous factors, such as strategic fit, vendor competence, delivery, and quality performance. Because a firm may have some competence in all areas and may have exceptional competence in only a few, selection can be challenging. Procurement policies also need to be established. Those might address issues such as percent of business done with any one supplier or with minority businesses. We now examine vendor selection as a three-stage process: (1) vendor evaluation, (2) vendor development, and (3) negotiations.

VENDOR EVALUATION

The first stage of vendor selection, *vendor evaluation*, involves finding potential vendors and determining the likelihood of their becoming good suppliers. This phase requires the development of evaluation criteria such as criteria shown in Example 2. However, both the criteria and the weights selected vary depending on the supply-chain strategy being implemented. (Refer to Table 6.1, on page 175.)

EXAMPLE 2

Weighted approach to vendor evaluation

Madhu Ranadive, president of Davisville Toys in Stratford, Ontario, is interested in evaluating suppliers who will work with her to make nontoxic, environmentally friendly paints and dyes for her line of children's toys. This is a critical strategic element of his supply chain, and she desires a firm that will contribute to his product.

APPROACH ▶ Madhu begins her analysis of one potential supplier, Faber Paint and Dye, by using the weighted approach to vendor evaluation.

SOLUTION ▶ Madhu first reviews the supplier-differentiation attributes in Table 6.1 and develops the following list of selection criteria. She then assigns the weights shown to help her perform an objective review of potential vendors. Her staff assigns the scores shown and computes the total weighted score.

Criteria	Weights	Scores (1–5) (5 highest)	Weight × Score
Engineering/research/innovation skills	.20	5	1.0
Production process capability (flexibility/technical assistance)	.15	4	0.6
Distribution/delivery capability	.05	4	0.2
Quality systems and performance	.10	2	0.2
Facilities/location	.05	2	0.1
Financial and managerial strength (stability and cost structure)	.15	4	0.6
Information systems capability (e-procurement, ERP)	.10	2	0.2
Integrity (environmental compliance/ethics)	.20	5	1.0
	1.00		3.9 Total

Faber Paint and Dye receives an overall score of 3.9.

INSIGHT ▶ Madhu now has a basis for comparison with other potential vendors, selecting the one with the highest overall rating.

LEARNING EXERCISE ▶ If Madhu believes that the weight for "engineering/research/innovation skills" should be increased to .25 and the weight for "financial and managerial strength" reduced to .10, what is the new score? [Answer: Faber Paint and Dye now goes to 3.95.]

RELATED PROBLEMS ▶ 6.2, 6.3, 6.4

The selection of competent suppliers is critical. If good suppliers are not selected, then all other supply-chain efforts are wasted. As firms move toward using fewer longer-term suppliers, the issues of financial strength, quality, management, research, technical ability, and potential for a close long-term relationship play an increasingly important role. These attributes should be noted in the evaluation process.

VENDOR DEVELOPMENT

The second stage of vendor selection is *vendor development.* Assuming that a firm wants to proceed with a particular vendor, how does it integrate this supplier into its system? The buyer makes sure the vendor has an appreciation of quality requirements, product specifications, schedules and delivery, the purchaser's payment system, and procurement policies. *Vendor development* may include everything from training, to engineering and production help, to procedures for information transfer.

NEGOTIATIONS

Regardless of the supply chain strategy adopted, negotiations regarding the critical elements of the contractual relationship must take place. These negotiations often focus on quality, delivery, payment, and cost. We will look at three classic types of **negotiation strategies**: the cost-based model, the market-based price model, and competitive bidding.

Negotiation strategies
Approaches taken by supply chain personnel to develop contractual relationships with suppliers.

COST-BASED PRICE MODEL The cost-based price model requires that the supplier open its books to the purchaser. The contract price is then based on time and materials or on a fixed cost with an escalation clause to accommodate changes in the vendor's labour and materials cost.

MARKET-BASED PRICE MODEL In the market-based price model, price is based on a published, auction, or index price. Many commodities (agriculture products, paper, metal, etc.) are priced this way. For instance, a market detail report is available for paperboard prices in Canada from Bharat Book Bureau at **www.bharatbook.com**. Nonferrous metal prices and prices of other metals can be found at **www.statcan.gc.ca**.

COMPETITIVE BIDDING When suppliers are not willing to discuss costs or where near-perfect markets do not exist, competitive bidding is often appropriate. Infrequent work (such as construction, tooling, and dies) is usually purchased based on a bid. Bidding may take place via mail, fax, or an internet auction. Competitive bidding is the typical policy in many firms for the majority of their purchases. Bidding policies usually require that the purchasing agent have several potential suppliers of the product (or its equivalent) and quotations from each. The major disadvantage of this method, as mentioned earlier, is that the development of long-term relations between buyer and seller is hindered. Competitive bidding may effectively determine initial cost. However, it may also make difficult the communication and performance that are vital for engineering changes, quality, and delivery.

Yet a fourth approach is *to combine one or more* of the preceding negotiation techniques. The supplier and purchaser may agree on review of certain cost data, accept some form of market data for raw material costs, or agree that the supplier will "remain competitive." In any case, a good supplier relationship is one in which both partners have established a degree of mutual trust and a belief in each other's competence, honesty, and fair dealing.

AUTHOR COMMENT
Time, cost, and reliability variables make logistic decisions demanding.

Logistics Management

Logistics management
An approach that seeks efficiency of operations through the integration of all material acquisition, movement, and storage activities.

Procurement activities may be combined with various shipping, warehousing, and inventory activities to form a logistics system. The purpose of **logistics management** is to obtain efficiency of operations through the integration of all material acquisition, movement, and storage activities. When transportation and inventory costs are substantial on both the input and output sides of the production process, an emphasis on logistics may be appropriate. When logistics issues are significant or expensive, many firms opt for outsourcing the logistics function. Logistics specialists can often bring expertise not available in-house. For instance, logistics companies often have tracking technology that reduces transportation losses and supports delivery schedules that adhere to precise delivery windows. The potential for competitive advantage is found via both reduced costs and improved customer service.

Firms recognize that the distribution of goods to and from their facilities can represent as much as 25% of the cost of products. In addition, the total distribution cost in Canada is over 10% of the gross national product (GNP). Because of this high cost, firms constantly evaluate their means of distribution. Five major means of distribution are trucking, railroads, airfreight, waterways, and pipelines.

DISTRIBUTION SYSTEMS

TRUCKING The vast majority of manufactured goods moves by truck. The flexibility of shipping by truck is only one of its many advantages. Companies that have adopted JIT programs in recent years have put increased pressure on truckers to pick up and deliver on time, with no damage, with paperwork in order, and at low cost. Trucking firms are using computers to monitor weather, find the most effective route, reduce fuel cost, and analyze the most efficient way to unload. In spite of these advances, the motor carrier industry averages a capacity utilization of only 50%. That underutilized space costs the Canadian economy over $3 billion per year. To improve logistics efficiency, the industry is establishing websites such as Schneider National's connection (**www.schneider.com**), which lets shippers and truckers find each other to use some of this idle capacity. Shippers may pick from thousands of approved North American carriers that have registered with Schneider logistics.

LO5: Explain major issues in logistics management

RAILROADS Canadian rail is the third-largest rail system in the world and it handles the fourth-largest volume of goods on the planet. Containerization has made intermodal shipping of truck trailers on railroad flat cars, often piggybacked as double-deckers, a popular means of distribution. Every year, Canadian rail moves over 70 million people and 70% of all surface goods. With the growth of JIT, however, rail transport has been the biggest loser because small-batch manufacture requires frequent, smaller shipments that are likely to move via truck or air.

AIRFREIGHT Airfreight represents less than 5% of tonnage shipped in Canada. However, the recent proliferation of airfreight carriers, such as Purolator, FedEx, UPS, and DHL, makes it a fast-growing mode of shipping. Clearly, for national and international movement of lightweight items, such as medical and emergency supplies, flowers, fruits, and electronic components, airfreight offers speed and reliability.

WATERWAYS Waterways are one of the nation's oldest means of freight transportation, dating back to construction of the Welland Canal in 1829. Included in Canadian waterways are the nation's rivers, canals, the Great Lakes, coastlines, and oceans connecting to other countries. The usual cargo on waterways is bulky, low-value cargo such as iron ore, grains, cement, coal, chemicals, limestone, and petroleum products. Internationally, millions of containers are shipped at very low cost via huge oceangoing ships each year. Water transportation is important when shipping cost is more important than speed.

PIPELINES Pipelines are an important form of transporting crude oil, natural gas, and other petroleum and chemical products. In 2010, the petroleum industry paid $10.3 billion to the province of Alberta. This accounted for 26% of that province's annual revenue. Much of the petroleum that was pumped through pipelines ran through Alberta.

THIRD-PARTY LOGISTICS

Supply-chain managers may find that outsourcing logistics is advantageous in driving down inventory investment and costs while improving delivery reliability and speed. Specialized logistics firms support this goal by coordinating the supplier's inventory system with the service capabilities of the delivery firm. FedEx, for example, has a successful history of using the internet for online tracking. At **www.FedEx.com**, a customer can compute shipping costs, print labels, adjust invoices, and track package status all on the same website. FedEx, UPS, and DHL play a core role in other firms' logistics processes. In some cases, they even run the server for retailer websites. In other cases, such as for Dell Computer, FedEx operates warehouses that pick, pack, test, and assemble products, then it handles delivery and customs

As this photo of the port of Vancouver suggests, with millions of containers entering Canada annually, tracking location, content, and condition of trucks and containers is a challenge. But new technology may improve both security and JIT shipments.

Seven farms within a 2-hour drive of Kenya's Nairobi Airport supply 300 tons of fresh beans, bok choy, okra, and other produce that is packaged at the airport and shipped overnight to Europe. The time between harvest and arrival in Europe is 2 days. When a good supply chain and good logistics work together, the results can be startling—and fresh food.

clearance when necessary. The *OM in Action* box, "DHL's Role in the Supply Chain," provides another example of how outsourcing logistics can reduce costs while shrinking inventory and delivery times.

OM *in Action* DHL's Role in the Supply Chain

It's the dead of night at DHL International's air express hub in Brussels, yet the massive building is alive with busy forklifts and sorting workers. The boxes going on and off the DHL plane range from Dell computers and Cisco routers to Caterpillar mufflers and Komatsu hydraulic pumps. Sun Microsystems computers from California are earmarked for Finland; DVDs from Teac's plant in Malaysia are destined for Bulgaria.

The door-to-door movement of time-sensitive packages is key to the global supply chain. JIT, short product life cycles, mass customization, and reduced inventories depend on logistics firms such as DHL, FedEx, and UPS. These powerhouses are in continuous motion.

With a decentralized network covering 225 countries and territories (more than are in the UN), DHL is a true multinational. The Brussels headquarters has only 450 of the company's 124 000 employees but includes 26 nationalities.

DHL has assembled an extensive global network of express logistics centres for strategic goods. In its Brussels logistics centre, for instance, DHL upgrades, repairs, and configures Fujitsu computers, InFocus projectors, and Johnson & Johnson medical equipment. It stores and provides parts for EMC and Hewlett-Packard and replaces Nokia and Philips phones. "If something breaks down on a Thursday at 4 o'clock, the relevant warehouse knows at 4:05, and the part is on a DHL plane at 7 or 8 that evening," says Robert Kuijpers, DHL International's CEO.

Sources: Journal of Commerce (August 15, 2005): 1; *Hoover's Company Records* (May 1, 2009): 40126; and *Forbes* (October 18, 1999): 120–124.

COST OF SHIPPING ALTERNATIVES

The longer a product is in transit, the longer the firm has its money invested. But faster shipping is usually more expensive than slow shipping. A simple way to obtain some insight into this trade-off is to evaluate holding cost against shipping options. We do this in Example 3.

Example 3 looks only at holding cost versus shipping cost. For the operations or logistics manager there are many other considerations, including coordinating shipments to maintain a schedule, getting a new product to market, and keeping a customer happy. Estimates of

EXAMPLE 3

Determining daily cost of holding

A shipment of new connectors for semiconductors needs to go from Vancouver to Singapore for assembly. The value of the connectors is $1750 and holding cost is 40% per year. One airfreight carrier can ship the connectors one day faster than its competitor, at an extra cost of $20.00. Which carrier should be selected?

APPROACH ▶ First we determine the daily holding cost and then compare the daily holding cost with the cost of faster shipment.

SOLUTION ▶ Daily cost of holding the product = (Annual holding cost × Product value)/365

= (0.40 × $1750)/365

= $1.92

Since the cost of saving one day is $20.00, which is much more than the daily holding cost of $1.92, we decide on the less costly of the carriers and take the extra day to make the shipment. This saves $18.08 ($20.00 – $1.92).

INSIGHT ▶ The solution becomes radically different if the one-day delay in getting the connectors to Singapore delays delivery (making a customer angry) or delays payment of a $150 000 final product. (Even one day's interest on $150 000 or an angry customer makes a savings of $18.08 insignificant.)

LEARNING EXERCISE ▶ If the holding cost is 100% per year, what is the decision? [Answer: Even with a holding cost of $4.79 per day, the less costly carrier is selected.]

RELATED PROBLEMS ▶ 6.8, 6.9, 6.10

these other costs can be added to the estimate of daily holding cost. Determining the impact and cost of these many other considerations makes the evaluation of shipping alternatives interesting.

SECURITY AND JIT

There is probably no society more open than that of Canada and the U.S. This includes the borders and ports—but they are swamped. Over 7 million containers enter these ports each year, along with thousands of planes, cars, and trucks each day. Even under the best of

Speed and accuracy in the supply chain are supported by bar-code tracking of shipments. At each step of a journey, from initial pickup to final destination, bar codes are read and stored. Within seconds, this tracking information is available online to customers worldwide.

conditions, some 5% of the container movements are misrouted, stolen, damaged, or excessively delayed.

Since the September 11, 2001, terrorist attacks, supply chains have become more complex. Technological innovations in the supply chain are improving security and JIT, making logistics more reliable. Technology is now capable of knowing truck and container location, content, and condition. New devices can detect whether someone has broken into a sealed container and can communicate that information to the shipper or receiver via satellite or radio. Motion detectors can also be installed inside containers. Other sensors can record interior data including temperature, shock, radioactivity, and whether a container is moving. Tracking lost containers, identifying delays, or just reminding individuals in the supply chain that a shipment is on its way will help expedite shipments. Improvements in security may aid JIT, and improvements in JIT may aid security—both of which can improve supply-chain logistics.

AUTHOR COMMENT
If you can't measure it, you can't control it.

Measuring Supply-Chain Performance

LO6: Compute the percentage of assets committed to inventory and inventory turnover

Like all other managers, supply-chain managers require standards (or *metrics*, as they are often called) to evaluate performance. Evaluation of the supply chain is particularly critical for these managers because they spend most of the organization's money. In addition, they make scheduling and quantity decisions that determine the assets committed to inventory. Only with effective metrics can managers determine: (1) how well the *supply chain is performing* and (2) *the assets committed to inventory.* We will now discuss these two metrics.

SUPPLY-CHAIN PERFORMANCE The benchmark metrics shown in Table 6.5 focus on procurement and vendor performance issues. World-class benchmarks are the result of well-managed supply chains that drive down costs, lead times, late deliveries, and shortages while improving quality.

ASSETS COMMITTED TO INVENTORY Three specific measures can be helpful here. The first is the amount of money invested in inventory, usually expressed as a percentage of assets, as shown in Equation (6-1) and Example 4:

$$\text{Percentage invested in inventory} = (\text{Total inventory investment/Total assets}) \times 100 \qquad (6\text{-}1)$$

EXAMPLE 4

Tracking Home Depot's inventory investment

Home Depot's management wishes to track its investment in inventory as one of its performance measures. Home Depot had $11.4 billion invested in inventory and total assets of $44.4 billion in 2006.

APPROACH ▶ Determine the investment in inventory and total assets and then use Equation (11-1).

SOLUTION ▶ Percent invested in inventory = (11.4/44.4) × 100 = 25.7%

INSIGHT ▶ Over one-fourth of Home Depot assets are committed to inventory.

LEARNING EXERCISE ▶ If Home Depot can drive its investment down to 20% of assets, how much money will it free up for other uses? [Answer: 11.4 − (44.4 × .2) = $2.52 billion.]

RELATED PROBLEMS ▶ 6.11b, 6.12b

TABLE 6.5
Metrics for Supply-Chain Performance

	Typical Firms	Benchmark Firms
Lead time (weeks)	15	8
Time spent placing an order	42 minutes	15 minutes
Percent of late deliveries	33%	2%
Percent of rejected material	1.5%	.0001%
Number of shortages per year	400	4

Source: Adapted from a McKinsey & Company report.

TABLE 6.6
Inventory as Percentage of Total Assets (with examples of exceptional performance)

Manufacturer (Toyota 5%)	15%
Wholesale (Coca-Cola 2.9%)	34%
Restaurants (McDonald's 0.05%)	2.9%
Retail (Home Depot 25.7%)	27%

TABLE 6.7
Examples of Annual Inventory Turnover

Food, Beverage, Retail	
Molson Coors	8
Coca-Cola	14
Home Depot	5
McDonald's	112
Manufacturing	
Dell Computer	90
Magna International	11
Toyota (overall)	13
Nissan (assembly)	150

Specific comparisons with competitors may assist evaluation. Total assets committed to inventory in manufacturing approach 15%, in wholesale 34%, and retail 27%—with wide variations, depending on the specific business model, the business cycle, and management (see Table 6.6).

The second common measure of supply chain performance is *inventory turnover* (see Table 6.7). Its reciprocal, *weeks of supply,* is the third. **Inventory turnover** is computed on an annual basis, using Equation (6-2):

Inventory turnover
Cost of goods sold divided by average inventory.

$$\text{Inventory turnover} = \text{Cost of goods sold/Inventory investment} \qquad (6\text{-}2)$$

Cost of goods sold is the cost to produce the goods or services sold for a given period. Inventory investment is the average inventory value for the same period. This may be the average of several periods of inventory or beginning and ending inventory added together and divided by 2. Often, average inventory investment is based on nothing more than the inventory investment at the end of the period—typically at year-end.[3]

In Example 5, we look at inventory turnover applied to PepsiCo.

EXAMPLE 5

Inventory turnover at PepsiCo, Inc.

PepsiCo, Inc., manufacturer and distributor of drinks, Frito-Lay, and Quaker Foods, provides the following in its 2005 annual report (shown here in $ billions). Determine PepsiCo's turnover.

Net revenue		$32.5
Cost of goods sold		$14.2
Inventory:		
Raw material inventory	$.74	
Work-in-process inventory	$.11	
Finished goods inventory	$.84	
Total inventory investment		$1.69

APPROACH ▶ Use the inventory turnover computation in Equation (6-2) to measure inventory performance. Cost of goods sold is $14.2 billion. Total inventory is the sum of raw material at $.74 billion, work-in-process at $.11 billion, and finished goods at $.84 billion, for total inventory investment of $1.69 billion.

SOLUTION ▶ Inventory Turnover = Cost of goods sold/Inventory investment

= 14.2/1.69

= 8.4

[3]Inventory quantities often fluctuate wildly, and various types of inventory exist (e.g., raw material, work-in-process, finished goods, and maintenance, repair, and operating supplies [MRO]). Therefore, care must be taken when using inventory values; they may reflect more than just supply-chain performance.

INSIGHT ▶ We now have a standard, popular measure by which to evaluate performance.

LEARNING EXERCISE ▶ If Coca-Cola's cost of goods sold is \$10.8 billion and inventory investment is \$.76 billion, what is its inventory turnover? [Answer: 14.2.]

RELATED PROBLEMS ▶ 6.11a, 6.12c, 6.13

Weeks of supply, as shown in Example 6, may have more meaning in the wholesale and retail portions of the service sector than in manufacturing. It is computed below as the reciprocal of inventory turnover:

$$\text{Weeks of supply} = \text{Inventory investment/(Annual cost of goods sold/52 weeks)} \quad (6\text{-}3)$$

EXAMPLE 6

Determining weeks of supply at PepsiCo, Inc.

Using the PepsiCo data in Example 5, management wants to know the weeks of supply.

APPROACH ▶ We know that inventory investment is \$1.69 billion and that weekly sales equal annual cost of goods sold (\$14.2 billion) divided by 52 = \$14.2/52 = \$.273 billion.

SOLUTION ▶ Using Equation (6-3), we compute weeks of supply as:

$$\text{Weeks of supply} = \text{(Inventory investment/Average weekly cost of goods sold)}$$
$$= 1.69/.273 = 6.19 \text{ weeks}$$

INSIGHT ▶ We now have a standard measurement by which to evaluate a company's continuing performance or by which to compare companies.

LEARNING EXERCISE ▶ If Coca-Cola's average inventory investment is \$.76 billion and its average weekly cost of goods sold is \$0.207 billion, what is the firm's weeks of supply? [Answer: 3.67 weeks.]

RELATED PROBLEMS ▶ 6.12a, 6.14

Supply-chain management is critical in driving down inventory investment. The rapid movement of goods is key. Walmart, for example, has set the pace in the retailing sector with its world-renowned supply-chain management. By doing so, it has established a competitive advantage. With its own truck fleet, distribution centres, and a state-of-the-art communication system, Walmart (with the help of its suppliers) replenishes store shelves an average of twice per week. Competitors resupply every other week. Economical and speedy resupply means both rapid response to product changes and customer preferences, as well as lower inventory investment. Similarly, while many manufacturers struggle to move inventory turnover up to 10 times per year, Dell Computer has inventory turns exceeding 90 and supply measured in *days*—not weeks. Supply-chain management provides a competitive advantage when firms effectively respond to the demands of global markets and global sources.

THE SCOR MODEL

In addition to the metrics presented above, the Supply-Chain Council (SCC) has developed 200 process elements, 550 metrics, and 500 best practices. The SCC (**www.supply-chain.org**) (**www.supplychaincanada.org**) is a 900-member not-for-profit association for the improvement of supply-chain effectiveness. The council has developed the five-part **Supply-Chain Operations Reference (SCOR) model.** The five parts are Plan, Source, Make, Deliver, and Return, as shown in Figure 6.3.

Supply-Chain Operations Reference (SCOR) model
A set of processes, metrics, and best practices developed by the Supply-Chain Council.

The council believes the model provides a structure for its processes, metrics, and best practices to be (1) implemented for competitive advantage; (2) defined and communicated precisely; (3) measured, managed, and controlled; and (4) fine-tuned as necessary to a specific application.

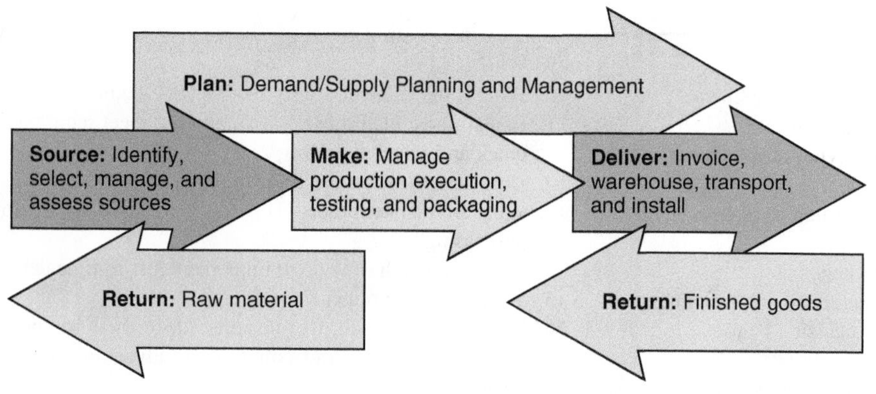

FIGURE 6.3
The Supply-Chain Operations Reference (SCOR) Model

CHAPTER SUMMARY

Competition is no longer between companies but between supply chains. For many firms, the supply chain determines a substantial portion of product cost and quality, as well as opportunities for responsiveness and differentiation. Six supply-chain strategies have been identified: (1) many suppliers, (2) few suppliers, (3) vertical integration, (4) joint ventures, (5) *keiretsu* networks, and (6) virtual companies. Skillful supply-chain management provides a great strategic opportunity for competitive advantage.

KEY TERMS

Supply-chain management (p. 153)
Make-or-buy decision (p. 158)
Outsourcing (p. 158)
Vertical integration (p. 160)
Keiretsu (p. 161)
Virtual companies (p. 161)
Bullwhip effect (p. 162)
Pull data (p. 163)
Single-stage control of replenishment (p. 163)
Vendor-managed inventory (VMI) (p. 163)
Collaborative planning, forecasting, and replenishment (CPFR) (p. 164)
Blanket order (p. 164)
Postponement (p. 165)
Drop shipping (p. 165)
Pass-through facility (p. 165)
Channel assembly (p. 165)
E-procurement (p. 165)
Electronic data interchange (EDI) (p. 165)
Advanced shipping notice (ASN) (p. 165)
Negotiation strategies (p. 167)
Logistics management (p. 168)
Inventory turnover (p. 173)
Supply-Chain Operations Reference (SCOR) model (p. 174)

Ethical Dilemma

For generations, the policy of Sears Roebuck and Company, the granddaddy of retailers, was not to purchase more than 50% of any of its suppliers' output. The rationale of this policy was that it allowed Sears to move to other suppliers, as the market dictated, without destroying the supplier's ability to stay in business. In contrast, Walmart purchases more and more of a supplier's output. Eventually, Walmart can be expected to sit down with that supplier and explain why the supplier no longer needs a sales force and that the supplier should eliminate the sales force, passing the cost savings on to Walmart.

Sears is losing market share, has been acquired by K-Mart, and is eliminating jobs; Walmart is gaining market share and hiring. What are the ethical issues involved, and which firm has a more ethical position?

Discussion Questions

1. Define *supply-chain management.*
2. What are the objectives of supply-chain management?
3. What is the objective of logistics management?
4. How do we distinguish between the types of risk in the supply chain?
5. What is vertical integration? Give examples of backward and forward integration.
6. What are three basic approaches to negotiations?
7. How does a traditional adversarial relationship with suppliers change when a firm makes a decision to move to a few suppliers?
8. What is the difference between postponement and channel assembly?
9. What is CPFR?
10. What is the value of online auctions in e-commerce?
11. Explain how FedEx uses the internet to meet requirements for quick and accurate delivery.
12. How does Walmart use drop shipping?
13. What are blanket orders? How do they differ from invoiceless purchasing?
14. What can purchasing do to implement just-in-time deliveries?
15. What is e-procurement?
16. How does Darden Restaurants, described in the *Global Company Profile*, find competitive advantage in its supply chain?
17. What is SCOR, and what purpose does it serve?

Solved Problem **Virtual Office Hours help is available at MyOMLab.**

▼ SOLVED PROBLEM 6.1

Jack's Pottery Outlet has total end-of-year assets of \$5 million. The first-of-the-year inventory was \$375 000, with a year-end inventory of \$325 000. The annual cost of goods sold was \$7 million. The owner, Eric Jack, wants to evaluate his supply chain performance by measuring his percentage of assets in inventory, his inventory turnover, and his weeks of supply. We use Equations (6-1), (6-2), and (6-3) to provide these measures.

▼ SOLUTION

First, determine *average inventory*:

$$(\$375\ 000 + \$325\ 000)/2 = \$350\ 000$$

Second, use Equation (11-1) to determine percent invested in inventory:

$$\text{Percent invested in inventory} = (\text{Total inventory investment/Total assets}) \times 100$$
$$= (350\ 000/5\ 000\ 000) \times 100$$
$$= 7\%$$

Third, determine inventory turnover, using Equation (11-2):

$$\text{Inventory turnover} = \text{Cost of goods sold/Inventory investment}$$
$$= 7\ 000\ 000/350\ 000$$
$$= 20$$

Finally, to determine weeks of inventory, use Equation (11-3), adjusted to weeks:

$$\text{Weeks of inventory} = \text{Inventory investment/Weekly cost of goods sold}$$
$$= 350\ 000/(7\ 000\ 000/52)$$
$$= 350\ 000/134\ 615$$
$$= 2.6$$

We conclude that Jack's Pottery Outlet has 7% of its assets invested in inventory, that the inventory turnover is 20, and that weeks of supply are 2.6.

Problems

•• **6.1** Choose a local establishment that is a member of a relatively large chain. From interviews with workers and information from the internet, identify the elements of the supply chain. Determine whether the supply chain represents a low-cost, rapid response, or differentiation strategy (refer to Chapter 2). Are the supply-chain characteristics significantly different from one product to another?

•• **6.2** As purchasing agent for Laurentian Enterprises in Quebec City, you ask your buyer to provide you with a ranking of "excellent," "good," "fair," or "poor" for a variety of characteristics for two potential vendors. You suggest that "Products" total be weighted 40% and the other three categories' totals be weighted 20% each. The buyer has returned the ranking shown at the top of the next page.

•• **6.3** Using the data in Problem 6.2, assume that both Donna, Inc. and Kay Corp. are able to move all their "poor" ratings to "fair." How would you then rank the two firms?

VENDOR RATING

Company	Excellent (4)	Good (3)	Fair (2)	Poor (1)
Financial Strength			K	D
Manufacturing Range			KD	
Research Facilities	K		D	
Geographical Locations		K	D	
Management		K	D	
Labour Relations			K	D
Trade Relations			KD	
Service				
Deliveries on Time		KD		
Handling of Problems		KD		
Technical Assistance		K	D	

Products	Excellent (4)	Good (3)	Fair (2)	Poor (1)
Quality	KD			
Price			KD	
Packaging			KD	
Sales				
Product Knowledge			D	K
Sales Calls			K	D
Sales Service		K	D	

DONNA INC. = D
KAY CORP. = K

Which of the two vendors would you select?

•• **6.4** Develop a vendor-rating form that represents your comparison of the education offered by universities in which you considered (or are considering) enrolling. Fill in the necessary data, and identify the "best" choice. Are you attending that "best" choice? If not, why not?

•• **6.5** Using sources from the internet, identify some of the problems faced by a company of your choosing as it moves toward, or operates as, a virtual organization. Does its operating as a virtual organization simply exacerbate old problems, or does it create new ones?

• **6.6** Using Table 6.4, determine the sales necessary to equal a dollar of savings on purchases for a company that has:
a) A net profit of 4% and spends 40% of its revenue on purchases.
b) A net profit of 6% and spends 80% of its revenue on purchases.

• **6.7** Using Table 6.4, determine the sales necessary to equal a dollar of savings on purchases for a company that has:
a) A net profit of 6% and spends 60% of its revenue on purchases.
b) A net profit of 8% and spends 80% of its revenue on purchases.

•• **6.8** Your options for shipping $100 000 of machine parts from Hamilton to Kuala Lumpur, Malaysia, are (1) use a ship that will take 30 days at a cost of $3800, or (2) truck the parts to Vancouver and then ship at a total cost of $4800. The second option will take only 20 days. You are paid via a letter of credit the day the parts arrive. Your holding cost is estimated at 30% of the value per year.
a) Which option is more economical?
b) What customer issues are not included in the data presented?

•• **6.9** If you have a third option for the data in Problem 6.8, and it costs only $4000 and also takes 20 days, what is your most economical plan?

•• **6.10** Monczka-Trent Shipping is the logistics vendor for Handfield Manufacturing Co. in New Brunswick. Handfield has daily shipments of a power-steering pump from its New Brunswick plant to an auto assembly line in Ontario. The value of the standard shipment is $250 000. Monczka-Trent has two options: (1) its standard 2-day shipment, or (2) a subcontractor who will team drive overnight with an effective delivery of one day. The extra driver costs $175. Handfield's holding cost is 35% annually for this kind of inventory.
a) Which option is more economical?
b) What production issues are not included in the data presented?

•• **6.11** Baker Mfg Inc. (see Table 6.8) wishes to compare its inventory turnover to those of industry leaders, who have turnover of about 13 times per year and 8% of their assets invested in inventory.
a) What is Baker's inventory turnover?
b) What is Baker's percentage of assets committed to inventory?
c) How does Baker's performance compare to the industry leaders?

TABLE 6.8 For Problems 6.11 and 6.12

Arrow Distributing Corp.	
Net revenue	$16 500
Cost of sales	$13 500
Inventory	$ 1000
Total assets	$ 8600
Baker Mfg. Inc.	
Net revenue	$27 500
Cost of sales	$21 500
Inventory	$ 1250
Total assets	$16 600

•• **6.12** Arrow Distributing Corp. (see Table 6.8) likes to track inventory by using weeks of supply as well as by inventory turnover.
a) What is its weeks of supply?
b) What percentage of Arrow's assets are committed to inventory?
c) What is Arrow's inventory turnover?
d) Is Arrow's supply-chain performance, as measured by these inventory metrics, better than that of Baker in Problem 6.11?

• **6.13** The grocery industry has an annual inventory turnover of about 14 times. Organic Grocers, Inc., had a cost of goods sold last year of $10.5 million; its average inventory was $1.0 million. What was Organic Grocers's inventory turnover, and how does that performance compare with that of the industry?

•• **6.14** Mattress Wholesalers, Inc. is constantly trying to reduce inventory in its supply chain. Last year, cost of goods sold was $7.5 million and inventory was $1.5 million. This year, costs of goods sold is $8.6 million and inventory investment is $1.6 million.
a) What were the weeks of supply last year?
b) What are the weeks of supply this year?
c) Is Mattress Wholesalers making progress in its inventory-reduction effort?

Refer to MyOMLab for this additional homework problem: 6.15

Case Studies

Dell's Value Chain

Dell Computer, with close supplier relationships, encourages suppliers to focus on their individual technological capabilities to sustain leadership in their components. Research and development costs are too high and technological changes are too rapid for any one company to sustain leadership in every component. Suppliers are also pressed to drive down lead times, lot sizes, and inventories. Dell, in turn, keeps its research customer-focused and leverages that research to help itself and suppliers. Dell also constructs special web pages for suppliers, allowing them to view orders for components they produce as well as current levels of inventory at Dell. This allows suppliers to plan based on actual end customer demand; as a result, it reduces the bullwhip effect. The intent is to work with suppliers to keep the supply chain moving rapidly, products current, and the customer order queue short. Then, with supplier collaboration, Dell can offer the latest options, can build to order, and can achieve rapid throughput. The payoff is a competitive advantage, growing market share, and low capital investment.

On the distribution side, Dell uses direct sales, primarily via the internet, to increase revenues by offering a virtually unlimited variety of desktops, notebooks, and enterprise products. Options displayed over the internet allow Dell to attract customers that value choice. Customers select recommended product configurations or customize them. Dell's customers place orders at any time of the day from anywhere in the world. And Dell's price is cheaper; retail stores have additional costs because of their brick-and-mortar model. Dell has also customized web pages that enable large business customers to track past purchases and place orders consistent with their purchase history and current needs. Assembly begins immediately after receipt of a customer order. Competing firms have previously assembled products filling the distribution channels (including shelves at retailers) before a product reaches the customer. Dell, in contrast, introduces a new product to customers over the internet as soon as the first of that model is ready. In an industry where products have life cycles measured in months, Dell enjoys a huge early-to-market advantage.

Dell's model also has cash flow advantages. Direct sales allow Dell to eliminate distributor and retailer margins and increase its own margin. Dell collects payment in a matter of days after products are sold. But Dell pays its suppliers according to the more traditional billing schedules. Given its low levels of inventory, Dell is able to operate its business with negative working capital because it manages to receive payment before it pays its suppliers for components. These more traditional supply chains often require 60 or more days for the cash to flow from customer to supplier—a huge demand on working capital.

Dell has designed its order processing, products, and assembly lines so that customized products can be assembled in a matter of hours. This allows Dell to postpone assembly until after a customer order has been placed. In addition, any inventory is often in the form of components that are common across a wide variety of finished products. Postponement, component modularity, and tight scheduling allow low inventory and support mass customization. Dell maximizes the benefit of postponement by focusing on new products for which demand is difficult to forecast. Manufacturers who sell via distributors and retailers find postponement virtually impossible. Therefore, traditional manufacturers are often stuck with product configurations that are not selling while simultaneously being out of the configurations that are selling. Dell is better able to match supply and demand.

One of the few negatives for Dell's model is that it results in higher outbound shipping costs than selling through distributors and retailers. Dell sends individual products directly to customers from its factories. But many of these shipments are small (often one or a few products), while manufacturers selling through distributors and retailers ship with some economy of scale, using large shipments via truck to warehouses and retailers, with the end user providing the final portion of delivery. As a result, Dell's outbound transportation costs are higher, but the relative cost is low (typically 2% to 3%), and, thus, the impact on the overall cost is low.

What Dell has done is build a collaborative supply chain and an innovative ordering and production system. The result is what Dell likes to refer to as its *value chain*—a chain that brings value from supplier to the customer and provides Dell with a competitive advantage.

Discussion Questions

1. How has Dell used its direct sales and build-to-order model to develop an exceptional supply chain?
2. How has Dell exploited the direct sales model to improve operations performance?
3. What are the main disadvantages of Dell's direct sales model?
4. How does Dell compete with a retailer who already has stock?
5. How does Dell's supply chain deal with the bullwhip effect?

Sources: Adapted from S. Chopra and P. Meindl, *Supply Chain Management*, 3rd ed. (Upper Saddle River, NJ: Prentice Hall, 2007); R. Kapuscinski, et al., "Inventory Decisions in Dell's Supply Chain," *Interfaces* 34, no. 3 (May–June 2004): 191–205; and A. A. Thompson, A. J. Strickland, and J. E. Gamble, "Dell, Inc. in 2006: Can Rivals Beat Its Strategy?" *Crafting and Executing Strategy*, 15th ed. (New York: McGraw-Hill, 2007).

Darden's Global Supply Chain

Darden Restaurants (subject of the *Global Company Profile* at the beginning of this chapter), owner of popular brands such as Olive Garden and Red Lobster, requires unique supply chains to serve more than 300 million meals annually. Darden's strategy is operations excellence, and senior VP Jim Lawrence's task is to ensure competitive advantage via Darden's supply chains. For a firm with purchases exceeding $1.5 billion annually, managing the supply chains is a complex and challenging task.

Darden, like other casual dining restaurants, has unique supply chains that reflect its menu options. Darden's supply chains are rather shallow, often having just one tier of suppliers. But it has four distinct supply chains.

First, "smallware" is a restaurant industry term for items such as linens, dishes, tableware, kitchenware, and silverware. These are purchased, with Darden taking title as they are received at the Darden Direct Distribution (DDD) warehouse in Orlando, Florida. From this single warehouse, smallware items are shipped via common carrier (trucking companies) to Olive Garden, Red Lobster, Bahama Breeze, and Seasons 52 restaurants.

Second, frozen, dry, and canned food products are handled economically by Darden's 11 distribution centres in North America, which are managed by major U.S. food distributors, such as MBM, Maines, and Sygma. This is Darden's second supply line.

Third, the fresh food supply chain (not frozen and not canned), where life is measured in days, includes dairy products, produce, and meat. This supply chain is B2B, where restaurant managers directly place orders with a preselected group of independent suppliers.

Fourth, Darden's worldwide seafood supply chain is the final link. Here Darden has developed independent suppliers of salmon, shrimp, tilapia, scallops, and other fresh fish that are source inspected by Darden's overseas representatives to ensure quality. These fresh products are flown to the U.S. and shipped to 16 distributors, with 22 locations, for quick delivery to the restaurants. With suppliers in 35 countries, Darden must be on the cutting edge when it comes to collaboration, partnering, communication, and food safety. It does this with heavy travel schedules for purchasing and quality control personnel, native-speaking employees onsite, and aggressive communication. Communication is a critical element; Darden tries to develop as much forecasting transparency as possible. "Point of sale (POS) terminals," says Lawrence, "feed actual sales every night to suppliers."

Discussion Questions*

1. What are the advantages of each of Darden's four supply chains?
2. What are the complications of having four supply chains?
3. Where would you expect ownership/title to change in each of Darden's four supply chains?
4. How do Darden's four supply chains compare with those of other firms, such as Dell or an automobile manufacturer? Why do the differences exist, and how are they addressed?

*You may wish to view the video that accompanies this case before answering these questions.

Arnold Palmer Hospital's Supply Chain

Arnold Palmer Hospital, one of the nation's top hospitals dedicated to serving women and children, is a large business with over 2000 employees working in a 431-bed facility totaling 676 000 square feet in Orlando, Florida. Like many other hospitals, and other companies, Arnold Palmer Hospital had been a long-time member of a large buying group, one servicing 900 members. But the group did have a few limitations. For example, it might change suppliers for a particular product every year (based on a new lower-cost bidder) or stock only a product that was not familiar to the physicians at Arnold Palmer Hospital. The buying group was also not able to negotiate contracts with local manufacturers to secure the best pricing.

So in 2003, Arnold Palmer Hospital, together with seven other partner hospitals in central Florida, formed its own much smaller, but still powerful (with $200 million in annual purchases) Healthcare Purchasing Alliance (HPA) corporation. The new alliance saved the HPA members $7 million in its first year with two main changes. First, it was structured and staffed to assure that the bulk of the savings associated with its contracting efforts went to its eight members. Second, it struck even better deals with vendors by guaranteeing a *committed* volume and signing not 1-year deals but 3- to 5-year contracts. "Even with a new internal cost of $400 000 to run HPA, the savings and ability to contract for what our member hospitals really want makes the deal a winner," says George DeLong, head of HPA.

Effective supply-chain management in manufacturing often focuses on development of new product innovations and efficiency through buyer–vendor collaboration. However, the approach in a service industry has a slightly different emphasis. At Arnold Palmer Hospital, supply-chain opportunities often manifest themselves through the Medical Economic Outcomes Committee. This committee (and its subcommittees) consists of users (including the medical and nursing staff) who evaluate purchase options with a goal of better medicine while achieving economic targets. For instance, the heart pacemaker negotiation by the cardiology subcommittee allowed for the standardization to two manufacturers, with annual savings of $2 million for just this one product.

Arnold Palmer Hospital is also able to develop custom products that require collaboration down to the third tier of the supply chain. This is the case with custom packs that are used in the operating room. The custom packs are delivered by a distributor, McKesson General Medical, but assembled by a pack company that uses materials the hospital wanted purchased from specific manufacturers. The HPA allows Arnold Palmer Hospital to be creative in this way. With major cost savings, standardization, blanket purchase orders, long-term contracts, and more control of product development, the benefits to the hospital are substantial.

Discussion Questions*

1. How does this supply chain differ from that in a manufacturing firm?
2. What are the constraints on making decisions based on economics alone at Arnold Palmer Hospital?
3. What role do doctors and nurses play in supply-chain decisions in a hospital? How is this participation handled at Arnold Palmer Hospital?
4. Dr. Smith just returned from the Annual Physician's Orthopedic Conference, where she saw a new hip joint replacement demonstrated. She decides she wants to start using the replacement joint at Arnold Palmer Hospital. What process will Dr. Smith have to go through at the hospital to introduce this new product into the supply chain for future surgical use?

*You may wish to view the video that accompanies this case before answering the questions.

Supply-Chain Management at Regal Marine

Like most other manufacturers, Regal Marine finds that it must spend a huge portion of its revenue on purchases. Regal has also found that the better its suppliers understand its end users, the better are both the supplier's product and Regal's final product. As one of the 10 largest U.S. powerboat manufacturers, Regal is trying to differentiate its products from the vast number of boats supplied by 300 other companies. Thus, the firm works closely with suppliers to ensure innovation, quality, and timely delivery.

Regal has done a number of things to drive down costs while driving up quality, responsiveness, and innovation. First, working on partnering relationships with suppliers ranging from providers of windshields to providers of instrument panel controls, Regal has brought timely innovation at reasonable cost to its product. Key vendors are so tightly linked with the company that they meet with designers to discuss material changes to be incorporated into new product designs.

Second, the company has joined about 15 other boat manufacturers in a purchasing group, known as American Boat Builders Association, to work with suppliers on reducing the costs of large purchases. Third, Regal is working with a number of local vendors to supply hardware and fasteners directly to the assembly line on a just-in-time basis. In some of these cases, Regal has worked out an arrangement with the vendor so that title does not transfer until parts are used by Regal. In other cases, title transfers when items are delivered to the property. This practice drives down total inventory and the costs associated with large-lot delivery.

Finally, Regal works with a personnel agency to outsource part of the recruiting and screening process for employees. In all these cases, Regal is demonstrating innovative approaches to supply-chain management that help the firm and, ultimately, the end user. The *Global Company Profile* featuring Regal Marine provides further background on Regal's operations.

Discussion Questions*

1. What other techniques might Regal use to improve supply-chain management?
2. What kind of response might members of the supply chain expect from Regal in response to their "partnering" in the supply chain?
3. Why is supply-chain management important to Regal?

*You may wish to view the video that accompanies this case before answering the questions.

Additional Case Study: Visit **MyOMLab** for this case study:
Amazon.com: Discusses opportunities and issues in an innovative business model for the internet.

Bibliography

Blackburn, Joseph, and Gary Scudder. "Supply Chain Strategies for Perishable Products." *Production and Operations Management* 18, no. 2 (March–April 2009): 129–137.

Boyer, Kenneth K., and G. Tomas M. Hult. "Extending the Supply Chain: Integrating Operations and Marketing in the Online Grocery Industry." *Journal of Operations Management* 23, no. 6 (September 2005): 642–661.

Chopra, Sunil, and Peter Meindl. *Supply Chain Management*, 4th ed. Upper Saddle River, NJ: Prentice Hall, 2010.

Crook, T. Russell, and James G. Combs. "Sources and Consequences of Bargaining Power in Supply Chains." *Journal of Operations Management* 25, no. 2 (March 2007): 546–555.

Hu, J., and C. L. Munson. "Speed versus Reliability Trade-offs in Supplier Selection." *International Journal Procurement Management* 1, no. 1/2 (2007): 238–259.

Kersten, Wolfgang, and Thorsten Blecker (eds.). *Managing Risk in Supply Chains*. Berlin: Erich Schmidt Verlag GmbH & Co., 2006.

Kreipl, Stephan, and Michael Pinedo."Planning and Scheduling in Supply Chains." *Production and Operations Management* 13, no. 1 (Spring 2004): 77–92.

Linton, J. D., R. Klassen, and V. Jayaraman. "Sustainable Supply Chains: An Introduction." *Journal of Operations Management* 25, no. 6 (November, 2007): 1075–1082.

Monczka, R. M., R. B. Handfield, L. C. Gianipero, and J. L. Patterson. *Purchasing and Supply Chain Management*, 4th ed. Mason, OH: Cengage, 2009.

Narayanan, Sriram, Ann S. Marucheck, and Robert B. Handfield. "Electronic Data Interchange: Research Review and Future Directions." *Decisions Sciences* 40, no. 1 (February 2009): 121–163.

Pisano, Gary P., and Roberto Verganti. "Which Kind of Collaboration Is Right for You?" *Harvard Business Review* 86, no. 12 (December, 2008): 78–86.

Sinha, K. K., and E. J. Kohnke. "Health Care Supply Chain Design." *Decision Sciences* 40, no. 2 (May 2009): 197–212.

Stanley, L. L., and V. R. Singhal. "Service Quality Along the Supply Chain." *Journal of Operations Management* 19, no. 3 (May 2001): 287–306.

Wisner, Joel, K. Tan, and G. Keong Leong. *Principles of Supply Chain Management*, 3rd ed., Mason, OH: Cengage, 2009.

CHAPTER 6 Rapid Review

<table>
<tr><th>Main Heading</th><th>Review Material</th><th>MyOMLab</th></tr>
<tr><td>THE SUPPLY CHAIN'S STRATEGIC IMPORTANCE
(pp. 153–156)</td><td>Most firms spend a huge portion of their sales dollars on purchases.<ul><li>Supply-chain management—Management of activities related to procuring materials and services, transforming them into intermediate goods and final products, and delivering them through a distribution system.</li></ul>The objective is to build a chain of suppliers that focuses on maximizing value to the ultimate customer.
Competition is no longer between companies; it is between supply chains.</td><td>VIDEO 6.1
Darden's Global Supply Chain</td></tr>
<tr><td>ETHICS AND SUSTAINABILITY
(pp. 156–157)</td><td>Ethics includes personal ethics, ethics within the supply chain, and ethical behaviour regarding the environment. The Institute for Supply Management has developed a set of principles and standards for ethical conduct.</td><td></td></tr>
<tr><td>SUPPLY-CHAIN ECONOMICS
(pp. 157–159)</td><td><ul><li>Make-or-buy decision—A choice between producing a component or service in-house or purchasing it from an outside source.</li><li>Outsourcing—Transferring to external suppliers a firm's activities that have traditionally been internal.</li></ul></td><td>Problems: 6.6, 6.7</td></tr>
<tr><td>SUPPLY-CHAIN STRATEGIES
(pp. 159–161)</td><td>Six supply-chain strategies for goods and services to be obtained from outside sources are:<ol><li>Negotiating with many suppliers and playing one supplier against another</li><li>Developing long-term partnering relationships with a few suppliers</li><li>Vertical integration</li><li>Joint ventures</li><li>Developing keiretsu networks</li><li>Developing virtual companies that use suppliers on an as-needed basis</li></ol><ul><li>Vertical integration—Developing the ability to produce goods or services previously purchased or actually buying a supplier or a distributor.</li><li>Keiretsu—A Japanese term that describes suppliers who become part of a company coalition.</li><li>Virtual companies—Companies that rely on a variety of supplier relationships to provide services on demand. Also known as hollow corporations or network companies.</li></ul></td><td>VIDEO 6.2
Supply-Chain Management at Regal Marine</td></tr>
<tr><td>MANAGING THE SUPPLY CHAIN
(pp. 161–165)</td><td>Supply-chain integration success begins with mutual agreement on goals, followed by mutual trust, and continues with compatible organizational cultures.
Three issues complicate the development of an efficient, integrated supply chain: local optimization, incentives, and large lots.<ul><li>Bullwhip effect—Increasing fluctuation in orders or cancellations that often occurs as orders move through the supply chain.</li><li>Pull data—Accurate sales data that initiate transactions to "pull" product through the supply chain.</li><li>Single stage control of replenishment—Fixing responsibility for monitoring and managing inventory for the retailer.</li><li>Vendor-managed inventory (VMI)—A system in which a supplier maintains material for the buyer, often delivering directly to the buyer's using department.</li><li>Collaborative planning, forecasting, and replenishment (CPFR)—A system in which members of a supply chain share information in a joint effort to reduce supply-chain costs.</li><li>Blanket order—A long-term purchase commitment to a supplier for items that are to be delivered against short-term releases to ship.</li><li>The purchasing department should make special efforts to increase levels of standardization.</li><li>Postponement—Delaying any modifications or customization to a product as long as possible in the production process.
Postponement strives to minimize internal variety while maximizing external variety.</li><li>Drop shipping—Shipping directly from the supplier to the end consumer rather than from the seller, saving both time and reshipping costs.</li><li>Pass-through facility—A facility that expedites shipment by holding merchandise and delivering from shipping hubs.</li><li>Channel assembly—A system that postpones final assembly of a product so the distribution channel can assemble it.</li></ul></td><td>VIDEO 6.3
Arnold Palmer Hospital's Supply Chain</td></tr>
</table>

Main Heading	Review Material	MyOMLab
E-PROCUREMENT (pp. 165–166)	• **E-procurement**—Purchasing facilitated through the internet. • **Electronic data interchange (EDI)**—A standardized data-transmittal format for computerized communications between organizations. • **Advanced shipping notice (ASN)**—A shipping notice delivered directly from vendor to purchaser. Online catalogues move companies from a multitude of individual phone calls, faxes, and emails to a centralized online system and drive billions of dollars of waste out of the supply chain.	
VENDOR SELECTION (pp. 166–168)	Vendor selection is a three-stage process: (1) vendor evaluation, (2) vendor development, and (3) negotiations. *Vendor evaluation* involves finding potential vendors and determining the likelihood of their becoming good suppliers. *Vendor development* may include everything from training, to engineering and production help, to procedures for information transfer. • **Negotiation strategies**—Approaches taken by supply-chain personnel to develop contractual relationships with suppliers. Three classic types of negotiation strategies are (1) the cost-based price model, (2) the market-based price model, and (3) competitive bidding.	Problems: 6.2, 6.3
LOGISTICS MANAGEMENT (pp. 168–172)	• **Logistics management**—An approach that seeks efficiency of operations through the integration of all material acquisition, movement, and storage activities. The total distribution cost in the United States is over 10% of the gross national product (GNP). Five major means of distribution are trucking, railroads, airfreight, waterways, and pipelines. The vast majority of manufactured goods move by truck.	Problems: 6.8–6.10
MEASURING SUPPLY-CHAIN PERFORMANCE (pp. 172–175)	Typical supply-chain benchmark metrics include lead time, time spent placing an order, percent of late deliveries, percent of rejected material, and number of shortages per year: Percent invested in inventory = (Total inventory investment/Total assets) × 100 (6-1) • **Inventory turnover**—Cost of goods sold divided by average inventory: Inventory turnover = Cost of goods sold ÷ Inventory investment (6-2) Weeks of supply = Inventory investment ÷ (Annual cost of goods sold/52 weeks) (6-3) • **Supply Chain Operations Reference (SCOR) Model**—A set of processes, metrics, and best practices developed by the Supply Chain Council. The five parts of the SCOR model are Plan, Source, Make, Deliver, and Return.	Problems: 6.11–6.15 Virtual Office Hours for Solved Problem: 6.1

Self Test

■ **Before taking the self-test,** refer to the learning objectives listed at the beginning of the chapter and the key terms listed at the end of the chapter.

LO1. The objective of supply-chain management is to __________.

LO2. The term *vertical integration* means to:
- **a)** develop the ability to produce products that complement or supplement the original product.
- **b)** produce goods or services previously purchased.
- **c)** develop the ability to produce the specified good more efficiently.
- **d)** all of the above.

LO3. The bullwhip effect can be aggravated by:
- **a)** local optimization.
- **b)** sales incentives.
- **c)** quantity discounts.
- **d)** promotions.
- **e)** all of the above.

LO4. Vendor selection requires:
- **a)** vendor evaluation and effective third-party logistics.
- **b)** vendor development and logistics.
- **c)** negotiations, vendor evaluation, and vendor development.
- **d)** an integrated supply chain.
- **e)** inventory and supply-chain management.

LO5. A major issue in logistics is:
- **a)** cost of purchases.
- **b)** vendor evaluation.
- **c)** product customization.
- **d)** cost of shipping alternatives.
- **e)** excellent suppliers.

LO6. Inventory turnover =
- **a)** Cost of goods sold ÷ Weeks of supply
- **b)** Weeks of supply ÷ Annual cost of goods sold
- **c)** Annual cost of goods sold ÷ 52 weeks
- **d)** Inventory investment ÷ Cost of goods sold
- **e)** Cost of goods sold ÷ Inventory investment

Answers: LO1. build a chain of suppliers that focuses on maximizing value to the ultimate customer; LO2. b; LO3. e; LO4. c; LO5. d; LO6. e.

The problems marked in red can be found on MyOMLab. Visit MyOMLab to access cases, videos, downloadable software, and much more. MyOMLab also features a personalized Study Plan that helps you identify which chapter concepts you've mastered and guides you towards study tools for additional practice.

Student Profile

Jaime Nicoll, CPIM, CSCP
Procurement & Subcontracts Supervisor, Innovative Steam Technologies
Business Administration Materials & Operations Management Program 2007

The Supply Chain field has proven to be an excellent career choice for me! I have spent the last five years managing international procurement for a world leader in the design and manufacture of heat recovery steam generators. My college experience led me to an exciting profession filled with stimulating challenges and world travel. In fact, I credit my college program for providing the networking opportunities that led me to the company I work for today. There are a wide range of career paths and employment opportunities in Operations management. My advice to you is to take advantage of membership and participation in a variety of networking events and professional associations to further your education and career. Since graduating, I have obtained my CPIM & CSCP certifications through APICS.

7

Outsourcing as a Supply-Chain Strategy

Supplement Outline

Contract manufacturers such as Flextronics provide outsourcing service to IBM, Cisco Systems, HP, Microsoft, Motorola, Sony, Nortel, Ericsson, and Sun, among many others. Flextronics is a high-quality producer that has won over 450 awards, including the Malcolm Baldrige Award. One of the side benefits of outsourcing is that client firms such as IBM can actually improve their performance by using the competencies of an outstanding firm like Flextronics. But there are risks involved in outsourcing. Outsourcing decisions, as part of the supply-chain strategy, are explored in this supplement.

Supplement 7 Learning Objectives

AUTHOR COMMENT
Outsourcing is a supply-chain strategy that can deliver tremendous value to an organization.

What Is Outsourcing?

Outsourcing is a creative management strategy. Indeed, some organizations use outsourcing to replace entire purchasing, information systems, marketing, finance, and operations departments. Outsourcing is applicable to firms throughout the world. And because outsourcing decisions are risky and many are not successful, making the right decision may mean the difference between success and failure.[1]

Because outsourcing grows by double digits every year, students and managers need to understand the issues, concepts, models, philosophies, procedures, and practices of outsourcing. This supplement describes current concepts, methodologies, and outsourcing strategies.

Outsourcing
Procuring from external sources services or products that are normally part of an organization.

Offshoring
Moving a business process to a foreign country but retaining control of it.

Outsourcing means procuring from external suppliers services or products that are normally a part of an organization. In other words, a firm takes functions it was performing in-house (such as accounting, janitorial, or call centre functions) and has another company do the same job. If a company owns two plants and reallocates production from the first to the second, this is not considered outsourcing. If a company moves some of its business processes to a foreign country but retains control, we define this move as **offshoring**, not outsourcing. For example, China's Haier Group recently offshored a $40 million refrigerator factory to South Carolina (with huge savings in transportation costs). Or, as Thomas Friedman wrote in his book *The World is Flat*,

[1]The authors wish to thank Professor Marc J. Schniederjans, of the University of Nebraska–Lincoln, for help with the development of this supplement. His book *Outsourcing and Insourcing in an International Context*, with Ashlyn Schniederjans and Dara Schniederjans (Armonk, NY: M.E. Sharpe, 2005), provided insight, content, and references that shaped our approach to the topic.

"Offshoring is when a company takes one of its factories that it is operating in Canton, Ohio, and moves the whole factory to Canton, China."

Early in their lives, many businesses handle their activities internally. As businesses mature and grow, however, they often find competitive advantage in the specialization provided by outside firms. They may also find limitations on locally available labour, services, materials, or other resources. So organizations balance the potential benefits of outsourcing with its potential risks. Outsourcing the wrong activities can cause major problems.

Outsourcing is not a new concept; it is simply an extension of the long-standing practice of *subcontracting* production activities. Indeed, the classic make-or-buy decision concerning products (which we discussed in Chapter 6) is an example of outsourcing.

So why has outsourcing expanded to become a major strategy in business the world over? From an economic perspective, it is due to the continuing move toward specialization in an increasingly technological society. More specifically, outsourcing's continuing growth is due to (1) increasing expertise, (2) reduced costs of more reliable transportation, and (3) the rapid development and deployment of advancements in telecommunications and computers. Low-cost communication, including the internet, permits firms anywhere in the world to provide previously limited information services.

Examples of outsourcing include:

- Call centres for Brazil in Angola (a former Portuguese colony in Africa) and for Canada, the U.S., and the U.K. in India.
- DuPont's legal services routed to the Philippines
- IBM handling travel services and payroll, and Hewlett-Packard providing IT services to P&G.
- ADP providing payroll services for thousands of firms.
- Production of the Audi A4 convertible and Mercedes CLK convertible by Wilheim Karmann in Osnabruck, Germany.
- Blue Cross sending hip-resurfacing-surgery patients to India.
- A Quebec medical service arranging for medical treatment in Cuba for Canadian residents.

VIDEO 7.1
Outsourcing Offshore at Darden

Outsourced manufacturing, also known as *contract manufacturing*, is becoming standard practice in many industries, from computers to automobiles.

Paralleling the growth of outsourcing is the growth of international trade. With the passage of landmark trade agreements like the North American Free Trade Agreement (NAFTA), the work of the World Trade Organization and the European Union, and other international trade zones established throughout the world, we are witnessing the greatest expansion of international commerce in history.

Table 7.1 provides a ranking of the top five and bottom five outsourcing locations (out of 50 countries) in the annual A.T. Kearney Global Options survey. Scores are based on a Global Services Location Index tallying financial attractiveness, workforce availability, employee skill set, and business environment.

TABLE 7.1
Desirable Outsourcing Destinations

Rank	Country	Score
1	India	6.9
2	China	6.6
3	Malaysia	6.1
4	Thailand	6.0
5	Brazil	5.9
⋮		
46	Ukraine	4.9
47	France	4.9
48	Turkey	4.8
49	Portugal	4.8
50	Ireland	4.2

Source: Based on A. T. Kearney, 2009.

TYPES OF OUTSOURCING Nearly any business activity can be outsourced. A general contractor in the building industry, who subcontracts various construction activities needed to build a home, is a perfect example of an outsourcer. Every component of the building process, including the architect's design, a consultant's site location analysis, a lawyer's work to obtain the building permits, plumbing, electrical work, dry walling, painting, furnace installation, landscaping, and sales, is usually outsourced. Outsourcing implies an agreement (typically a legally binding contract) with an external organization.

Among the business processes outsourced are (1) purchasing, (2) logistics, (3) R&D, (4) operation of facilities, (5) management of services, (6) human resources, (7) finance/accounting, (8) customer relations, (9) sales/marketing, (10) training, and (11) legal processes. Note that the first six of these are OM functions that we discuss in this text.

Strategic Planning and Core Competencies

As we saw in Chapter 2, organizations develop missions, long-term goals, and strategies as general guides for operating their businesses. The strategic planning process begins with a basic mission statement and establishing goals. Given the mission and goals, strategic planners next undertake an internal analysis of the organization to identify how much or little each business activity contributes to the achievement of the mission.

AUTHOR COMMENT
Ford Motor used to mine its own ore, make and ship its own steel, and sell cars directly, but those days are long gone.

FIGURE 7.1
Sony, an Outsourcing Company

Based on J. B. Quinn. "Outsourcing Innovation." *Sloan Management Review* (Summer 2000): 20.

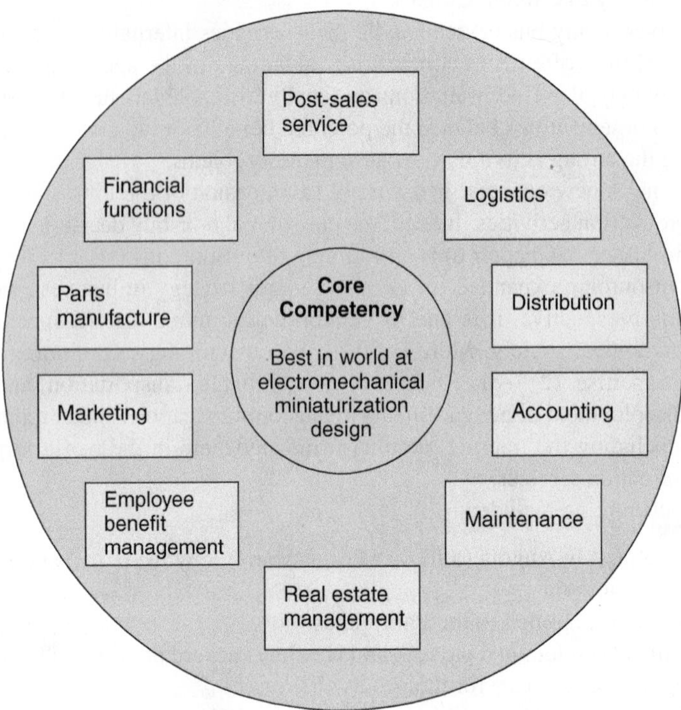

Core competencies
An organization's unique skills, talents, and capabilities.

LO 1: Explain how core competencies relate to outsourcing

During such an analysis, firms identify their strengths—what they do well or better than their competitors. These unique skills, talents, and capabilities are called **core competencies**. Core competencies may include specialized knowledge, proprietary technology or information, and unique production methods. The trick is to identify what the organization does better than anyone else. Common sense dictates that core competencies are the activities that a firm should perform. By contrast, *non-core activities*, which can be a sizable portion of an organization's total business, are good candidates for outsourcing.

Sony's core competency, for example, is electromechanical design of chips. This is its core, and Sony is one of the best in the world when it comes to rapid response and specialized production of these chips. But, as Figure 7.1 suggests, outsourcing could offer Sony continuous innovation and flexibility. Leading specialized outsource providers are likely to come up with major innovations in such areas as software, human resources, and distribution. That is their business, not Sony's.

Managers evaluate their strategies and core competencies and ask themselves how to use the assets entrusted to them. Do they want to be the offshore company that does low-margin work at 3%–4% or the innovative firm that makes a 30%–40% margin? PC or iPod assemblers in China and Taiwan earn 3%–4%, but Apple, which innovates, designs, and sells, has a margin 10 times as large.

To summarize, management must be cautious in outsourcing those elements of the product or service that provide a competitive advantage.

AUTHOR COMMENT
Author James Champy writes, "Although you may be good at something tactically, someone else may do it better and at lower cost."

THE THEORY OF COMPARATIVE ADVANTAGE

Theory of comparative advantage
A theory which states that countries benefit from specializing in (and exporting) products and services in which they have relative advantage, and importing goods in which they have a relative disadvantage.

The motivation for international outsourcing comes from the **theory of comparative advantage**. This theory focuses on the basic economics of outsourcing internationally. According to the theory, if an external provider, regardless of its geographic location, can perform activities more productively than the purchasing firm, then the external provider should do the work. This allows the purchasing firm to focus on what it does best, its core competencies.

However, comparative advantage is not static. Companies, and indeed countries, strive to find comparative advantage. Countries such as India, China, and Russia have made it a government priority and set up agencies to support the easy transition of foreign firms into their outsourcing markets. Work and jobs go to countries that reduce risk through the necessary legal structures, effective infrastructure, and an educated workforce.

The dynamics of comparative advantage are evident from a recent study of five manufactured products. In an effort to meet "optimal" prices on auto parts in 2005, companies were moving

In the ultimate outsourcing risk, NASA awarded contracts of $3.5 billion (USD) to a team, led by Orbital Sciences Corp., to ship cargo to the International Space Station starting in 2011. The company is solely responsible for designing, building, and launching rockets on a regular basis. NASA hopes to save time and money by outsourcing.

work from Mexico to China. At that time China had a 22% price advantage on these parts over Canada and the U.S. But by 2009 that gap had dropped to 5.5%—and in some instances manufacturing in China was 20% more expensive than Mexico. As a result, some manufacturing began migrating back to North America; the price gap wasn't large enough to merit the hassle of manufacturing halfway around the world.[2]

Nonetheless, consistent with the theory of comparative advantage, the trend toward outsourcing continues to grow. This does not mean all existing outsourcing decisions are perfect. The term **backsourcing** has been used to describe the return of business activity to the original firm. We will now discuss the risks associated with outsourcing.

Backsourcing
The return of business activity to the original firm.

Risks of Outsourcing

AUTHOR COMMENT
The substantial risk in outsourcing requires managers to invest the effort to make sure they do it right.

Risk management starts with a realistic analysis of risks and results in a strategy that minimizes the impact of these uncertainties. Indeed, outsourcing can look very risky. And it is. Perhaps half of all outsourcing agreements fail because of inappropriate planning and analysis. For one thing, few promoters of international outsourcing mention the erratic power grids in some foreign countries or the difficulties with local government officials, inexperienced managers, and unmotivated employees. On the other hand, when managers set an outsourcing goal of 75% cost reduction and receive only a 30%–40% cost reduction, they view the outsourcing as a failure, when, in fact, it may be a success.

Quality can also be at risk. A recent survey of 150 North American companies found that, as a group, those that outsourced customer service saw a drop in their score on the American Consumer Satisfaction Index. We should point out that the declines were roughly the same whether companies outsourced domestically or overseas.[3]

Another risk is the political backlash that results from outsourcing to foreign countries. The perceived loss of North American jobs (as well as the loss of jobs in European countries) has fuelled anti-outsourcing rhetoric and action from government officials. (See the *OM in Action* box, "Backsourcing to Small-Town Canada").

LO 2: Describe the risks of outsourcing

Despite the negative impression created by government actions, the press, and public opinion, data suggest that foreigners outsource far more services to North America than North American companies send abroad. And while North American jobs are outsourced, a minuscule few are outsourced offshore. A recent Organisation for Economic Cooperation and Development (OECD) report on the subject shows that outsourcing is not as big a cause in job losses as, say, improved technology, and has an overall positive effect.[4] It is also a two-way street. India's cartoon producer Jadoo Works, for example, outsources projects to North American animators.

[2] "China's Eroding Advantage" *Business Week* (June 15, 2009): 54:55. The report dealt with five categories of machined products, ranging from large engine parts requiring significant labour to small plastic components that need little.
[3] J. Whitaker, M. S. Krishnan, and C. Fornell. "How Offshore Outsourcing Affects Customer Satisfaction." *The Wall Street Journal* (July 7, 2008): R4.
[4] "Outsourcing: Old Assumptions Are Being Challenged as the Outsourcing Industry Matures," *The Economist* (July 28, 2007): 65–66.

OM *in Action* Backsourcing to Small-Town Canada

Canadian companies continue their global search for efficiency by outsourcing call centres and back-office operations, but many find they need to look no farther than a place like Edmundston, New Brunswick or Markham, Ontario.

To Canadian firms facing quality problems with their outsourcing operations overseas and bad publicity at home, small-town Canada is emerging as a pleasant alternative. Edmundston (population 16 643) or Markham (population 300 000) may be the perfect call centre location. Even though the pay is often close to minimum wage, the jobs are a welcome addition to the local communities.

American Express Canada recently moved 200 call centre jobs back from India to Markham. Primus Telecommunications Canada made a similar change, shifting 125 jobs from Mumbai, India, to its call centres in Edmundston, Ottawa, and Toronto between 2009 and 2011.

By moving out of big cities to the cheaper labour and real estate of smaller towns, companies can achieve another advantage and save millions while still increasing productivity. A call centre located in a town that just lost its major manufacturing plant finds the jobs easy to fill.

Taking advantage of even cheaper wages in other countries will not stop soon, though. Is India the unstoppable overseas call centre capital that people think it is? Not at all. Despite its population of over 1.2 billion, only a small percentage of the workers have the language skills and technical education to work in Western-style industries. Already, India has been warned that if call centres can't recruit at reasonable wages, its jobs will move to the Philippines, South Africa, and Ghana. And indeed, Dell, Apple, and Britain's Powergen have backsourced from Indian call centres, claiming their costs had become too high.

Table 7.2 lists some of the risks inherent in outsourcing.

In addition to the external risks, operations managers must deal with other issues that outsourcing brings. These include (1) changes in employment levels, (2) changes in facilities and processes needed to receive components in a different state of assembly, and (3) vastly expanded logistics issues, including insurance, customs, and timing.

What can be done to mitigate the risks of outsourcing? Research indicates that of all the reasons given for outsourcing failure, the most common is that the decision was made without sufficient understanding and analysis. The next section provides a methodology that helps analyze the outsourcing decision process.

TABLE 7.2
The Outsourcing Process and Related Risks

Outsourcing Process	Examples of Possible Risks
Identify non-core competencies	Can be incorrectly identified as a non-core competency
Identify non-core activities that should be outsourced	Just because the activity is not a core competency for your firm does not mean an outsource provider is more competent and efficient
Identify impact on existing facilities, capacity, and logistics	Failing to understand the change in resources and talents needed internally
Establish goals and draft outsourcing agreement specifications	Setting goals so high that failure is certain
Identify and select outsource provider	Selecting the wrong outsource provider
Negotiate goals and measures of outsourcing performance	Misinterpreting measures and goals, how they are measured, and what they mean
Monitor and control current outsourcing program	Being unable to control product development, schedules, and quality
Evaluate and give feedback to outsource provider	Having a non-responsive provider (i.e., one that ignores feedback)
Evaluate international political and currency risks	Country's currency may be unstable; a country may be politically unstable; cultural and language differences may inhibit successful operations
Evaluate coordination needed for shipping and distribution	Understanding of the timing necessary to manage flows to different facilities and markets

AUTHOR COMMENT Cultural differences may indeed be why companies are less frequently outsourcing their call centres.

Evaluating Outsourcing Risk with Factor Rating

The factor-rating method is an excellent tool for dealing with both country risk assessment and provider selection problems.

AUTHOR COMMENT
The factor-rating model adds objectivity to decision making.

RATING INTERNATIONAL RISK FACTORS

Suppose a company has identified for outsourcing an area of production that is a non-core competency. Example 1 shows how to rate several international risk factors using an *unweighted* factor-rating approach.

EXAMPLE 1

Establishing risk factors for four countries

Toronto Airbags produces auto and truck airbags for Nissan, Chrysler, Mercedes, and BMW. It wants to conduct a risk assessment of outsourcing manufacturing. Four countries—the U.K., Mexico, Spain, and Canada (the current home nation)—are being considered. Only English- or Spanish-speaking countries are included because they "fit" with organizational capabilities.

APPROACH ▶ Toronto's management identifies nine factors, listed in Table 7.3, and rates each country on a 0–3 scale, where 0 is no risk and 3 is high risk. Risk ratings are added to find the lowest-risk location.

TABLE 7.3
Toronto Airbag's International Risk Factors, by Country (an unweighted approach)*

Risk Factor	U.K.	Mexico	Spain	Canada (home country)
Economic: Labour cost/laws	1	0	2	1
Economic: Capital availability	0	2	1	0
Economic: Infrastructure	0	2	2	0
Culture: Language	0	0	0	0
Culture: Social norms	2	0	1	2
Migration: Uncontrolled	0	2	0	0
Politics: Ideology	2	0	1	2
Politics: Instability	0	1	2	2
Politics: Legalities	3	0	2	3
Total risk rating scores	8	7	11	10

*Risk rating scale: 0 = no risk, 1 = minor risk, 2 = average risk, 3 = high risk

SOLUTION ▶ Based on these ratings, Mexico is the least risky of the four locations being considered.

INSIGHT ▶ As with many other quantitative methods, assessing risk factors is not easy and may require considerable research, but the technique adds objectivity to a decision.

LEARNING EXERCISE ▶ Social norms in the U.K. have just been rescored by an economist, and the new rating is "no risk." How does this affect Toronto's decision? [Answer: The U.K. now has the lowest rating, at 6, for risk.]

RELATED PROBLEMS ▶ 7.1, 7.3

In Example 1, Toronto Airbags considered only English- and Spanish-speaking countries. But countries like China, India, and Russia have millions of English-speaking personnel. This may have an impact on the final decision.

LO3: Use factor rating to evaluate both country and provider outsourcers

Example 1 considered the home country of the outsourcing firm. This inclusion helps document the risks that a domestic outsourcing provider poses compared to the risks posed by international providers. Including the home country in the analysis also helps justify final strategy selection to stakeholders who might question it.

Indeed, **nearshoring** (i.e., choosing an outsource provider located in the home country or in a nearby country) can be a good strategy for businesses and governments seeking both control and cost advantages. Firms in the U.S. are interested in nearshoring to Canada because of Canada's cultural similarity and geographic nearness. This allows the company wanting to outsource to exert more control than would be possible when outsourcing to most other countries. Nearshoring represents a compromise in which some cost savings are sacrificed for greater control because Canada's smaller wage differential limits the labour cost reduction advantage.

Nearshoring
Choosing an outsource provider in the home country or in a nearby country.

RATING OUTSOURCE PROVIDERS

We illustrated the factor-rating method's computations when each factor has its own importance weight. In Example 2, we now apply that concept in Example 1 to compare outsourcing providers being considered by a firm.

EXAMPLE 2

Rating provider selection criteria

National Architects, Inc., a Vancouver-based designer of high-rise buildings, has decided to outsource its information technology (IT) function. Three outsourcing providers are being actively considered: one in Canada, one in India, and one in Israel.

APPROACH ▶ National's VP of operations, Susan Cholette, has made a list of seven criteria she considers critical. After putting together a committee of four other VPs, she has rated each firm (on a 1–5 scale, with 5 being highest) and has also placed an importance weight on each of the factors, as shown in Table 7.4.

TABLE 7.4
Factor Ratings Applied to National Architects' Potential IT Outsourcing Providers

		Outsource Providers		
Factor (criterion)*	**Importance Weight**	**BIM (Canada)**	**S.P.C. (India)**	**Telco (Israel)**
1. Can reduce operating costs	.2	3	3	5
2. Can reduce capital investment	.2	4	3	3
3. Skilled personnel	.2	5	4	3
4. Can improve quality	.1	4	5	2
5. Can gain access to technology not in company	.1	5	3	5
6. Can create additional capacity	.1	4	2	4
7. Aligns with policy/philosophy/culture	.1	2	3	5
Totals	1.0	3.9	3.3	3.8

*These seven major criteria are based on a survey of 165 procurement executives, as reported in J. Schildhouse, "Outsourcing Ins and Outs," *Inside Supply Management* (December 2005): 22–29.

SOLUTION ▶ Susan multiplies each rating by the weight and sums the products in each column to generate a total score for each outsourcing provider. She selects BIM, which has the highest overall rating.

INSIGHT ▶ When the total scores are as close (3.9 vs. 3.8) as they are in this case, it is important to examine the sensitivity of the results to inputs. For example, if one of the importance weights or factor scores changes even marginally, the final selection may change. Management preference may also play a role here.

LEARNING EXERCISE ▶ Susan decides that "Skilled personnel" should instead get a weight of 0.1 and "Aligns with policy/philosophy/culture" should increase to 0.2. How do the total scores change? [Answer: BIM = 3.6, S.P.C. = 3.2, and Telco = 4.0, so Telco is selected.]

RELATED PROBLEMS ▶ 7.2, 7.4, 7.5, 7.6, 7.7

Most North American toy companies now outsource their production to Chinese manufacturers. Cost savings are significant, but there are several downsides, including loss of control over such issues as quality. In 2007 alone, Mattel had to recall 10.5 million Elmos, Big Birds, and SpongeBobs. These made-in-China toys contained excessive levels of lead in their paint. In 2008, the quality headlines dealt with poisonous pet food from China, and in 2009 it was tainted milk products.

Advantages and Disadvantages of Outsourcing

ADVANTAGES OF OUTSOURCING

LO4: List the advantages and disadvantages of outsourcing

As mentioned earlier, companies outsource for five main reasons. They are, in order of importance: (1) cost savings, (2) gaining outside expertise, (3) improving operations and service, (4) focusing on core competencies, and (5) gaining outside technology.

COST SAVINGS The number-one reason driving outsourcing for many firms is the possibility of significant cost savings, particularly for labour. (See the *OM in Action* box, "Walmart's Link to China.")

GAINING OUTSIDE EXPERTISE In addition to gaining access to a broad base of skills that are unavailable in-house, an outsourcing provider may be a source of innovation for improving products, processes, and services.

IMPROVING OPERATIONS AND SERVICE An outsourcing provider may have production flexibility. This may allow the firm outsourcing its work to win orders by more quickly introducing new products and services.

FOCUSING ON CORE COMPETENCIES An outsourcing provider brings *its* core competencies to the supply chain. This frees up a firm's human, physical, and financial resources to reallocate to core competencies.

GAINING OUTSIDE TECHNOLOGY Firms can outsource to state-of-the-art providers instead of retaining old (legacy) systems. This means they do not have to invest in new technology, thereby cutting risks.

OTHER ADVANTAGES There are additional advantages in outsourcing. For example, a firm may improve its performance and image by associating with an outstanding supplier. Outsourcing can also be used as a strategy for downsizing, or "re-engineering," a firm.

DISADVANTAGES OF OUTSOURCING

There are a number of potential disadvantages in outsourcing. Here are just a few.

INCREASED TRANSPORTATION COSTS Delivery costs may rise substantially if distance increases from an outsourcing provider to a firm using that provider.

LOSS OF CONTROL This disadvantage can permeate and link to all other problems with outsourcing. When managers lose control of some operations, costs may increase because it's harder to assess and control them. For example, production of most of the world's laptops is now outsourced. This means that companies like Dell and HP find themselves using the same contractor (Quanta) to make their machines in China. This can leave them struggling to maintain control over the supplier.

OM *in Action* Walmart's Link to China

No other company has a more efficient supply chain, and no other company has embraced outsourcing to China more vigorously than Walmart. Perhaps as much as 85% of Walmart's merchandise is made abroad, and Chinese factories are by far the most important and fastest growing of these sources.

A whopping 10%–13% of everything China sends to the U.S. ends up on Walmart's shelves—over $15 billion (USD) worth of goods a year. Walmart has almost 600 people on the ground in China just to negotiate and make purchases.

As much as Walmart has been demonized for its part in offshoring jobs, its critical mass allows Chinese firms to build assembly lines that are so huge that they drive prices down through economies of scale.

Walmart's Chinese suppliers achieve startling, market-shaking price cuts. For example, the price of portable DVD players with 17cm LCD screens dropped in half when Walmart found a Chinese factory to build in giant quantities. Walmart's success in going abroad and pressing suppliers for price breaks has forced both retailers and manufacturers to re-evaluate their supply chains.

The company has also led the way to sustainability and product safety through its "Responsible Sourcing" program, announced in 2008. Because Chinese products have been riddled with safety issues, Walmart in 2009 required "an identifiable trail" from raw materials to suppliers.

It also told its top 200 Chinese suppliers that they had until 2012 to become energy and resource efficient, cutting energy use by 20%.

Sources: The Wall Street Journal (October 22, 2008): B1; **About.com:** Logistics/Supply Chain (November 26, 2008); and *Financial Times* (December 12, 2008): 9.

CREATING FUTURE COMPETITION Intel, for example, outsourced a core competency, chip production, to AMD when it could not keep up with early demands. Within a few years, AMD became a leading competitor, manufacturing its own chips.

NEGATIVE IMPACT ON EMPLOYEES Employee morale may drop when functions are outsourced, particularly when friends lose their jobs. Employees believe they may be next, and indeed they may be. Productivity, loyalty, and trust—all of which are needed for a healthy, growing business—may suffer.

LONGER-TERM IMPACT Some disadvantages of outsourcing tend to be longer term than the advantages of outsourcing. In other words, many of the risks firms run by outsourcing may not show up on the bottom line until some time in the future. This permits CEOs who prefer short-term planning and are interested only in bottom-line improvements to use the outsourcing strategy to make quick gains at the expense of longer-term objectives.

The advantages and disadvantages of outsourcing may or may not occur but should be thought of as possibilities to be managed effectively.

Audits and Metrics to Evaluate Performance

Regardless of the techniques and success in selection of outsourcing providers, agreements must specify results and outcomes. Whatever the outsourced component or service, management needs an evaluation process to ensure satisfactory continuing performance. At a minimum, the product or service must be defined in terms of quality, customer satisfaction, delivery, cost, and improvement. The mix and detail of the performance measures will depend on the nature of the product.

In situations where the outsourced product or service plays a major role in strategy and winning orders, the relationship needs to be more than after-the-fact audits and reports. It needs to be based on continuing communication, understanding, trust, and performance. The relationship should manifest itself in the mutual belief that "we are in this together" and go well beyond the written agreement.

However, when outsourcing is for less critical components, agreements that include the traditional mix of audits and metrics (such as cost, logistics, quality, and delivery) may be reported weekly or monthly. When a *service* has been outsourced, more imaginative metrics may be necessary. For instance, in an outsourced call centre, these metrics may deal with personnel evaluation and training, call volume, call type, and response time, as well as tracking complaints. In this dynamic environment, reporting of such metrics may be required daily.

AUTHOR COMMENT
Because outsourcing is rife with potential abuse, companies have to be careful not to harm individuals, societies, or nature.

Ethical Issues in Outsourcing

Laws, trade agreements, and business practices are contributing to a growing set of international, ethical practices for the outsourcing industry. Table 7.5 presents several tenets of conduct that have fairly universal acceptance.

In the electronics industry, HP, Dell, IBM, Intel and twelve other companies have created the Electronics Industry Code of Conduct (EICC). The EICC sets environmental standards, bans child labour and excessive overtime, and audits outsourcing producers to ensure compliance.

TABLE 7.5
Ethical Principles and Related Outsourcing Linkages

Ethics Principle	Outsourcing Linkage
Do no harm to indigenous cultures	Avoid outsourcing in a way that violates religious holidays (e.g., making employees work during religious holidays).
Do no harm to the ecological systems	Don't use outsourcing to move pollution from one country to another.
Uphold universal labour standards	Don't use outsourcing to take advantage of cheap labour that leads to employee abuse.
Uphold basic human rights	Don't accept outsourcing that violates basic human rights.
Pursue long-term involvement	Don't use outsourcing as a short-term arrangement to reduce costs; view it as a long-term partnership.
Share knowledge and technology	Don't think outsourcing agreements will prevent loss of technology, but use the inevitable sharing to build good relationships.

SUPPLEMENT SUMMARY

Companies can give many different reasons why they outsource, but the reality is that outsourcing's most attractive feature is that it helps firms cut costs. Workers in low-cost countries simply work much more cheaply, with fewer fringe benefits, work rules, and legal restrictions, than their U.S. and European counterparts. For example, a comparable hourly wage of $20 in the U.S. and $30 in Europe is well above the $1.26 per hour in China. Yet China often achieves quality levels equivalent to (or even higher than) plants in the West.

There is a growing economic pressure to outsource. But there is also a need for planning outsourcing to make it acceptable to all participants. When outsourcing is done in the right way, it creates a win–win situation.

Key Terms

Outsourcing (p. 186)
Offshoring (p. 186)
Core competencies (p. 188)
Theory of comparative advantage (p. 188)
Backsourcing (p. 189)
Nearshoring (p. 191)

Discussion Questions

1. How would you summarize outsourcing trends?
2. What potential cost saving advantages might firms experience by using outsourcing?
3. What internal issues must managers address when outsourcing?
4. How should a company select an outsourcing provider?
5. What are international risk factors in the outsourcing decision?
6. How can ethics be beneficial in an outsourcing organization?
7. What are some of the possible consequences of poor outsourcing?

Using Software to Solve Outsourcing Problems

Excel, Excel OM, and POM for Windows may be used to solve most of the problems in this supplement.

Excel OM and POM for Windows both contain Factor Rating modules that can address issues such as the ones we saw in Examples 1 and 2.

Problems*

• **7.1** Claudia Program Technologies, Inc., has narrowed its choice of outsourcing provider to two firms located in different countries. Program wants to decide which one of the two countries is the better choice, based on risk-avoidance criteria. She has polled her executives and established four criteria. The resulting ratings for the two countries are presented in the table below, where 1 is a lower risk and 3 is a higher risk.

a) Using the unweighted factor-rating method, which country would you select?
b) If the first two factors (price and nearness) are given a weight of 2, and the last two factors (technology and history) are given a weight of 1, how does your answer change? PX

Selection Criterion	U.K.	Canada
Price of service from outsourcer	2	3
Nearness of facilities to client	3	1
Level of technology	1	3
History of successful outsourcing	1	2

*Note: PX means the problem may be solved with POM for Windows and/or Excel OM.

• **7.2** Using the same ratings given in Problem 7.1, assume that the executives have determined four criteria weightings: Price, with a weight of 0.1; Nearness, with 0.6; Technology, with 0.2; and History, with 0.1.

a) Using the weighted factor-rating method, which country would you select?
b) Double each of the weights used in part (a) (to 0.2, 1.2, 0.4, and 0.2, respectively). What effect does this have on your answer? Why? PX

• **7.3** Ranga Ramasesh is the operations manager for a firm that is trying to decide which one of four countries it should research for possible outsourcing providers. The first step is to select a country based on cultural risk factors, which are critical to eventual business success with the provider. Ranga has reviewed outsourcing provider directories and found that the four countries in the table that follows have an ample number of providers from which they can choose. To aid in the country selection step, he has enlisted the aid of a cultural expert, John Wang, who has provided ratings of the various criteria in the table that follows. The resulting ratings are on a 1 to 10 scale, where 1 is a low risk and 10 is a high risk.

a) Using the unweighted factor-rating method, which country should Ranga select based on risk avoidance?

b) If Peru's ratings for "Society value of quality work" and "Individualism attitudes" are each lowered by 50%, how does your answer to part (a) change? PX

Culture Selection Criterion	Mexico	Panama	Costa Rica	Peru
Trust	1	2	2	1
Society value of quality work	7	10	9	10
Religious attitudes	3	3	3	5
Individualism attitudes	5	2	4	8
Time orientation attitudes	4	6	7	3
Uncertainty avoidance attitudes	3	2	4	2

•• **7.4** Using the same ratings given in Problem 7.3(a), assume that John Wang has determined six criteria weightings: trust, with a weight of 0.4; quality, with 0.2; religious, with 0.1; individualism, with 0.1; time, with 0.1; and uncertainty, with 0.1. Using the weighted factor-rating method, which country should Ranga select? PX

•• **7.5** Charles Teplitz's firm wishes to use factor rating to help select an outsourcing provider of logistics services.

a) With weights from 1–5 (5 highest) and ratings 1–100 (100 highest), use the following table to help Teplitz make his decision:

		Rating of Logistics Providers		
Criterion	**Weight**	**Atlanta Shipping**	**Seattle Delivery**	**Utah Freight**
Quality	5	90	80	75
Delivery	3	70	85	70
Cost	2	70	80	95

b) Teplitz decides to increase the weights for quality, delivery, and cost to 10, 6, and 4, respectively. How does this change your conclusions? Why?

c) If Atlanta Shipping's ratings for each of the factors increase by 10%, what are the new results? PX

• **7.6** Walker Accounting Software is marketed to small accounting firms throughout Canada and the U.S. Owner George Walker has decided to outsource the company's help desk and is considering three providers: Manila Call Centre (Philippines), Delhi Services (India), and Moscow Bell (Russia). The following table summarizes the data Walker has assembled. Which outsourcing firm has the best rating? (Higher weights imply higher importance and higher ratings imply more desirable providers.) PX

		Provider Ratings		
Criterion	**Importance Weight**	**Manila**	**Delhi**	**Moscow**
Flexibility	0.5	5	1	9
Trustworthiness	0.1	5	5	2
Price	0.2	4	3	6
Delivery	0.2	5	6	6

••• **7.7** Price Technologies, a Nova Scotia-based high-tech manufacturer, is considering outsourcing some of its electronics production. Four firms have responded to its request for bids, and CEO Willard Price has started to perform an analysis on the scores his OM team has entered in the table below.

		Ratings of Outsource Providers			
Factor	**Weight**	**A**	**B**	**C**	**D**
Labour	w	5	4	3	5
Quality procedures	30	2	3	5	1
Logistics system	5	3	4	3	5
Price	25	5	3	4	4
Trustworthiness	5	3	2	3	5
Technology in place	15	2	5	4	4
Management team	15	5	4	2	1

Weights are on a scale from 1 through 30, and the outsourcing provider scores are on a scale of 1 through 5. The weight for the labour factor is shown as a w because Price's OM team cannot agree on a value for this weight. For what range of values of w, if any, is company C a recommended outsourcing provider, according to the factor-rating method?

Case Studies

Outsourcing to Mumbai

Some provinces in Canada have discouraged the outsourcing of certain functions on the part of the provincial government to firms in other countries. Yet others have been more open to the idea as a means of saving taxpayers' money. The government of Prince Edward Island (PEI) thought it might work for them while they sought advice on a new payroll system. In so doing, PEI accepted the lowest bid from Mumbai Consultants Inc., a firm residing in India and one with non-specialized experience.

The specifications of the project called for the completion and launch of the new system within nine months. Once the agreement was signed, no one from the PEI government office kept a close eye on the progress of the implementation, and assumed no news was good news. As the launch date approached, a new manager from Mumbai Consultants contacted the appropriate person in the PEI government indicating the project would be over budget and about 4 months late. The reason provided for the delay and the budget challenges included high employee turnover at Mumbai and a lack of knowledge-transfer throughout this turnover. Moreover, it was suggested that they did not have the necessary expertise in-house, and the little they did have was swept away during the turnover. The Mumbai manager advised that if the province wished to shorten the new timeline they would have to pay an additional 35% of the original contract price because Mumbai Consultants Inc. would also have additional costs.

Discussion Questions

1. Use the process in Table 7.2 to analyze what the pfrovincial government of PEI could have done to achieve a more successful outcome.
2. Is this a case of cultural misunderstanding, or could the same result have occurred if a Canadian firm, such as Accenture Canada, had been selected?
3. Conduct your own research to assess the risks of outsourcing any information technology project. (*Computerworld* is one good source.)

Outsourcing Offshore at Darden

Darden Restaurants, owner of popular brands such as Olive Garden and Red Lobster, serves more than 300 million meals annually in over 1700 restaurants across the U.S. and Canada. To achieve competitive advantage via its supply chain, Darden must achieve excellence at each step. With purchases from 35 countries, and seafood products with a shelf life as short as 4 days, this is a complex and challenging task.

Those 300 million meals annually mean 15 million kilograms of shrimp and huge quantities of tilapia, swordfish, and other fresh purchases. Fresh seafood is typically flown to North America and monitored each step of the way to ensure that 1 degree Celsius is maintained.

Darden's purchasing agents travel the world to find competitive advantage in the supply chain. Darden personnel from supply chain and development, quality assurance, and environmental relations contribute to developing, evaluating, and checking suppliers. Darden also has seven native-speaking representatives living on other continents to provide continuing support and evaluation of suppliers. All suppliers must abide by Darden's food standards, which typically exceed FDA and other industry standards. Darden expects continuous improvement in durable relationships that increase quality and reduce cost.

Darden's aggressiveness and development of a sophisticated supply chain provides an opportunity for outsourcing. Much food preparation is labour intensive and is often more efficient when handled in bulk. This is particularly true where large volumes may justify capital investment. For instance, Tyson and Iowa Beef prepare meats to Darden's specifications much more economically than can individual restaurants. Similarly, Darden has found that it can outsource both the cutting of salmon to the proper portion size and the cracking/peeling of shrimp more cost-effectively offshore than in U.S. distribution centres or individual restaurants.

Discussion Questions*

1. What are some outsourcing opportunities in a restaurant?
2. What supply-chain issues are unique to a firm sourcing from 35 countries?
3. Examine how other firms or industries develop international supply chains as compared to Darden.
4. Why does Darden outsource harvesting and preparation of much of its seafood?

*You may wish to view the video that accompanies this case study before answering these questions.

Bibliography

Aron, R., and J. V. Singh. "Getting Offshoring Right." *Harvard Business Review* (December 2005): 135–143.

Bravard, J., and R. Morgan. *Smarter Outsourcing*. Upper Saddle River, NJ: Pearson, 2006.

Champy, James. *Avoiding the Seven Deadly Sins of Outsourcing Relationships*. Plano, TX: Perot Systems, 2005.

Friedman, Thomas. *The World Is Flat: A Brief History of the 21st Century*. New York: Farrar, Straus, and Giroux, 2005.

Greenwald, Bruce C., and Judd Kahn. *Globalization: The Irrational Fear That Someone in China Will Take Your Job*. New York: Wiley, 2009.

Halvey, J. K., and B. M. Melby. *Business Process Outsourcing*, 2nd ed. New York: Wiley, 2007.

Hirschheim, R., A. Heinzl, and J. Dibbern. *Information Systems Outsourcing*. Secaucus, NJ: Springer, 2009.

Lee, Hau L., and Chung-Yee Lee. *Building Supply Chain Excellence in Emerging Economies*. Secaucus, NJ: Springer, 2007.

Messner, W. *Working with India*, Secaucus, NJ: Springer, 2009.

Midler, Paul. *Poorly Made in China: An Insider's Account of the Tactics behind China's Production Game*. New York: Wiley, 2009.

Thomas, A. R., and T. J. Wilkinson. "The Outsourcing Compulsion." *MIT Sloan Management Review* 48, no. 1 (Fall 2006): 10.

Webb, L., and J. Laborde. "Crafting a Successful Outsourcing Vendor/Client Relationship." *Business Process Management Journal* 11, no. 5 (2005): 437–443.

Whitten, Dwayne, and Dorothy Leidner. "Bringing IT Back: An Analysis of the Decision to Backsource or Switch Vendors." *Decision Sciences* 37, no. 4 (November 2006): 605–621.

Yourdon, Edward. *Outsource: Competing in the Global Productivity Race*. Upper Saddle River, NJ: Prentice Hall, 2005.

CHAPTER 7 Rapid Review

Main Heading	Review Material	MyOMLab
WHAT IS OUTSOURCING? (pp. 186–187)	• **Outsourcing**—Procuring from external sources services or products that are normally part of an organization Some organizations use outsourcing to replace entire purchasing, information systems, marketing, finance, and operations departments. • **Offshoring**—Moving a business process to a foreign country but retaining control of it. Outsourcing is not a new concept; it is simply an extension of the long-standing practice of *subcontracting* production activities. Outsourced manufacturing, also known as contract manufacturing, is becoming standard practice in many industries. Outsourcing implies an agreement (typically a legally binding contract) with an external organization.	**VIDEO 7.1** Outsourcing Offshore at Darden
STRATEGIC PLANNING AND CORE COMPETENCIES (pp. 187–189)	• **Core competencies**—An organization's unique skills, talents, and capabilities. Core competencies may include specialized knowledge, proprietary technology or information, and unique production methods. *Non-core activities*, which can be a sizable portion of an organization's total business, are good candidates for outsourcing. • **Theory of comparative advantage**—A theory which states that countries benefit from specializing in (and exporting) products and services in which they have relative advantage and importing goods in which they have a relative disadvantage. • **Backsourcing**—The return of business activity to the original firm.	
RISKS OF OUTSOURCING (pp. 189–190)	Perhaps half of all outsourcing agreements fail because of inappropriate planning and analysis. Potential risks of outsourcing include: • In some countries, erratic power grids, difficult local government officials, inexperienced managers, or unmotivated employees. • A drop in quality or customer service. • Political backlash that results from outsourcing to foreign countries. • Changes in employment levels. • Changes in facilities and processes needed to receive components in a different state of assembly. • Vastly expanded logistics issues, including insurance, customs, and timing. The most common reason given for outsourcing failure is that the decision was made without sufficient understanding and analysis.	
EVALUATING OUTSOURCING RISK WITH FACTOR RATING (pp. 191–192)	The factor-rating method is an excellent tool for dealing with both country risk assessment and provider-selection problems. Including the home country of the outsourcing firm in a factor-rating analysis helps document the risks that a domestic outsourcing provider poses compared to the risks posed by international providers. Including the home country in the analysis also helps justify final strategy selection to stakeholders who might question it. • **Nearshoring**—Choosing an outsource provider in the home country or in a nearby country. Nearshoring can be a good strategy for businesses and governments seeking both control and cost advantages.	Problems: 7.1–7.7
ADVANTAGES AND DISADVANTAGES OF OUTSOURCING (pp. 193–194)	Advantages of outsourcing include: • *Cost savings:* The number-one reason driving outsourcing for many firms is the possibility of significant cost savings, particularly for labour. • *Gaining outside expertise:* In addition to gaining access to a broad base of skills that are unavailable in-house, an outsourcing provider may be a source of innovation for improving products, processes, and services. • *Improving operations and service:* An outsourcing provider may have production flexibility. This may allow the client firm to win orders by more quickly introducing new products and services. • *Focusing on core competencies:* An outsourcing provider brings *its* core competencies to the supply chain. This frees up the firm's human, physical, and financial resources to reallocate to the firm's own core competencies. • *Gaining outside technology:* Firms can outsource to state-of-the-art providers instead of retaining old (legacy) systems. These firms do not have to invest in new technology, thereby cutting risks.	

Main Heading	Review Material	MyOMLab
	• *Other advantages:* The client firm may improve its performance and image by associating with an outstanding supplier. Outsourcing can also be used as a strategy for downsizing, or "re-engineering," a firm. Potential disadvantages of outsourcing include: • *Increased transportation costs:* Delivery costs may rise substantially if distance increases from an outsourcing provider to a client firm. • *Loss of control:* This disadvantage can permeate and link to all other problems with outsourcing. When managers lose control of some operations, costs may increase because it's harder to assess and control them. • *Creation of future competitors* • *Negative impact on employees:* Employee morale may drop when functions are outsourced, particularly when friends lose their jobs. • *Longer-term impact:* Some disadvantages of outsourcing tend to be longer term than the advantages of outsourcing. In other words, many of the risks firms run by outsourcing may not show up on the bottom line until some time in the future.	
AUDITS AND METRICS TO EVALUATE PERFORMANCE (p. 194)	Outsourcing agreements must specify results and outcomes. Management needs an evaluation process to ensure satisfactory continuing performance. At a minimum, the product or service must be defined in terms of quality, customer satisfaction, delivery, cost, and improvement. When the outsourced product or service plays a major role in strategy and winning orders, the relationship needs to be based on continuing communication, understanding, trust, and performance.	
ETHICAL ISSUES IN OUTSOURCING (p. 194)	Some outsourcing policies linked to ethical principles include: avoid outsourcing in a way that violates religious holidays; don't use outsourcing to move pollution from one country to another; don't use outsourcing to take advantage of cheap labour that leads to employee abuse; don't accept outsourcing that violates basic human rights; don't use outsourcing as a short-term arrangement to reduce costs—view it as a long-term partnership; and don't think an outsourcing agreement will prevent loss of technology, but use the inevitable sharing to build a good relationship with outsourcing firms.	

Self Test

■ **Before taking the self-test,** refer to the learning objectives listed at the beginning of the supplement and the key terms listed at the end of the supplement.

LO1. Core competencies are those strengths in a firm that include:
- **a)** specialized skills.
- **b)** unique production methods.
- **c)** proprietary information/knowledge.
- **d)** things a company does better than others.
- **e)** all of the above.

LO2. Outsourcing can be a risky proposition because:
- **a)** about half of all outsourcing agreements fail.
- **b)** it saves only about 30% in labour costs.
- **c)** labour costs are increasing throughout the world.
- **d)** a non-core competency is outsourced.
- **e)** shipping costs are increasing.

LO3. Evaluating outsourcing providers by comparing their weighted average scores involves:
- **a)** factor-rating analysis.
- **b)** cost-volume analysis.
- **c)** transportation model analysis.
- **d)** linear regression analysis.
- **e)** crossover analysis.

LO4. Advantages of outsourcing include:
- **a)** focusing on core competencies and cost savings.
- **b)** gaining outside technology and creating new markets in India for U.S. products.
- **c)** improving operations by closing plants in Malaysia.
- **d)** employees wanting to leave the firm.
- **e)** reduced problems with logistics

Answers: LO1. e; LO2. a; LO3. a; LO4. a.

MyOMLab — The problems marked in red can be found on MyOMLab. Visit MyOMLab to access cases, videos, downloadable software, and much more. MyOMLab also features a personalized Study Plan that helps you identify which chapter concepts you've mastered and guides you towards study tools for additional practice.

Students Profile

Michelle Parronchi Supply Chain Specialist, Blackberry
Business Administration – Materials and Operations Management Co-op, 2009

Following graduation I was immediately hired as a Supply Chain Specialist for a high tech company that sells in markets around the globe. Our Supply Chain department is responsible for all material supply in each of our plants around the world. Our role is to ensure that we always have sufficient material to keep the plants running while balancing global inventory to minimize all costs related to it. The Supply Chain department gives visibility to all

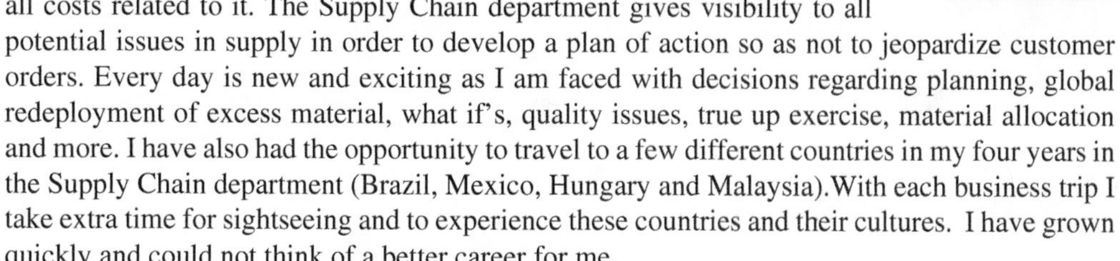

potential issues in supply in order to develop a plan of action so as not to jeopardize customer orders. Every day is new and exciting as I am faced with decisions regarding planning, global redeployment of excess material, what if's, quality issues, true up exercise, material allocation and more. I have also had the opportunity to travel to a few different countries in my four years in the Supply Chain department (Brazil, Mexico, Hungary and Malaysia).With each business trip I take extra time for sightseeing and to experience these countries and their cultures. I have grown quickly and could not think of a better career for me.

8

Managing Inventory throughout the Supply Chain

Chapter Outline

BAUMGARTEN/VARIO IMAGES/SIPA/Newscom

Employees pick items off the shelves at an Amazon.com warehouse in Leipzig, Germany.

When they first started appearing in the late 1990s, Web-based "e-tailers" such as Amazon.com hoped to replace the "bricks" of traditional retailing with the "clicks" of online ordering via computer keyboards. Rather than opening dozens or even hundreds of stores filled with expensive inventory, an e-tailer could run a single virtual store that served customers around the globe. Their business model suggested that inventory could be kept at a few key sites, chosen to minimize costs and facilitate quick delivery to customers. In theory, e-tailers were highly "scalable" businesses that could add new customers with little or no additional investment in inventory or facilities. (Traditional retailers usually need to add stores to gain significant increases in their customer base.)

TABLE 8.1
Amazon.com Financial Results, 1997–2009

Year	Net Sales ($Millions)	Inventory ($Millions) (Dec. 31)	Inventory Turns
1997	$148	$9	16.4
1998	$610	$30	20.3
1999	$1,640	$221	7.4
2000	$2,762	$175	15.8
2001	$3,122	$143	21.8
2002	$3,933	$202	19.5
2003	$5,264	$294	17.9
2004	$6,921	$480	14.4
2005	$8,490	$566	15.0
2006	$10,711	$877	12.2
2007	$14,835	$1,200	12.4
2008	$19,166	$1,399	13.7
2009	$24,509	$2,171	11.3

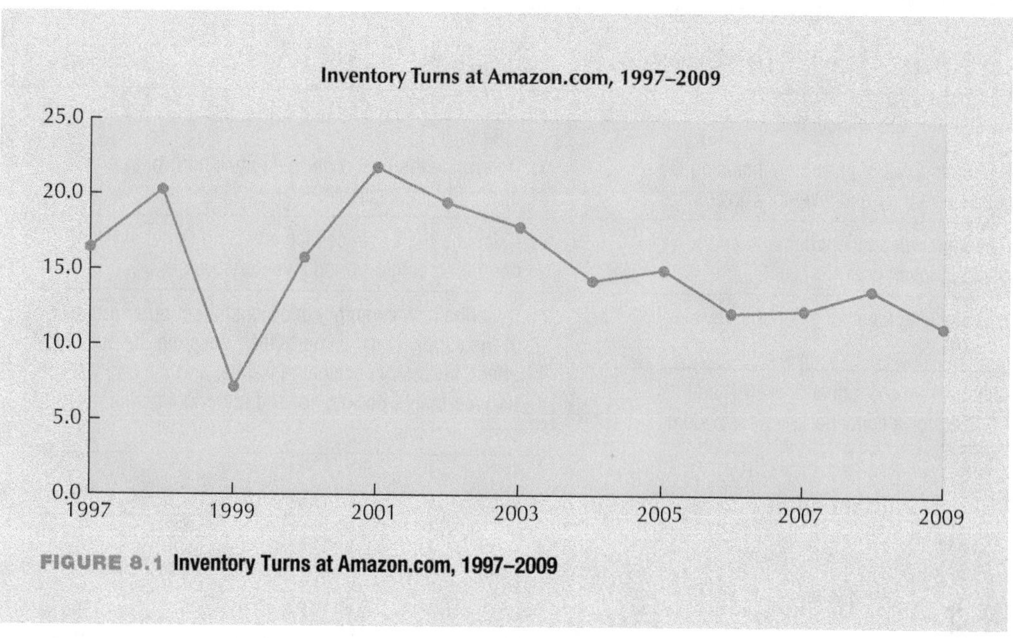

FIGURE 8.1 Inventory Turns at Amazon.com, 1997–2009

But how has this actually played out for Amazon? Table 8.1 contains sales and inventory figures, pulled from the company's annual reports, for Amazon for the years 1997 through 2009. The first column reports net sales for each calendar year, and the second column contains the amount of inventory on hand at the end of the year. The third column shows inventory turns, which is calculated as (net sales/ending inventory). Retailers generally want higher inventory turns, which indicate that they can support the same level of sales with less inventory.

Graphing these results provides some interesting insights. Consider Figure 8.1. In late 1999, Amazon learned that managing inventory can be challenging even for e-tailers. That was the year the company expanded into new product lines, such as electronics and housewares, with which it had little experience. Amazon's purchasing managers were faced with the question of how many of these items to hold in inventory. Too little, and they risked losing orders and alienating customers; too much, and they could lock up the company's resources in unsold products. Only later, when sales for the 1999 holiday season fell flat and Amazon's inventory levels skyrocketed did the purchasing managers realize they had overstocked. In fact, as the figures show, by the end of 1999, Amazon's inventory turnover ratio was 7.4—*worse* than that of the typical brick-and-mortar retailer.

After 1999, Amazon seemed to learn its lesson. Inventory turns rose to nearly 22 in 2001, but they have fallen steadily ever since, to 11.3 turns for 2009. But why? The decline in inventory turns since 2001 is due to a shift in Amazon's business strategy. Instead of trying to build competitive advantage based on low-cost books, Amazon now seeks to provide customers with convenient shopping and fast delivery for a much wider range of products. Such a strategy requires more inventory to support the same level of sales.

So today, how does Amazon compare to its brick-and-mortar competitors? Amazon handily beats traditional book retailer Barnes & Noble, whose inventory turns for 2009 were just 4.2. Yet Best Buy, which sells computers, video games, and appliances, generated 9.1 inventory turns in 2009—not bad, especially considering all the retail stores Best Buy must support.

Chapter 8 Learning Objectives

By the end of this chapter, you will be able to:

1: Describe the various roles of inventory, including the different types of inventory and inventory drivers.

2: Distinguish between independent demand and dependent demand inventory.

3: Calculate the restocking level for a periodic review system.

4: Calculate the economic order quantity (*EOQ*) and reorder point (*ROP*) for a continuous review system.

5: Determine the best order quantity when volume discounts are available.

6: Calculate the target service level and target stocking point for a single-period inventory system.

7: Describe how inventory decisions affect other areas of the supply chain. In particular, describe the bullwhip effect, inventory positioning issues, and the impacts lof transportation, packaging, and material handling considerations.

Introduction

Inventory
According to APICS, "those stocks or items used to support production (raw materials and work-inprocess items), supporting activities (maintenance, repair, and operating supplies) and customer service (finished goods and spare parts)."

APICS defines **inventory** as "those stocks or items used to support production (raw materials and work-in-process items), supporting activities (maintenance, repair, and operating supplies) and customer service (finished goods and spare parts)."[1] In this chapter, we discuss the critical role of inventory—why it is necessary, what purposes it serves, and how it is controlled.

As Amazon's experience suggests, inventory management is still an important function, even in the Internet age. In fact, many managers seem to have a love–hate relationship with inventory. Michael Dell talks about inventory velocity—the speed at which components move through Dell Computer's operations—as a key measure of his company's performance.[2] In his mind, the less inventory the company has sitting in the warehouse, the better. Victor Fung of the Hong Kong-based trading firm Li & Fung, goes so far as to say, "Inventory is the root of all evil."[3]

Yet look what happened to the price of gasoline in the United States during the spring of 2007. It skyrocketed, primarily because refineries were shut down for maintenance and suppliers were caught with inadequate reserves. And if you have ever visited a store only to find that your favorite product is sold out, you might think the *lack* of inventory is the root of all evil. The fact is, inventory is both a valuable resource and a potential source of waste.

The Role of Inventory

Consider WolfByte Computers, a fictional manufacturer of desktop computers and servers. Figure 8.2 shows the supply chain for WolfByte Computers. WolfByte assembles the machines from components purchased from companies throughout the world, three of which are shown in the figure. Supplier 1 provides the display unit, Supplier 2 manufactures the integrated circuit board (ICB), and Supplier 3 produces the mouse.

Looking downstream, WolfByte sells its computers through independent retail stores and through its own Web site. At retail stores, customers can buy a computer off the shelf, or they can order one to be customized and shipped directly to them. On average, WolfByte takes about a week to ship a computer from its assembly plant to a retail store or a customer. Both WolfByte and the retail stores keep spare parts on hand to handle customers' warranty claims and other service requirements.

With this background, let's discuss the basic types of inventory and see how they fit into WolfByte's supply chain.

[1]J. H. Blackstone, ed., *APICS Dictionary*, 13th ed. (Chicago, IL: APICS, 2010).

[2]J. Magretta, "The Power of Virtual Integration: An Interview with Dell Computer's Michael Dell," *Harvard Business Review* 76, no. 2 (March–April 1998): 72–84.

[3]J. Magretta, "Fast, Global, and Entrepreneurial: Supply Chain Management, Hong Kong Style," *Harvard Business Review* 76, no. 5 (September–October 1998): 102–109.

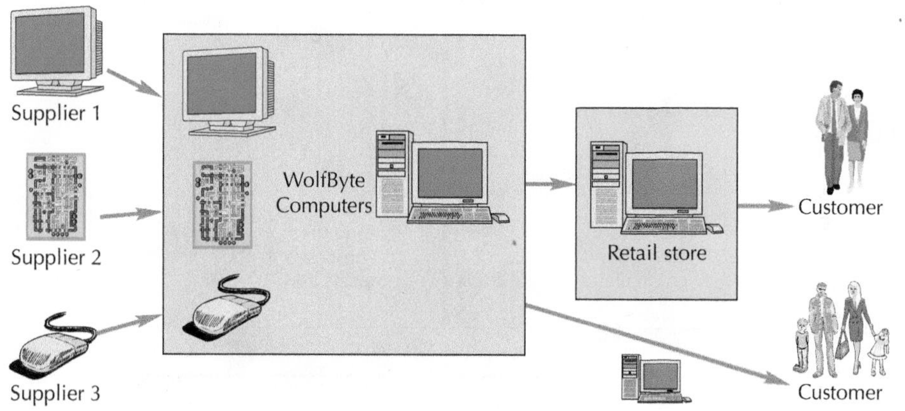

FIGURE 8.2
WolfByte Computers's Supply Chain

INVENTORY TYPES

Cycle stock
Components or products that are received in bulk by a downstream partner, gradually used up, and then replenished again in bulk by the upstream partner.

Two of the most common types of inventory are cycle stock and safety stock. **Cycle stock** refers to components or products that are received in bulk by a downstream partner, gradually used up, and then replenished again in bulk by the upstream partner. For example, suppose Supplier 3 ships 20,000 mouse devices at a time to WolfByte. Of course, WolfByte can't use all those devices at once. More likely, workers pull them out of inventory as needed. Eventually, the inventory runs down, and WolfByte places another order for mouse devices. When the new order arrives, the inventory level rises and the cycle is repeated. Figure 8.3 shows the classic sawtooth pattern associated with cycle stock inventories.

Cycle stock exists at other points in WolfByte's supply chain. Almost certainly, Suppliers 1 through 3 have cycle stocks of raw materials that they use to make components. And retailers need to keep cycle stocks of both completed computers and spare parts in order to serve their customers.

Safety stock
Extra inventory that a company holds to protect itself against uncertainties in either demand or replenishment time.

Cycle stock is often thought of as active inventory because companies are constantly using it up, and their suppliers constantly replenishing it. **Safety stock**, on the other hand, is extra inventory that companies hold to protect themselves against uncertainties in either demand levels or replenishment time. Companies do not plan on using their safety stock any more than you plan on using the spare tire in the trunk of your car; it is there *just in case*.

Let's return to the mouse example in Figure 8.3. WolfByte has timed its orders so that a new batch of mouse devices comes in just as the old batch is used up. But what if Supplier 3 is late in delivering the devices? What if demand is higher than expected? If either or both these conditions occur, WolfByte could run out of mouse devices before the next order arrives.

Imagine the resulting chaos: Assembly lines would have to shut down, customers' orders couldn't be filled, and WolfByte would have to notify customers, retailers, and shippers about the delays.

One solution is to hold some extra inventory, or safety stock, of mouse devices to protect against fluctuations in demand or replenishment time. Figure 8.4 shows what WolfByte's inventory levels would look like if the company decided to hold safety stock of 1,000 mouse devices.

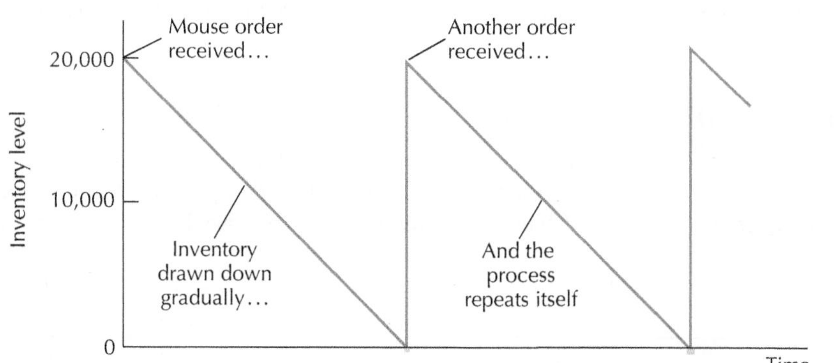

FIGURE 8.3
Cycle Stock at WolfByte Computers

FIGURE 8.4
Safety Stock at WolfByte Computers

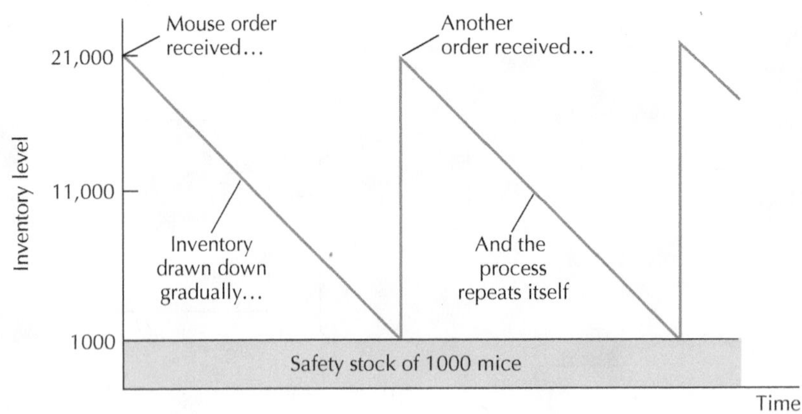

As you can see, safety stock provides valuable protection, but at the cost of higher inventory levels. Later in the chapter, we discuss ways of calculating appropriate safety stock levels.

There are four other common types of inventory: anticipation, hedge, transportation, and smoothing. Anticipation inventory, as the name implies, is inventory that is held in anticipation of customer demand. **Anticipation inventory** allows instant availability of items when customers want them. **Hedge inventory**, according to APICS, is "a form of inventory buildup to buffer against some event that may not happen. Hedge inventory planning involves speculation related to potential labor strikes, price increases, unsettled governments, and events that could severely impair the company's strategic initiatives."[4] In this sense, hedge inventories can be thought of as a special form of safety stock. WolfByte has stockpiled a hedge inventory of three months' worth of ICBs because managers have heard that Supplier 2 may experience a labor strike in the next few months.

Anticipation inventory
Inventory that is held in anticipation of customer demand.

Hedge inventory
According to APICS, a "form of inventory buildup to buffer against some event that may not happen. Hedge inventory planning involves speculation related to potential labor strikes, price increases, unsettled governments, and events that could severely impair the company's strategic initiatives."

Transportation inventory
Inventory that is moving from one link in the supply chain to another.

Smoothing inventory
Inventory that is used to smooth out differences between upstream production levels and downstream demand.

Transportation inventory represents inventory that is "in the pipeline," moving from one link in the supply chain to another. When the physical distance between supply chain partners is long, transportation inventory can represent a considerable investment. Suppose, for example, that Supplier 2 is located in South Korea, and WolfByte is located in Texas. ICBs may take several weeks to travel the entire distance between the two companies. As a result, multiple orders could be in the pipeline on any particular day. One shipment of ICBs might be sitting on the docks in Kimhae, South Korea; two others might be halfway across the Pacific; a fourth might be found on Route I-10, just outside Phoenix, Arizona. In fact, the transportation inventory of ICBs alone might dwarf the total cycle and safety stock inventories in the rest of the supply chain.

Finally, **smoothing inventory** is used to smooth out differences between upstream production levels and downstream demand. Suppose management has determined that WolfByte's assembly plant is most productive when it produces 3,000 computers a day (where productivity output in dollars/input in dollars). Unfortunately, demand from retailers and customers will almost certainly vary from day to day. As a result, WolfByte's managers may decide to produce a constant 3,000 computers per day, building up finished goods inventory during periods of slow demand and drawing it down during periods of high demand. (Figure 8.5 illustrates this approach.) Smoothing inventories allow individual links in the supply chain to stabilize their production at the most efficient level and to avoid the costs and headaches associated with constantly changing workforce levels and/or production rates. If you think you may have heard of this idea before, you have: It's part of the rationale for following a level production strategy in developing a sales and operations plan.

INVENTORY DRIVERS

From this discussion, we can see that inventory is a useful resource. However, companies don't want to hold more inventory than necessary. Inventory ties up space and capital: A dollar invested in inventory is a dollar that cannot be used somewhere else. Likewise, the space used to

[4]Blackstone, APICS Dictionary.

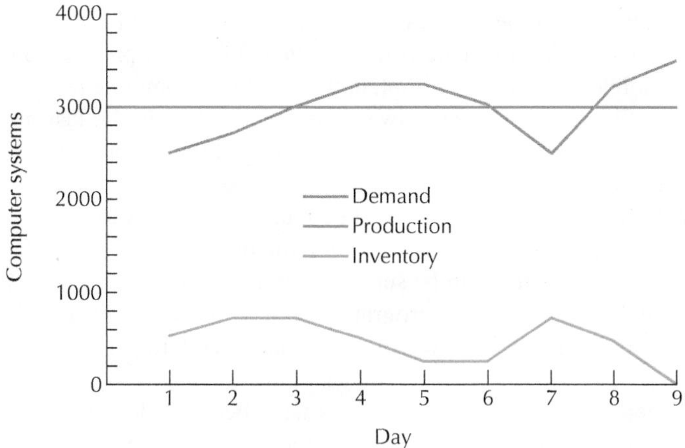

FIGURE 8.5
Smoothing Inventories at WolfByte Computers

store inventory can often be put to more productive use. Inventory also poses a significant risk of obsolescence, particularly in supply chains with short product life cycles. Consider what happens when Intel announces the next generation of processor chips. Would you want to be stuck holding the old-generation chips when the new ones hit the market?

Finally, inventory is too often used to hide problems that management really should resolve. In this sense, inventory can serve as a kind of painkiller, treating the symptom without solving the underlying problem. Consider our discussion of safety stock. Suppose WolfByte's managers decide to hold additional safety stock of ICBs because of quality problems they have been experiencing with units received from Supplier 2. While the safety stock may buffer WolfByte from these quality problems, it does so at a cost. A better solution might be to improve the quality of incoming ICBs, thereby reducing both quality-related costs and the need for additional safety stock.

With these concerns in mind, let's turn our attention to **inventory drivers**—business conditions that force companies to hold inventory. Table 8.2 summarizes the ways in which various inventory drivers affect different types of inventory. To the extent that organizations can manage and control the drivers of inventories, they can reduce the supply chain's need for inventory.

Inventory drivers
Business conditions that force companies to hold inventory.

In managing inventory, organizations face uncertainty throughout the supply chain. On the upstream (supplier) end, they face **supply uncertainty**, or the risk of interruptions in the flow of components they need for their internal operations. In assessing supply uncertainty, managers need to answer questions such as these:

Supply uncertainty
The risk of interruptions in the flow of components from upstream suppliers.

- How consistent is the quality of the goods being purchased?
- How reliable are the supplier's delivery estimates?
- Are the goods subject to unexpected price increases or shortages?

Problems in any of these areas can drive up supply uncertainty, forcing an organization to hold safety stock or hedging inventories.

TABLE 8.2
Inventory Drivers and Their Impact

Inventory Driver	Impact
Uncertainty in supply or demand	Safety stock, hedge inventory
Mismatch between a downstream partner's demand and the most efficient production or shipment volumes for an upstream partner	Cycle stock
Mismatch between downstream demand levels and upstream production capacity	Smoothing inventory
Mismatch between timing of customer demand and supply chain lead times	Anticipation inventory Transportation inventory

Demand uncertainty
The risk of significant and unpredictable fluctuations in downstream demand.

On the downstream (customer) side, organizations face **demand uncertainty**, or the risk of significant and unpredictable fluctuations in the demand for their products. For example, many suppliers of automobile components complain that the big automobile manufacturers' forecasts are unreliable and that order sizes are always changing, often at the last minute. Under such conditions, suppliers are forced to hold extra safety stock to meet unexpected jumps in demand or changes in order size.

In dealing with uncertainty in supply and demand, the trick is to determine what types of uncertainty can be reduced and then to focus on reducing them. For example, poor quality is a source of supply uncertainty that can be substantially reduced or even eliminated through business process or quality improvement programs, such as those we discussed in Chapter 3. On the other hand, forecasting may help to reduce demand uncertainty, but it can never completely eliminate it.

Another common inventory driver is the mismatch between demand and the most efficient production or shipment volumes. Let's start with a simple example—facial tissue. When you blow your nose, how many tissues do you use? Most people would say 1, yet tissues typically come in boxes of 200 or more. Clearly, a mismatch exists between the number of tissues you need at any one time and the number you need to purchase. The reason, of course, is that packaging, shipping, and selling facial tissues one at a time would be highly inefficient, especially because the cost of holding a cycle stock of facial tissues is trivial. On an organizational scale, mismatches between demand and efficient production or shipment volumes are the main drivers of cycle stocks. As we will see later in this chapter, managers can often alter their business processes to reduce production or shipment volumes, thereby reducing the mismatch with demand and the resulting need for cycle stocks.

Likewise, mismatches between overall demand levels and production capacity can force companies to hold smoothing inventories (Figure 8.5). Of course, managers can reduce smoothing inventories by varying their capacity to better match demand or by smoothing demand to better match capacity.

The last inventory driver we will discuss is a mismatch between the timing of the customer's demand and the supply chain's lead time. When you go to the grocery store, you expect to find fresh produce ready to buy; your expected waiting time is zero. But produce can come from almost anywhere in the world, depending on the season. To make sure that bananas and lettuce will be ready and waiting for you at your local store, someone has to initiate their movement through the supply chain days or even weeks ahead of time and determine how much anticipation inventory to hold. Whenever the customer's maximum waiting time is shorter than the supply chain's lead time, companies must have transportation and anticipation inventories to ensure that the product will be available when the customer wants it.

How can businesses reduce the need to hold anticipation inventory? Often they do so both by shrinking their own lead time and by persuading customers to wait longer. It's hard to believe now, but personal computers once took many weeks to work their way through the supply chain. As a result, manufacturers were forced to hold anticipation inventories to meet customer demand. Today manufacturers assemble and ship a *customized* computer directly to the customer's front door in just a few days. Customers get fast and convenient delivery of a product that meets their exact needs. At the same time, the manufacturer can greatly reduce or even eliminate anticipation inventory.

In the remainder of this chapter, we examine the systems that are used in managing various types of inventory. Before beginning a detailed discussion of these tools and techniques of inventory management, however, we need to distinguish between two basic inventory categories: independent demand and dependent demand inventory. The distinction between the two is crucial because the tools and techniques needed to manage each are *very* different.

Independent demand inventory
Inventory items whose demand levels are beyond a company's complete control.

Dependent demand inventory
Inventory items whosedemand levels are tied directly to a company's planned production of another item.

INDEPENDENT VERSUS DEPENDENT DEMAND INVENTORY

In general, **independent demand inventory** refers to inventory items whose demand levels are beyond a company's complete control. **Dependent demand inventory**, on the other hand, refers to inventory items whose demand levels are tied directly to the company's planned production of another item. Because the required quantities and timing of dependent demand inventory items can be predicted with great accuracy, they are under an company's *complete* control.

A simple example of an independent demand inventory item is a kitchen table. While a furniture manufacturer may use forecasting models to predict the demand for kitchen tables and may try to use pricing and promotions to manipulate demand, the actual demand for kitchen tables is unpredictable. The fact is that *customers* determine the demand for these items, so finished tables clearly fit the definition of independent demand inventory.

But what about the components that are used to make the tables, such as legs? Suppose that a manufacturer has decided to produce 500 tables five weeks from now. With this information, a manager can quickly calculate exactly how many legs will be needed:

$$500 \times 4 \text{ legs per table} = 2{,}000 \text{ legs}$$

Furthermore, the manager can determine exactly when the legs will be needed, based on the company's production schedule. Because the timing and quantity of the demand for table legs are completely predictable and under the manager's total control, the legs fit the definition of dependent demand items. Dependent demand items require an entirely different approach to managing than do independent demand items.

Three basic approaches are used to manage independent demand inventory items: periodic review systems, continuous review systems, and single-period inventory systems. We examine all three approaches in the following sections.

Periodic Review Systems

One of the simplest approaches to managing independent demand inventory is based on a periodic review of inventory levels. In a **periodic review system**, a company checks the inventory level of an item at regular intervals and restocks to some predetermined level, R. The actual order quantity, Q, is the amount required to bring the inventory level back up to R. Stated more formally:

Periodic review system
An inventory system that is used to manage independent demand inventory. The inventory level for an item is checked at regular intervals and restocked to some predetermined level.

$$Q = R - I \qquad (8\text{-}1)$$

where:

Q = order quantity
R = restocking level
I = inventory level at the time of review

Figure 8.6 shows the fluctuations in the inventory levels of a single item under a two-week periodic review system. As the downward-sloping line shows, the inventory starts out full and then slowly drains down as units are pulled from it. (Note that the line will be straight only if demand is constant.) After two weeks, the inventory is replenished, and the process begins again.

A periodic review system nicely illustrates the use of both cycle stock and safety stock. By replenishing inventory every two weeks, rather than daily or even hourly, the organization spreads the cyclical cost of restocking across more units. And the need to hold safety stock helps to determine the restocking level. Increasing the restocking level effectively increases safety stock: The higher the level, the less likely the organization is to run out of inventory before the next replenishment period. On the flip side, because inventory is checked only at regular intervals, the company could run out of an item before the inventory is replenished. In fact, that is exactly what happens just before week 6 in Figure 8.6. If you have ever visited your favorite

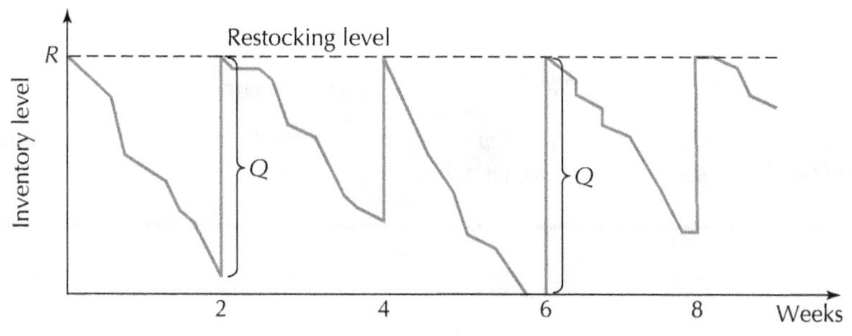

FIGURE 8.6
Periodic Review System

vending machine, only to find that the item you wanted has been sold out, you have been the victim of a periodic review system stockout.

As you might imagine, a periodic review system is best suited to items for which periodic restocking is economical and the cost of a high restocking level (and hence a large safety stock) is not prohibitive. A classic example is a snack food display at a grocery store. Constantly monitoring inventory levels for low-value items such as pretzels or potato chips makes no economic sense. Rather, a vendor will stop by a store regularly and top off the supply of all the items, usually with more than enough to meet demand until the next replenishment date.

RESTOCKING LEVELS

The key question in setting up a periodic review system is determining the restocking level, *R*. In general, *R* should be high enough to meet all but the most extreme demand levels during the reorder period (*RP*) and the time it takes for the order to come in (L). Specifically:

$$R = \mu_{RP+L} + z\sigma_{RP+L} \qquad (8\text{-}2)$$

where:

μ_{RP+L} = average demand during the reorder period and the order lead time
σ_{RP+L} = standard deviation of demand during the reorder period and the order lead time
z = number of standard deviations above the average demand (higher z values increase the restocking level, thereby lowering the probability of a stockout)

Service level
A term used to indicate the amount of demand to be met under conditions of demand and supply uncertainty.

Equation (8-2) assumes that the demand during the reorder period and the order lead time is normally distributed. By setting *R* a certain number of standard deviations above the average, a firm can establish a **service level**, which indicates what percentage of the time inventory levels will be high enough to meet demand during the reorder period. For example, setting $z = 1.28$ would make *R* large enough to meet expected demand 90% of the time (i.e., provide a 90% service level), while setting $z = 2.33$ would provide a 99% service level. Different z values and the resulting service levels are listed in the following table.

z Value	Resulting Service Level
1.28	90%
1.65	95
2.33	99
3.08	99.9

EXAMPLE 1

Establishing a Periodic Review System for McCreery's Chips

McCreery's Chips sells large tins of potato chips at a grocery superstore. Every 10 days, a McCreery's deliveryperson stops by and checks the inventory level. He then places an order, which is delivered 3 days later. Average demand during the reorder period and order lead time (13 days total) is 240 tins. The standard deviation of demand during this same time period is 40 tins. The grocery superstore wants enough inventory on hand to meet demand 95% of the time. In other words, the store is willing to take a 5% chance that it will run out of tins before the next order arrives.

Using this information, McCreery's establishes the following restocking level:

$$R = \mu_{RP+L} + z\sigma_{RP+L}$$
$$= 240 \text{ tins} + 1.65*40 \text{ tins} = 306 \text{ tins}$$

Suppose the next time the deliveryperson stops by, he counts 45 tins. Based on this information, he will order $Q = 306 - 45 = 261$ tins, which will be delivered in 3 days.

Continuous Review Systems

While the periodic review system is straightforward, it is *not* well suited to managing critical and/or expensive inventory items. A more sophisticated approach is needed for these types of inventory. In a **continuous review system**, the inventory level for an item is constantly monitored, and when the reorder point is reached, an order is released.

Continuous review system
An inventory system used to manage independent demand inventory. The inventory level for an item is constantly monitored, and when the reorder point is reached, an order is released.

A continuous review system has several key features:

1. Inventory levels are monitored constantly, and a replenishment order is issued only when a preestablished reorder point has been reached.
2. The size of a replenishment order is typically based on the trade-off between holding costs and ordering costs.
3. The reorder point is based on both demand and supply considerations, as well as on how much safety stock managers want to hold.

To simplify our discussion of continuous review systems, we will begin by assuming that the variables that underlie the system are constant. Specifically:

1. The inventory item we are interested in has a constant demand per period, d. That is, there is no variability in demand from one period to the next. Demand for the year is D.
2. L is the lead time, or number of periods that must pass before a replenishment order arrives. L is also constant.
3. H is the cost of holding a single unit in inventory for a year. It includes the cost of the space needed to store the unit, the cost of potential obsolescence, and the opportunity cost of tying up the organization's funds in inventory. H is known and fixed.
4. S is the cost of placing an order, regardless of the order quantity. For example, the cost to place an order might be \$100, whether the order is for 2 or 2,000 units. S is also known and fixed.
5. P, the price of each unit, is fixed.

Under these assumptions, the fluctuations in the inventory levels for an item will look like those in Figure 8.7. Inventory levels start out at Q, the order quantity, and decrease at a constant rate, d. Because this is a continuous review system, the next order is issued when the reorder point, labeled R, is reached. What should the reorder point be? In this simple model, in which the demand rate and lead time are constant, we should reorder when the inventory level reaches the point where there are just enough units left to meet requirements until the next order arrives:

$$R = dL \tag{8-3}$$

For example, if the demand rate is 50 units a week and the lead time is 3 weeks, the manager should place an order when the inventory level drops to 150 units. If everything goes according to plan, the firm will run out of units just as the next order arrives. Finally, because the inventory level in this model goes from Q to 0 over and over again, the average inventory level is $\frac{Q}{2}$.

THE ECONOMIC ORDER QUANTITY (*EOQ*)

How do managers of a continuous review system choose the order quantity (Q)? Is there a "best" order quantity, and if so, how do holding costs (H) and ordering costs (S) affect it? To understand the role of holding and ordering costs in a continuous review system, let's see what happens if the order quantity is sliced in half, to Q', as shown in Figure 8.8. The result: With quantity Q' the manager ends up ordering twice as often, which doubles the company's ordering costs. On the other hand, cutting the order quantity in half also halves the average inventory level, which lowers holding costs.

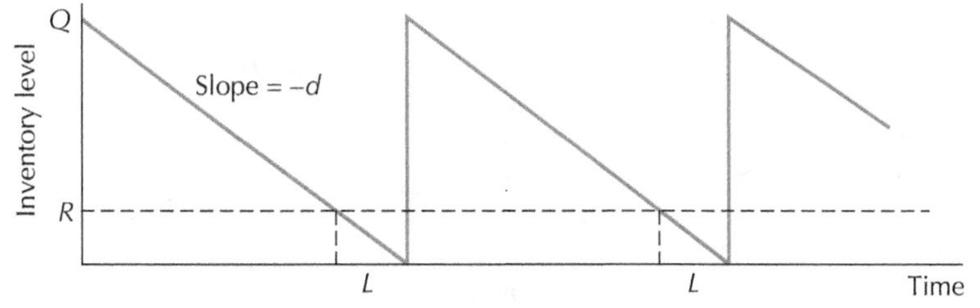

FIGURE 8.7
Continuous Review System (with Constant Demand Rate *d*)

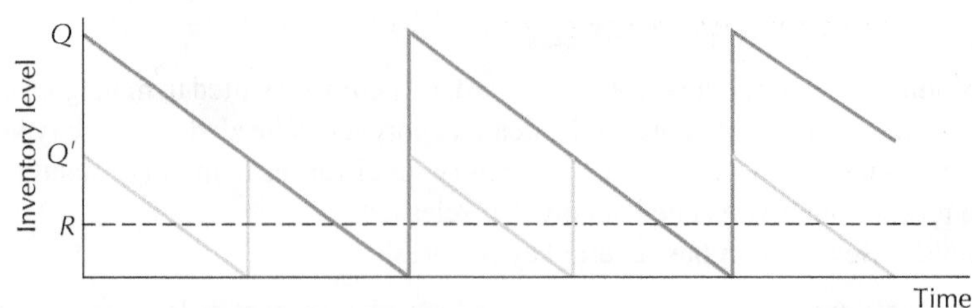

FIGURE 8.8
The Effect of Halving the Order Quantity

The relationship between holding costs and ordering costs can be seen in the following equation:

$$\text{Total holding and ordering cost for the year} = \text{total yearly holding cost} + \text{total yearly ordering cost}$$

$$= \left(\frac{Q}{2}\right)H + \left(\frac{D}{Q}\right)S \qquad \text{(8-4)}$$

Yearly holding cost is calculated by taking the average inventory level ($Q/2$) and multiplying it by the per-unit holding cost. Yearly ordering cost is calculated by calculating the number of times we order per year (D/Q) and multiplying this by the fixed ordering cost.

As Equation (8-4) suggests, there is a trade-off between yearly holding costs and ordering costs. Reducing the order quantity, Q, will decrease holding costs, but force the organization to order more often. Conversely, increasing Q will reduce the number of times an order must be placed, but result in higher average inventory levels.

Figure 8.9 shows graphically how yearly holding and ordering costs react as the order quantity, Q, varies. In addition to showing the cost curves for yearly holding costs and yearly ordering costs, Figure 8.9 includes a total cost curve that combines these two. If you look closely, you can see that the lowest point on the total cost curve also happens to be where yearly holding costs equal yearly ordering costs.

Economic order quantity (*EOQ*)
The order quantity that minimizes annual holding and ordering costs for an item.

Figure 8.9 illustrates the **economic order quantity** (*EOQ*), the particular order quantity (Q) that minimizes holding costs and ordering costs for an item. This special order quantity is found by setting yearly holding costs equal to yearly ordering costs and solving for Q:

$$\left(\frac{Q}{2}\right)H = \left(\frac{D}{Q}\right)S$$

$$Q^2 = \frac{2DS}{\text{H}}$$

$$Q = \sqrt{\frac{2DS}{\text{H}}} = EOQ \qquad \text{(8-5)}$$

where:

Q = order quantity
H = annual holding cost per unit
D = annual demand
S = ordering cost

As Figure 8.9 shows, order quantities that are higher than the *EOQ* will result in annual holding costs that are higher than ordering costs. Conversely, order quantities that are lower than the *EOQ* will result in annual ordering costs that are higher than holding costs.

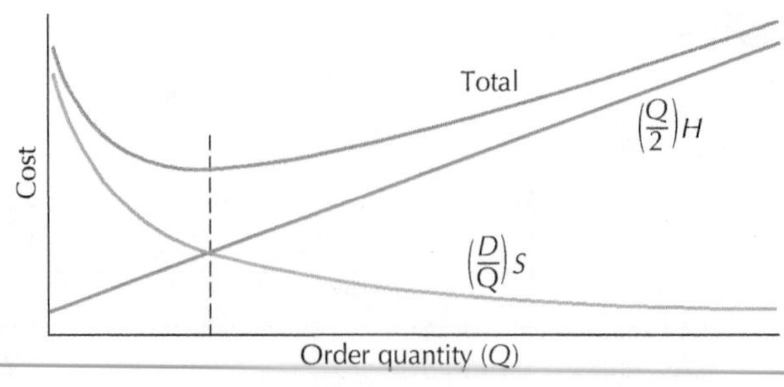

FIGURE 8.9
The Relationships among Yearly Holding Costs, Yearly Ordering Costs, and the Order Quantity, *Q*

EXAMPLE 2

Calculating the *EOQ* at Boyer's Department Store

You are in charge of ordering items for Boyer's Department Store, located in Seattle. For one of the products Boyer's carries, the Hudson Valley Model Y ceiling fan, you have the following information:

$$\text{Annual demand } (D) = 4{,}000 \text{ fans a year}$$
$$\text{Annual holding cost } (H) = \$15 \text{ per fan}$$
$$\text{Ordering cost } (S) = \$50 \text{ per order}$$

Your predecessor ordered fans four times a year, in quantities (Q) of 1,000. The resulting annual holding and ordering costs were:

$$\text{Holding costs for the year} + \text{ordering costs for the year}$$
$$= (1{,}000/2)\ \$15 + (4{,}000/1{,}000)\ \$50$$
$$= \$7{,}500 + \$200 = \$7{,}700$$

Because holding costs are much higher than ordering costs, we know that the *EOQ* must be much lower than 1,000 fans. In fact:

$$EOQ = \sqrt{\frac{2*4{,}000*\$50}{\$15}} \text{ which rounds to 163 fans per order}$$

The number 163 seems strange, so let's check to see if it results in lower annual costs:

$$\text{Holding costs} + \text{ordering costs}$$
$$= (163/2)\ \$15 + (4{,}000/163)\ \$50$$
$$= \$1{,}222.50 + \$1{,}226.69 = \$2{,}449.49$$

Notice that holding costs and ordering costs are essentially equal, as we would expect. More important, *simply by ordering the right quantity*, you could reduce annual holding and ordering costs for this item by

$$\$7{,}700 - \$2{,}449 = \$5{,}251$$

Now suppose Boyer's carries 250 other products with cost and demand structures similar to that of the Hudson Valley Model Y ceiling fan. In that case, you might be able to save 250*$5,251 = $1,312,750 per year just by ordering the right quantities!

Of course, the *EOQ* has some limitations. Holding costs (H) and ordering costs (S) cannot always be estimated precisely, so managers may not always be able to calculate the true *EOQ*. However, as Figure 8.9 suggests, total holding and ordering costs are relatively flat over a wide range around the *EOQ*. So order quantities can be off a little and still yield total costs that are close to the minimum.

A more valid criticism of the *EOQ* is that it does not take into account volume discounts, which can be particularly important if suppliers offer steep discounts to encourage customers to order in large quantities. Later in the chapter, we examine how volume discounts affect the order quantity decision.

Other factors that limit the application of the *EOQ* model include ordering costs that are not always fixed and demand rates that vary throughout the year. However, the *EOQ* is a good starting point for understanding the impact of order quantities on inventory-related costs.

REORDER POINTS AND SAFETY STOCK

The *EOQ* tells managers *how much* to order but not *when to* order. We saw in Equation (8.3) that when the demand rate (d) and lead time (L) are constant, the reorder point is easily calculated as:

$$ROP = dL$$

But d and L are rarely fixed. Consider the data in Table 8.3, which lists 10 different combinations of demand rates and lead times. The average demand rate, $\overline{d}$ and average lead time, $\overline{L}$ are 50 units and 3 weeks, respectively. Our first inclination in this case might be to set the reorder point at $\overline{d}\,\overline{L}$ = 50 units. Yet 5 out of 10 times, dL exceeds 150 units (see Table 8.3). A better solution—one that takes into account the variability in demand rate and lead time—is needed.

TABLE 8.3
Sample Variations in Demand Rate and Lead Time

Demand Rate (D) in Units Per Week	Lead Time (L), In Weeks	Demand During Lead Time (DL), in Units
60	3	180*
40	4	160*
55	2	110
45	3	135
50	3	150
65	3	195*
35	3	105
55	3	165*
45	4	180*
50	2	100
Average = 50 units	Average = 3 weeks	Average = 148 units

* Demand greater than $\bar{d}\,\bar{L}$

When either lead time or demand—or both—varies, a better solution is to set the reorder point higher than $ROP = dL$. Specifically:

$$ROP = \bar{d}\,\bar{L} + SS \qquad (8\text{-}6)$$

where:

SS = safety stock

Recall that WolfByte Computers carried a safety stock of 1,000 mouse devices (Figure 8.4). Again, safety stock (SS) is an extra amount beyond that needed to meet average demand during lead time. This is added to the reorder point to protect against variability in both demand and lead time. Safety stock raises the reorder point, forcing a company to reorder earlier than usual. In doing so, it helps to ensure that future orders will arrive before the existing inventory runs out.

Figure 8.10 shows how safety stock works when both the demand rate and the lead time vary. We start with an inventory level of Q plus the safety stock ($Q + SS$) When we reach the new reorder point of $\bar{d}\,\bar{L} + SS$ an order is released. But look what happens during the first reorder period: Demand exceeds $\bar{d}\,\bar{L}$ forcing workers to dip into the safety stock. If the safety stock had not been there, the inventory would have run out. In the second reorder period, even though the lead time is longer than before, demand flattens out so much that workers do not need the safety stock.

In general, the decision of how much safety stock to hold depends on five factors:

1. The variability of demand;
2. The variability of lead time;
3. The average length of lead time;
4. The desired service level; and
5. The average demand.

Let's talk about each of these factors. First, the more the demand level and the lead time vary, the more likely it is that inventory will run out. Therefore, higher variability in demand and lead time will tend to force a company to hold more safety stock. Furthermore, a longer average lead

FIGURE 8.10
The Impact of Varying Demand Rates and Lead Times

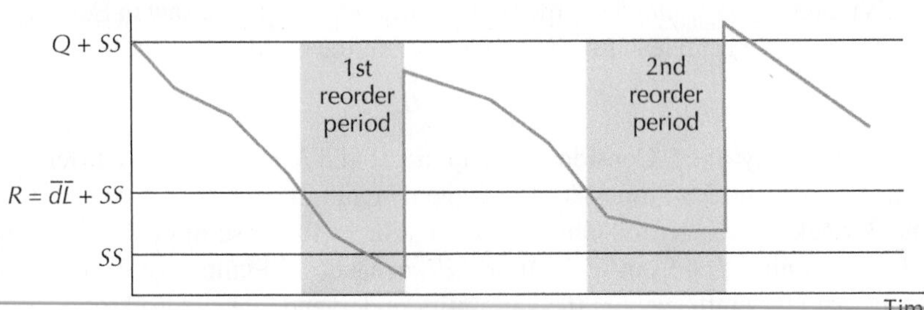

time exposes a firm to this variability for a longer period. When lead times are extremely short, as they are in just-in-time (JIT) environments, safety stocks can be very small.

The service level is a managerial decision. Service levels are usually expressed in statistical terms, such as "During the reorder period, we should have stock available 90% of the time." While the idea that management might agree to accept even a small percentage of stockouts may seem strange, in reality, whenever demand or lead time varies, the *possibility* exists that a firm will run out of an item, no matter how large the safety stock. The higher the desired service level, the less willing management is to tolerate a stockout, and the more safety stock is needed.

EXAMPLE 3

Calculating the Reorder Point and Safety Stock at Boyer's Department Store

Let's look at one approach to calculating the reorder point with safety stock. Like other approaches, this one is based on simple statistics. To demonstrate the math, we'll return to Boyer's Department Store and the Hudson Valley Model Y ceiling fan. Boyer's sells, on average, 16 Hudson Valley Model Y ceiling fans a day ($\bar{d} = 16$) with a standard deviation in daily demand of 3 fans ($\sigma_d = 3$). This demand information can be estimated easily from past sales history.

If the store reorders fans directly from the manufacturer, the fans will take, on average, 9 days to arrive ($\bar{L} = 9$) with a standard deviation in lead time of 2 days ($\sigma_L = 3$). The store manager has decided to maintain a 95% service level. In other words, the manager is willing to run out of fans only 5% of the time before the next order arrives.

From these numbers, we can see that:

$$\text{Average demand during the reorder period} = \bar{d}\,\bar{L} = 144 \text{ fans}$$

Taking the analysis a step further, we can show using basic statistics that:

$$\begin{aligned} &= \sigma_{dL} \\ &= \sqrt{\bar{L}\sigma_d^2 + \bar{d}^2\sigma_L^2} = \sqrt{9*9 + 256*4} \qquad (8\text{-}7) \\ &= 33.24 \end{aligned}$$

To ensure that Boyer's meets its desired service level, we need to set the reorder point high enough to meet demand during the reorder period 95% of the time. Put another way, the reorder point (*ROP*) should be set at the ninety-fifth percentile of demand during the reorder period. Because demand during the reorder period is often normally distributed, basic statistics tells us that:

$$\begin{aligned} \text{Reorder point } (ROP) &= \text{ninety-fifth percentile of demand during the reorder period} \\ &= \bar{d}\,\bar{L} + z\sigma_{dL} \\ &= 144 + 1.65*33.24 \\ &= 198.8, \text{ or } 199 \end{aligned}$$

In this equation, 1.65 represents the number of standard deviations (z) above the mean that corresponds to the ninety-fifth percentile of a normally distributed variable. (Other z values and their respective service levels are shown in Table 8.4.) The more general formula for calculating the reorder point is, therefore:

$$ROP = \bar{d}\,\bar{L} + z\sqrt{\bar{L}\sigma_d^2 + \bar{d}^2\sigma_L^2} \qquad (8\text{-}8)$$

where:

$\bar{d}$ = average demand per time period
$\bar{L}$ = average lead time
σ_d^2 = variance of demand per time period
σ_L^2 = variance of lead time
z = number of standard deviations above the average demand during lead time (higher z values lower the probability of a stockout)

TABLE 8.4
***z* Values Used in Calculating Safety Stock**

z Value	Associated Service Level
0.84	80%
1.28	90
1.65	95
2.33	99

Notice that the first part of the equation, $\bar{d}\bar{L}$ covers only the average demand during the reorder period. The second part of the equation, $z\sqrt{\bar{L}\sigma_d^2 + \bar{d}^2\sigma_L^2}$, represents the safety stock. For Boyer's, then, the amount of safety stock needed is:

$$z\sqrt{\bar{L}\sigma_d^2 + \bar{d}^2\sigma_L^2} = 1.65 * 33.24 = 54.88, \text{ or } 55 \text{ fans}$$

Of course, there are other methods for determining safety stock. Some managers consider variations in both the lead time and the demand rate; others use a definition of service level that includes the frequency of reordering. (Firms that reorder less often than others are less susceptible to stockouts.) In practice, many firms take an unscientific approach to safety stock, such as setting the reorder point equal to 150% of expected demand. Whatever the method used, however, these observations will still hold: The amount of safety stock needed will be affected by the variability of demand and lead time, the length of the average lead time, and the desired service level.

QUANTITY DISCOUNTS

In describing the economic order quantity, one of our assumptions was that the price per unit, P, was fixed. This was a convenient assumption because it allowed us to focus on minimizing just the total holding and ordering costs for the year (Equation [8.3]). But what if a supplier offers a price discount for ordering larger quantities? How will this affect the EOQ?

When quantity discounts are in effect, we must modify our analysis to look at total ordering, holding, *and item costs* for the year:

Total holding, ordering, and item costs for the year =

$$\left(\frac{Q}{2}\right)H + \left(\frac{D}{Q}\right)S + DP \tag{8-9}$$

where:

Q = order quantity
H = holding cost per unit
D = annual demand
P = price per unit (which can now vary)
S = ordering cost

Because the EOQ formula (Equation [8.5]) considers only holding and ordering costs, the EOQ may not result in lowest total costs when quantity discounts are in effect. To illustrate, suppose we have the following information:

D = 1,200 units per year
H = \$10 per unit per year
S = \$30 per order
P = \$35 per unit for orders less than 90; \$32.50 for orders of 90 or more

If we ignore the price discounts and calculate the EOQ, we get the following:

$$EOQ = \sqrt{\frac{2*1{,}200*\$30}{\$10}}, \text{ which round to 85 units}$$

Total annual holding, ordering, and item costs for an order quantity of 85 are:

$$\left(\frac{85}{2}\right)\$10 + \left(\frac{1{,}200}{85}\right)\$30 + \$35x1200$$
$$= \$425 + \$423.53 + \$42{,}000$$
$$= \$42{,}848.53$$

But note that if we increase the order size by just 5 units, to 90, we can get a discount of \$35 − \$32.50 = \$2.50 per unit. Selecting an order quantity of 90 would give us the following annual holding, ordering, and item costs:

$$\left(\frac{90}{2}\right)\$10 + \left(\frac{1{,}200}{90}\right)\$30 + \$32.50x1200$$
$$= \$450 + \$400 + \$39{,}000$$
$$= \$39{,}850.00$$

When volume price discounts are in effect, we must follow a two-step process:

1. Calculate the *EOQ*. If the *EOQ* number represents a quantity that can be purchased for the lowest price, stop—we have found the lowest cost order quantity. Otherwise, we go to step 2.
2. Compare total holding, ordering, and item costs at the *EOQ* quantity with total costs at each price break *above* the *EOQ*. There is no reason to look at quantities below the *EOQ*, as these would result in higher holding and ordering costs, as well as higher item costs

EXAMPLE 4

Volume Discounts at Hal's Magic Shop

© Annavee | Dreamstime.com

Hal's Magic Shop purchases masks from a Taiwanese manufacturer. The manufacturer has quoted the following price breaks to Hal:

Order Quantity	Price per Mask
1–100	\$15
101–200	\$12.50
201 or more	\$10

Hal sells 1,000 masks a year. The cost to place an order is \$20, and the holding cost per mask is about \$3 per year. How many masks should Hal order at a time?

Solving for the *EOQ*, Hal gets the following:

$$EOQ = \sqrt{\frac{2*1{,}000*\$20}{\$3}} = 115 \text{ masks}$$

Unfortunately, Hal cannot order 115 masks and get the lowest price of \$10 per mask. Therefore, he compares total holding, ordering, and item costs at $Q = 115$ masks to those at the next highest price break, 201 masks:

Total annual holding, ordering, and item costs for an order quantity of 115 masks =

$$\left(\frac{115}{2}\right)\$3 + \left(\frac{1{,}000}{115}\right)\$20 + \$12.50x1000$$
$$= \$172.50 + \$173.91 + \$12{,}500$$
$$= \$12{,}846.41$$

Total annual holding, ordering, and item costs for an order quantity of 201 masks =

$$\left(\frac{201}{2}\right)\$3 + \left(\frac{1{,}000}{201}\right)\$20 + \$10.00x1000$$
$$= \$301.50 + \$99.50 + \$10{,}000$$
$$= \$10{,}401.00$$

So even though an order quantity of 115 would minimize holding and ordering costs, the price discount associated with ordering 201 masks more than offsets this. Hal should use an order quantity of 201 masks.

Single-Period Inventory Systems

So far, our discussions have assumed that any excess inventory we order can be held for future use. But this is not always true. In some situations, excess inventory has a very limited life and must be discarded, sold at a loss, or even hauled away at additional cost if not sold in the period intended. Examples include fresh fish, magazines and newspapers, and Christmas trees. In other cases, inventory might have such a specialized purpose (such as spare parts for a specialized machine) that any unused units cannot be used elsewhere. When such conditions apply, a company must weigh the cost of being short against the cost of having excess units, where:

$$\text{Shortage cost} = C_{\text{Shortage}} = \text{value of the item } \textit{if} \text{ demanded} - \text{item cost} \quad \text{(8-10)}$$

$$\text{Excess cost} = C_{\text{Excess}} = \text{item cost} + \text{disposal cost} - \text{salvage value} \quad \text{(8-11)}$$

For example, say that an item that sells for $200 costs $50 but must be disposed of at a cost of $5 if not used. This item has the following shortage and excess costs:

$$C_{\text{Shortage}} = \$200 - \$50 = \$150$$

$$C_{\text{Excess}} = \$50 + \$5 = \$55$$

Single-period inventory system
A system used when demand occurs in only a single point in time.

Target service level
For a single-period inventory system, the service level at which the expected cost of a shortage equals the expected cost of having excess units.

Target stocking point
For a single-period inventory system, the stocking point at which the expected cost of a shortage equals the expected cost of having excess units.

The goal of a **single-period inventory system** is to establish a stocking level that strikes the *best balance* between expected shortage costs and expected excess costs. Developing a single-period system for an item is a two-step process:

1. Determine a **target service level** (**SL$_T$**) that strikes the best balance between shortage costs and excess costs.
2. Use the target service level to determine the **target stocking point** (**TS**) for the item.

We describe each of these steps in more detail in the following sections.

TARGET SERVICE LEVEL

For the single-period inventory system, service level is simply the probability that there are enough units to meet demand. Unlike a periodic and continuous review system, there is no reorder period to consider here—either there is enough inventory or there isn't. The target service level, then, is the service level at which the expected cost of a shortage equals the expected cost of having excess units:

$$\text{Expected shortage cost} = \text{expected excess cost}$$

or:

$$(1 - p)C_{\text{Shortage}} = pC_{\text{Excess}} \quad \text{(8-12)}$$

where:

p = probability that there are enough units to meet demand
$(1 - p)$ = probability that there is a shortage
C_{Shortage} = shortage cost
C_{Excess} = excess cost

The target service level (SL_T) is the p value at which Equation (8-12) holds true:

$$(1 - SL_T)C_{\text{Shortage}} = SL_T C_{\text{Excess}}$$

$$SL_T = \frac{C_{\text{Shortage}}}{C_{\text{Shortage}} + C_{\text{Excess}}} \quad \text{(8-13)}$$

where:

C_{Shortage} = shortage cost
C_{Excess} = excess cost

Let's use Equation (8.13) to test our intuition. Suppose the shortage cost and the excess cost for an item are both $10. In this case, we would be indifferent to either outcome, and we would set the inventory level so that each outcome would be equally likely. Equation (8.13) confirms our logic:

$$SL_T = \frac{C_{\text{Shortage}}}{C_{\text{Shortage}} + C_{\text{Excess}}} = \frac{\$10}{\$10 + \$10} = 0.50, \text{ or } 50\%$$

But what if the cost associated with a shortage is much higher—say, $90? In this case, we would want a much higher target service level because shortage costs are so much more severe than excess costs. Again, Equation (8.13) supports our reasoning:

$$\frac{C_{\text{Shortage}}}{C_{\text{Shortage}} + C_{\text{Excess}}} = \frac{\$90}{\$90 + \$10} = 0.9, \text{ or } 90\%$$

EXAMPLE 5

Determining the Target Service Level at Don's Lemonade Stands

Don Washing is trying to determine how many gallons of lemonade to make each day. Don needs to consider a single-period system because whatever lemonade is left over at the end of the day must be thrown away due to health concerns. Every gallon he mixes costs him $2.50 but will generate $10 in revenue if sold.

In terms of the single-period inventory problem, Dan's shortage and excess costs are defined as follows:

$$C_{\text{Shortage}} = \text{revenue per gallon} - \text{cost per gallon} = \$10.00 - \$2.50 = \$7.50$$

$$C_{\text{Excess}} = \text{cost per gallon} = \$2.50$$

From this information, Don can calculate his target service level:

$$SL_T = \frac{C_{\text{Shortage}}}{C_{\text{Shortage}} + C_{\text{Excess}}} = \frac{\$7.50}{\$7.50 + \$2.50} = 0.75, \text{ or } 75\%$$

Interpreting the results, Don should make enough lemonade to meet demand approximately 75% of the time.

EXAMPLE 6

Determining the Target Service Level at Fran's Flowers

Every day, Fran Chapman of Fran's Flowers makes floral arrangements for sale at the local hospital. The arrangements cost her approximately $12 to make, but they sell for $25. Any leftover arrangements can be sold at a heavily discounted price of $5 the following day. Fran wants to know what her target service level should be.

Fran's shortage and excess costs are as follows:

$$C_{\text{Shortage}} = \text{revenue per arrangement} - \text{cost per arrangement} = \$25 - \$12 = \$13$$

$$C_{\text{Excess}} = \text{cost per arrangement} - \text{salvage value} = \$12 - \$5 = \$7$$

Fran's target service level is, therefore:

$$SL_T = \frac{C_{\text{Shortage}}}{C_{\text{Shortage}} + C_{\text{Excess}}} = \frac{\$13}{\$13 + \$7} = 0.65, \text{ or } 65\%$$

Fran should make enough arrangements to meet demand approximately 65% of the time.

TARGET STOCKING POINT

To complete the development of a single-period inventory system, we next have to translate the target service level (a probability) into a target stocking point. To do so, we have to know something about how demand is distributed. Depending on the situation, we can approximate the demand distribution from historical records, or we can use a theoretical distribution, such as the normal distribution or Poisson distribution. Furthermore, the distribution may be continuous (i.e., demand can take on fractional values) or discrete (i.e., demand can take on only integer values). Example 7 shows how the process works when we can model demand by using the normal distribution, while Example 8 demonstrates the process for a historically based discrete distribution.

EXAMPLE 7

Determining the Target Stocking Point for Normally Distributed Demand

In Example 5, Don Washing determined that the target service level for lemonade was:

$$\frac{C_{\text{Shortage}}}{C_{\text{Shortage}} + C_{\text{Excess}}} = \frac{\$7.50}{\$7.50 + \$2.50} = 0.75, \text{ or } 75\%$$

Don knows from past experience that the daily demand follows a normal distribution. Therefore, Don wants to set a target stocking point (TS) that is higher than approximately 75% of the area under the normal curve. Figure 8.11 illustrates the idea.

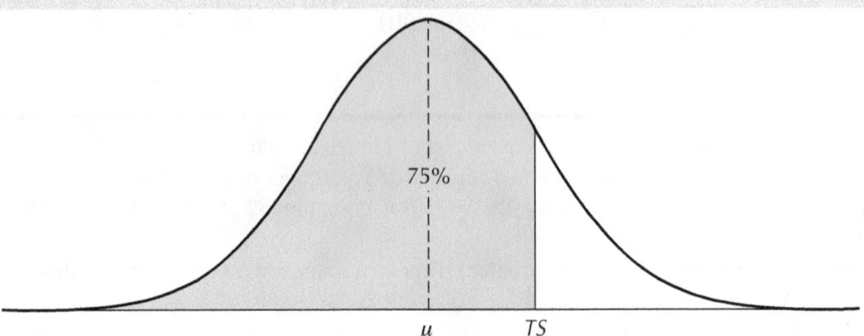

FIGURE 8.11
Target Stocking Point for Don's Lemonade Stands

The general formula for calculating the target stocking point when demand is normally distributed is:

$$\text{Target stocking point (normally distributed demand)} = \mu + z_{SLT}{*}\sigma \qquad \textbf{(8-14)}$$

where:

μ = mean demand per time period
z_{SLT} = number of standard deviations above the mean required to meet the target service level
σ = standard deviation of demand per period

To further complicate things, Don also knows that the mean values and standard deviations for demand differ by day of the week (Table 8.5). Therefore, he will have to calculate different target stocking points for Monday through Friday, Saturday, and Sunday.

TABLE 8.5
Demand Values for Don's Lemonade Stands

Day of the Week	Mean Demand, μ	Standard Deviation of Demand, σ
Monday–Friday	422 gallons	67 gallons
Saturday	719 gallons	113 gallons
Sunday	528 gallons	85 gallons

Using Equation (8-14) and the cumulative normal table, Don quickly determines that a service level of 75% would require the target stocking point to be approximately 0.68 standard deviations above the mean. Therefore, the target stocking points are as follows:

	$\mu + z_{SLT}{*}\sigma$
Monday–Friday:	422 + 0.68*67 = 467.56 gallons
Saturday	719 + 0.68*113 = 795.84 gallons
Sunday	528 + 0.68*85 = 585.8 gallons

EXAMPLE 8

Determining the Target Stocking Point for Non-Normally Distributed Demand

In Example 6 , Fran Chapman calculated her target service level for floral arrangements:

$$\frac{C_{\text{Shortage}}}{C_{\text{Shortage}} + C_{\text{Excess}}} = \frac{\$13}{\$13 + \$7} = 0.65, \text{ or } 65\%$$

Fran has kept track of arrangement sales for the past 34 days and has recorded the demand numbers shown in Table 8.6.

TABLE 8.6
Demand History for Fran's Flowers

Daily Demand	No. of Days With This Demand Level During the Past 34 Days	Percentage of Days Experiencing This Demand Level	Cumulative Percentage
10 or fewer	0	0/34 = 0%	0%
11	2	2/34 = 5.9%	5.9%
12	5	5/34 = 14.7%	20.6%
13	5	5/34 = 14.7%	35.3%
14	6	6/34 = 17.6%	52.9%
15	7	7/34 = 20.6%	**73.5%**
16	5	5/34 = 14.7%	88.2%
17	3	3/34 = 8.8%	97.0%
18	1	1/34 = 2.9%	100%
19 or more	0	0%	100%

Looking at Table 8.6, Fran realizes that if she wants to meet her target service level of 65%, she will need to stock 15 arrangements each day. This is because 15 arrangements is the first stocking point at which the probability of meeting expected demand (73.5%) is greater than the target service level of 65%. Conversely, if Fran stocked just 14 arrangements, according to Table 8.6, she would meet demand only 52.9% of the time.

Inventory in the Supply Chain

So far, we have discussed the functions and drivers of inventory, and we have identified some basic techniques for managing independent demand inventory items. In this section, we broaden our scope to consider the ramifications of inventory decisions for the rest of the supply chain.

THE BULLWHIP EFFECT

A major limitation of the *EOQ* model is that it considers the impact on costs for only a single firm. No consideration is given to how order quantity decisions for one firm affect other members of the supply chain. Therefore, even though the *EOQ* minimizes costs for a particular firm, it can cause problems for other partners and may actually increase *overall* supply chain costs. An example of this is the bullwhip effect.[5] APICS defines the **bullwhip effect** as "an extreme change in the supply position upstream in a supply chain generated by a small change in demand downstream in the supply chain."[6]

Bullwhip effect
According to APICS, "an extreme change in the supply position upstream in a supply chain generated by a small change in demand downstream in the supply chain."

To illustrate, suppose the ABC plant makes pool cleaners that are sold through six distributors. The distributors have similar demand patterns and identical *EOQ* and *ROP* quantities:

Average weekly demand = 500 pool cleaners (standard deviation = 100)
Order quantity = 1,500
Reorder point = 750

Figure 8.12 shows the results of a simulation covering 50 weeks of simulated demand across the six distributors. Even though total weekly demand across the six distributors ranged from 2,331 to 3,641, the quantities ordered from the plant ranged from 0 to 7,500.

What causes this? Quite simply, if a distributor reaches its reorder point, it places a large order. Otherwise, it does nothing. Therefore, a single-unit change in demand may determine whether

[5]Hau L. Lee, V. Padmanabhan, and S. Whang, "The Bullwhip Effect in Supply Chain," *Sloan Management Review* 38, no. 3 (Spring 1997): 70–77.

[6]Blackstone, *APICS Dictionary*.

FIGURE 8.12
Total Demand across the Six Distributors

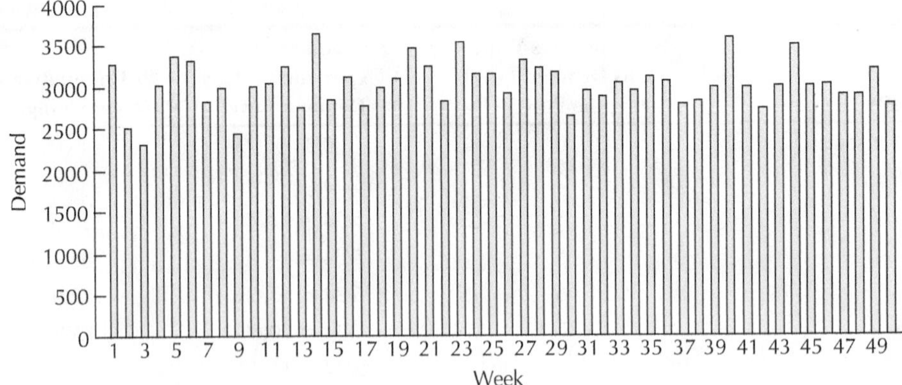

Resulting Total Quantities (Q = 1,500 for Each Distributor) Ordered from the ABC Plant

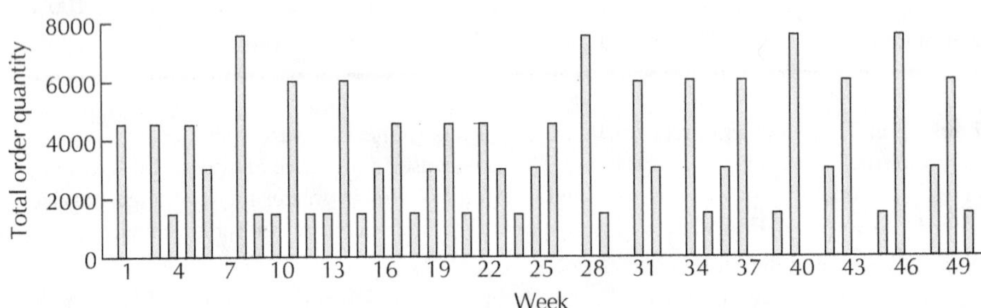

the distributor places an order. So even though the distributors may be following good inventory practice by ordering in quantities of 1,500, the impact on the supply chain is to increase demand variability at the plant. Ultimately, this demand variability will drive up costs at the plant, which will then be forced to pass on at least some of these costs to the distributors.

In order to reduce the bullwhip effect, many supply chain partners are working together to reduce order quantities by removing volume discount incentives and reducing ordering costs. Figure 8.13 shows, for example, what the quantities ordered from the plant would look like if order quantities were cut in half, to 750. Now the orders range from 750 to 4,500; this is not perfect, but it's a big improvement over what the range was before.

INVENTORY POSITIONING

Managers must decide *where* in the supply chain to hold inventory. In general, the decision about where to position inventory is based on two general truths:

1. The cost and value of inventory increase as materials move down the supply chain.
2. The flexibility of inventory decreases as materials move down the supply chain.

That is, as materials work their way through the supply chain, they are transformed, packaged, and moved closer to their final destination. All these activities add both cost and value. Take breakfast cereal, for example. By the time it reaches the stores, cereal has gone through such a significant transformation and repackaging that it appears to have little in common with the basic materials that went into it. But the value added goes beyond transformation and packaging; it includes location as well. A product that is in stock and available immediately is always worth more to the customer than the same product available later.

FIGURE 8.13
Resulting Total Quantities (Q = 750 for Each Distributor) Ordered from the ABC Plant

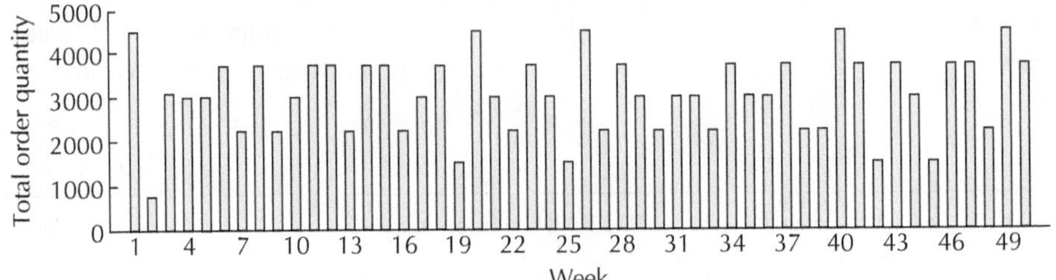

What keeps organizations from pushing inventory as far down the supply chain as possible? Cost, for one thing. By delaying the transformation and movement of materials, organizations can postpone the related costs. Another reason for holding inventory back in the supply chain is flexibility. Once materials have been transformed, packaged, and transported down the chain, reversing the process becomes very difficult, if not impossible. Wheat that has been used to make a breakfast cereal cannot be changed into flour that is suitable for making a cake. Likewise, repackaging shampoo into a different-sized container is impractical once it has been bottled. The same goes for transportation: Repositioning goods from one location to another can be quite expensive, especially compared to the cost of delaying their movement until demand has become more certain. This loss of flexibility is a major reason materials are often held back in the supply chain. In short, supply chain managers are constantly trying to strike a balance between costs on the one hand and flexibility on the other in deciding where to position inventory.

EXAMPLE 9

Pooling Safety Stock at Boyer's Department Store

An especially good case for holding back inventory can be made if an organization can hold all of its safety stock in a single central location. This is one example of **inventory pooling**, in which several locations share safety stock inventories in order to lower overall holding costs. Suppose, for instance, that Boyer's has eight stores in the Chicago area. Each store sells, on average, 10 ceiling fans a day. Suppose that the standard deviation of daily demand at each store is ($\sigma_d = 3$) and the average lead time is 9 days, with a standard deviation of 2 days. We showed in Example 3 that to maintain a 95% service level ($z = 1.65$) a store would need to maintain a safety stock of 55 fans. The total safety stock across all eight stores would therefore be 8*55 = 440 fans.

But what if Boyer's could pool the safety stock for all eight stores at a single store, which could provide same-day service to the other seven stores? Because a single location would have a demand variance equal to n times that of n individual stores:

$$\text{Standard deviation of demand during lead time, across } n \text{ locations} = \sqrt{n}*\sigma_{dL}$$

For Boyer's, this calculates out to:

$$= \sqrt{8}*\sqrt{L*\sigma_d^2 + d^2*\sigma_L^2}$$
$$= \sqrt{8}*33.24$$
$$= 94 \text{ fans}$$

And the pooled safety stock would be:

$$z*94 = 1.65*94 = 155.1, \text{ or } 155 \text{ fans}$$

By pooling its safety stock, Boyer's could reduce the safety stock level by (440 − 155) = 285 fans, or 65%. Considering the *thousands* of items stocked in Boyer's eight stores, centralizing Boyer's safety stock could produce significant savings.

Inventory pooling
Holding safety stock in a single location instead of multiple locations. Several locations then share safety stock inventories to lower overall holding costs by reducing overall safety stock levels.

TRANSPORTATION, PACKAGING, AND MATERIAL HANDLING CONSIDERATIONS

We will wrap up our discussion of inventory in the supply chain by considering how inventory decisions—most notably, order quantities—are intertwined with transportation, packaging, and material handling issues. The point of this discussion is to recognize that, in the real world, there is more to determining order quantities than just holding, ordering, and item costs.

Consider an example. Borfax Industries buys specialized chemicals from a key supplier. These chemicals can be purchased in one of two forms:

Form	Quantity	Weight	Dimensionality (Width/Depth/Height)	Price Per Bag
Carton	144 bags	218 lb.	2′ × 2′ × 1′	$25
Pallet	12 cartons; 1,728 bags	2,626 lb.	4′ × 4′ × 3.5′	$18

Supply Chain Connections Inventory Management and Pooling Groups at Automotive Dealerships

Automobile dealerships face a classic dilemma in deciding how to manage their inventories of service parts. On the one hand, customers expect their cars to be fixed promptly. On the other hand, dealerships typically do not have the space or financial resources to stock all the possible items a customer's car may need. If this wasn't difficult enough, most dealerships do not have the inventory expertise on site to deal with these issues.

To address these concerns, many automotive manufacturers have developed information systems in which the manufacturer makes inventory decisions for dealerships, based on calculated reorder points. Of course, the dealerships may override these recommendations if they like. And if a part placed in the dealership under the recommendation of the system sits at the dealership too long, the manufacturer will typically buy it back.

In addition, dealerships in the same geographic region typically establish "pooling groups." These dealerships agree to share safety stocks for expensive or slow-moving items. If one dealership runs out of the part, it can instantly check on the part's availability within the pooling group (via an information system) and arrange to have the item picked up. The result is lower overall inventories and better parts availability for customers.

First, notice that the chemicals can be purchased in multiples of 144 (cartons) or 1,728 (pallets). It is highly unlikely that any *EOQ* value calculated by Borfax will fit perfectly into either of these packaging alternatives.

If Borfax purchases a full pallet, it can get a substantial price discount. The supplier will also make a direct truck shipment if Borfax purchases five or more pallets at a time. This will reduce the lead time from 15 days to 5. However, pallets require material handling equipment capable of carrying nearly 3,000 pounds, as well as suitable storage space. On the other hand, the cartons are less bulky but will still require some specialized handling due to their weight. In choosing the best order quantity, Borfax must not only look at the per-bag price but also consider its material handling capabilities, transportation costs, and inventory holding costs.

CHAPTER SUMMARY

Inventory is an important resource in supply chains, serving many functions and taking many forms. But like any other resource, it must be managed well if an organization is to remain competitive. We started this chapter by examining the various types of inventory in a simple supply chain. We also discussed what drives inventory. To the extent that organizations can leverage inventory drivers, they can bring down the amount of inventory they need to hold in order to run their supply chains smoothly.

In the second part of this chapter, we introduced some basic tools for managing independent demand inventory. These tools provide managers with simple models for determining how much to order and when to order. We then examined the relationship between inventory decisions and the bullwhip effect, the decision about where to position inventory in the supply chain, and how transportation, packaging, and material handling considerations might impact inventory decisions.

KEY FORMULAS

Restocking level under a periodic review system (page 212):

$$R = \mu_{RP+L} + z\sigma_{RP+L} \quad (8\text{-}2)$$

where:

μ_{RP+L} = average demand during the reorder period and the order lead time

σ_{RP+L} = standard deviation of demand during the reorder period and the order lead time

z = number of standard deviations above the average demand (higher z values lower the probability of a stockout)

Total holding and ordering costs for the year (page 214):

$$\left(\frac{Q}{2}\right)H + \left(\frac{D}{Q}\right)S \qquad (8\text{-}4)$$

where:

Q = order quantity
H = annual holding cost per unit
D = annual demand
S = ordering cost

Economic order quantity (*EOQ*) (page 214):

$$Q = \sqrt{\frac{2DS}{\mathrm{H}}} = EOQ \qquad (8\text{-}5)$$

where:

Q = order quantity
H = annual holding cost per unit
D = annual demand
S = ordering cost

Reorder point under a continuous review system (page 217):

$$ROP = \bar{d}\,\bar{L} + z\sqrt{\bar{L}\sigma_d^2 + \bar{d}^2\sigma_L^2} \qquad (8\text{-}8)$$

where:

$\bar{d}$ = average demand per time period
$\bar{L}$ = average lead time
σ_d^2 = variance of demand per time period
σ_L^2 = variance of lead time
z = number of standard deviations above the average demand during lead time (higher z values lower the probability of a stockout)

Total holding, ordering, and item costs for the year (page 218):

$$\left(\frac{Q}{2}\right)H + \left(\frac{D}{Q}\right)S + DP \qquad (8\text{-}9)$$

where:

Q = order quantity
H = holding cost per unit
D = annual demand
P = price per unit
S = ordering cost

Target service level under a single-period inventory system (page 220):

$$SL_T = \frac{C_{\text{Shortage}}}{C_{\text{Shortage}} + C_{\text{Excess}}} \qquad (8\text{-}13)$$

where:

C_{Shortage} = shortage cost
C_{Excess} = excess cost

Key Terms

Anticipation inventory (p. 208)
Bullwhip effect (p. 223)
Continuous review system (p. 213)
Cycle stock (p. 207)
Demand uncertainty (p. 210)
Dependent demand inventory (p. 210)
Economic order quantity (*EOQ*) (p. 213)
Hedge inventory (p. 208)
Independent demand inventory (p. 210)
Inventory (p. 206)
Inventory drivers (p. 208)
Inventory pooling (p. 225)
Periodic review system (p. 211)
Safety stock (p. 207)
Service level (p. 212)
Single-period inventory system (p. 220)
Smoothing inventory (p. 208)
Supply uncertainty (p. 209)
Target service level (p. 220)
Target stocking point (p. 220)
Transportation inventory (p. 208)

USING EXCEL IN INVENTORY MANAGEMENT

Several of the models described in this chapter depend on estimates of average demand and average lead time and on associated measures of variance (σ^2) or standard deviation (σ). The spreadsheet model in Figure 8.14 shows how such values can be quickly estimated from historical data, using Microsoft Excel's built-in functions. The spreadsheet contains historical demand data for 20 weeks, as well as lead time information for 15 prior orders. From this information, the spreadsheet calculates average values and variances and then uses these values to calculate average demand during lead time, safety stock, and the reorder point. The highlighted cells represent the input values. The calculated cells are as follows:

Cell C32 (average weekly demand):	= AVERAGE(C12:C31)
Cell C33 (variance of weekly demand):	= VAR(C12:C31)
Cell G27 (average order lead time):	= AVERAGE(G12:G26)
Cell G28 (variance of lead time):	= VAR(G12:G26)
Cell F5 (average demand during lead time):	= C32*G27
Cell F6 (safety stock):	= F3*SQRT(G27*C33+C32^2*G28)
Cell F7 (reorder point):	= F5+F6

	A	B	C	D	E	F	G	H	I
1	**Calculating the Reorder Point from Demand and Order History**								
2									
3		z value (for desired service level:)				1.65			
4									
5					Average demand during lead time:	280.72	units		
6					+ Safety stock:	125.47	units		
7					Reorder point:	406.19	units	(Equation 10-6)	
8									
9		*** Demand History ***				*** Order History ***			
10							Lead time		
11		Week	Demand			Order	(days)		
12		1	33			1	10		
13		2	14			2	6		
14		3	18			3	12		
15		4	37			4	9		
16		5	34			5	10		
17		6	53			6	8		
18		7	31			7	8		
19		8	21			8	8		
20		9	19			9	7		
21		10	44			10	3		
22		11	43			11	8		
23		12	37			12	9		
24		13	45			13	7		
25		14	43			14	8		
26		15	36			15	8		
27		16	40			Average:	8.07		
28		17	28			Variance:	4.07		
29		18	41						
30		19	36						
31		20	43						
32		Average:	34.80						
33		Variance:	106.27						

FIGURE 8.14
Excel Solution to the Reorder Point Problem

Solved Problems

▼ SOLVED PROBLEM 8.1

Jake Fleming sells graphic card update kits for computers. Jake purchases these kits for $20 and sells about 250 kits a year. Each time Jake places an order, it costs him $25 to cover shipping and paperwork. Jake figures that the cost of holding an update kit in inventory is about $3.50 per kit per year. What is the economic order quantity? How many times per year will Jake place an order? How much will it cost Jake to order and hold these kits each year?

▼ SOLUTION

The economic order quantity for the kits is:

$$\sqrt{\frac{2*250*\$25}{\$3.50}} = 59.76\text{, or } 60 \text{ kits}$$

The number of orders placed per year is:

$$\frac{250}{60} = 4.17 \text{ orders per year}$$

The total holding and ordering costs for the year (not counting any safety stock Jake might hold) are:

$$\frac{60}{2}\$3.50 + \frac{250}{60}\$25 = \$105 + \$104.17 = \$209.17$$

▼ SOLVED PROBLEM 8.2

The manufacturer of the graphic card update kits has agreed to charge Jake just $15 per kit if Jake orders 250 kits at a time. Should Jake accept the manufacturer's offer?

▼ SOLUTION

For the *EOQ*, the total holding, ordering, and item costs for the year are:

$$\frac{60}{2}\$3.50 + \frac{250}{60}\$25 = 250*\$20 = \$105 + \$104.17 + \$5{,}000 = \$5{,}209.17$$

If Jake takes the volume discount, he will order 250 kits at a time (after all, ordering more than 250 would only move him further away from the *EOQ*, which minimizes holding and ordering costs):

$$\frac{250}{2}\$3.50 + \frac{250}{250}\$25 + 250*\$15 = \$437.50 + \$25 + \$3{,}750 = \$4{,}212.50$$

Therefore, Jake should take the volume discount and order just once a year.

Discussion Questions

1. You hear someone comment that *any* inventory is a sign of waste. Do you agree or disagree? Can managers simultaneously justify holding inventories and still seek out ways to lower inventory levels?
2. In your own words, what is an inventory driver? What is the difference between a controllable inventory driver and an uncontrollable inventory driver? Give examples.
3. Which of the following are independent demand inventory items? Dependent demand inventory items?
   a. Bicycles in a toy store
   b. Bicycle wheels in a bicycle factory
   c. Blood at a blood bank
   d. Hamburgers at a fast-food restaurant
   e. Hamburger buns at a plant that produces frozen dinners
4. In a supply chain, what are the pros and cons of pushing inventory downstream, closer to the final customer? How might modular product designs make it more profitable for companies to postpone the movement of inventory down the supply chain?
5. (Use the *EOQ* and *ROP* formulas to answer this question.) Which variables could you change if you wanted to reduce inventory costs in your organization? Which ones would you prefer to change? Why?
6. The JIT movement has long argued that firms should:
   a. Maximize their process flexibility so that ordering costs are minimized;
   b. Stabilize demand levels;
   c. Shrink lead times as much as possible; and
   d. Assign much higher holding costs to inventory than has traditionally been the case.

   Using the *EOQ* and *ROP* formulas, explain how such efforts would be consistent with JIT's push for lower inventory levels.

Problems

Additional homework problems are available at www.pearsonhighered.com/bozarth. These problems use Excel to generate customized problems for different class sections or even different students. (* = easy; ** = moderate; *** = advanced)

•• **8.1** (*) Pam runs a mail-order business for gym equipment. Annual demand for TricoFlexers is 16,000. The annual holding cost per unit is $2.50, and the cost to place an order is $50. What is the economic order quantity?

•• **8.2** (**) Using the same holding and ordering costs as in problem 1, suppose demand for TricoFlexers doubles, to 32,000. Does the *EOQ* also double? Explain what happens.

•• **8.3** (**) The manufacturer of TricoFlexers has agreed to offer Pam a price discount of $5 per unit ($45 rather than $50) if she buys 1,500. Assuming that annual demand is still 16,000, how many units should Pam order at a time?

•• **8.3** (*) Jimmy's Delicatessen sells large tins of Tom Tucker's Toffee. The deli uses a periodic review system, checking inventory levels every 10 days, at which time an order is placed for more tins. Order lead time is 3 days. Average daily demand is 7 tins, so average demand during the reorder period and order lead time (13 days) is 91 tins. The standard deviation of demand during this same 13-day period is 17 tins. Calculate the restocking level. Assume that the desired service level is 90%.

•• **8.5** (**) For problem 4, suppose that the standard deviation of demand during the 13-day period drops to 4 tins. What happens to the restocking level? Explain why.

•• **8.6** (***) For Tom Tucker's Toffee in problem 4, draw a sawtooth diagram similar to the one in Figure 8.3. Assume that the beginning inventory level is equal to the restocking level and that the demand rate is a *constant* 7 tins per day. What is the safety stock level? (*Hint:* Look at the formula for calculating restocking level.) What is the average inventory level?

•• **8.7** (*) KraftyCity is a large retailer that sells power tools and other hardware supplies. One of its products is the KraftyMan workbench. Information on the workbench is as follows:

Annual demand = 1,200
Holding cost = $15 per year
Ordering cost = $200 per order

What is the economic order quantity for the workbench?

•• **8.8** (**) Suppose that KraftyCity has to pay $50 per workbench for orders under 200 but only $42 per workbench for orders of 201 or more. Using the information provided in problem 7, what order quantity *should* KraftyCity use?

•• **8.9** (*) The lead time for KraftyCity workbenches is 3 weeks, with a standard deviation of 1.2 weeks, and the average weekly demand is 24, with a standard deviation of 8 workbenches. What should the reorder point be if KraftyCity wants to provide a 95% service level?

•• **8.10** (**) Now suppose the supplier of workbenches guarantees KraftyCity that the lead time will be a constant 3 weeks, with no variability (i.e., standard deviation of lead time = 0). Recalculate the reorder point, using the demand and service level information in problem 9. Is the reorder point higher or lower? Explain why.

•• **8.11** (*) Ollah's Organic Pet Shop sells about 4,000 bags of free-range dog biscuits every year. The fixed ordering cost is $15, and the cost of holding a bag in inventory for a year is $2. What is the economic order quantity for the biscuits?

•• **8.12** (**) Suppose Ollah decides to order 200 bags at a time. What would the total ordering and holding costs for the year be? (For this problem, don't consider safety stock when calculating holding costs.)

•• **8.13** (**) Average weekly demand for free-range dog biscuits is 80 bags per week, with a standard deviation of 16 bags. Ollah uses a continuous inventory review system to manage inventory of the biscuits. Ollah wants to set the reorder point high enough that there is only a 5% chance of running out before the next order comes in. Assuming that the lead time is a constant 2 weeks, what should the reorder point be?

•• **8.14** (**) Suppose Ollah decides to use a periodic review system to manage the free-range dog biscuits, with the vendor checking inventory levels every week. Under this scenario, what would the restocking level be, assuming the same demand and lead time characteristics listed in problem 13 and the same 95% service level? (Note that because the standard deviation of weekly demand is 16, basic statistics tells us the standard deviation of demand over 3 weeks will be $\sqrt{3} \times 16 \approx 28$.)

•• **8.15** Ollah's Organic Pet Shop sells bags of cedar chips for pet bedding or snacking (buyer's choice). The supplier has offered Ollah the following terms:

Order 1–100 bags, and the price is $6.00 a bag.
Order 101 or more bags, and the price is $4.50 a bag.

Annual demand is 630, fixed ordering costs are $9 per order, and the per-bag holding cost is estimated to be around $2 per year.

a. (*) What is the economic order quantity for the bags?
b. (**) What order quantity should Ollah order, based on the volume discount? Is this different from the *EOQ*? If so, how could this be?
c. (**) Suppose the lead time for bags is a constant 2 weeks, and average weekly demand is 12.6 bags, with a standard deviation of 3.2 bags. If Ollah wants to maintain a 98% service level, what should her reorder point be?

•• **8.16** (**) David Polston prints up T-shirts to be sold at local concerts. The T-shirts sell for $20 each but cost David only $6.50 each. However, because the T-shirts have concert-specific information on them, David can sell a leftover shirt for only $3. Suppose the demand for shirts can be approximated with a normal distribution and the mean demand is 120 shirts, with a standard deviation of 35. What is the target service level? How many shirts should David print up for a concert?

•• **8.17** Sherry Clower is trying to figure out how many custom books to order for her class of 25 students. In the past, the number of students buying books has shown the following demand pattern:

Number of Students Who Bought a Book	Percentage of Observations
16 or fewer	0%
17	4%
18	15%
19	17%
20	18%
21	26%
22	10%
23	6%
24	4%
25	0%

a. (**) Suppose each custom book costs Sherry $12 to print, and she sells the books to the students for $50 each. Excess books must be scrapped. What is the target service level? What is the target stocking point?

b. (**) Suppose printing costs increase to $22. Recalculate the new target service level and target stocking point. What happens?

•• **8.18** One of the products sold by OfficeMax is a Hewlett-Packard DeskJet Z4480 printer. As purchasing manager, you have the following information for the printer:

Average weekly demand (52 weeks per year):	60 printers
Standard deviation of weekly demand:	12 printers
Order lead time:	3 weeks
Standard deviation of order lead time:	0 (lead times are constant)
Item cost:	$120 per printer
Cost to place an order:	$2
Yearly holding cost per printer:	$48
Desired service level during reordering period:	99% (z = 2.33)

a. (*) What is the economic order quantity for the printer?

b. (**) Calculate annual ordering costs and holding costs (ignoring safety stock) for the *EOQ*. What do you notice about the two?

c. (**) Suppose OfficeMax currently orders 120 printers at a time. How much more or less would OfficeMax pay in holding and ordering costs per year if it ordered just 12 printers at a time? Show your work.

d. (**) What is the reorder point for the printer? How much of the reorder point consists of safety stock?

For parts e and f, use the following formula to consider the impact of safety stock (SS) on average inventory levels and annual holding costs:

$$\left(\frac{Q}{2} + SS\right)H$$

e. (***) What is the annual cost of holding inventory, including the safety stock? How much of this cost is due to the safety stock?

f. (***) Suppose OfficeMax is able to cut the lead time to a constant 1 week. What would the new safety stock level be? How much would this reduce annual holding costs?

•• **8.19** (***) OfficeMax is considering using the Internet to order printers from Hewlett-Packard. The change is expected to make the cost of placing orders drop to almost nothing, although the lead time will remain the same. What effect will this have on the order quantity? On the holding and ordering costs for the year? Explain, using any formulas and examples you find helpful.

•• **8.20** Through its online accessory store, Gateway sells its own products, as well as products made by other companies. One of these products is the Viewsonic VX150 LCD monitor:

Estimated *annual* demand:	15,376 monitors (50 weeks per year)
Cost:	$640 per monitor
Lead time:	2 weeks
Standard deviation of weekly demand:	16 monitors
Standard deviation of lead time:	0.3 weeks
Holding cost per unit per year:	40% of item cost
Ordering cost:	$25 per order
Desired service level:	95% (z = 1.65)

a. (*) What is the economic order quantity for the monitor? Calculate annual ordering costs and holding costs (ignoring safety stock) for the *EOQ*.

b. (**) What is the reorder point for the monitor? How much of the reorder point consists of safety stock?

c. (**) Suppose Gateway decides to order 64 monitors at a time. What would its yearly ordering and holding costs (ignoring safety stock) for the monitor be?

d. (**) Because computer technologies become obsolete so quickly, Gateway is thinking about raising holding costs from 40% of item cost to some higher percentage. What will be the impact on the economic order quantity for monitors? Explain why.

For parts e and f, use the following formula to consider the impact of safety stock (*SS*) on average inventory levels and annual holding costs:

$$\left(\frac{Q}{2} + SS\right)H$$

e. (***) What is the annual cost of holding inventory, including the safety stock? How much of this cost is due to the safety stock?

f. (***) Suppose Gateway is able to cut the lead time to a constant 1 week. What would the new safety stock level be? How much would this reduce annual holding costs?

•• **8.21** One of the products stocked by a Sam's Club store is *Sams Cola*, which is sold in cases. The demand level for *Sams Cola* is highly seasonal:

- During the *slow season*, the demand rate is approximately 650 cases a month, which is the same as a yearly demand rate of $650*12 = 7,800$ cases.
- During the *busy season*, the demand rate is approximately 1,300 cases a month, or 15,600 cases a year.
- The cost to place an order is $5, and the yearly holding cost for a case of *Sams Cola* is $12.

a. (**) According to the *EOQ* formula, how many cases of *Sams Cola* should be ordered at a time during the slow season? How many cases of *Sams Cola* should be ordered during the busy season?

b. (**) Suppose Sam's Club decides to use the same order quantity, $Q = 150$, throughout the year. Calculate total holding and ordering costs for the year. Do not consider safety stock in your calculations. (Annual demand can be calculated as an average of the slow and busy rates given above.)

•• **8.22** (**) During the busy season, the store manager has decided that 98% of the time, he does not want to run out of *Sams Cola* before the next order arrives. Use the following data to calculate the reorder point for *Sams Cola*:

Weekly demand during the busy season:	325 cases per week
Lead time:	0.5 weeks
Standard deviation of weekly demand:	5.25
Standard deviation of lead time:	0 (lead time is constant)
Number of standard deviations above the mean needed to provide a 98% service level (z):	2.05

•• **8.23** Mountain Mouse makes freeze-dried meals for hikers. One of Mountain Mouse's biggest customers is a sporting goods superstore. Every 5 days, Mountain Mouse checks the inventory level at the superstore and places an order to restock the meals. These meals are delivered by UPS in 2 days. Average demand during the reorder period and order lead time is 100 meals, and the standard deviation of demand during this same time period is about 20 meals.

a. (**) Calculate the restocking level for Mountain Mouse. Assume that the superstore wants a 90% service level. What happens to the restocking level if the superstore wants a higher level of service—say, 95%?

b. (*) Suppose there are 20 meals in the superstore when Mountain Mouse checks inventory levels. How many meals should be ordered, assuming a 90% service level?

•• **8.24** (**) Dave's Sporting Goods sells Mountain Mouse freeze-dried meals. Dave's uses a continuous review system to manage meal inventories. Suppose Mountain Mouse offers the following volume discounts to its customers:

1–500 meals: $7 per meal
501 or more meals: $6.50 per meal

Annual demand is 2,000 meals, and the cost to place an order is $15. Suppose the holding cost is $2 per meal per year. How many meals should Dave's order at a time? What are the total holding, ordering, and item costs associated with this quantity?

•• **8.25** (***) (*Microsoft Excel problem*) The following figure shows an Excel spreadsheet that compares total ordering and holding costs for some current order quantity to the same costs for the *EOQ* and calculates how much could be saved by switching to the *EOQ*. **Re-create this spreadsheet in Excel.** You should develop the spreadsheet so that the results will be recalculated if any of the values in the highlighted cells are changed. Your formatting does not have to be exactly the same, but the numbers should be. (As a test, see what happens if you just change the annual demand and cost per order to 5,000 and $25, respectively. Your new *EOQ* should be 91.29, and the total savings under the *EOQ* should be $5,011.39.)

	A	B	C	D	E	F
1	**Calculating Savings under EOQ**					
2						
3			Annual demand:	4000		
4			Annual holding cost, per unit:	$30.00		
5			Cost per order:	$30.00		
6						
7			Current order quantity:	500		
8			Current annual holding cost:	$7500.00		
9			Current annual ordering cost:	$240.00		
10			Total cost:	$7740.00		
11						
12			Economic order quantity:	89.44		
13			EOQ annual holding cost:	$1341.64		
14			EOQ annual ordering cost:	$1341.64		
15			Total cost:	$2683.28		
16						
17			**Total savings under EOQ:**	**$5056.72**		
18						

•• **8.26** (***) (*Microsoft Excel problem*) The following figure shows an Excel spreadsheet that calculates the benefit of pooling safety stock. Specifically, the sheet calculates how much could be saved in annual holding costs if the safety stocks for three locations were held in a single location. **Re-create this spreadsheet in Excel.** You should develop the spreadsheet so that the results will be recalculated if any of the values in the highlighted cells are changed. Your formatting does not have to be exactly the same, but the numbers should be. (As a test, see what happens if you change Location 1's average daily demand and variance of daily demand to 100 and 15, respectively. Your new pooled safety stock should be 30.34, and the total savings due to pooling safety stock should be $108.21.)

	A	B	C	D	E	F	G
1	**Calculating Savings Due to Pooling Safety Stock**						
2							
3	Annual holding cost per unit:			$5.00			
4	Lead time (fixed):			8	days		
5	z value (for desired service level):			2.33			
6							
7						Average demand	
8			Average	Variance of	Reorder	during	
9			daily demand	daily demand	point	lead time	Safety stock
10		Location 1	50	4.5	413.98	400.00	13.98
11		Location 2	40	6.2	336.41	320.00	16.41
12		Location 3	30	5	254.74	240.00	14.74
13						Total units:	45.13
14						**Total annual holding cost:**	**$225.63**
15							
16						Average demand	
17			Average	Variance of	Reorder	during	
18			daily demand	daily demand	point	lead time	Safety stock
19		**Pooled SS**	120	15.7	986.11	960.00	26.11
20						**Total annual holding cost:**	**$130.56**
21							
22						**Savings due to pooling safety stock:**	**$95.07**

Case Studies

Northcutt Bikes: The Service Department

silver-john/Shutterstock.com

Introduction

Several years ago, Jan Northcutt, owner of Northcutt Bikes, recognized the need to organize a separate department to deal with service parts for the bikes her company makes. Because the competitive strength of her company was developed around customer responsiveness and flexibility, she felt that creating a separate department focused exclusively on aftermarket service was critical in meeting that mission.

When she established the department, she named Ann Hill, one of her best clerical workers at the time, to establish and manage the department. At first, the department occupied only a corner of the production warehouse, but now it has grown to occupy its own 100,000-square-foot warehouse. The service business has also grown significantly, and it now represents over 15% of the total revenue of Northcutt Bikes. The exclusive mission of the service department is to provide parts (tires, seats, chains, etc.) to the many retail businesses that sell and service Northcutt Bikes.

While Ann has turned out to be a very effective manager (and now holds the title of Director of Aftermarket Service), she still lacks a basic understanding of materials management. To help her develop a more effective materials management program, she hired Mike Alexander, a recent graduate of an outstanding business management program at North Carolina State University, to fill the newly created position of Materials Manager of Aftermarket Service.

The Current Situation

During the interview process, Mike got the impression that there was a lot of opportunity for improvement at Northcutt Bikes. It was only after he selected his starting date and requested some information that he started to see the full extent of the challenges that lay ahead. His first day on the job really opened his eyes. One of the first items he had requested was a status report on inventory history and shipped orders. In response, the following note was on his desk the first day from the warehouse supervisor, Art Demming:

> *We could not compile the history you requested, as we keep no such records. There's just too much stuff in here to keep a close eye on it all. Rest assured, however, that we think the inventory positions on file are accurate, as we just completed our physical count of inventory last week. I was able to track down a demand history for a couple of our items, and that is attached to this memo. Welcome to the job!*

Mike decided to investigate further. Although the records were indeed difficult to track down and compile, by the end of his second week, he had obtained a fairly good picture of the situation, based on an investigation of 100 parts selected at random. He learned, for example, that although there was an average of over 70 days' worth of inventory (annual sales/average inventory), the fill rate for customer orders was less than 80%, meaning that only 80% of the items requested were in inventory; the remaining orders were back-ordered. Unfortunately, the majority of customers viewed service parts as generic and would take their business elsewhere when parts were not available from Northcutt Bikes.

What really hurt was when those businesses sometimes canceled their entire order for parts and placed it with another parts supplier. The obvious conclusion was that while there was plenty of inventory overall, the timing and quantities were misplaced. Increasing the inventory did not appear to be the answer, not only because a large amount was already being held but also because the space in the warehouse (built less than two years ago) had increased from being 45% utilized just after they moved in to its present utilization of over 95%.

Mike decided to start his analysis and development of solutions on the two items for which Art had already provided demand history. He felt that if he could analyze and correct any problems with those two parts, he could expand the analysis to most of the others. The two items on which he had history and concentrated his initial analysis were the FB378 Fender Bracket and the GS131 Gear Sprocket. Northcutt Bikes purchases the FB378 from a Brazilian source. The lead time has remained constant, at three weeks, and the estimated cost of a purchase order for these parts is given at $35 per order. Currently Northcutt Bikes uses an order lot size of 120 for the FB378 and buys the items for $5 apiece.

The GS131 part, on the other hand, is a newer product only recently being offered. A machine shop in Nashville, Tennessee, produces the part for Northcutt Bikes, and it gives Northcutt Bikes a fairly reliable six-week lead time. The cost of placing an order with the machine shop is only about $15, and currently Northcutt Bikes orders 850 parts at a time. Northcutt Bikes buys the item for $10.75.

Following is the demand information that Art gave to Mike on his first day for the FB378 and the GS131:

	FB378		GS131	
Week	Forecast	Actual Demand	Forecast	Actual Demand
1	30	34		
2	32	44		
3	35	33		
4	34	39		
5	35	48		
6	38	30		
7	36	26		
8	33	45		
9	37	33		
10	37	30		
11	36	47	10	16
12	37	40	18	27
13	38	31	30	35
14	36	38	42	52
15	36	32	55	51
16	35	49	54	44
17	37	24	52	57
18	35	41	53	59
19	37	34	53	46
20	36	24	52	62
21	34	52	53	51
22	36	41	53	60
23	37	30	54	46
24	36	37	53	58
25	36	31	54	42
26	35	45	53	57
27	36		53	

(continued)

Mike realized he also needed input from Ann about her perspective on the business. She indicated that she felt strongly that with better management, Northcutt Bikes should be able to use the existing warehouse for years to come, even with the anticipated growth in business. Currently, however, she views the situation as a crisis because "we're bursting at the seams with inventory. It's costing us a lot of profit, yet our service level is very poor, at less than 80%. I'd like to see us maintain a 95% or better service level without back orders, yet we need to be able to do that with a net reduction in total inventory. What do you think, Mike? Can we do better?"

Questions

1. Use the available data to develop inventory policies (order quantities and reorder points) for the FB378 and GS131. Assume that the holding cost is 20% of unit price.
2. Compare the inventory costs associated with your suggested order quantities with those of the current order quantities. What can you conclude?
3. Do you think the lost customer sales should be included as a cost of inventory? How would such an inclusion impact the ordering policies you established in question 1?

References

Books and Articles

Blackstone, J. H., ed., *APICS Dictionary*, 13th ed. (Chicago, IL: APICS, 2010).

Lee, H. L., V. Padmanabhan, and S. Whang, "The Bullwhip Effect in Supply Chain," *Sloan Management Review* 38, no. 3 (Spring 1997): 70–77.

Magretta, J., "Fast, Global, and Entrepreneurial: Supply Chain Management, Hong Kong Style," *Harvard Business Review* 76, no. 5 (September–October 1998): 102–109.

Magretta, J., "The Power of Virtual Integration: An Interview with Dell Computer's Michael Dell," *Harvard Business Review* 76, no. 2 (March–April 1998): 72–84.

Index

Index usage notes: boldface = key term, *f* = figure, *t* = table, *n* = note